MATSURI AK

2

Genju no Seiza

Genju no Seiza Vol. 2
Created by Matsuri Akino

Translation - Mike Kiefl
English Adaptation - Christine Boylan
Retouch and Lettering - Starprint Brokers
Production Artist - Bowen Park
Cover Design - John Lo

Editor - Tim Beedle
Digital Imaging Manager - Chris Buford
Production Manager - Elisabeth Brizzi
Managing Editor - Vy Nguyen
Pre-Press Supervisor - Erika Terriquez
Art Director - Anne Marie Horne
VP of Production - Ron Klamert
Editor-in-Chief - Rob Tokar
Publisher - Mike Kiley
President and C.O.O. - John Parker
C.E.O. and Chief Creative Officer - Stuart Levy

A  Manga

TOKYOPOP Inc.
5900 Wilshire Blvd. Suite 2000
Los Angeles, CA 90036

E-mail: info@TOKYOPOP.com
Come visit us online at www.TOKYOPOP.com

ISBN: 1-59816-608-5

First TOKYOPOP printing: December 2006
10 9 8 7 6 5 4 3 2 1
Printed in the USA

Genju no Seiza

VOLUME 2

CREATED BY
MATSURI AKINO

HAMBURG // LONDON // LOS ANGELES // TOKYO

Genju no Seiza

TABLE OF CONTENTS

Story So Far

An empty throne...

Not in the literal sense (but I'll get to that in a moment), but for the past forty years, that is in truth what Dhalashar has had. For forty years, we've been without a king. But that has all changed now. We have found our heir to the throne. He is the half-Sherpa son of a world-famous photographer, and his name is Fuuto Kamishina. Currently living in Japan with his mother, young Fuuto has already begun to exhibit some of the powers of our king, and although he is unaware of this, his use of them has affirmed to me that he will be a good king. However, he is also a tad stubborn, and to this he refuses to accept his role as our new sovereign and religious leader.

There are further complications as well. While the people of Dhalashar have been without their TRUE king for quite some time, they have not been without a king. The Snake-God, Naga, a treacherous and deceitful deity, recently sensed opportunity upon our vacant throne. He has instilled an impostor king—little more than a puppet to Naga's ambitions—to rule Dhalashar. And much to my chagrin, many people of my nation have accepted this false sovereign as our next heir to the throne. However, Naga knows his king is false and that the emergence of the true sovereign will prove that to the people of Dhalashar. He fears young Fuuto Kamishina, and will do what he can to ensure he never ascends to the throne. He has already dispatched several assassins, and I fear more may be on the way.

—Garuda, Guardian Beast of the true King of Dhalashar

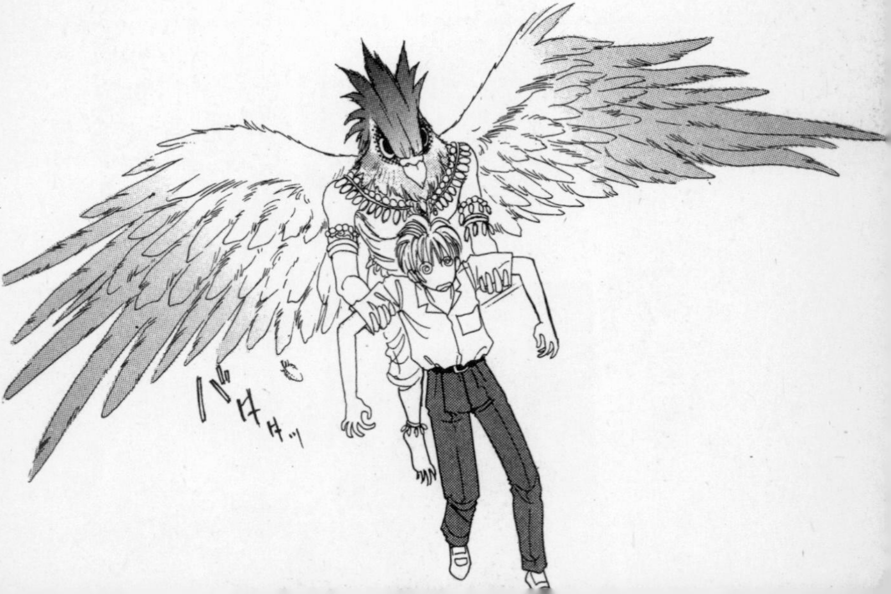
バササッ

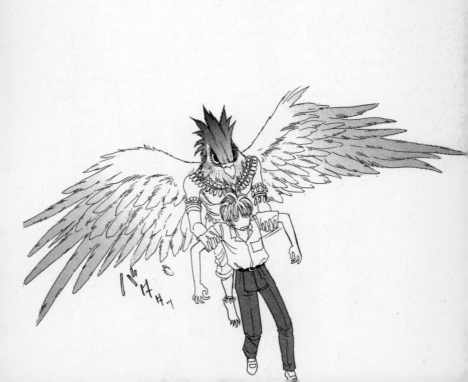

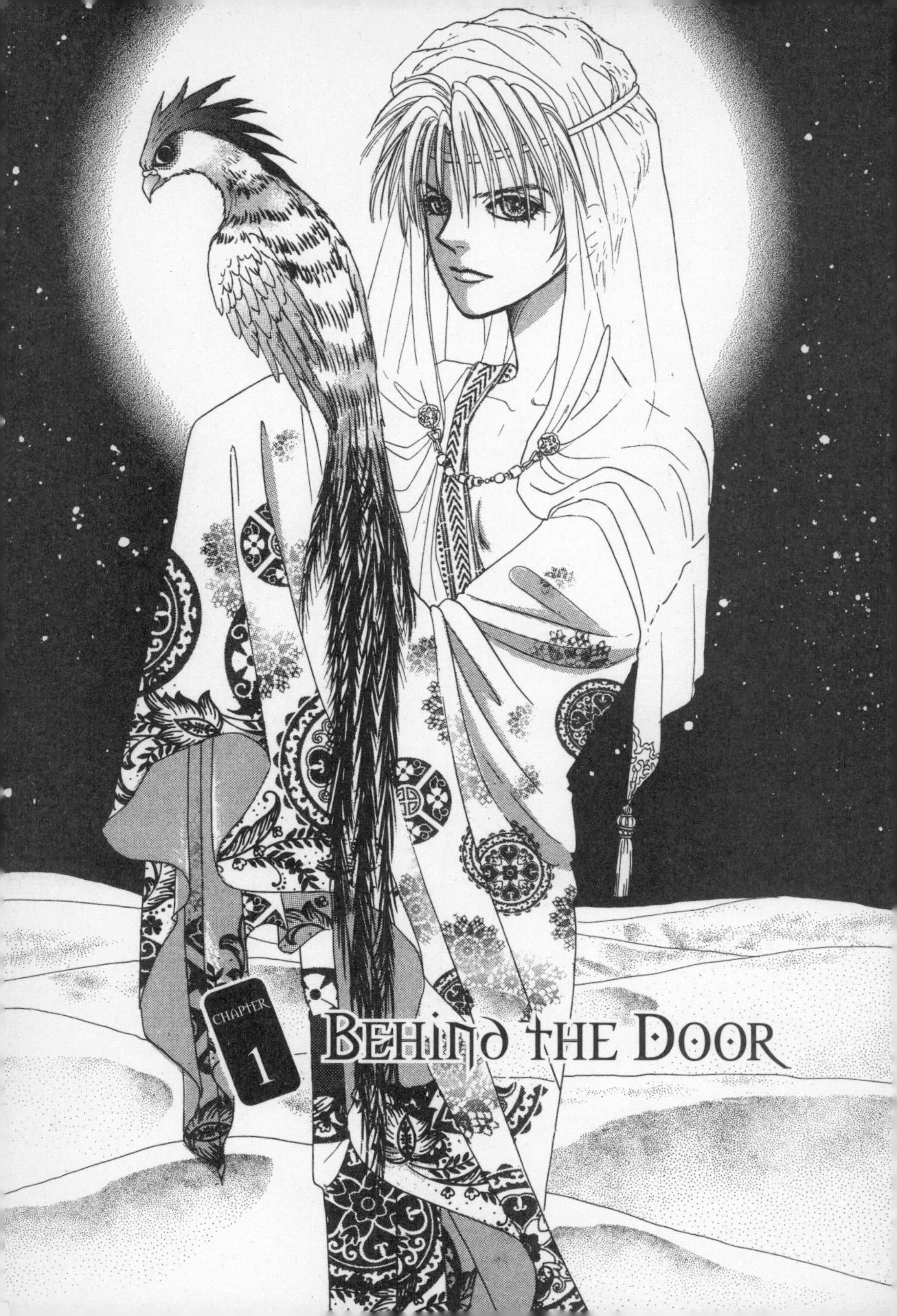
CHAPTER 1
BEHIND THE DOOR

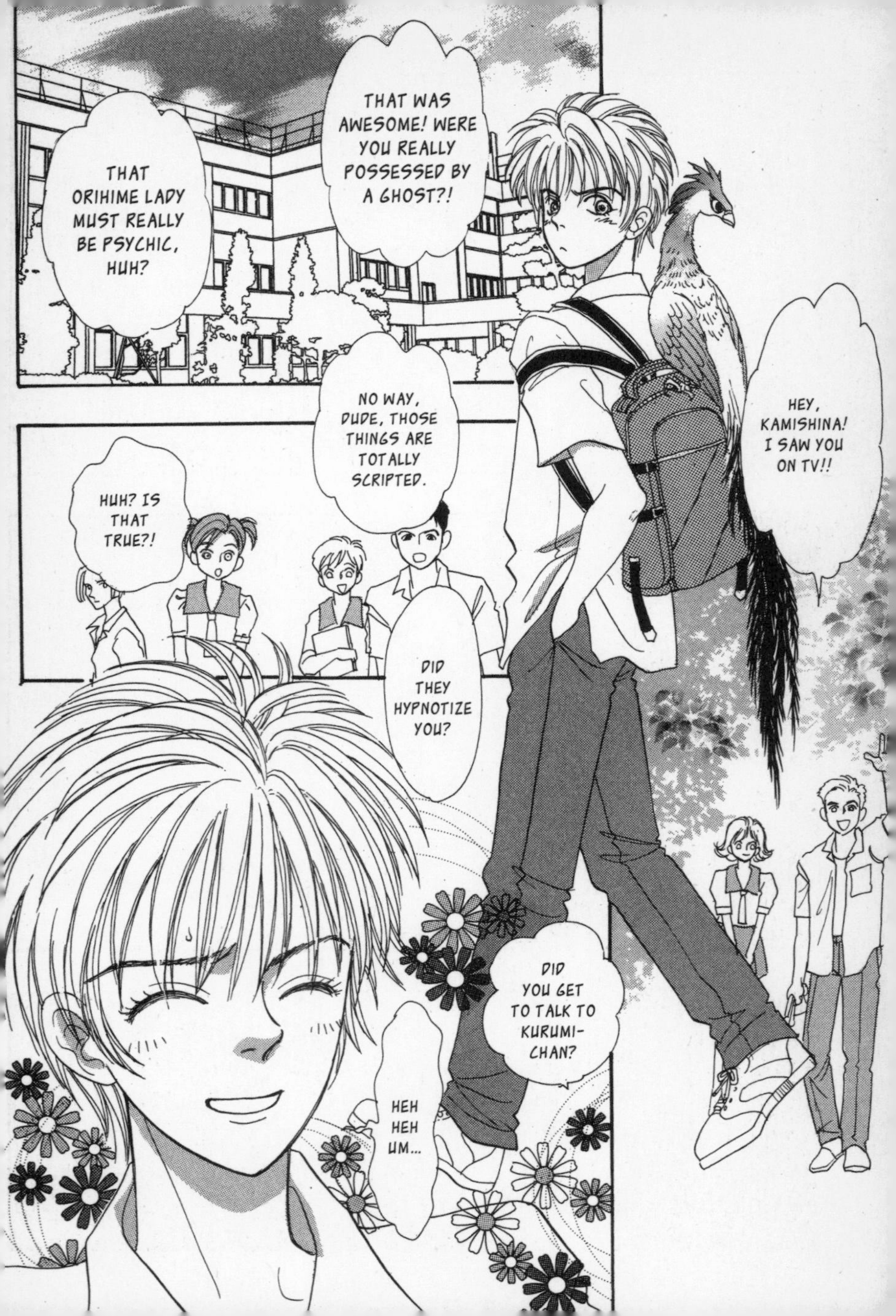
HEY, KAMISHINA! I SAW YOU ON TV!!
THAT WAS AWESOME! WERE YOU REALLY POSSESSED BY A GHOST?!
THAT ORIHIME LADY MUST REALLY BE PSYCHIC, HUH?
NO WAY, DUDE, THOSE THINGS ARE TOTALLY SCRIPTED.
HUH? IS THAT TRUE?!
DID THEY HYPNOTIZE YOU?
DID YOU GET TO TALK TO KURUMI-CHAN?
HEH HEH UM...

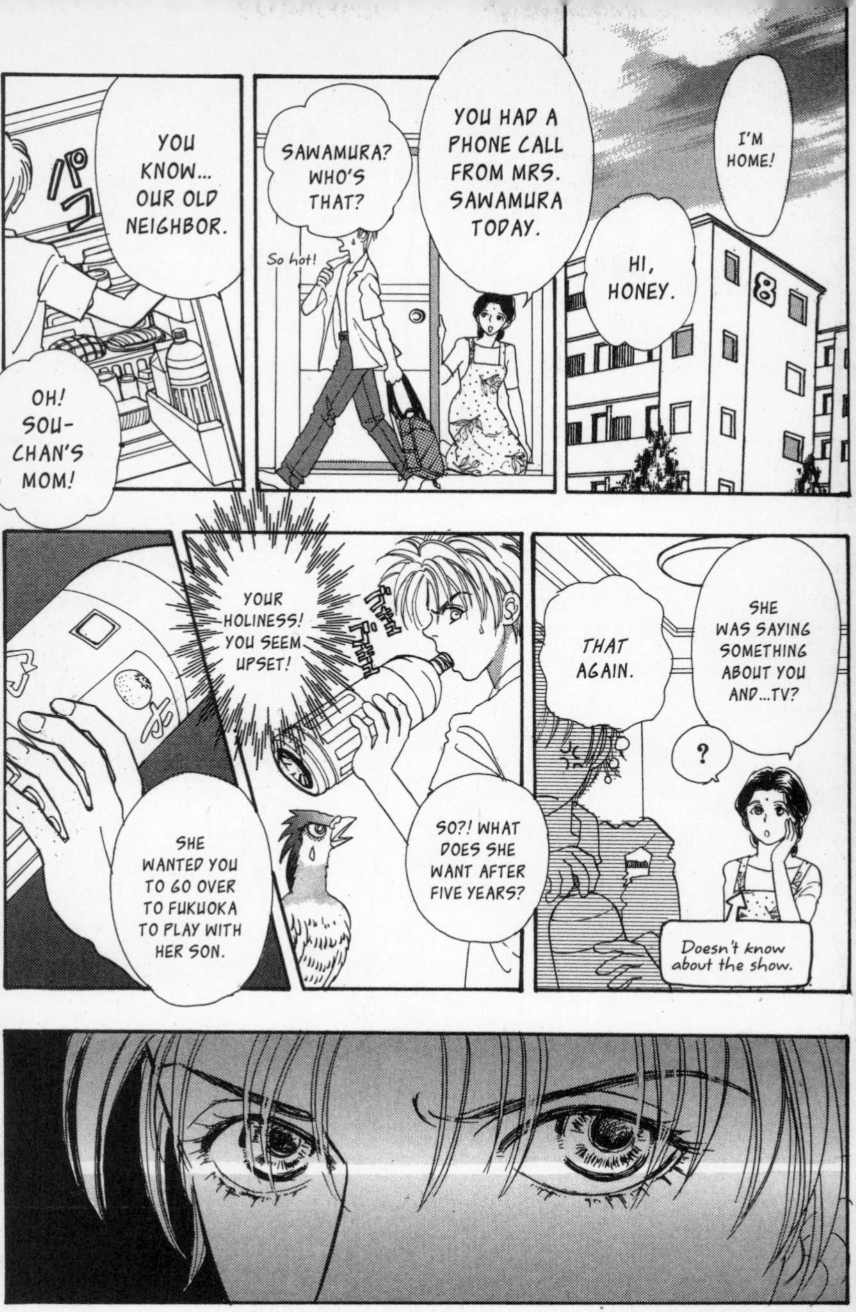
I'M HOME!
HI, HONEY.
YOU HAD A PHONE CALL FROM MRS. SAWAMURA TODAY.
SAWAMURA? WHO'S THAT?
So hot!
YOU KNOW... OUR OLD NEIGHBOR.
OH! SOU-CHAN'S MOM!
SHE WAS SAYING SOMETHING ABOUT YOU AND...TV?
THAT AGAIN.
?
Doesn't know about the show.
YOUR HOLINESS! YOU SEEM UPSET!
SO?! WHAT DOES SHE WANT AFTER FIVE YEARS?
SHE WANTED YOU TO GO OVER TO FUKUOKA TO PLAY WITH HER SON.

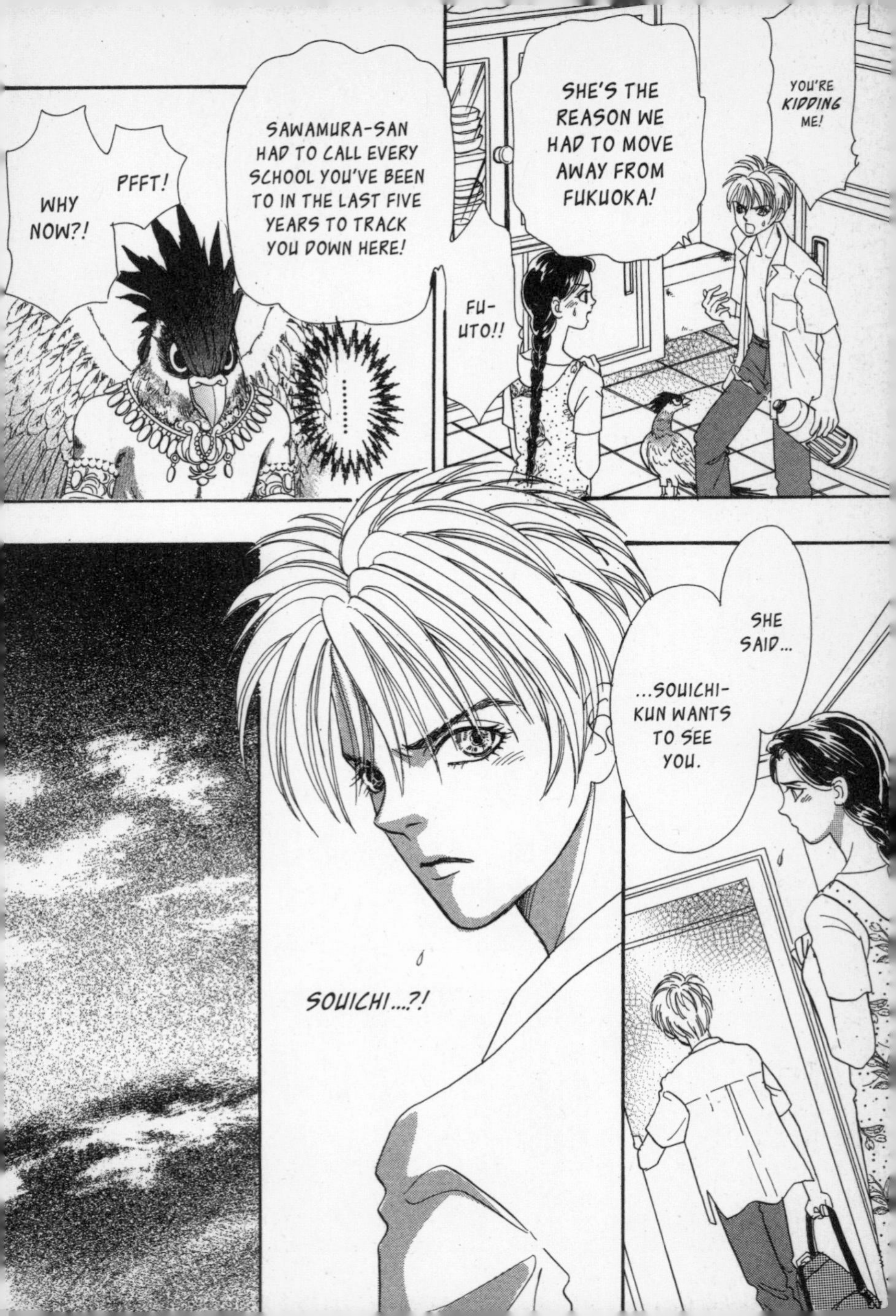
YOU'RE KIDDING ME!
SHE'S THE REASON WE HAD TO MOVE AWAY FROM FUKUOKA!
FU-UTO!!
SAWAMURA-SAN HAD TO CALL EVERY SCHOOL YOU'VE BEEN TO IN THE LAST FIVE YEARS TO TRACK YOU DOWN HERE!
PFFT!
WHY NOW?!
......
SHE SAID...
...SOUICHI-KUN WANTS TO SEE YOU.
SOUICHI...?!

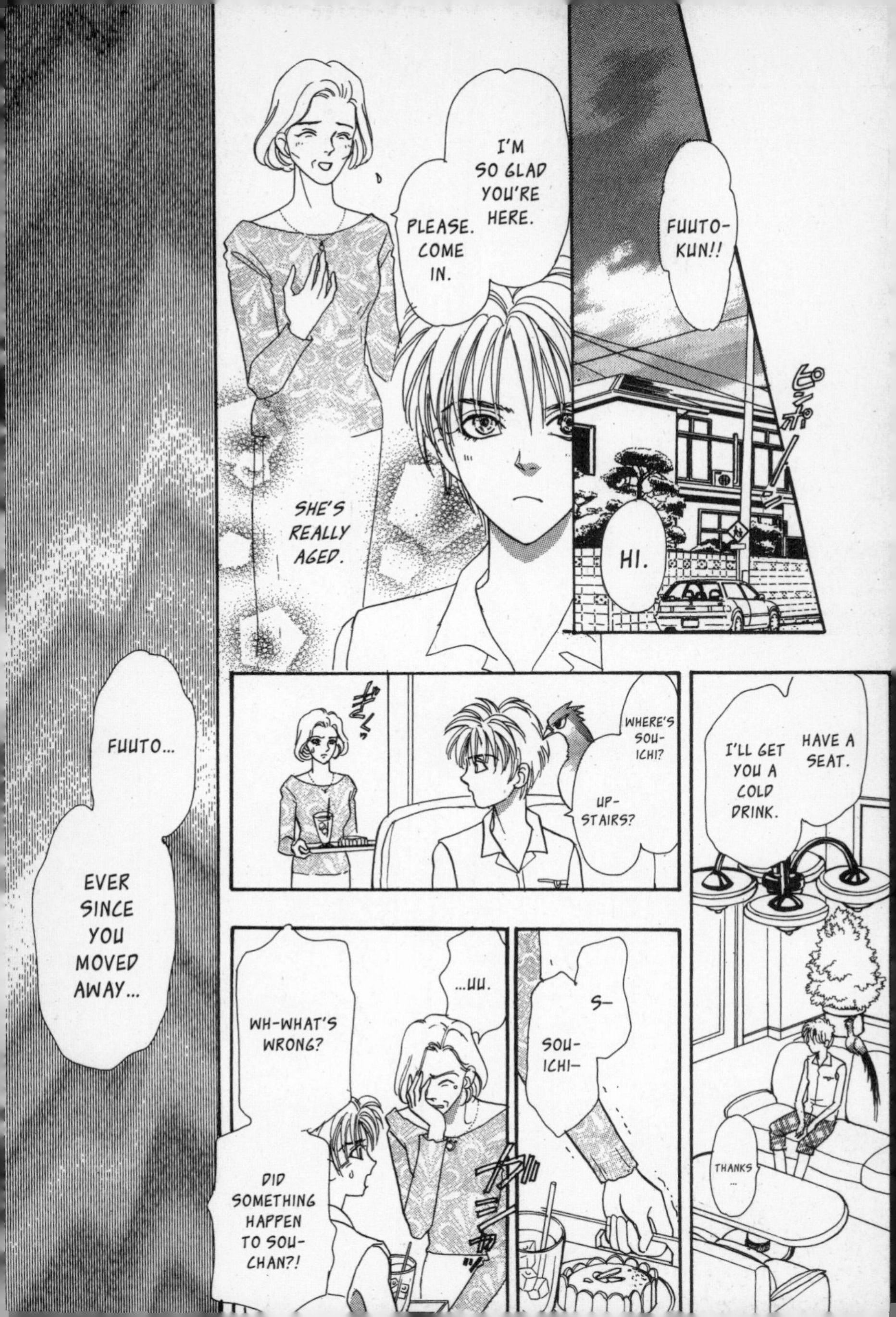
FUUTO-KUN!!
HI.
I'M SO GLAD YOU'RE HERE.
PLEASE. COME IN.
SHE'S REALLY AGED.
HAVE A SEAT.
I'LL GET YOU A COLD DRINK.
THANKS ...
WHERE'S SOU-ICHI?
UP-STAIRS?
S- SOU-ICHI-
...UU.
WH-WHAT'S WRONG?
DID SOMETHING HAPPEN TO SOU-CHAN?!
FUUTO...
EVER SINCE YOU MOVED AWAY...

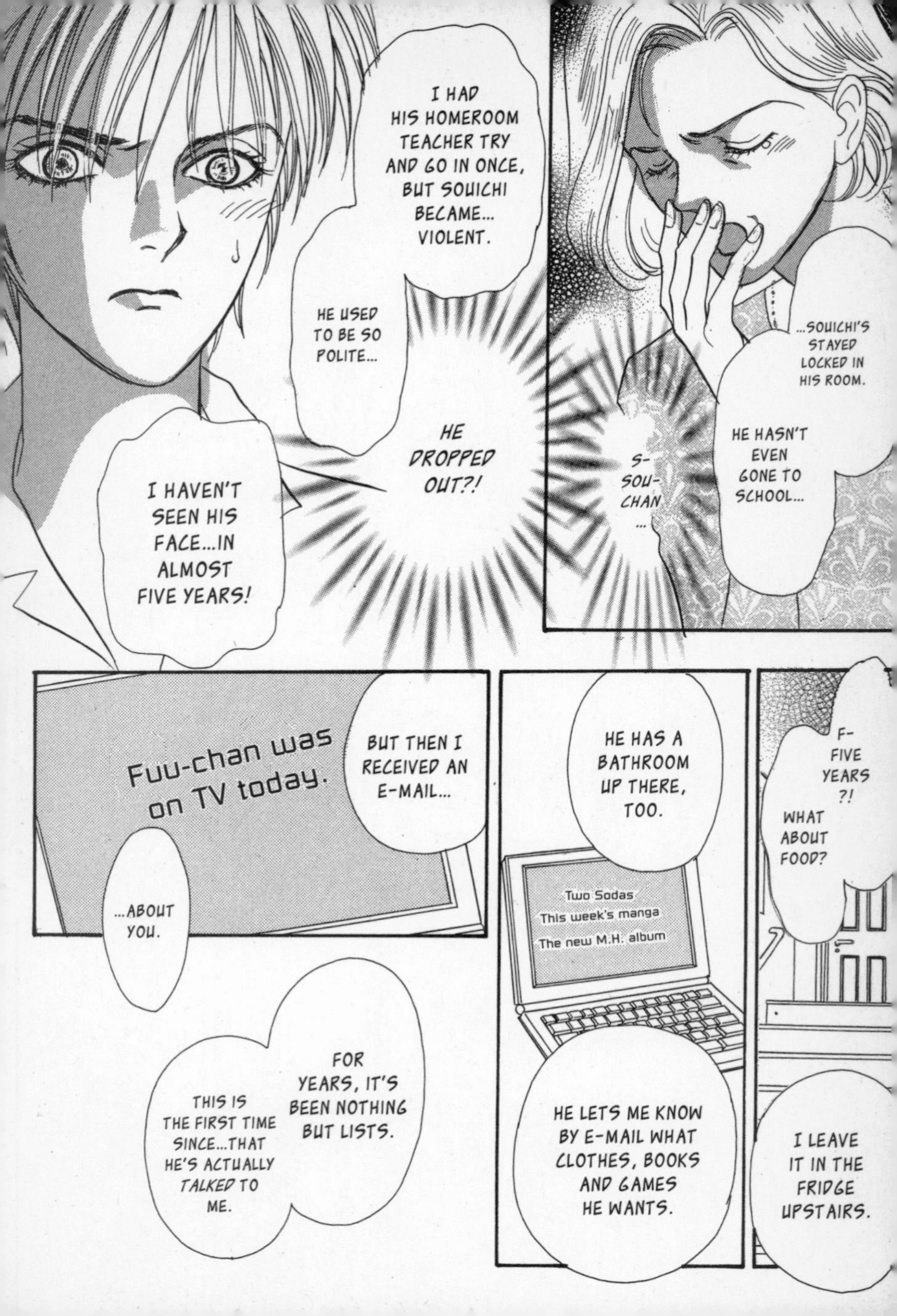
...SOUICHI'S STAYED LOCKED IN HIS ROOM.
HE HASN'T EVEN GONE TO SCHOOL...
S-SOU-CHAN...
HE DROPPED OUT?!
I HAD HIS HOMEROOM TEACHER TRY AND GO IN ONCE, BUT SOUICHI BECAME... VIOLENT.
HE USED TO BE SO POLITE...
I HAVEN'T SEEN HIS FACE...IN ALMOST FIVE YEARS!
F-FIVE YEARS?!
WHAT ABOUT FOOD?
I LEAVE IT IN THE FRIDGE UPSTAIRS.
HE HAS A BATHROOM UP THERE, TOO.
Two Sodas
This week's manga
The new M.H. album
HE LETS ME KNOW BY E-MAIL WHAT CLOTHES, BOOKS AND GAMES HE WANTS.
BUT THEN I RECEIVED AN E-MAIL...
Fuu-chan was on TV today.
...ABOUT YOU.
FOR YEARS, IT'S BEEN NOTHING BUT LISTS.
THIS IS THE FIRST TIME SINCE...THAT HE'S ACTUALLY *TALKED* TO ME.

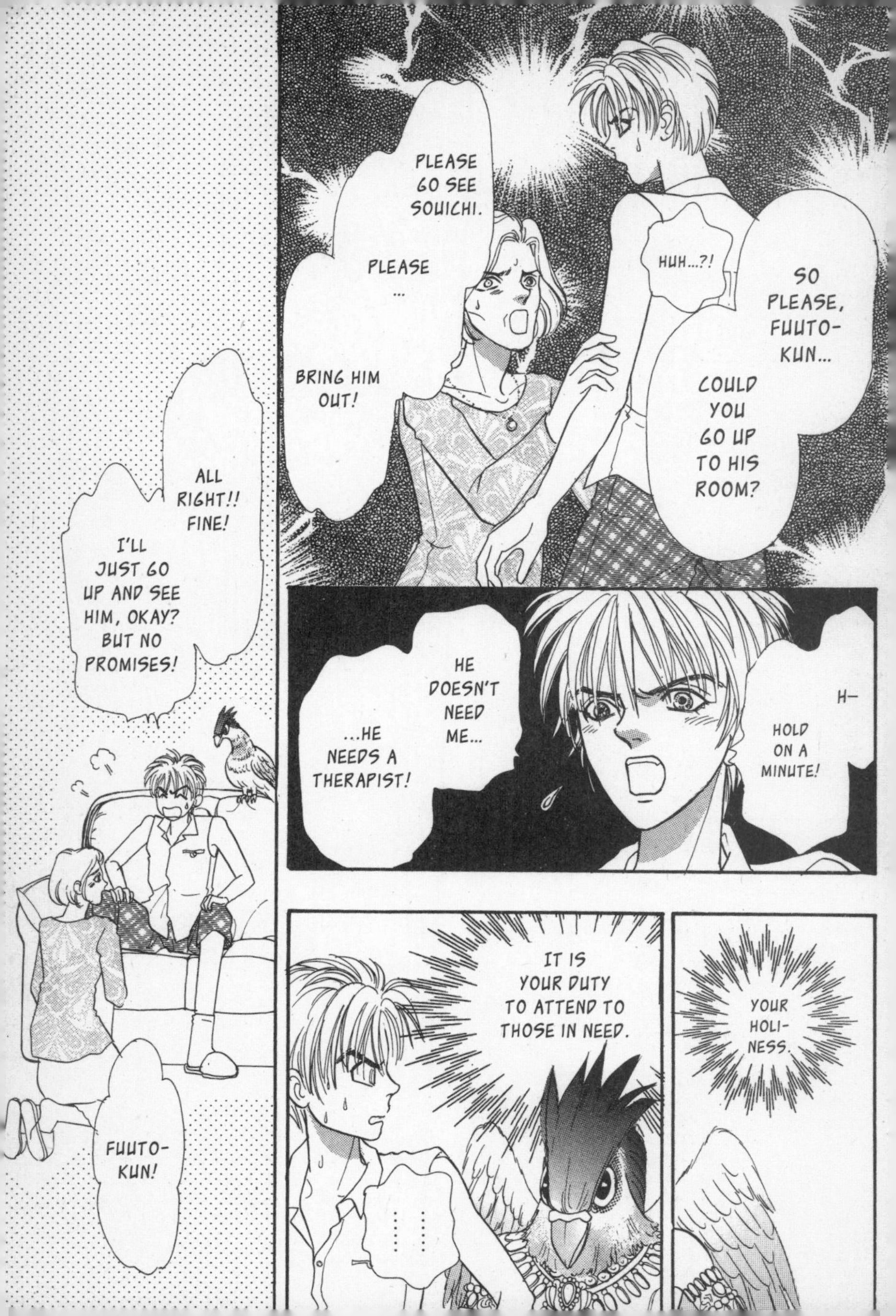
SO PLEASE, FUUTO-KUN... COULD YOU GO UP TO HIS ROOM?
HUH...?!
PLEASE GO SEE SOUICHI. PLEASE ... BRING HIM OUT!
H— HOLD ON A MINUTE!
HE DOESN'T NEED ME... ...HE NEEDS A THERAPIST!
YOUR HOLINESS.
IT IS YOUR DUTY TO ATTEND TO THOSE IN NEED.
……
ALL RIGHT!! FINE!
I'LL JUST GO UP AND SEE HIM, OKAY? BUT NO PROMISES!
FUUTO-KUN!

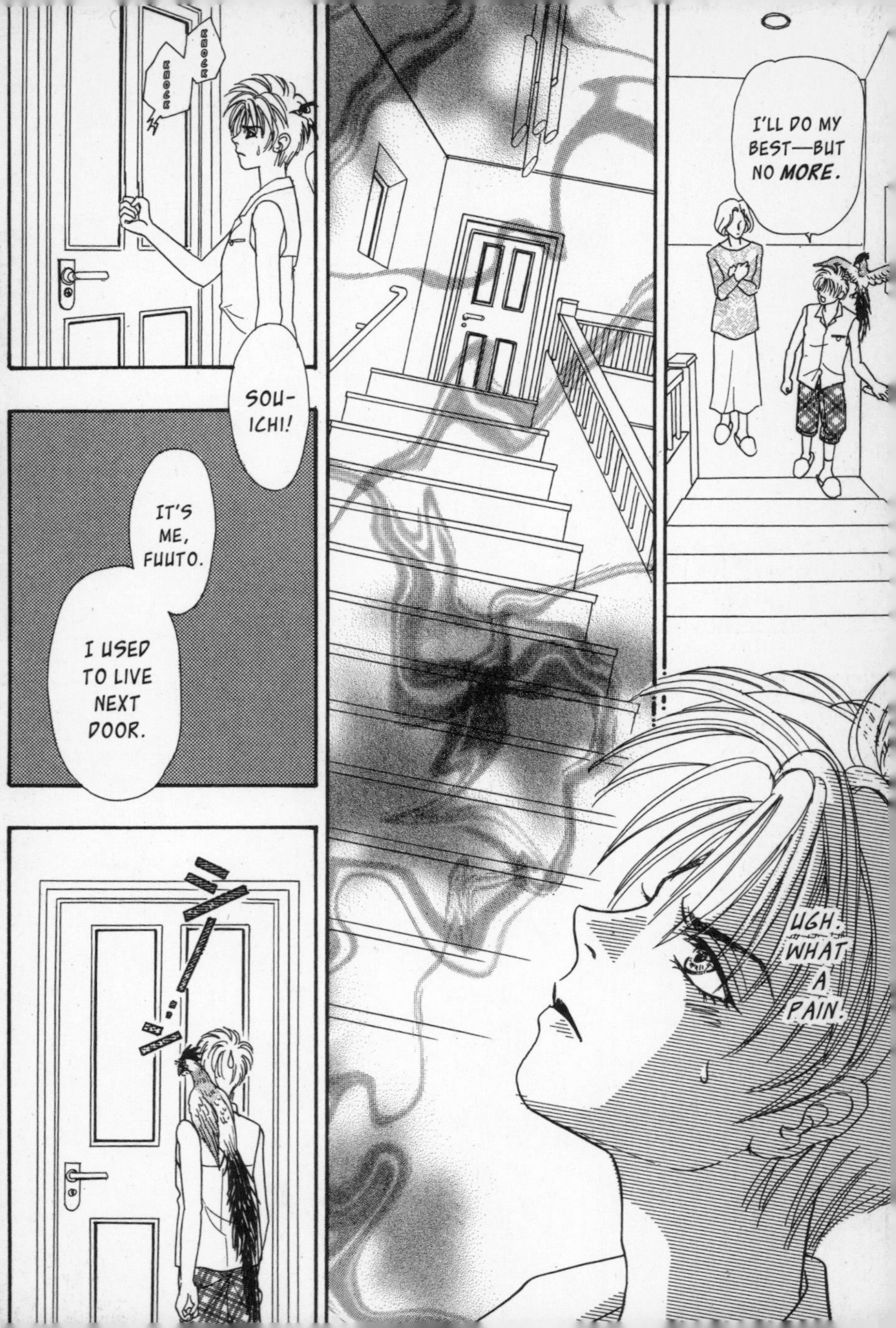
I'LL DO MY BEST—BUT NO MORE.
UGH. WHAT A PAIN.
KNOCK KNOCK
SOU-ICHI!
IT'S ME, FUUTO.
I USED TO LIVE NEXT DOOR.

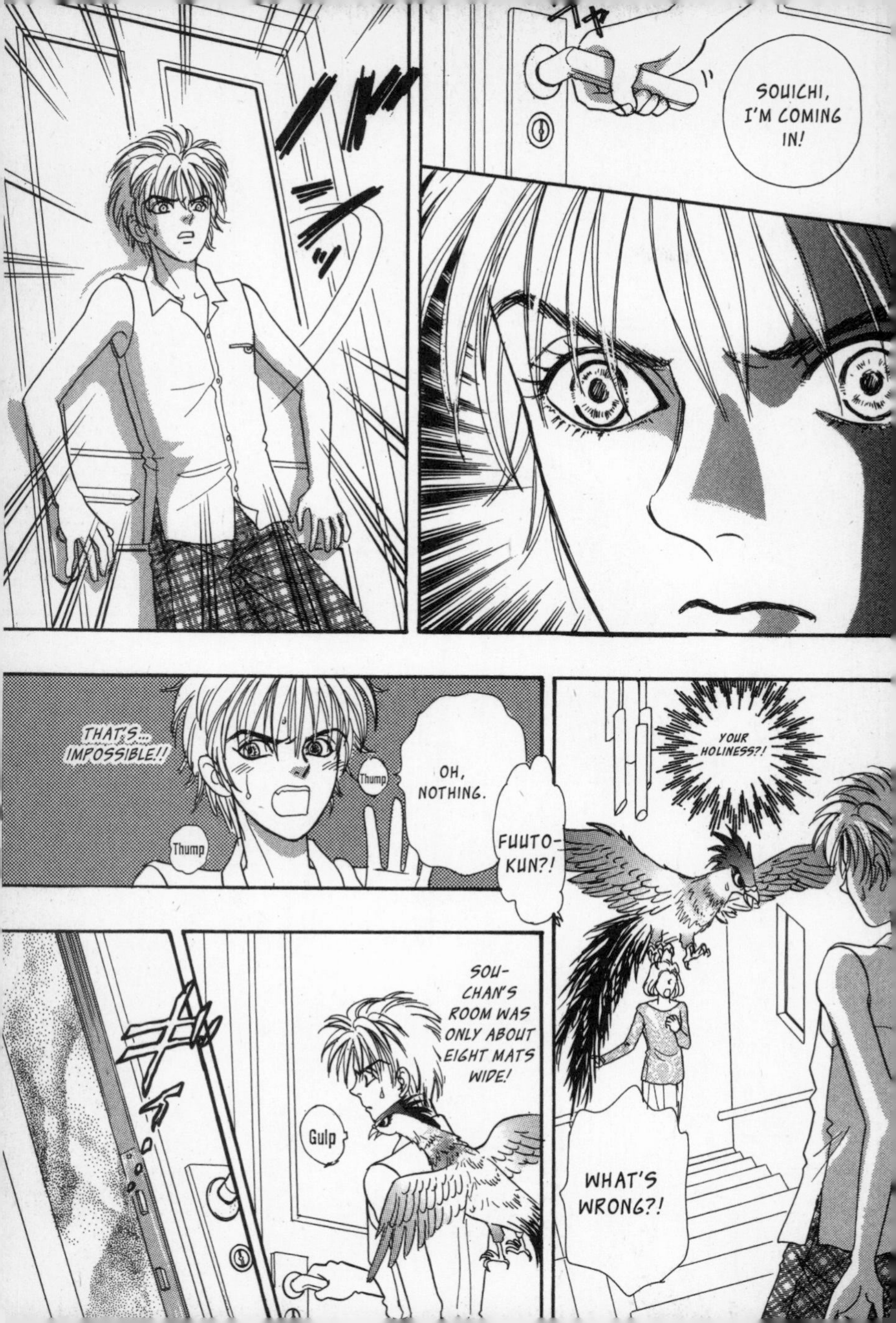
SOUICHI, I'M COMING IN!
YOUR HOLINESS?!
FUUTO-KUN?!
WHAT'S WRONG?!
OH, NOTHING.
Thump
THAT'S... IMPOSSIBLE!!
Thump
SOU-CHAN'S ROOM WAS ONLY ABOUT EIGHT MATS WIDE!
Gulp

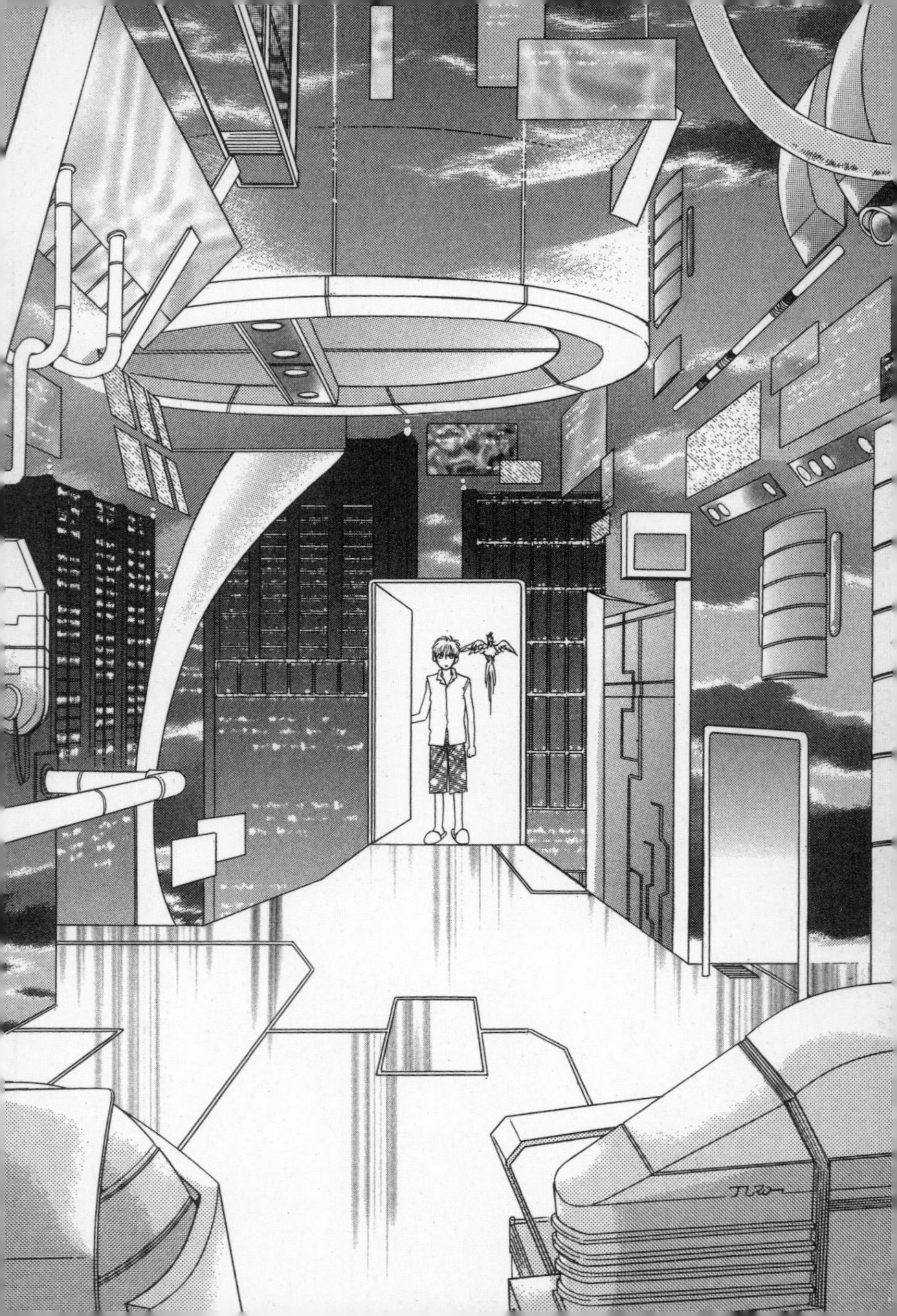

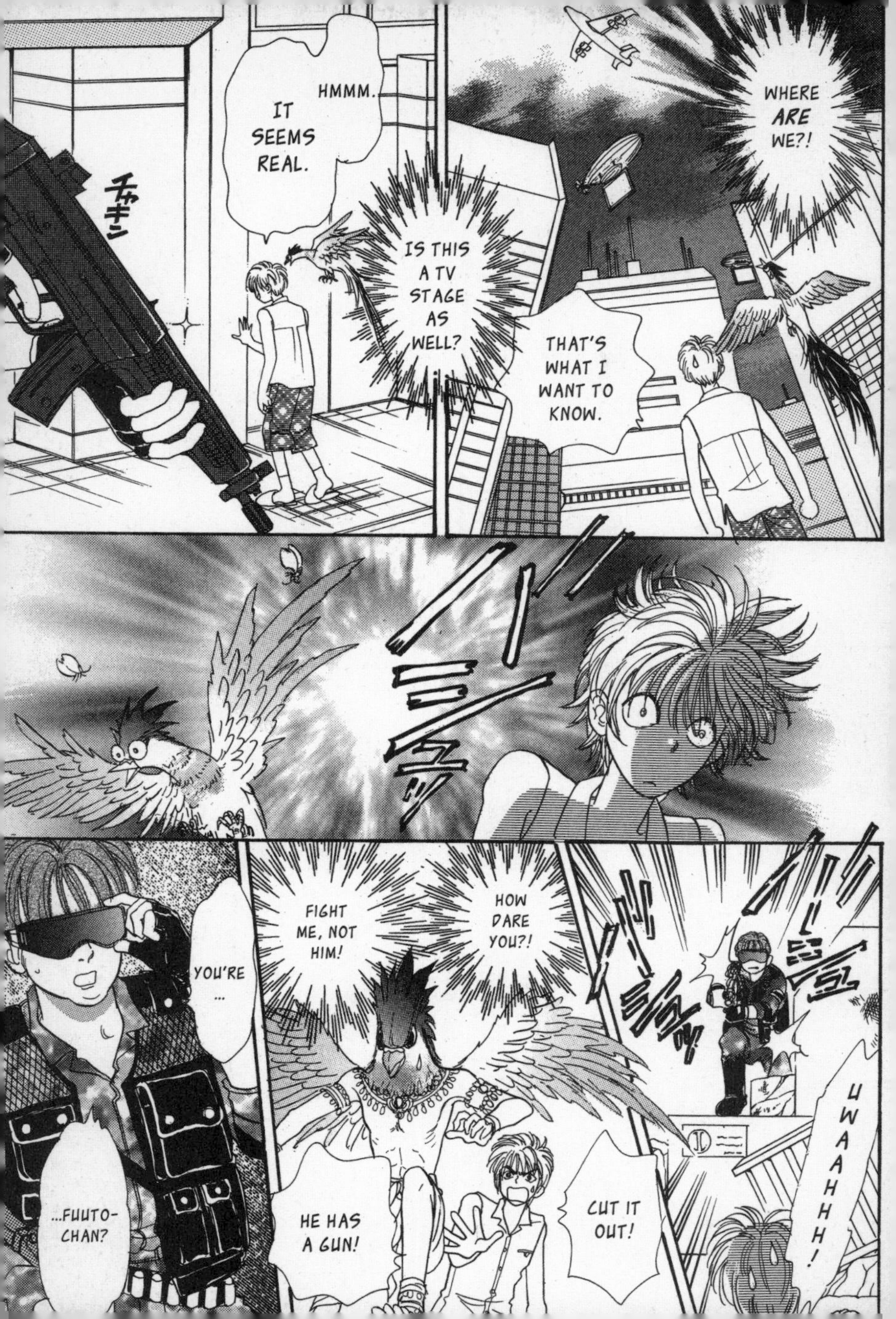
WHERE ARE WE?!
IS THIS A TV STAGE AS WELL?
THAT'S WHAT I WANT TO KNOW.
HMMM. IT SEEMS REAL.
チャキン
UWAAAHHHH!
HOW DARE YOU?!
FIGHT ME, NOT HIM!
CUT IT OUT!
HE HAS A GUN!
YOU'RE ...
...FUUTO-CHAN?

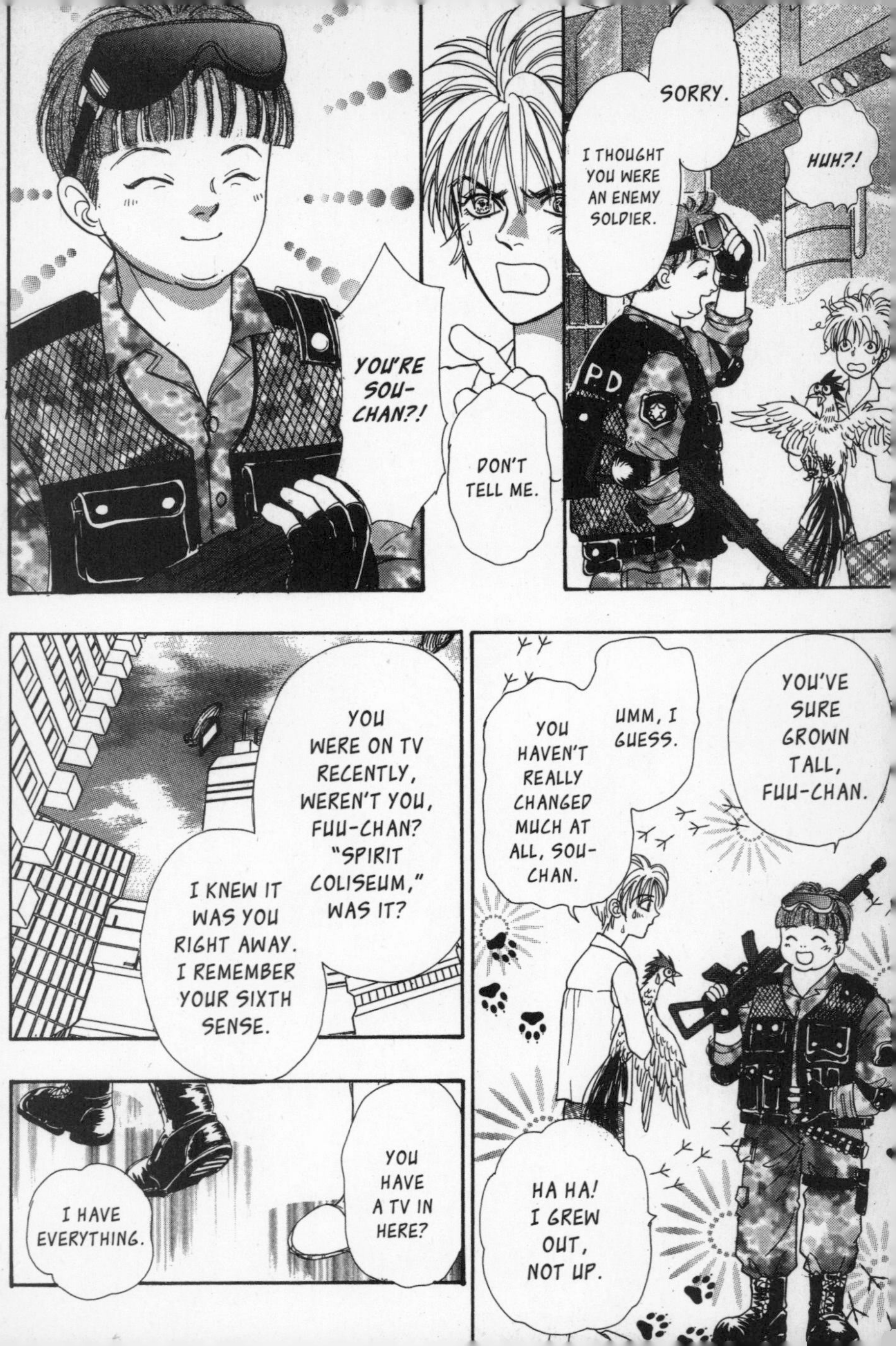
SORRY.
I THOUGHT YOU WERE AN ENEMY SOLDIER.
HUH?!
DON'T TELL ME.
YOU'RE SOU-CHAN?!
YOU'VE SURE GROWN TALL, FUU-CHAN.
UMM, I GUESS.
YOU HAVEN'T REALLY CHANGED MUCH AT ALL, SOU-CHAN.
HA HA! I GREW OUT, NOT UP.
YOU WERE ON TV RECENTLY, WEREN'T YOU, FUU-CHAN? "SPIRIT COLISEUM," WAS IT?
I KNEW IT WAS YOU RIGHT AWAY. I REMEMBER YOUR SIXTH SENSE.
YOU HAVE A TV IN HERE?
I HAVE EVERYTHING.

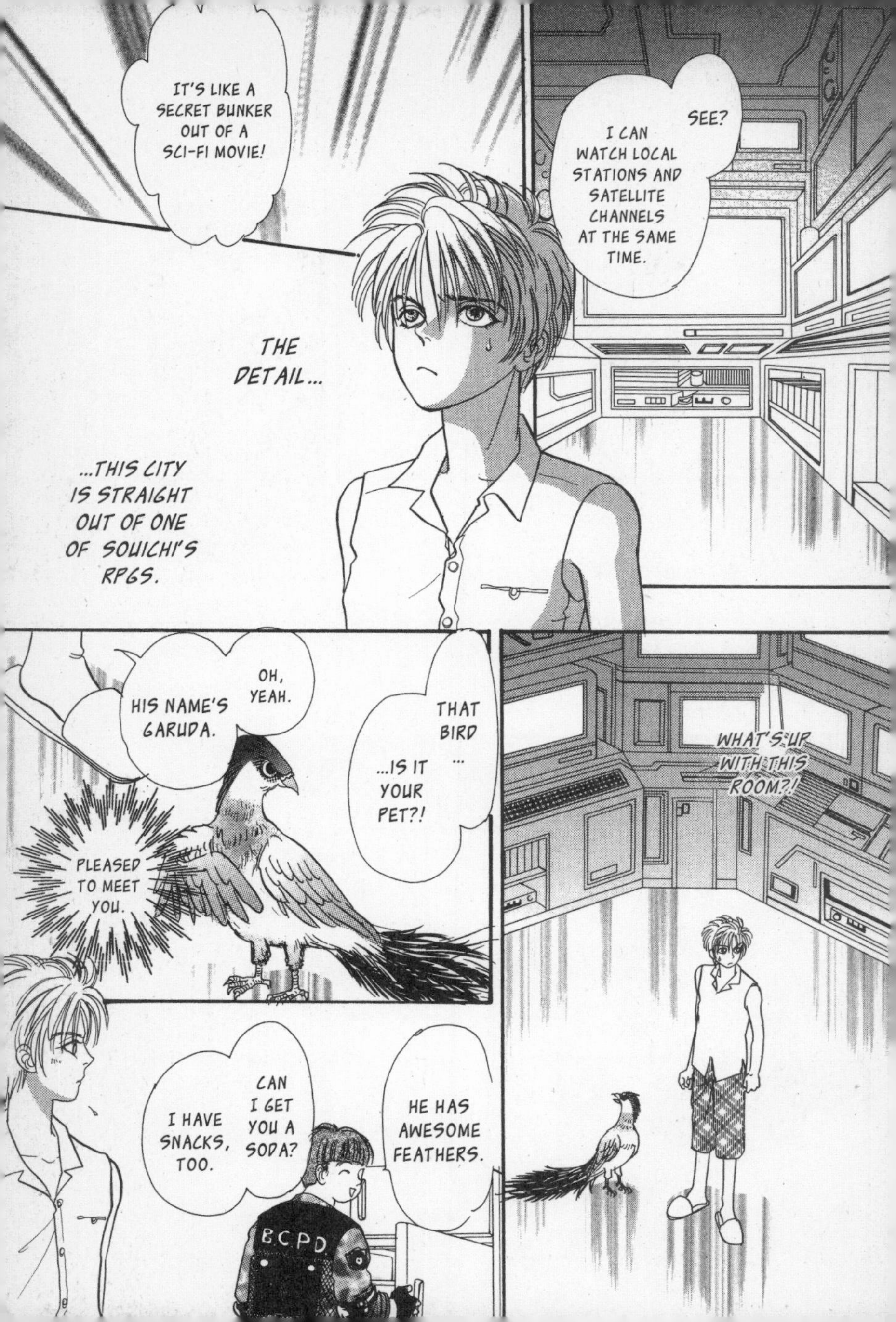
SEE?
I CAN WATCH LOCAL STATIONS AND SATELLITE CHANNELS AT THE SAME TIME.
IT'S LIKE A SECRET BUNKER OUT OF A SCI-FI MOVIE!
THE DETAIL...
...THIS CITY IS STRAIGHT OUT OF ONE OF SOUICHI'S RPGS.
WHAT'S UP WITH THIS ROOM?!
THAT BIRD...
...IS IT YOUR PET?!
OH, YEAH.
HIS NAME'S GARUDA.
PLEASED TO MEET YOU.
HE HAS AWESOME FEATHERS.
CAN I GET YOU A SODA?
I HAVE SNACKS, TOO.
B.C.P.D

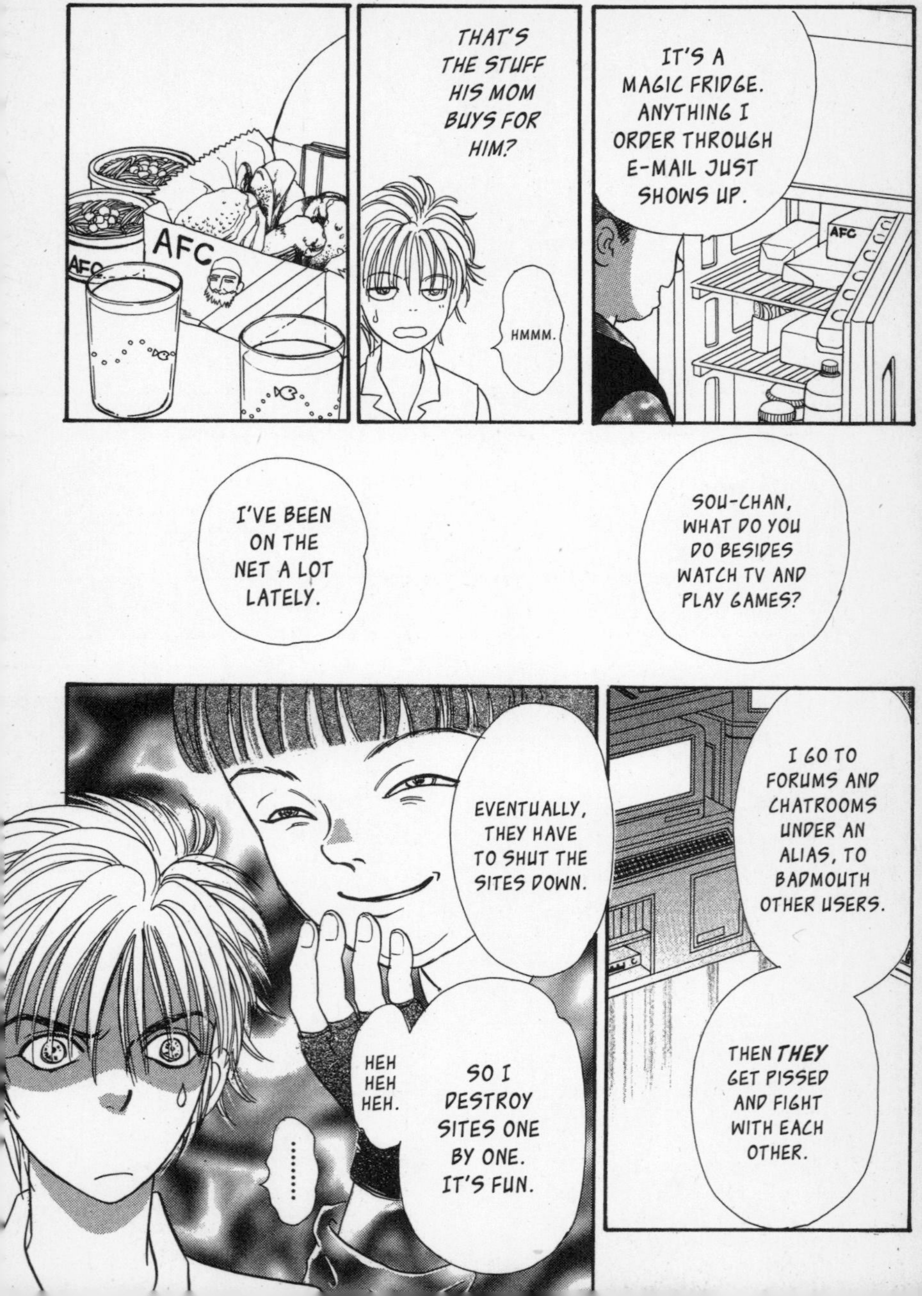
IT'S A MAGIC FRIDGE. ANYTHING I ORDER THROUGH E-MAIL JUST SHOWS UP.
AFC
THAT'S THE STUFF HIS MOM BUYS FOR HIM?
HMMM.
AFC
SOU-CHAN, WHAT DO YOU DO BESIDES WATCH TV AND PLAY GAMES?
I'VE BEEN ON THE NET A LOT LATELY.
I GO TO FORUMS AND CHATROOMS UNDER AN ALIAS, TO BADMOUTH OTHER USERS.
THEN *THEY* GET PISSED AND FIGHT WITH EACH OTHER.
EVENTUALLY, THEY HAVE TO SHUT THE SITES DOWN.
SO I DESTROY SITES ONE BY ONE. IT'S FUN.
HEH HEH HEH.
....

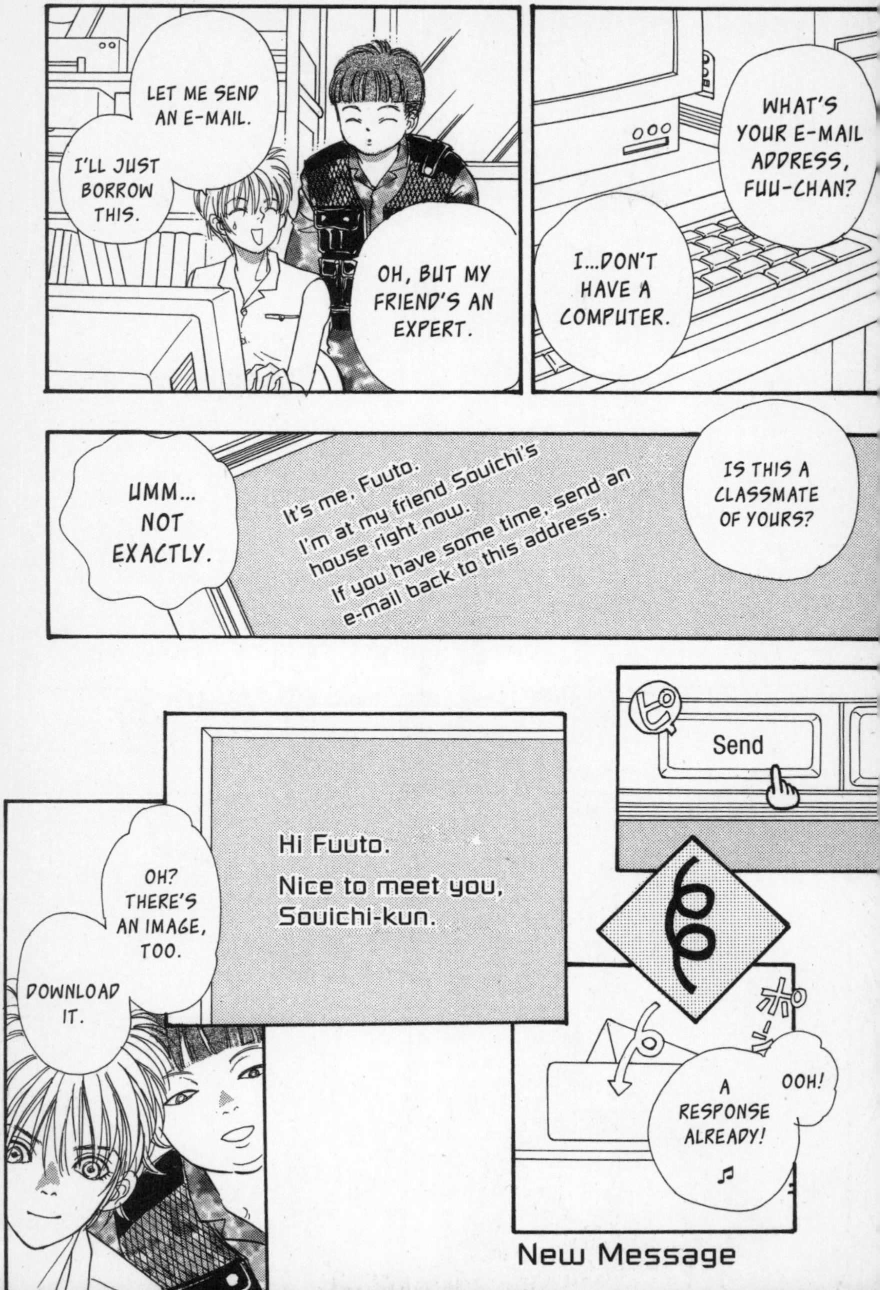
WHAT'S YOUR E-MAIL ADDRESS, FUU-CHAN?
I...DON'T HAVE A COMPUTER.
LET ME SEND AN E-MAIL.
I'LL JUST BORROW THIS.
OH, BUT MY FRIEND'S AN EXPERT.
IS THIS A CLASSMATE OF YOURS?
It's me, Fuuto.
I'm at my friend Souichi's house right now.
If you have some time, send an e-mail back to this address.
UMM... NOT EXACTLY.
ピ
Send
OOH!
A RESPONSE ALREADY! ♪
New Message
Hi Fuuto.
Nice to meet you, Souichi-kun.
OH? THERE'S AN IMAGE, TOO.
DOWNLOAD IT.

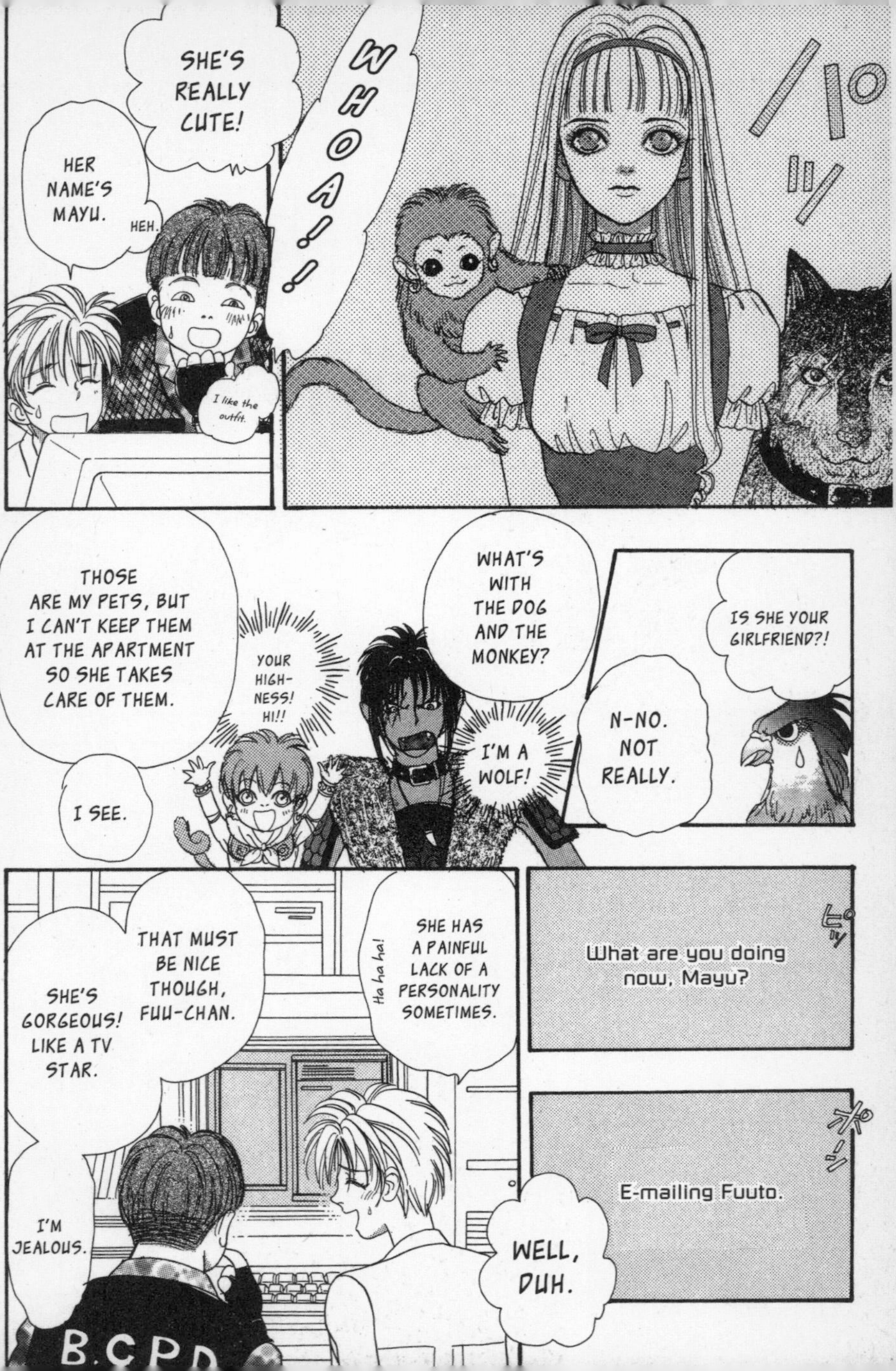
WHOA!!
SHE'S REALLY CUTE!
HER NAME'S MAYU.
HEH.
I like the outfit.
IS SHE YOUR GIRLFRIEND?!
N-NO. NOT REALLY.
WHAT'S WITH THE DOG AND THE MONKEY?
I'M A WOLF!
YOUR HIGHNESS! HI!!
THOSE ARE MY PETS, BUT I CAN'T KEEP THEM AT THE APARTMENT SO SHE TAKES CARE OF THEM.
I SEE.
What are you doing now, Mayu?
E-mailing Fuuto.
SHE HAS A PAINFUL LACK OF A PERSONALITY SOMETIMES.
Ha ha ha!
THAT MUST BE NICE THOUGH, FUU-CHAN.
SHE'S GORGEOUS! LIKE A TV STAR.
I'M JEALOUS.
WELL, DUH.
B.C.P.D

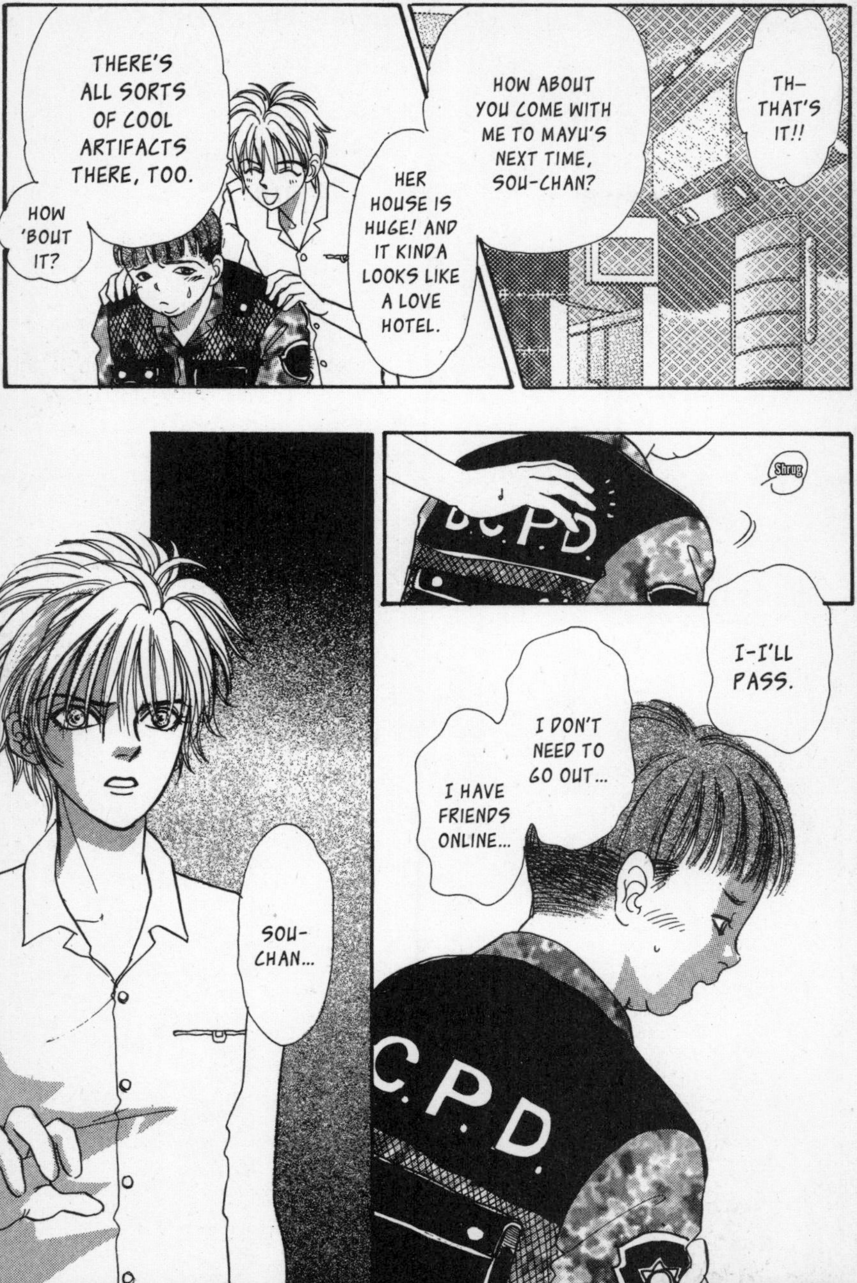
TH— THAT'S IT!!
HOW ABOUT YOU COME WITH ME TO MAYU'S NEXT TIME, SOU-CHAN?
HER HOUSE IS HUGE! AND IT KINDA LOOKS LIKE A LOVE HOTEL.
THERE'S ALL SORTS OF COOL ARTIFACTS THERE, TOO.
HOW 'BOUT IT?
Shrug
I-I'LL PASS.
I DON'T NEED TO GO OUT...
I HAVE FRIENDS ONLINE...
SOU-CHAN...

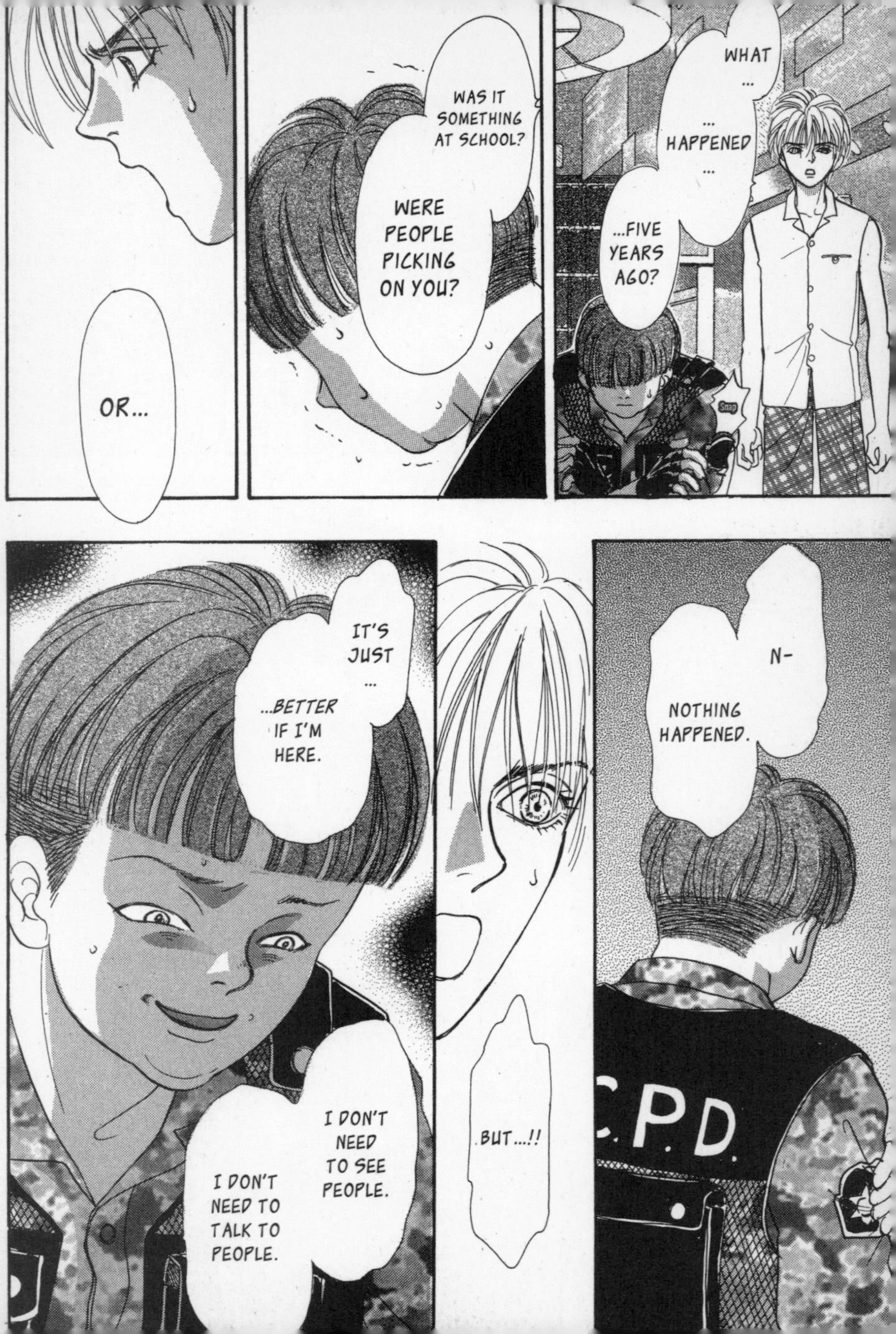
WHAT ... ... HAPPENED ...
...FIVE YEARS AGO?
Snap
WAS IT SOMETHING AT SCHOOL?
WERE PEOPLE PICKING ON YOU?
OR...
N- NOTHING HAPPENED.
C.P.D.
BUT...!!
IT'S JUST ...
...BETTER IF I'M HERE.
I DON'T NEED TO SEE PEOPLE.
I DON'T NEED TO TALK TO PEOPLE.

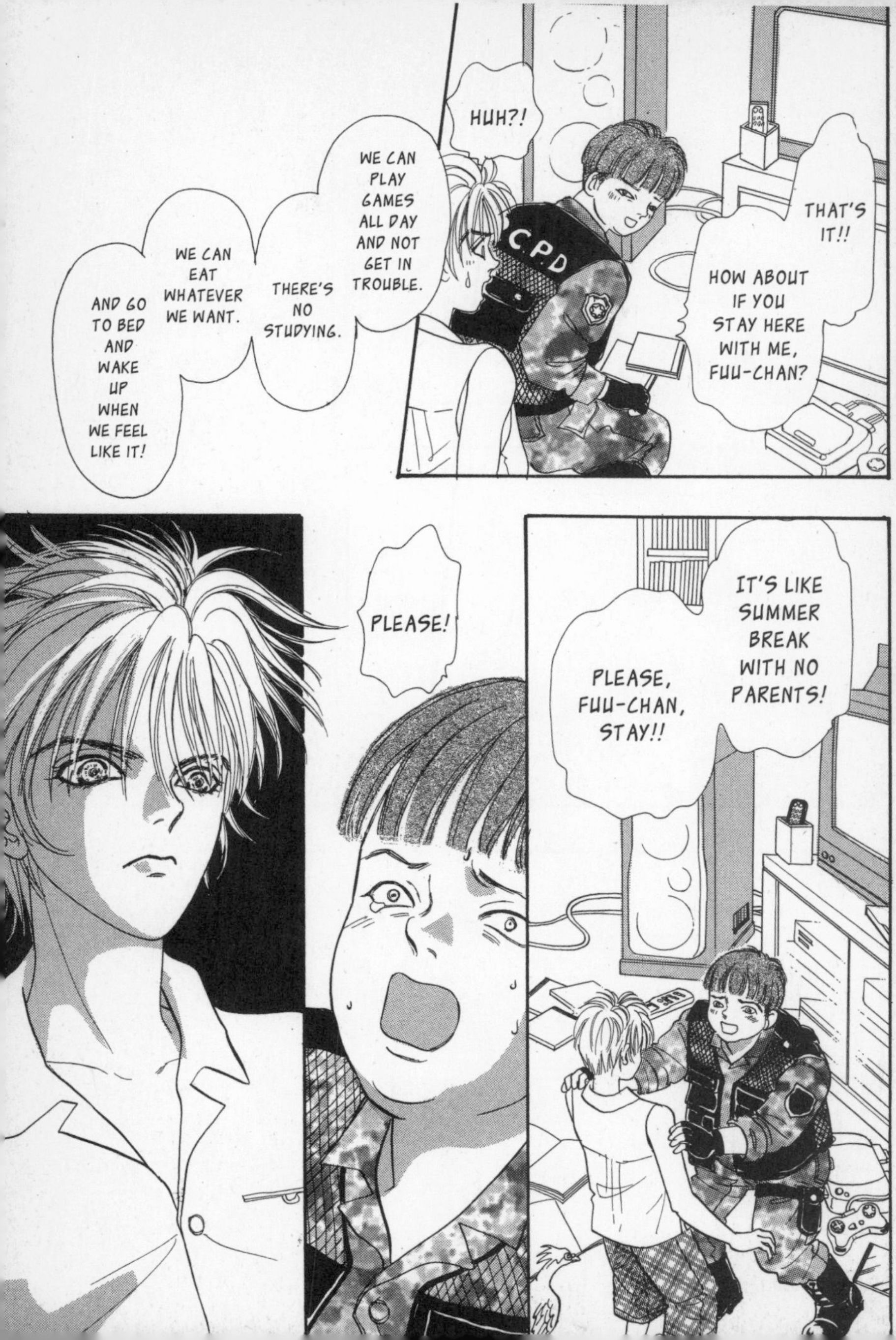
THAT'S IT!! HOW ABOUT IF YOU STAY HERE WITH ME, FUU-CHAN?
HUH?!
WE CAN PLAY GAMES ALL DAY AND NOT GET IN TROUBLE.
THERE'S NO STUDYING.
WE CAN EAT WHATEVER WE WANT.
AND GO TO BED AND WAKE UP WHEN WE FEEL LIKE IT!
IT'S LIKE SUMMER BREAK WITH NO PARENTS!
PLEASE, FUU-CHAN, STAY!!
PLEASE!

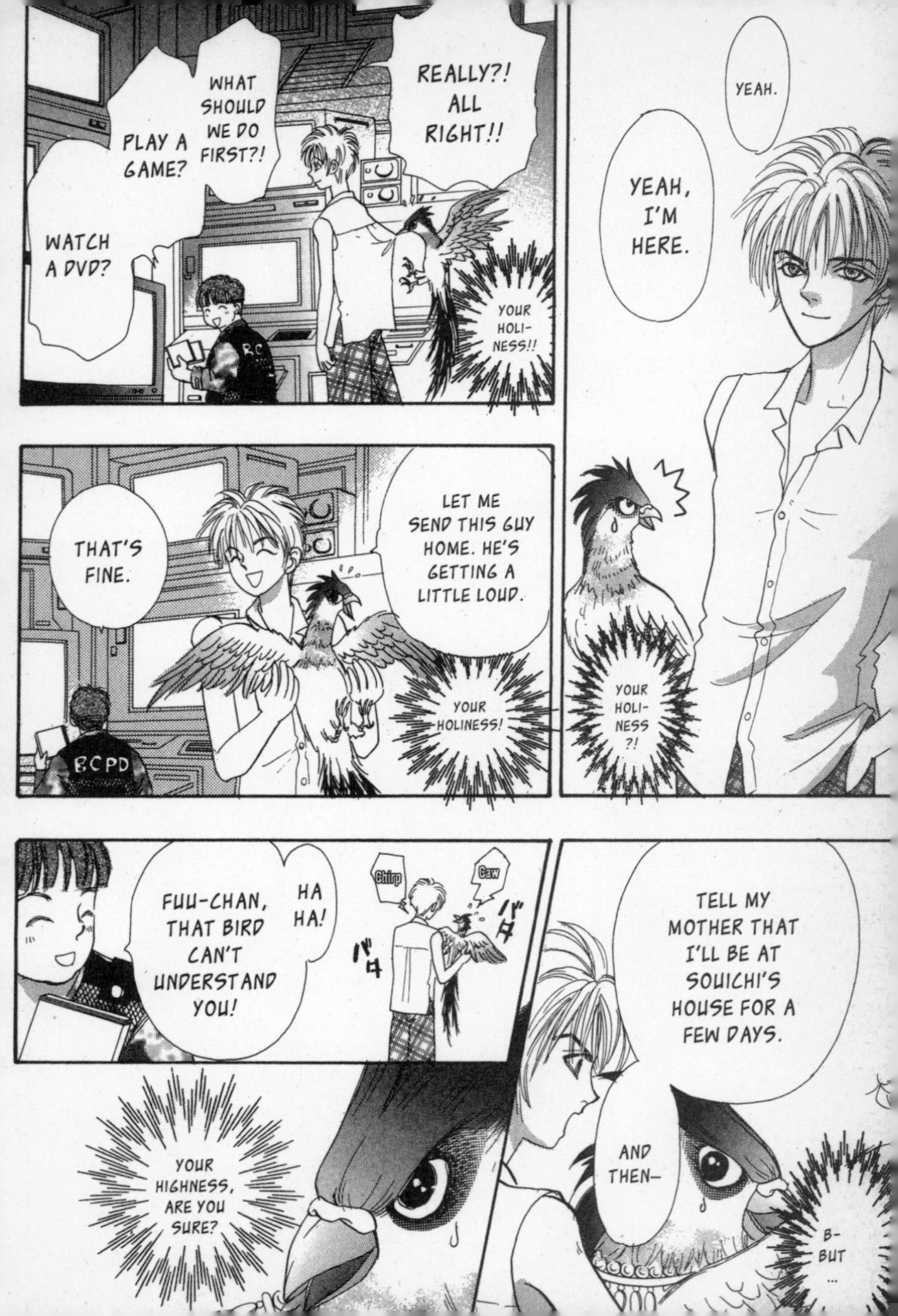
YEAH.
YEAH, I'M HERE.
YOUR HOLI-NESS ?!
REALLY?! ALL RIGHT!!
WHAT SHOULD WE DO FIRST?!
PLAY A GAME?
YOUR HOLINESS!!
WATCH A DVD?
LET ME SEND THIS GUY HOME. HE'S GETTING A LITTLE LOUD.
YOUR HOLINESS!
THAT'S FINE.
TELL MY MOTHER THAT I'LL BE AT SOUICHI'S HOUSE FOR A FEW DAYS.
AND THEN—
B-BUT...
Caw
バタ
Chirp
バタ
HA HA!
FUU-CHAN, THAT BIRD CAN'T UNDERSTAND YOU!
YOUR HIGHNESS, ARE YOU SURE?

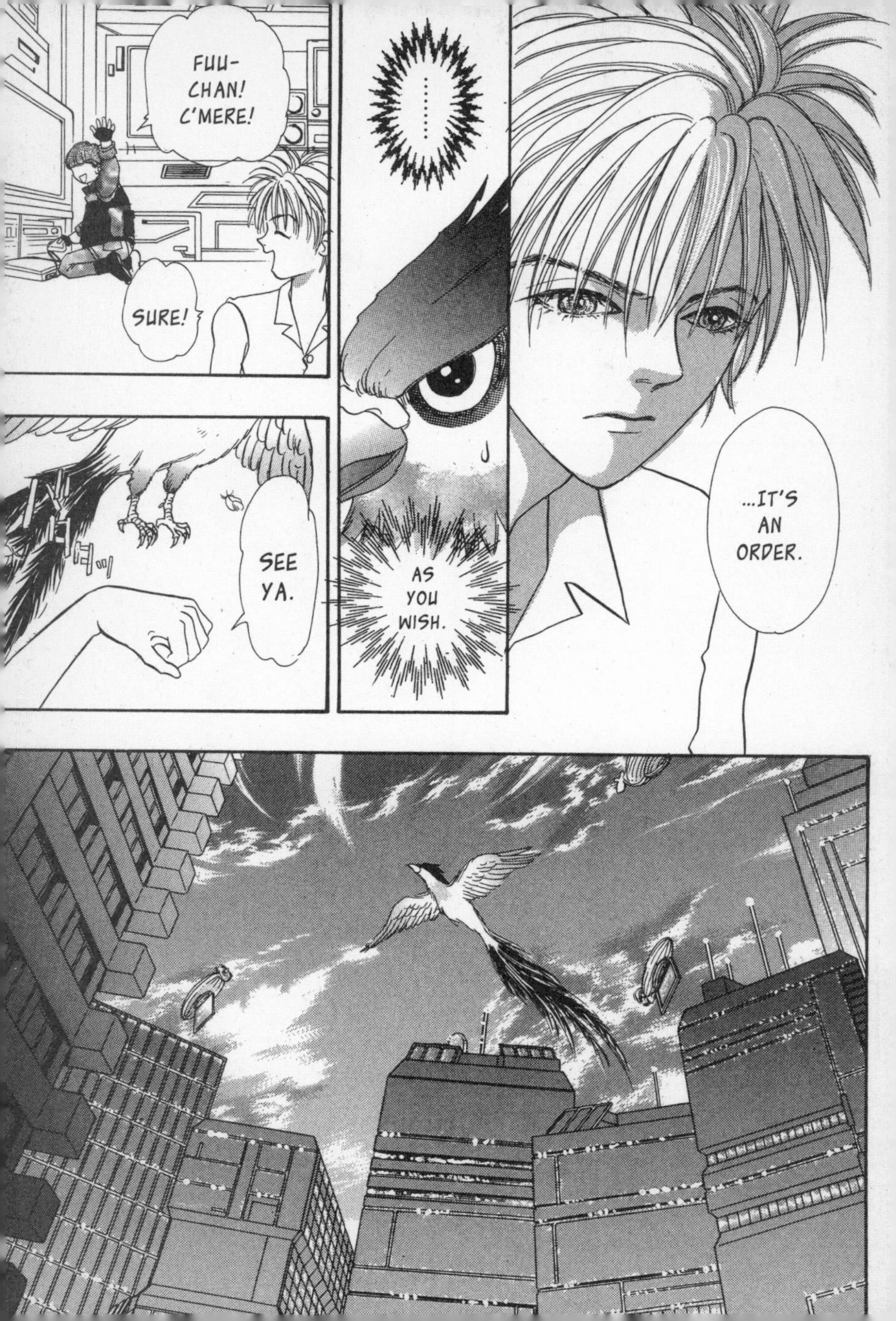
...IT'S AN ORDER.
......
AS YOU WISH.
FUU-CHAN! C'MERE!
SURE!
SEE YA.

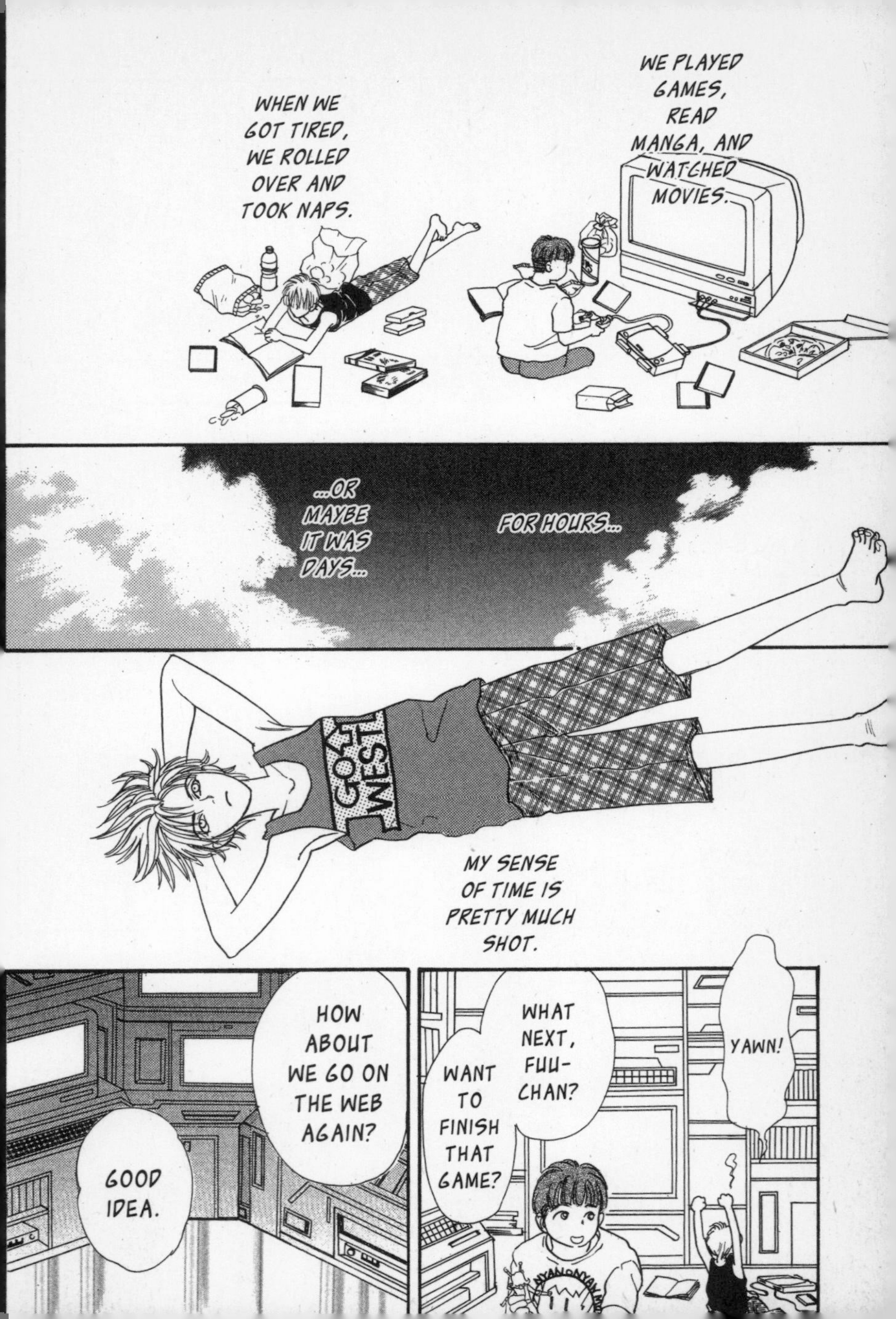
WE PLAYED GAMES, READ MANGA, AND WATCHED MOVIES.
WHEN WE GOT TIRED, WE ROLLED OVER AND TOOK NAPS.
FOR HOURS...
...OR MAYBE IT WAS DAYS...
MY SENSE OF TIME IS PRETTY MUCH SHOT.
YAWN!
WHAT NEXT, FUU-CHAN?
WANT TO FINISH THAT GAME?
HOW ABOUT WE GO ON THE WEB AGAIN?
GOOD IDEA.

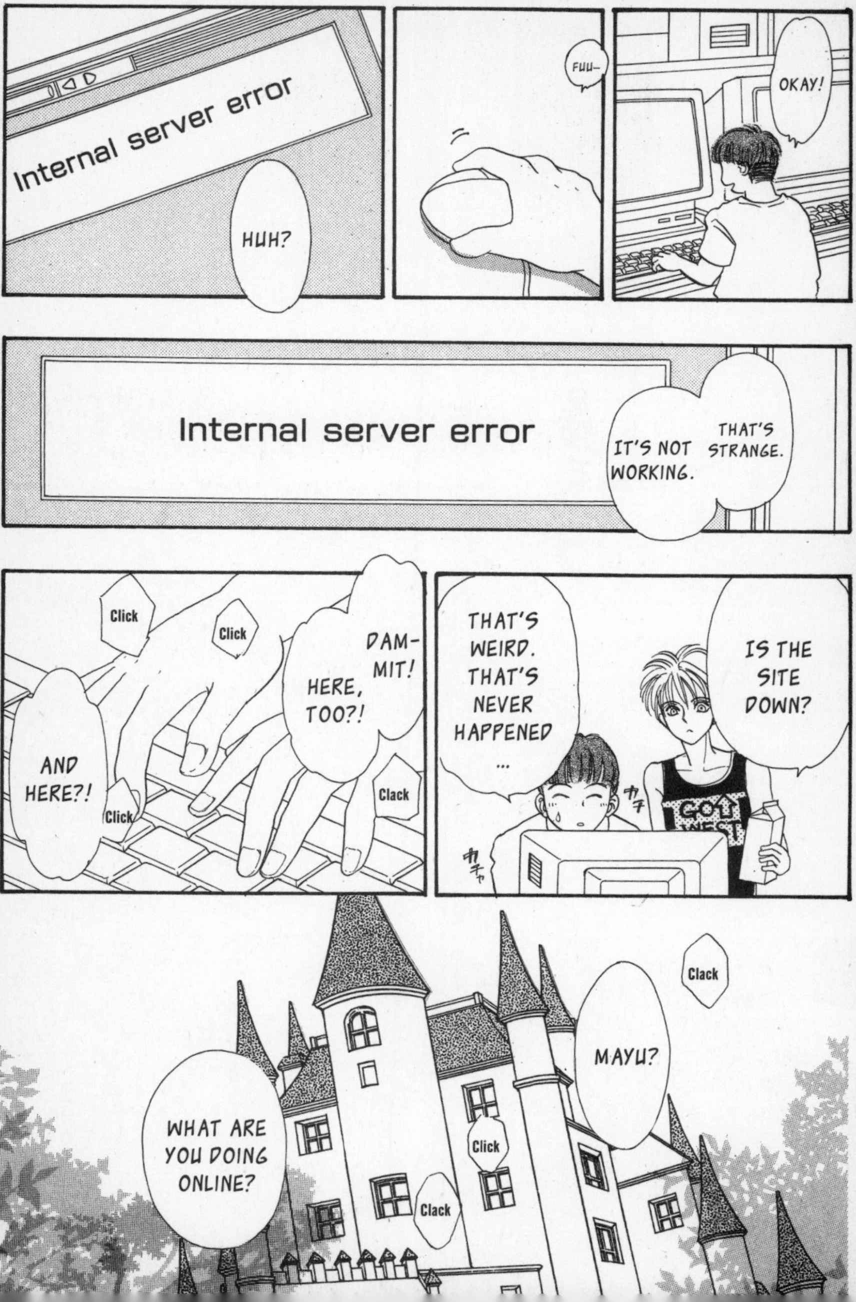
OKAY!
FUU–
Internal server error
HUH?
THAT'S STRANGE. IT'S NOT WORKING.
Internal server error
IS THE SITE DOWN?
THAT'S WEIRD. THAT'S NEVER HAPPENED ...
カチ
カチャ
DAM-MIT!
HERE, TOO?!
Click
Click
Clack
AND HERE?!
Click
Clack
MAYU?
Click
Clack
WHAT ARE YOU DOING ONLINE?

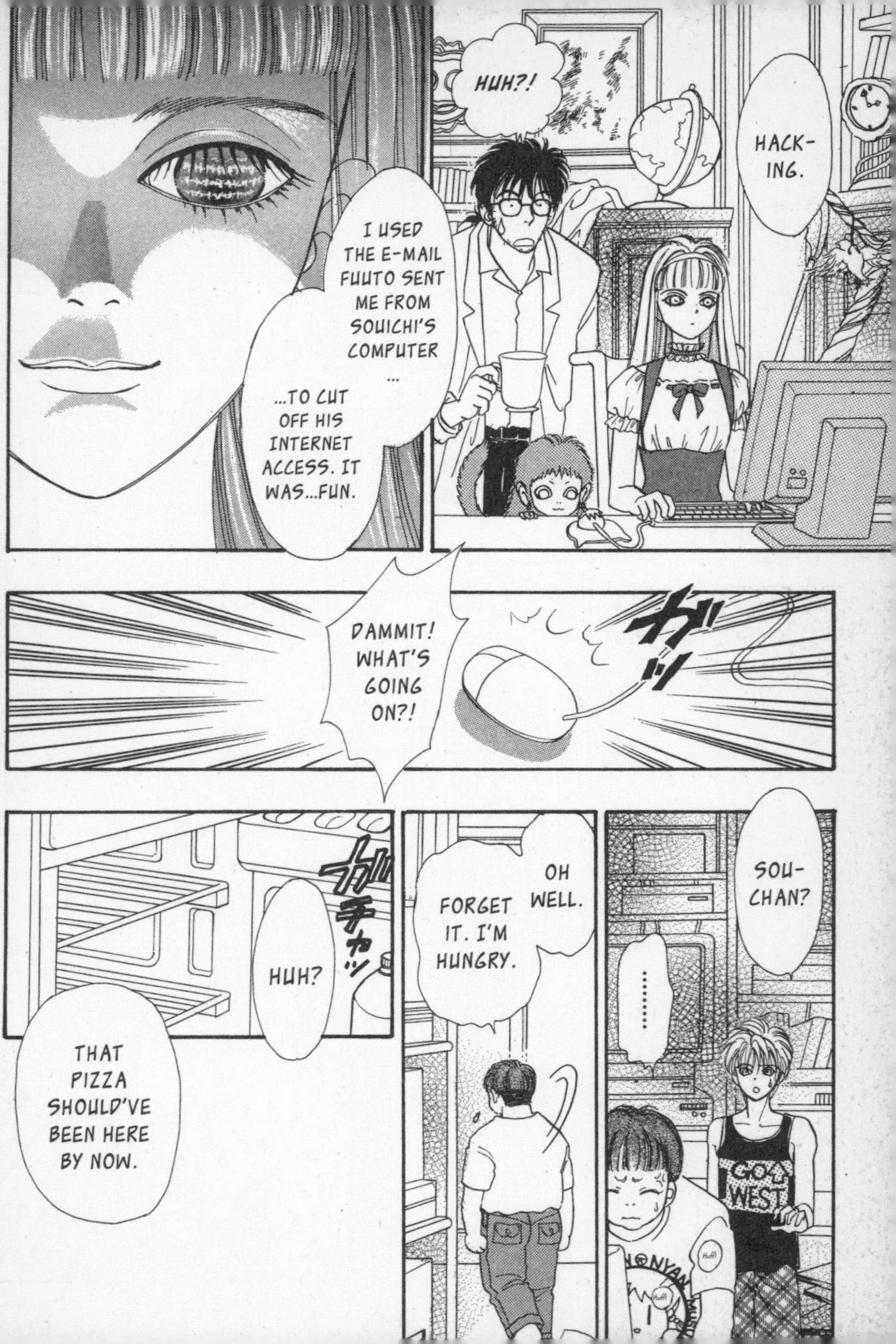
HACK-ING.
HUH?!
I USED THE E-MAIL FUUTO SENT ME FROM SOUICHI'S COMPUTER ...
...TO CUT OFF HIS INTERNET ACCESS. IT WAS...FUN.
ガッ
DAMMIT! WHAT'S GOING ON?!
SOU-CHAN?
......
GO WEST
OH WELL.
FORGET IT. I'M HUNGRY.
HUH?
THAT PIZZA SHOULD'VE BEEN HERE BY NOW.

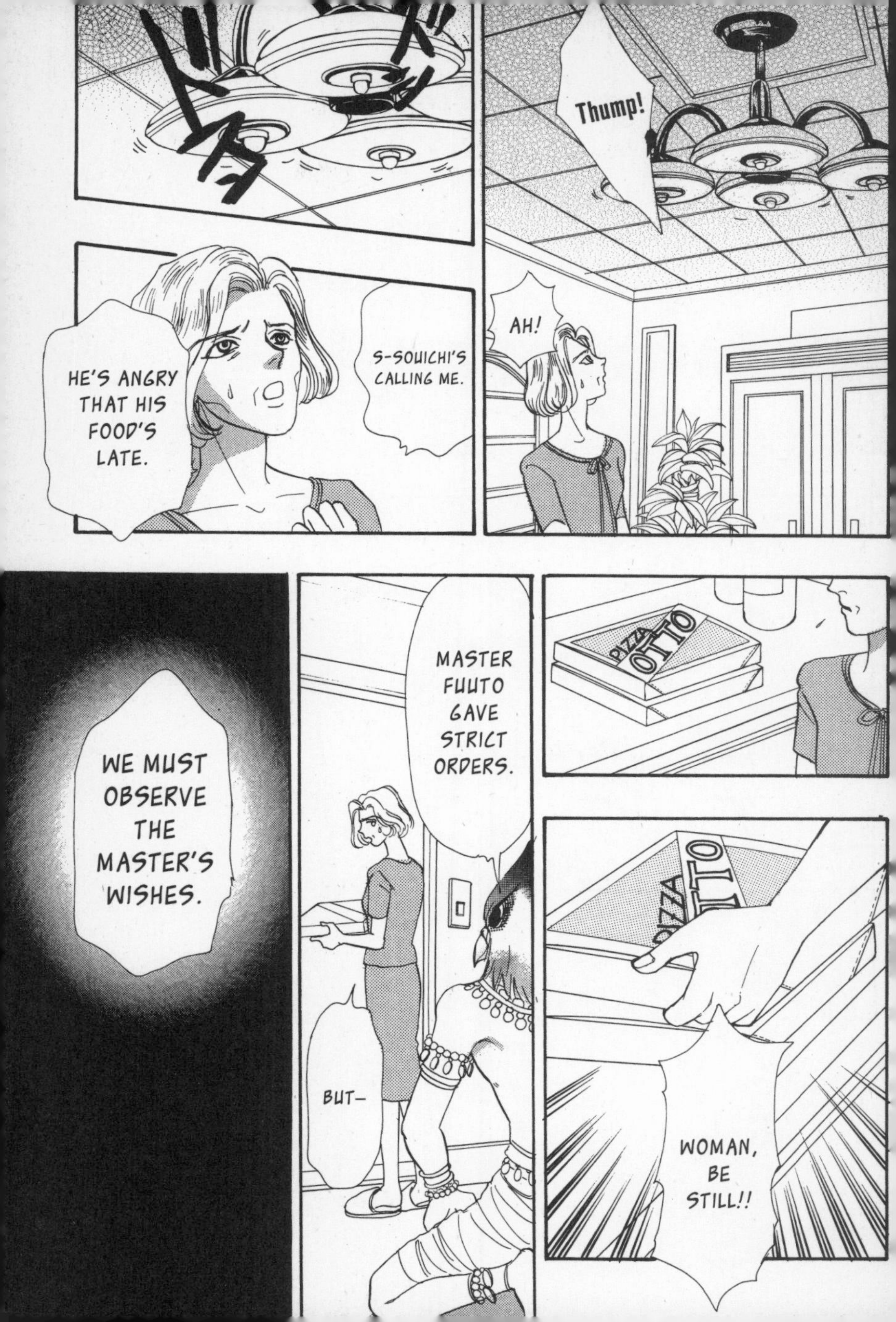
Thump!
AH!
S-SOUICHI'S CALLING ME.
HE'S ANGRY THAT HIS FOOD'S LATE.
PIZZA OTTO
PIZZA OTTO
WOMAN, BE STILL!!
MASTER FUUTO GAVE STRICT ORDERS.
BUT—
WE MUST OBSERVE THE MASTER'S WISHES.

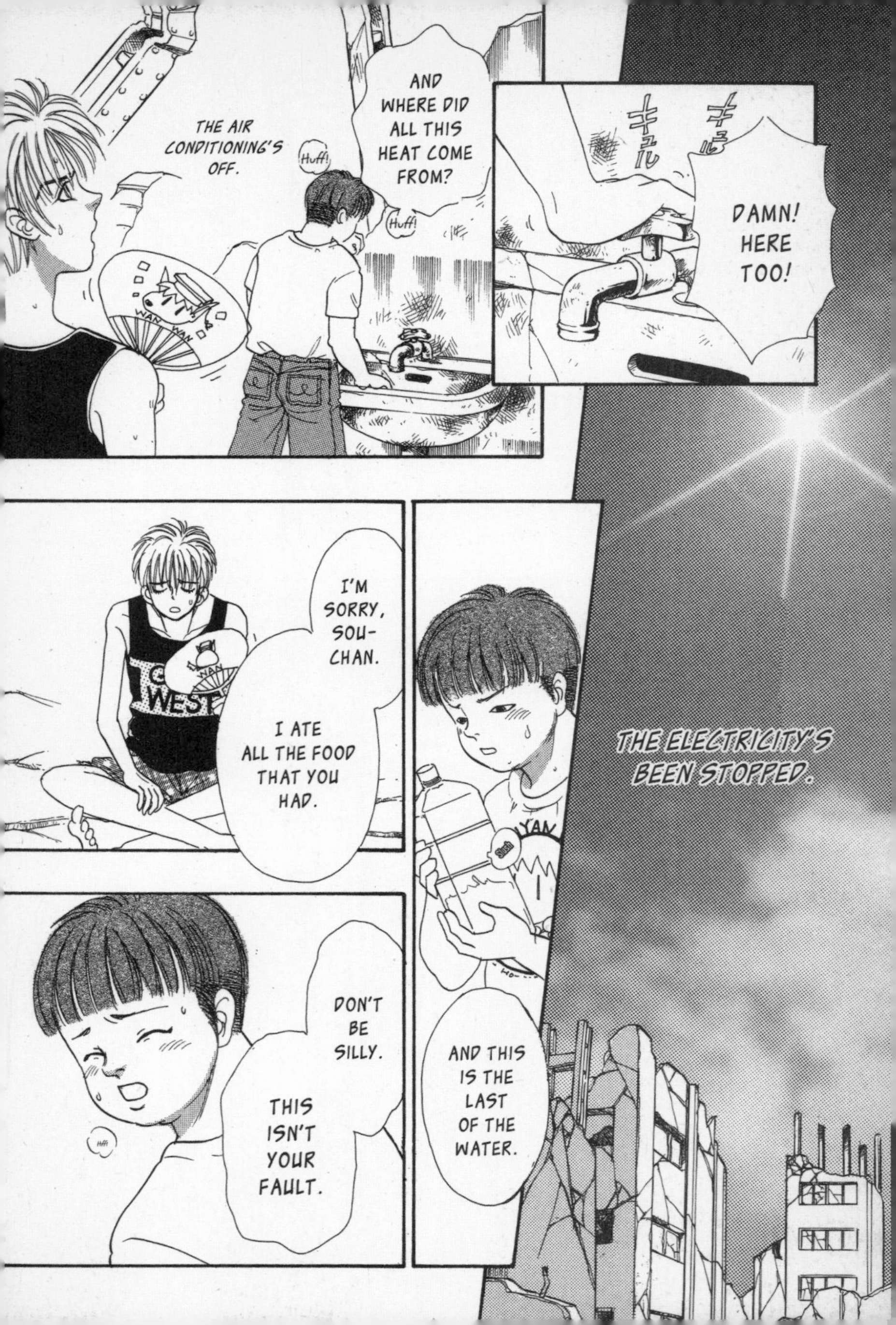

THE AIR CONDITIONING'S OFF.
Huff!
AND WHERE DID ALL THIS HEAT COME FROM?
Huff!
WAN WAN
キュ
キュル
DAMN! HERE TOO!
THE ELECTRICITY'S BEEN STOPPED.
Slosh
AND THIS IS THE LAST OF THE WATER.
I'M SORRY, SOU-CHAN.
I ATE ALL THE FOOD THAT YOU HAD.
DON'T BE SILLY.
THIS ISN'T YOUR FAULT.

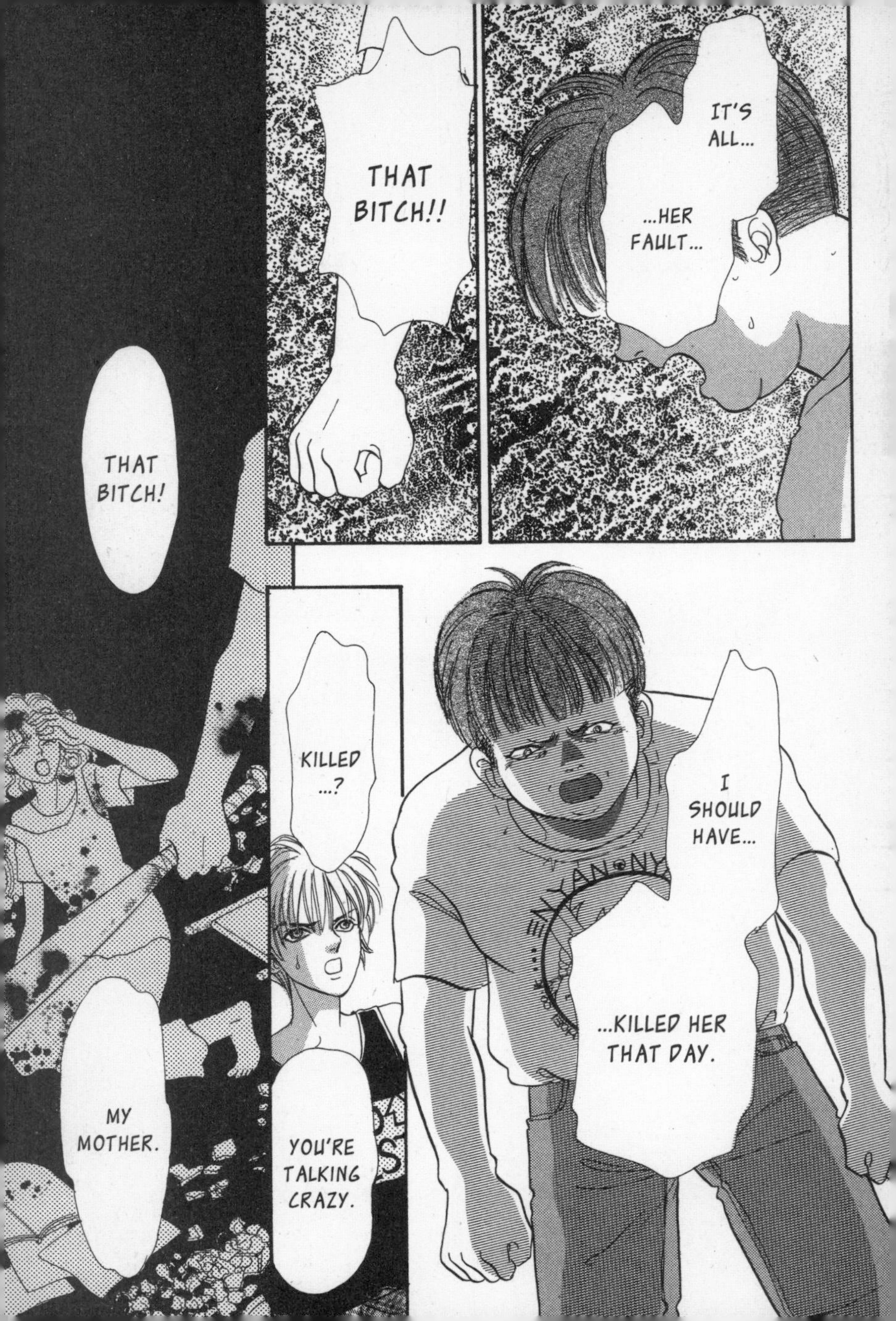
IT'S ALL...
...HER FAULT...
THAT BITCH!!
I SHOULD HAVE...
...KILLED HER THAT DAY.
KILLED ...?
YOU'RE TALKING CRAZY.
THAT BITCH!
MY MOTHER.

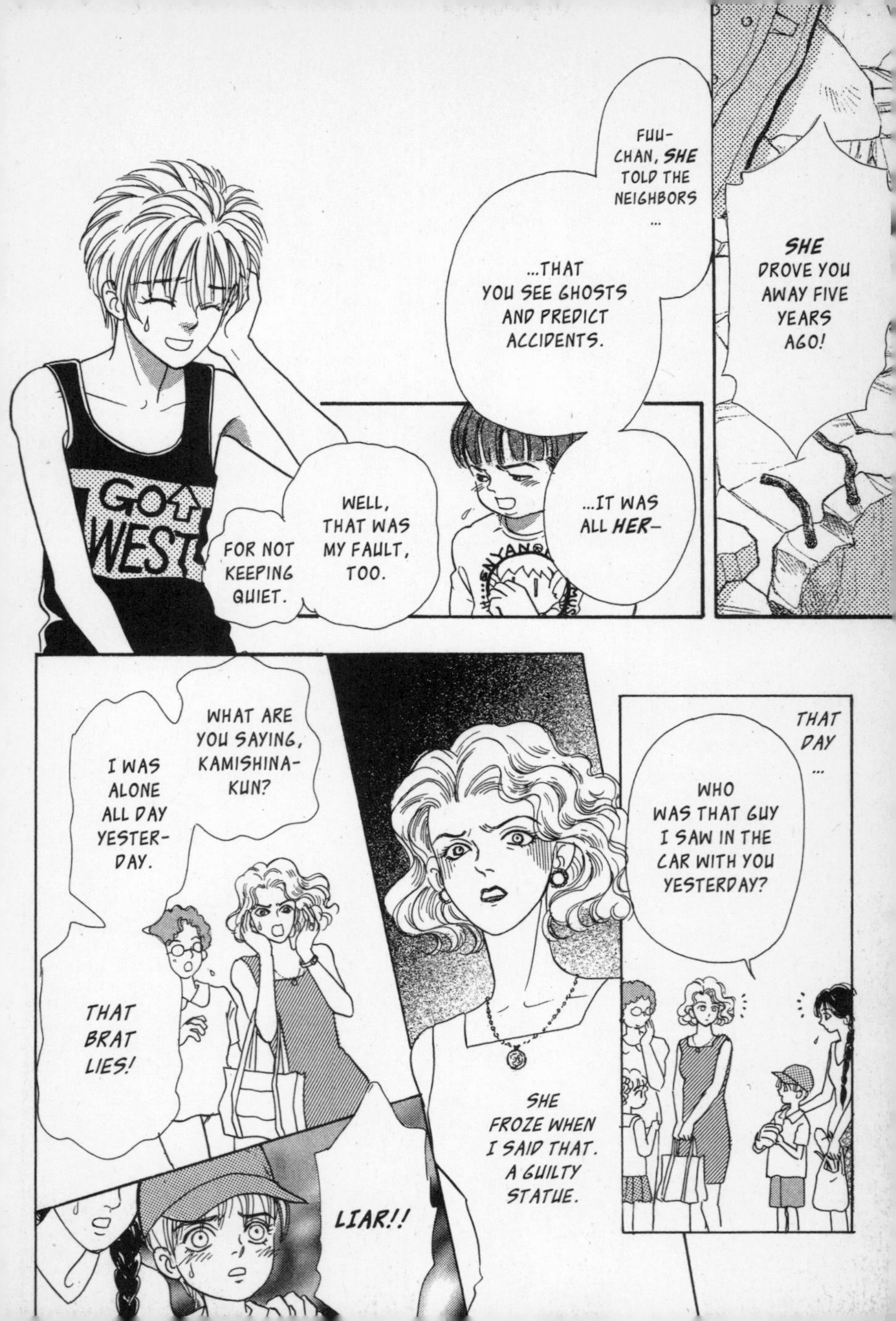
SHE DROVE YOU AWAY FIVE YEARS AGO!
FUU-CHAN, SHE TOLD THE NEIGHBORS ...
...THAT YOU SEE GHOSTS AND PREDICT ACCIDENTS.
...IT WAS ALL HER–
WELL, THAT WAS MY FAULT, TOO.
FOR NOT KEEPING QUIET.
THAT DAY ...
WHO WAS THAT GUY I SAW IN THE CAR WITH YOU YESTERDAY?
SHE FROZE WHEN I SAID THAT. A GUILTY STATUE.
WHAT ARE YOU SAYING, KAMISHINA-KUN?
I WAS ALONE ALL DAY YESTER-DAY.
THAT BRAT LIES!
LIAR!!

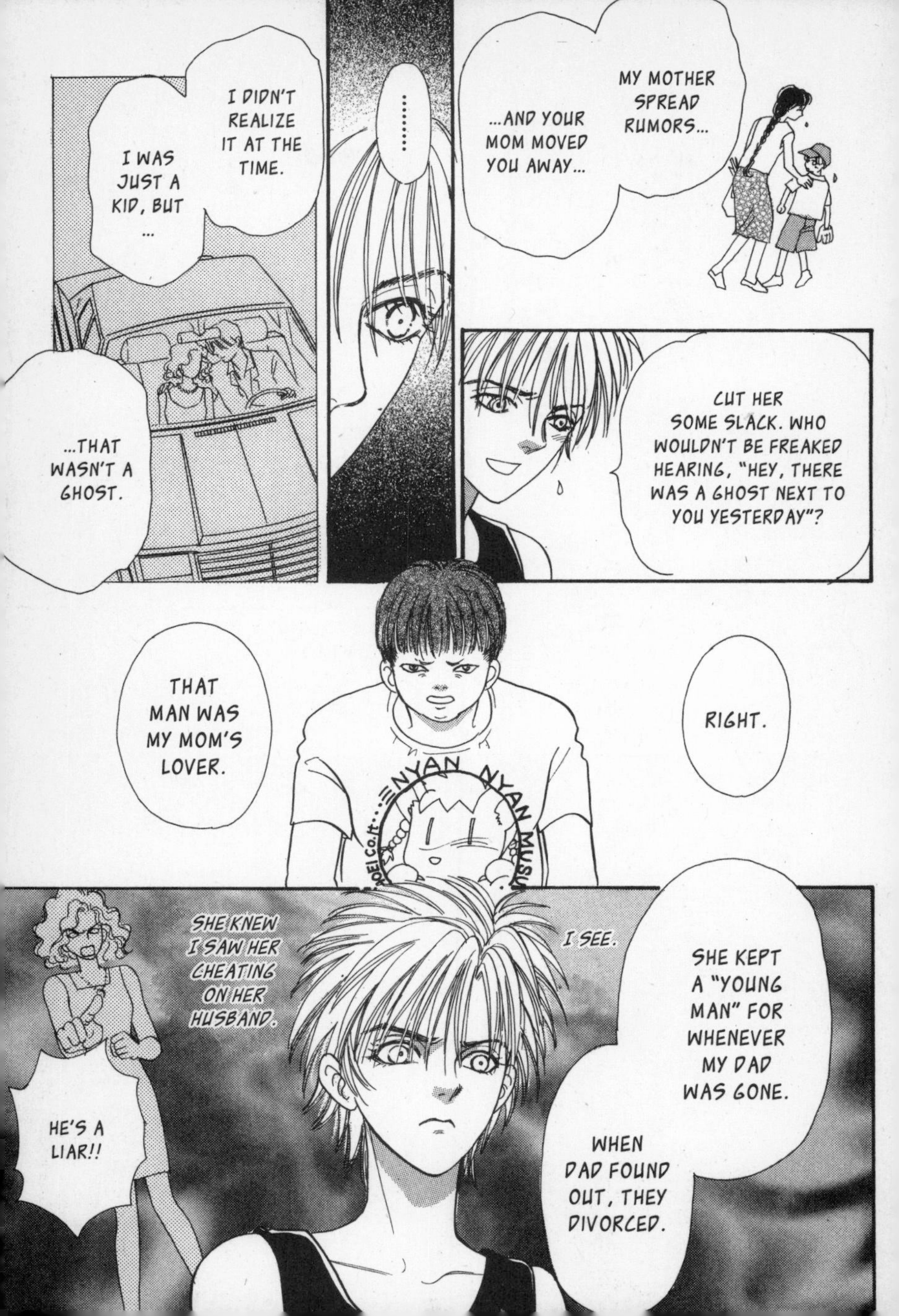
MY MOTHER SPREAD RUMORS...
...AND YOUR MOM MOVED YOU AWAY...
CUT HER SOME SLACK. WHO WOULDN'T BE FREAKED HEARING, "HEY, THERE WAS A GHOST NEXT TO YOU YESTERDAY"?
......
I DIDN'T REALIZE IT AT THE TIME.
I WAS JUST A KID, BUT ...
...THAT WASN'T A GHOST.
THAT MAN WAS MY MOM'S LOVER.
RIGHT.
NYAN NYAN MUSU
SHE KEPT A "YOUNG MAN" FOR WHENEVER MY DAD WAS GONE.
I SEE.
WHEN DAD FOUND OUT, THEY DIVORCED.
SHE KNEW I SAW HER CHEATING ON HER HUSBAND.
HE'S A LIAR!!

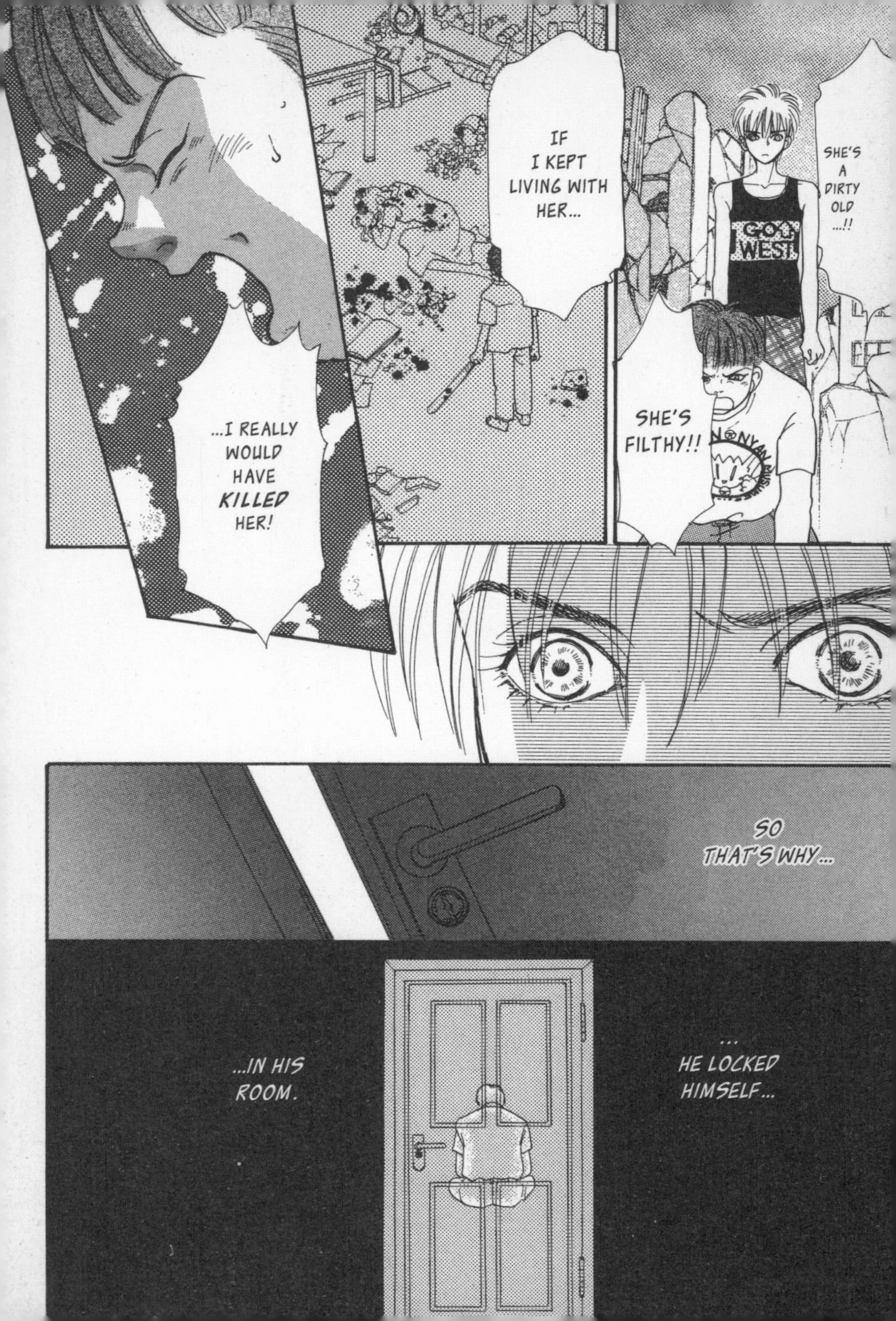
SHE'S A DIRTY OLD ...!!
SHE'S FILTHY!!
IF I KEPT LIVING WITH HER...
...I REALLY WOULD HAVE KILLED HER!
SO THAT'S WHY...
... HE LOCKED HIMSELF...
...IN HIS ROOM.

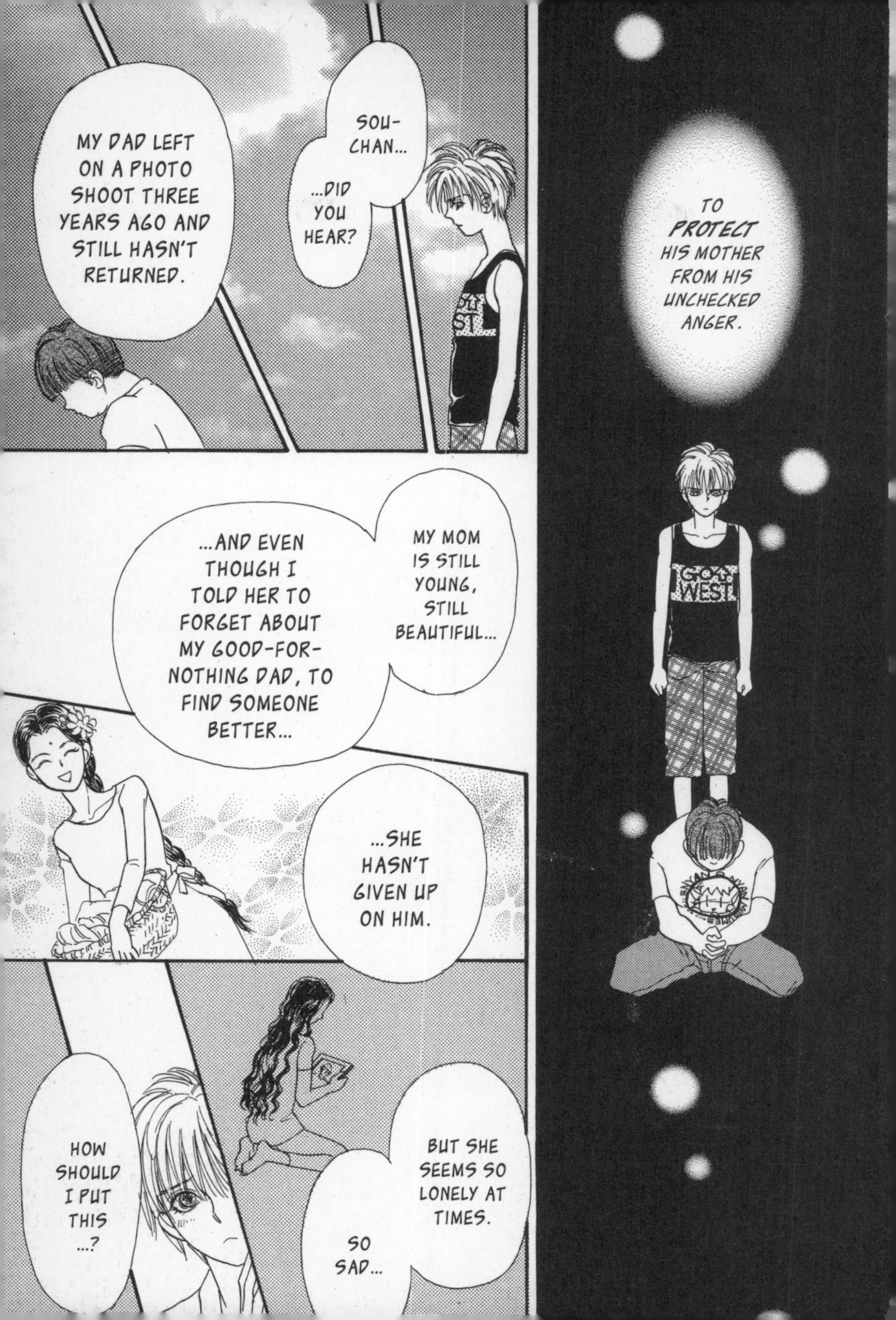
TO *PROTECT* HIS MOTHER FROM HIS UNCHECKED ANGER.
SOU-CHAN...
...DID YOU HEAR?
MY DAD LEFT ON A PHOTO SHOOT THREE YEARS AGO AND STILL HASN'T RETURNED.
MY MOM IS STILL YOUNG, STILL BEAUTIFUL...
...AND EVEN THOUGH I TOLD HER TO FORGET ABOUT MY GOOD-FOR-NOTHING DAD, TO FIND SOMEONE BETTER...
...SHE HASN'T GIVEN UP ON HIM.
BUT SHE SEEMS SO LONELY AT TIMES.
SO SAD...
HOW SHOULD I PUT THIS ...?

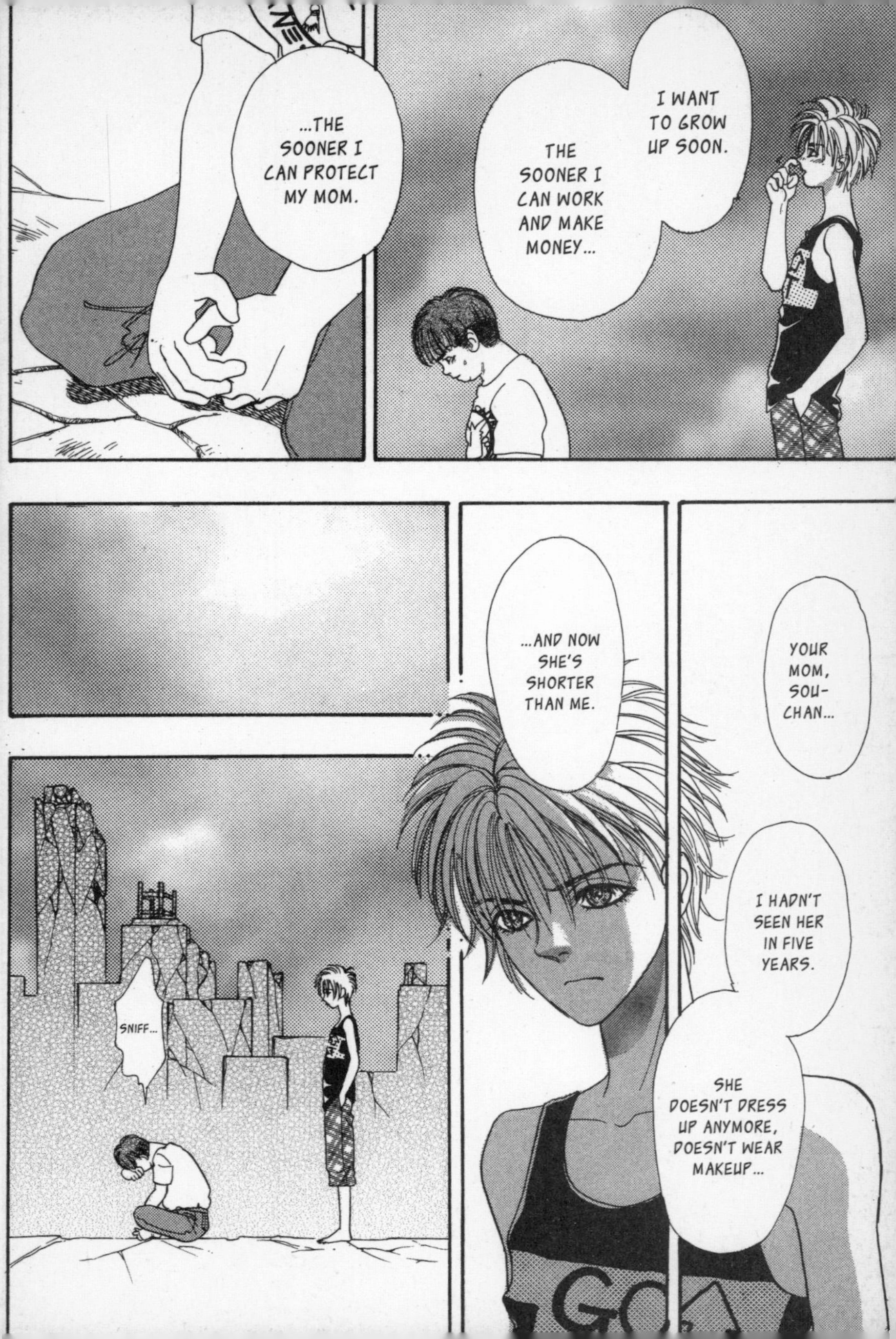
I WANT TO GROW UP SOON.
THE SOONER I CAN WORK AND MAKE MONEY...
...THE SOONER I CAN PROTECT MY MOM.
YOUR MOM, SOU-CHAN...
I HADN'T SEEN HER IN FIVE YEARS.
SHE DOESN'T DRESS UP ANYMORE, DOESN'T WEAR MAKEUP...
...AND NOW SHE'S SHORTER THAN ME.
SNIFF...

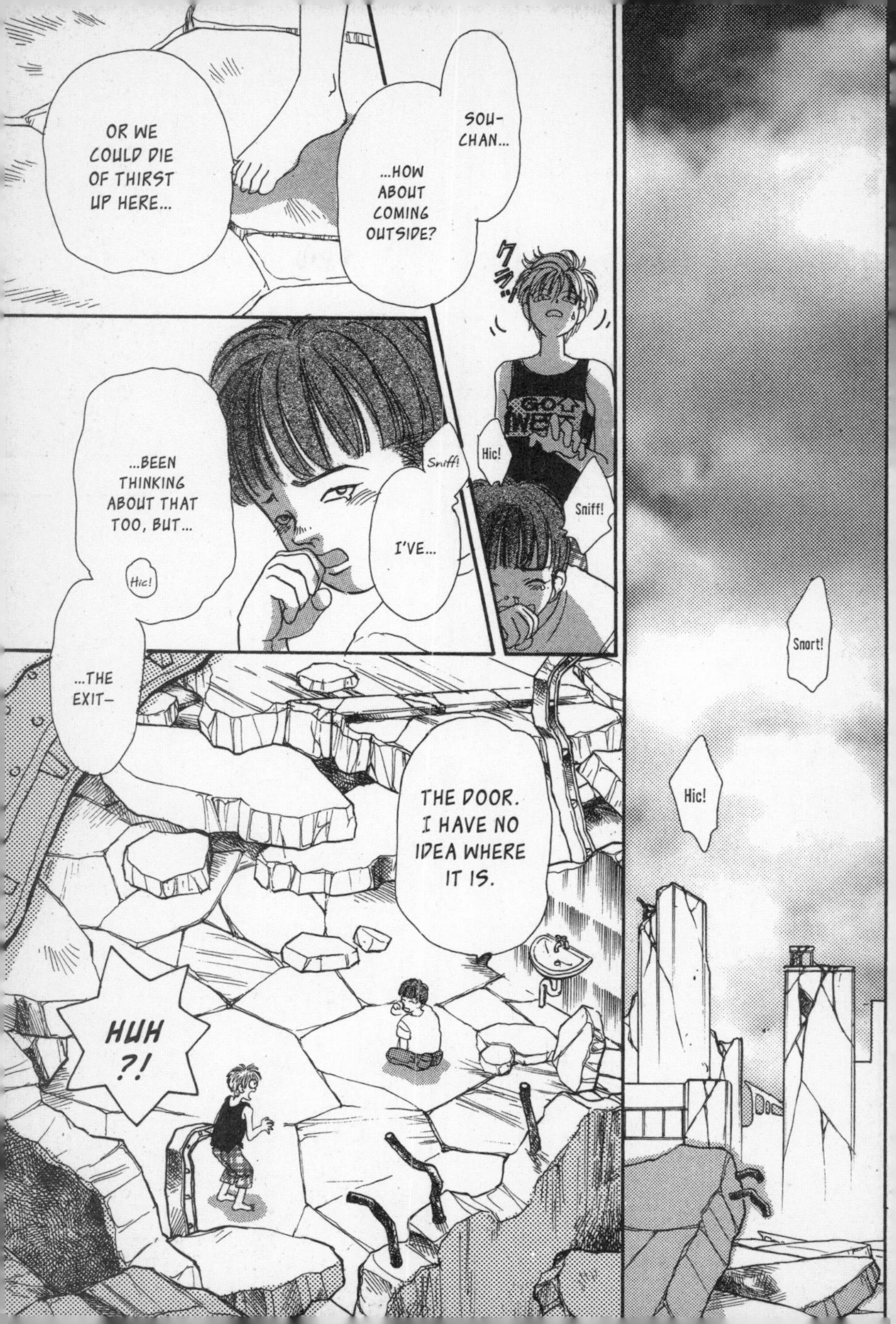
Snort!
Hic!
SOU-CHAN...
...HOW ABOUT COMING OUTSIDE?
OR WE COULD DIE OF THIRST UP HERE...
クラッ
Hic!
Sniff!
Sniff!
I'VE...
...BEEN THINKING ABOUT THAT TOO, BUT...
Hic!
...THE EXIT—
THE DOOR. I HAVE NO IDEA WHERE IT IS.
HUH ?!

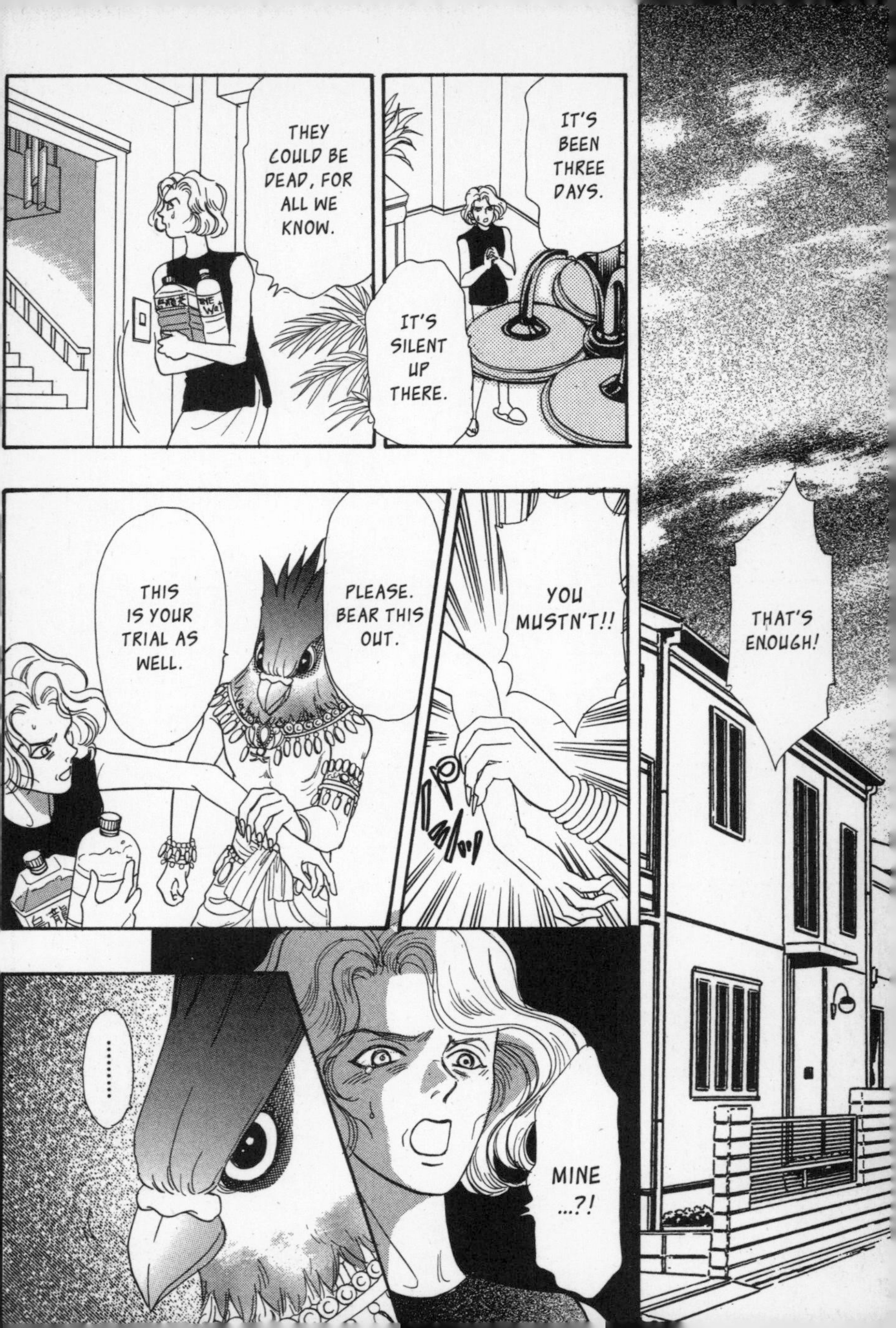

THAT'S ENOUGH!
IT'S BEEN THREE DAYS.
IT'S SILENT UP THERE.
THEY COULD BE DEAD, FOR ALL WE KNOW.
YOU MUSTN'T!!
PLEASE. BEAR THIS OUT.
THIS IS YOUR TRIAL AS WELL.
MINE ...?!
....

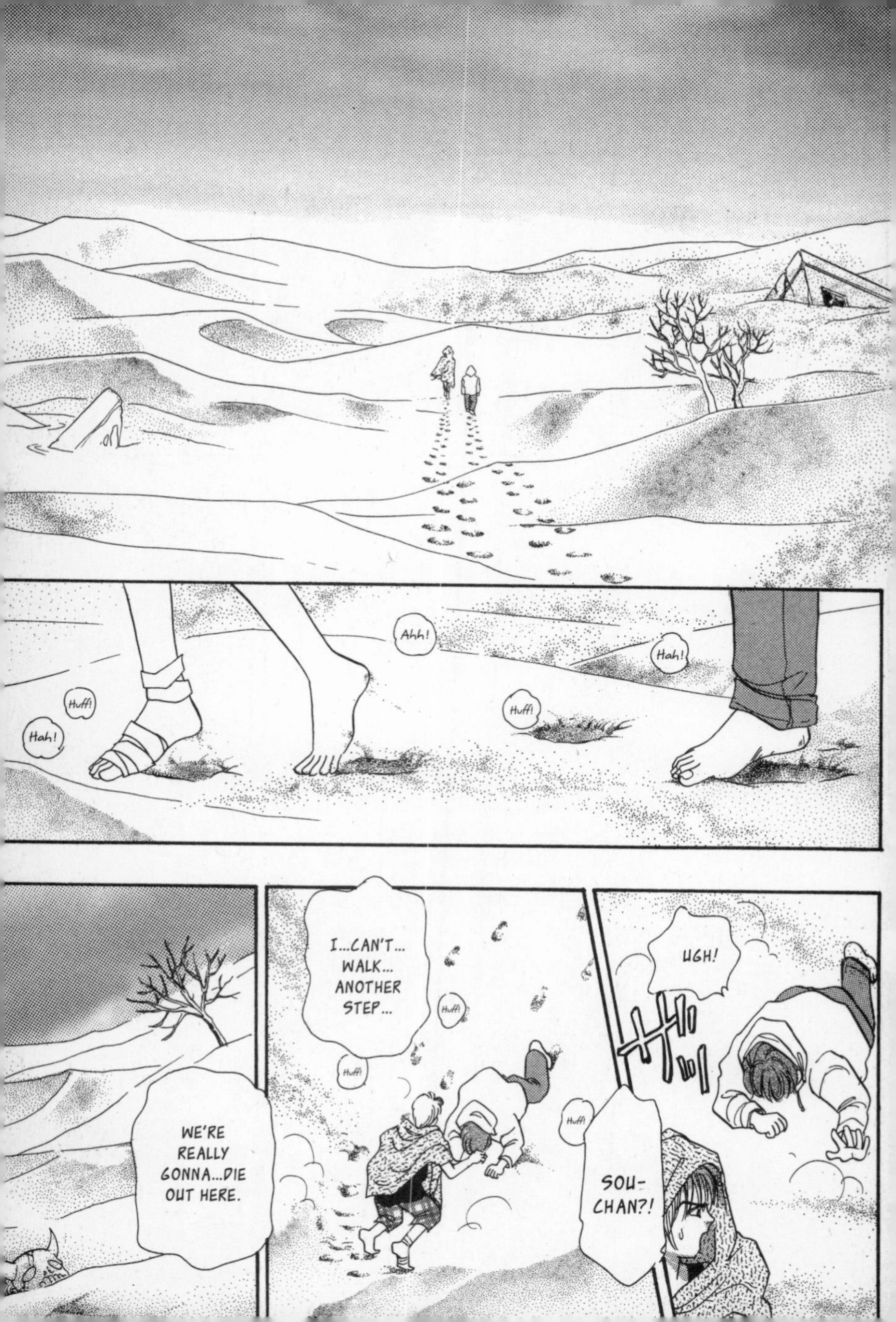
Hah!
Huff!
Ahh!
Huff!
Hah!
UGH!
SOU-CHAN?!
I...CAN'T... WALK... ANOTHER STEP...
Huff!
Huff!
Huff!
WE'RE REALLY GONNA...DIE OUT HERE.

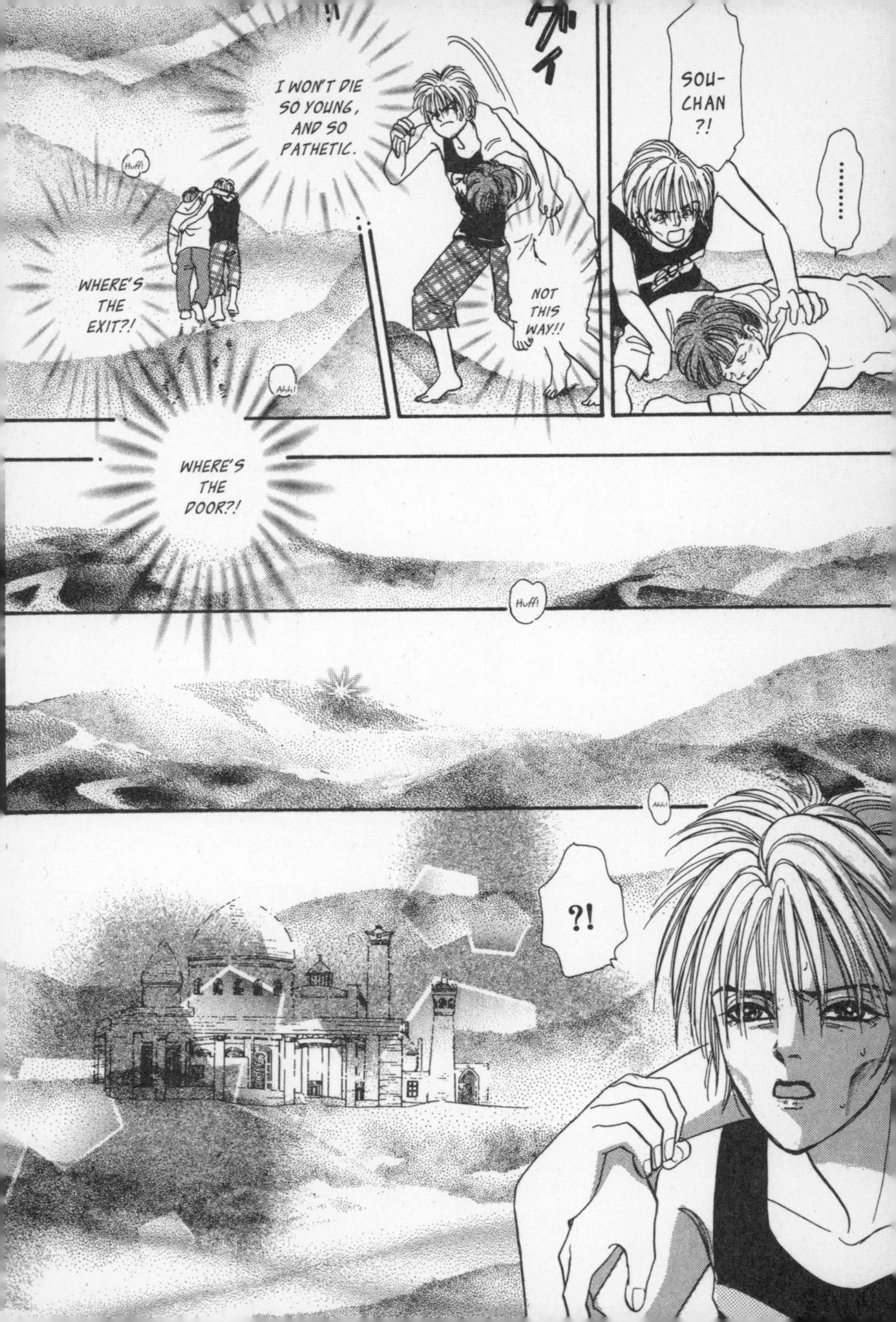
SOU-CHAN ?!
......
グイ
I WON'T DIE SO YOUNG, AND SO PATHETIC.
NOT THIS WAY!!
Huff!
WHERE'S THE EXIT?!
Ahh!
WHERE'S THE DOOR?!
Huff!
Ahh!
?!

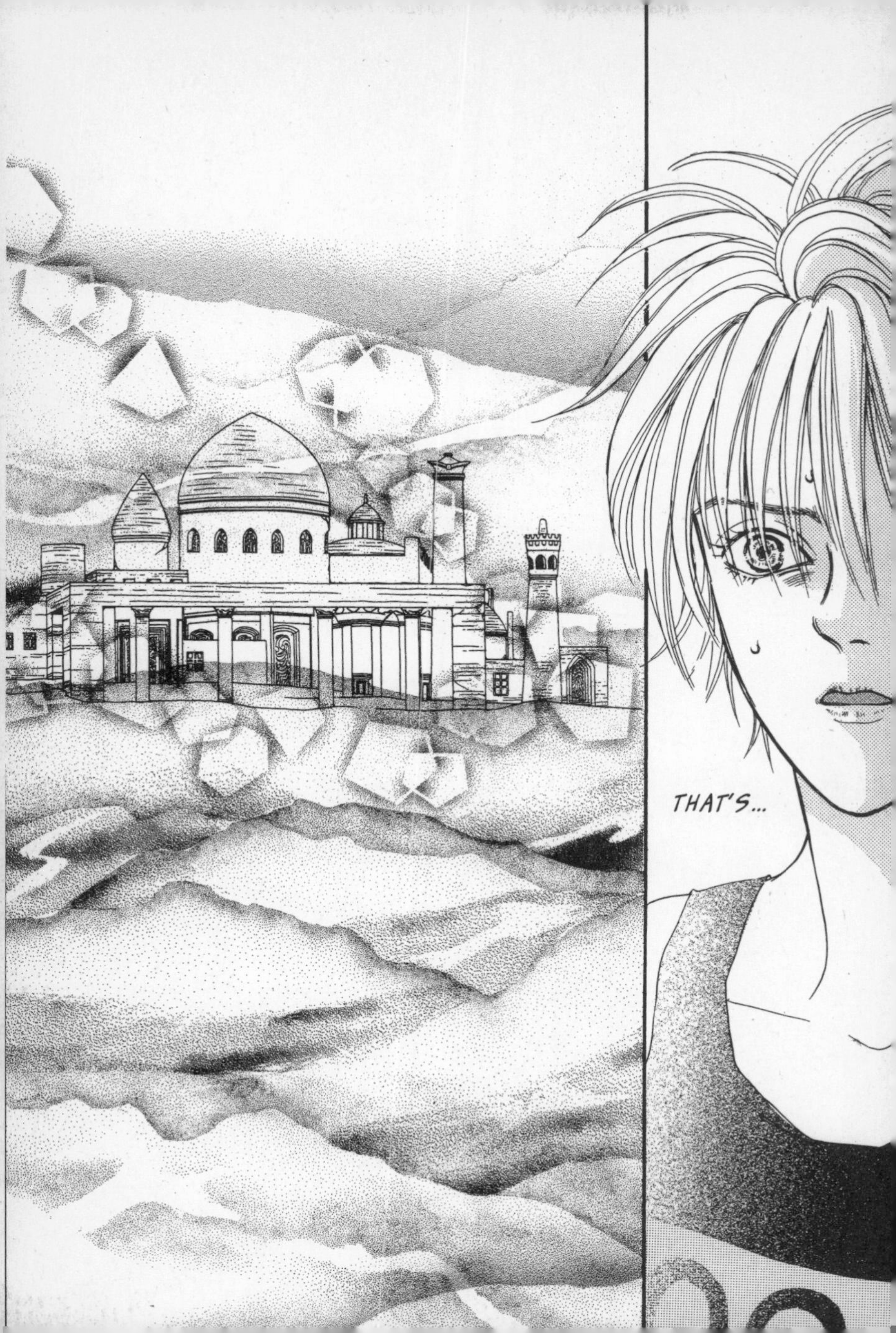
THAT'S...

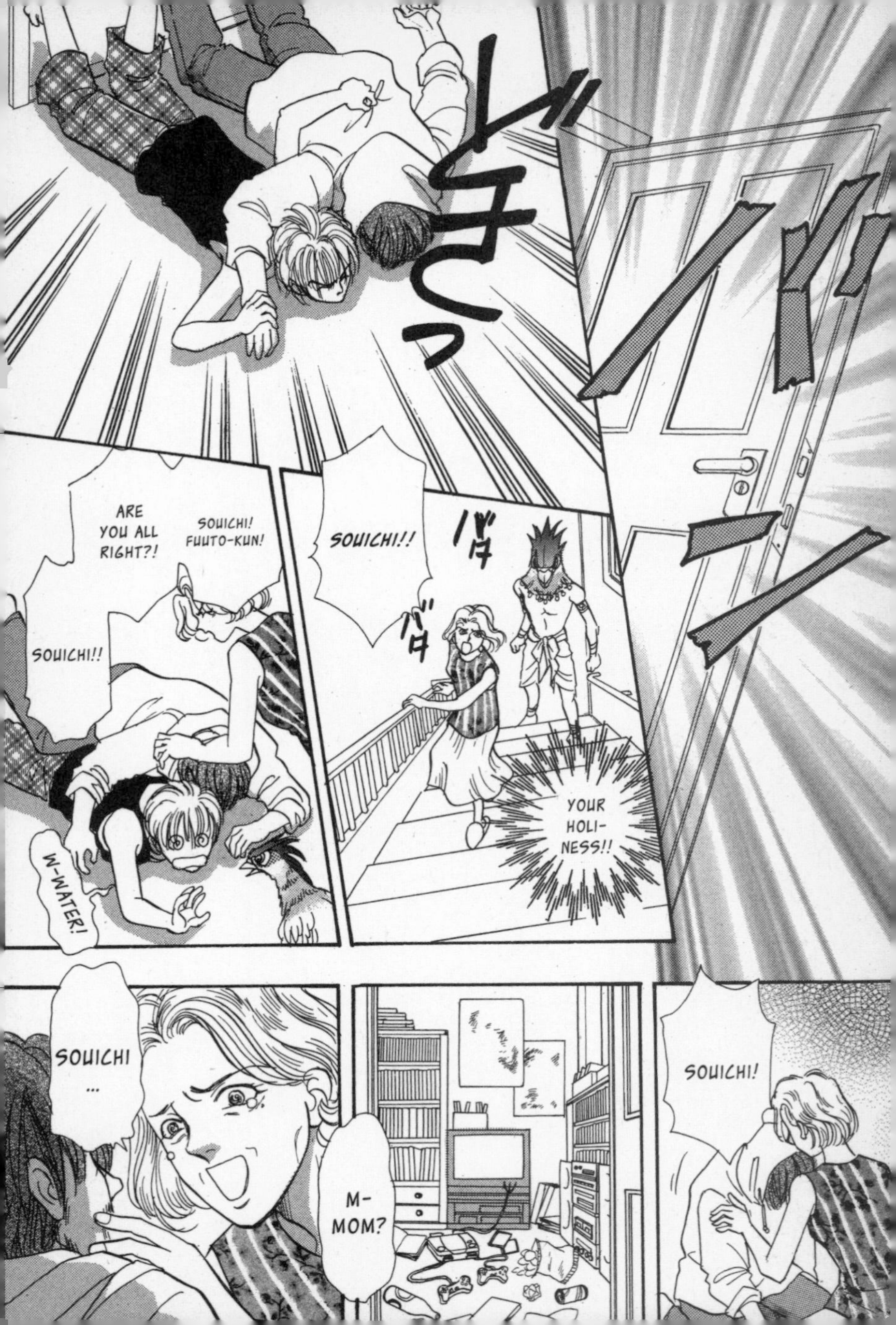
どさっ
バン
SOUICHI!!
バタ
バタ
YOUR HOLI-NESS!!
SOUICHI! FUUTO-KUN!
ARE YOU ALL RIGHT?!
SOUICHI!!
W-WATER!
SOUICHI!
M-MOM?
SOUICHI ...

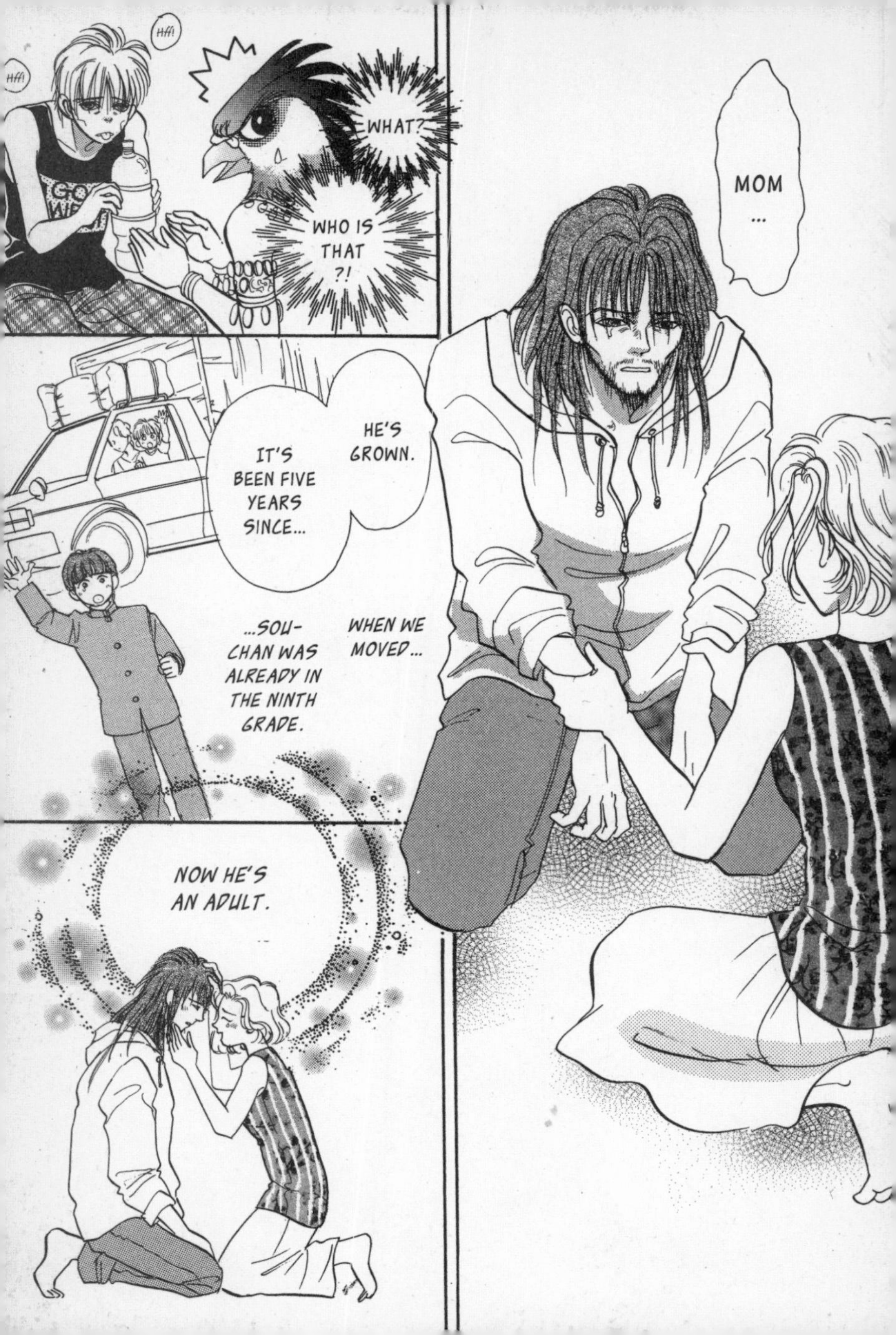
MOM ...
WHAT?
WHO IS THAT ?!
Hff!
Hff!
HE'S GROWN.
IT'S BEEN FIVE YEARS SINCE...
WHEN WE MOVED...
...SOU-CHAN WAS ALREADY IN THE NINTH GRADE.
NOW HE'S AN ADULT.

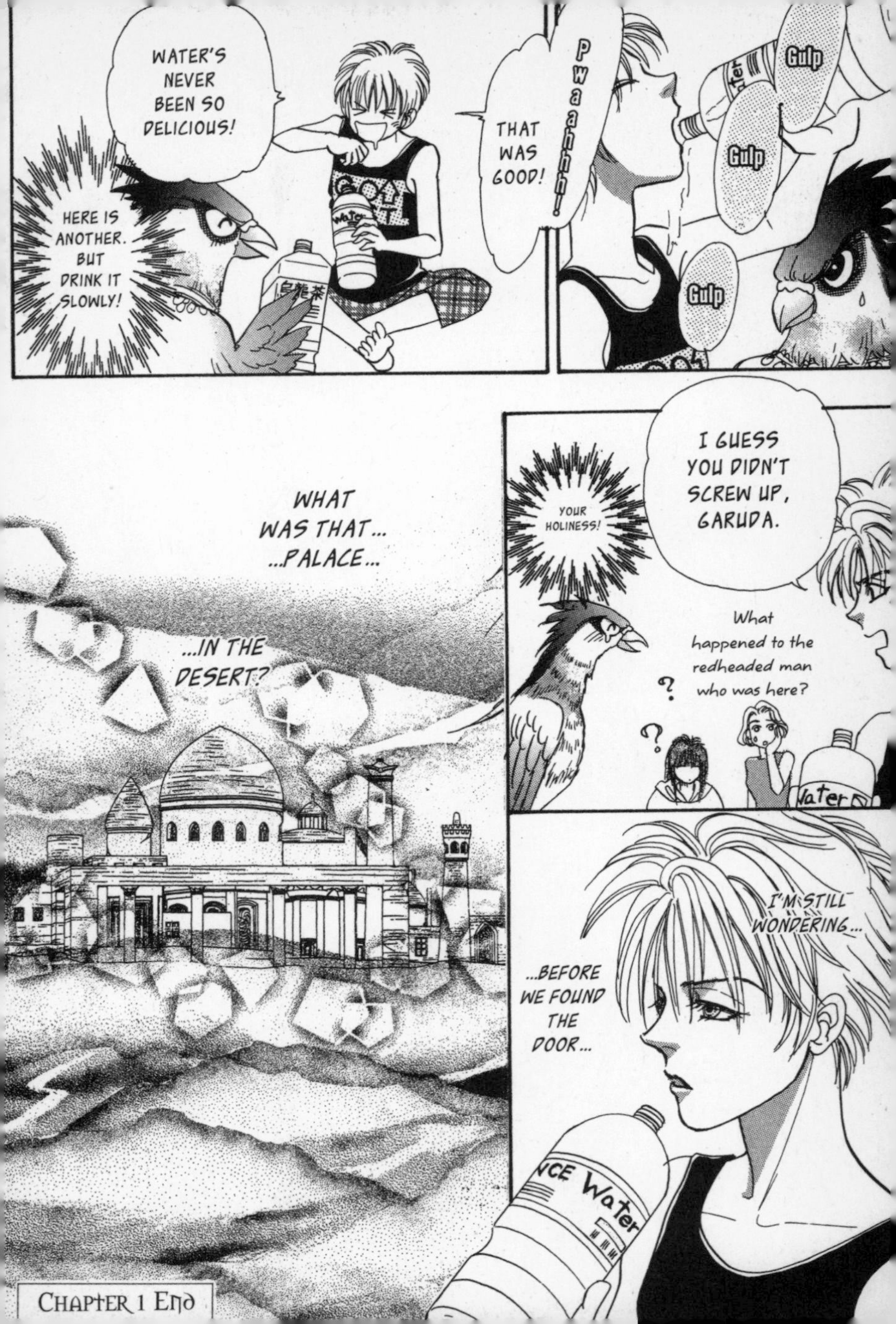
Gulp
Gulp
Gulp
Pwaannhh!
THAT WAS GOOD!
WATER'S NEVER BEEN SO DELICIOUS!
HERE IS ANOTHER. BUT DRINK IT SLOWLY!
I GUESS YOU DIDN'T SCREW UP, GARUDA.
YOUR HOLINESS!
What happened to the redheaded man who was here?
I'M STILL WONDERING...
...BEFORE WE FOUND THE DOOR...
WHAT WAS THAT... ...PALACE...
...IN THE DESERT?
CHAPTER 1 END

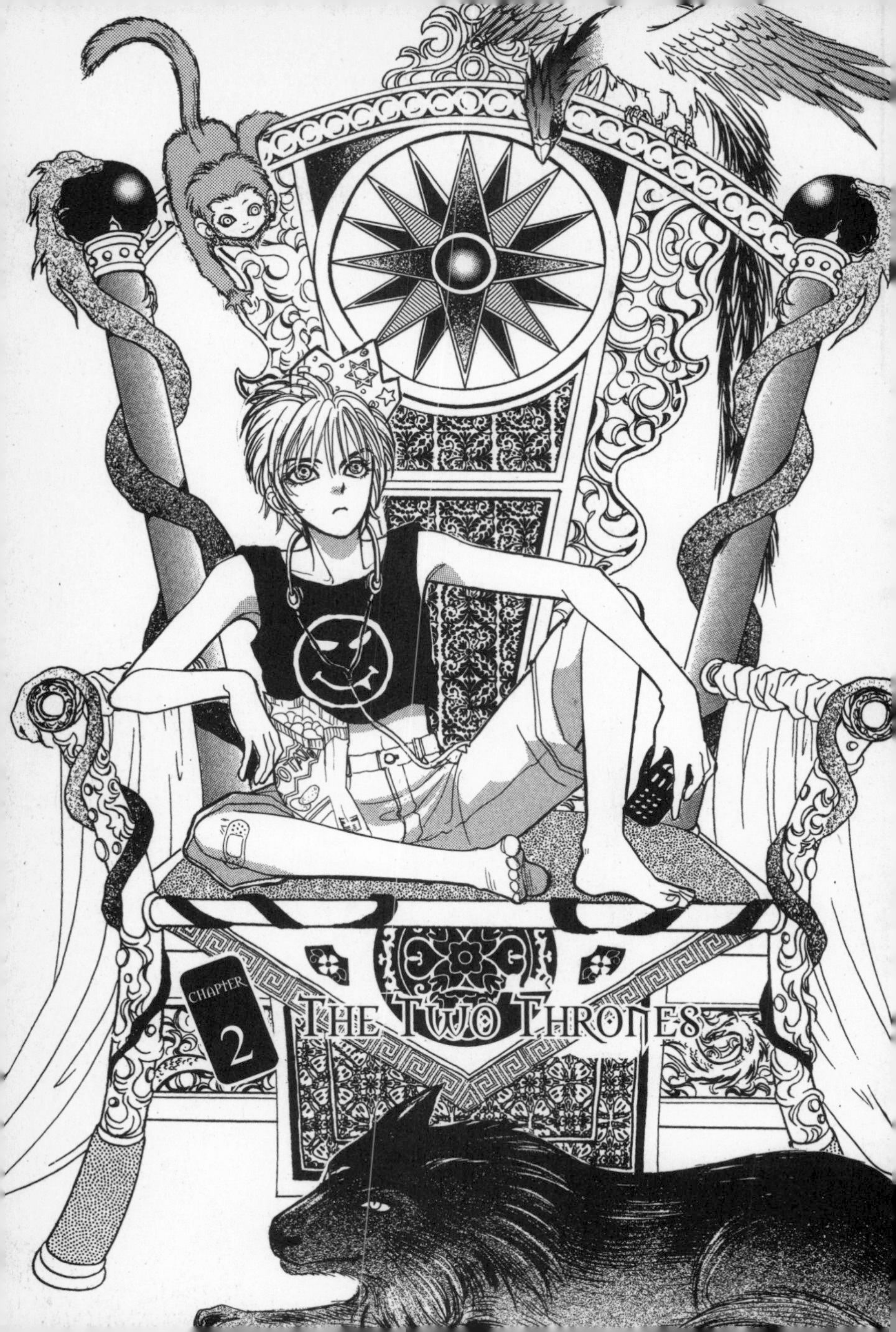
CHAPTER 2
THE TWO THRONES
OTAKU

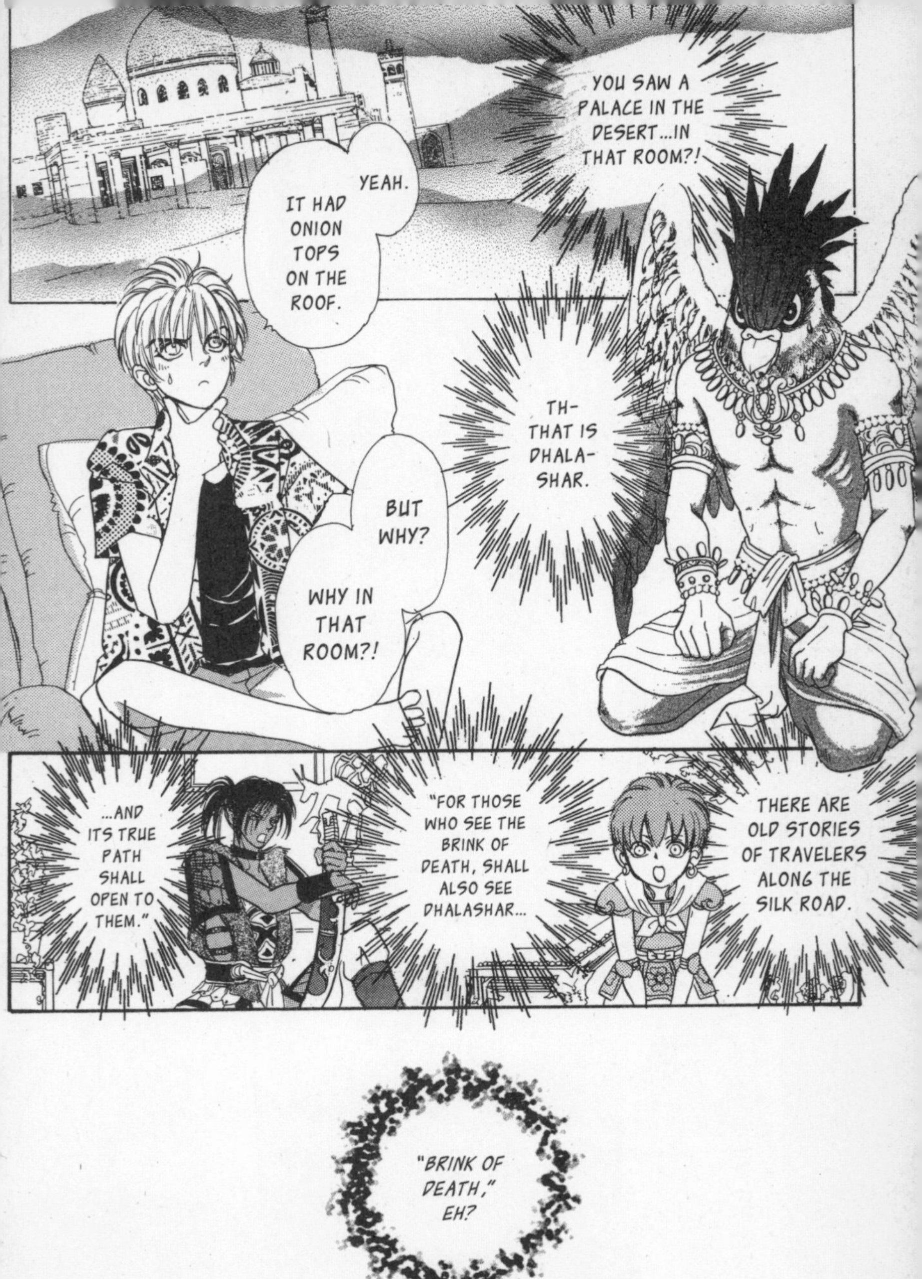
YOU SAW A PALACE IN THE DESERT...IN THAT ROOM?!
YEAH.
IT HAD ONION TOPS ON THE ROOF.
TH-THAT IS DHALA-SHAR.
BUT WHY?
WHY IN THAT ROOM?!
THERE ARE OLD STORIES OF TRAVELERS ALONG THE SILK ROAD.
"FOR THOSE WHO SEE THE BRINK OF DEATH, SHALL ALSO SEE DHALASHAR...
...AND ITS TRUE PATH SHALL OPEN TO THEM."
"BRINK OF DEATH," EH?

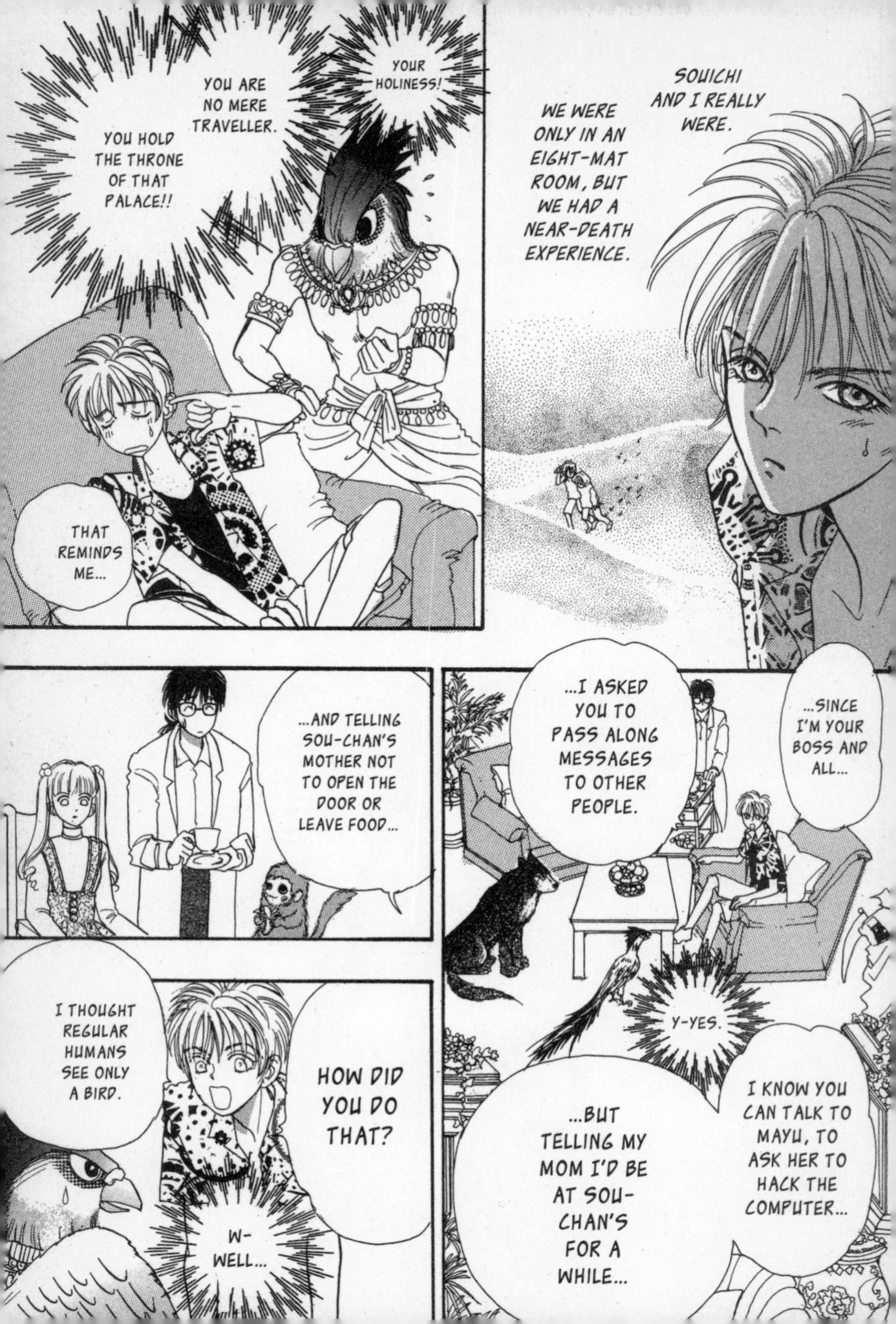
SOUICHI AND I REALLY WERE.
WE WERE ONLY IN AN EIGHT-MAT ROOM, BUT WE HAD A NEAR-DEATH EXPERIENCE.
YOUR HOLINESS!
YOU ARE NO MERE TRAVELLER.
YOU HOLD THE THRONE OF THAT PALACE!!
THAT REMINDS ME...
...SINCE I'M YOUR BOSS AND ALL...
...I ASKED YOU TO PASS ALONG MESSAGES TO OTHER PEOPLE.
Y-YES.
I KNOW YOU CAN TALK TO MAYU, TO ASK HER TO HACK THE COMPUTER...
...BUT TELLING MY MOM I'D BE AT SOU-CHAN'S FOR A WHILE...
...AND TELLING SOU-CHAN'S MOTHER NOT TO OPEN THE DOOR OR LEAVE FOOD...
HOW DID YOU DO THAT?
I THOUGHT REGULAR HUMANS SEE ONLY A BIRD.
W-WELL...

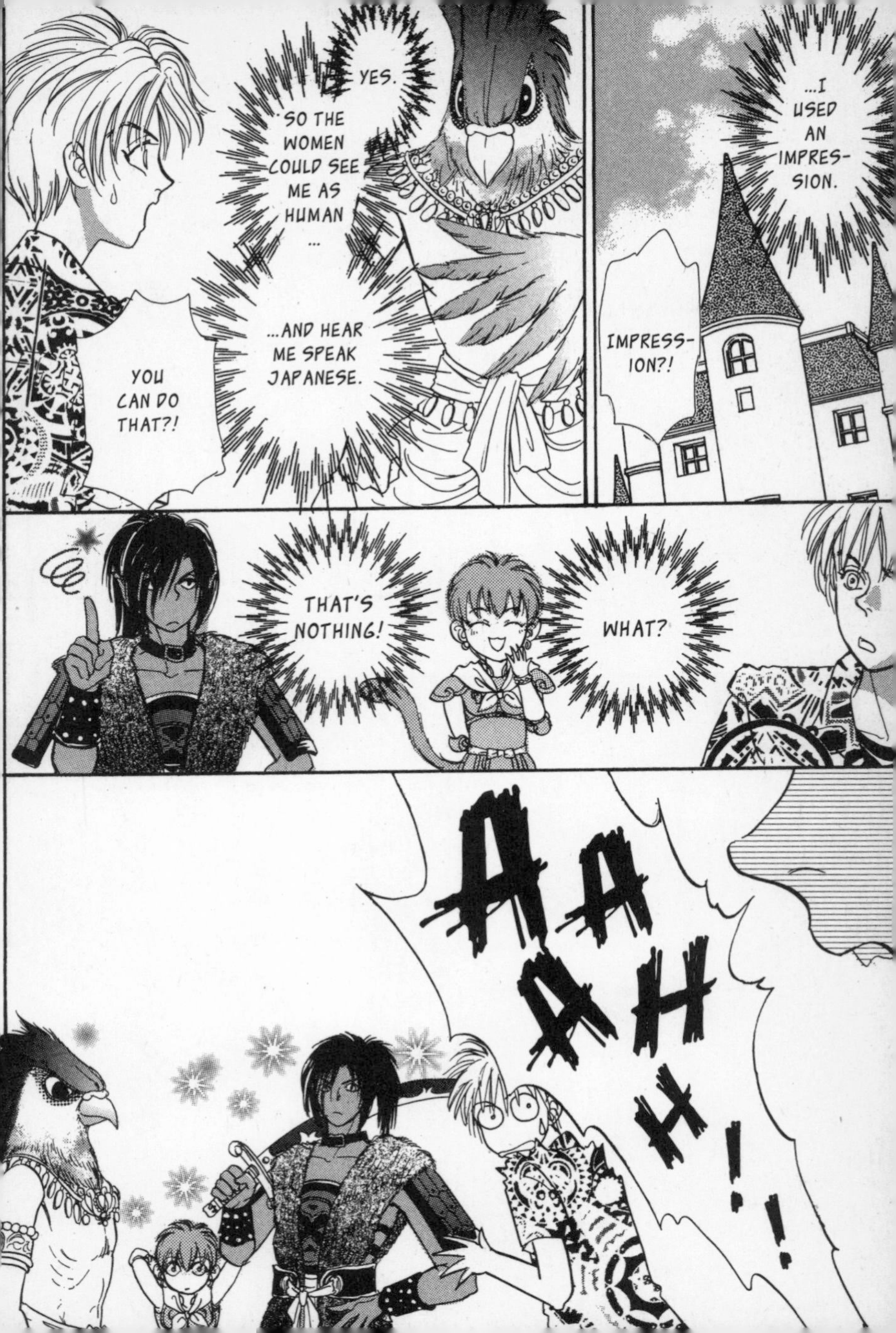
...I USED AN IMPRESSION.
IMPRESSION?!
YES.
SO THE WOMEN COULD SEE ME AS HUMAN ...
...AND HEAR ME SPEAK JAPANESE.
YOU CAN DO THAT?!
WHAT?
THAT'S NOTHING!
AAAH!!!

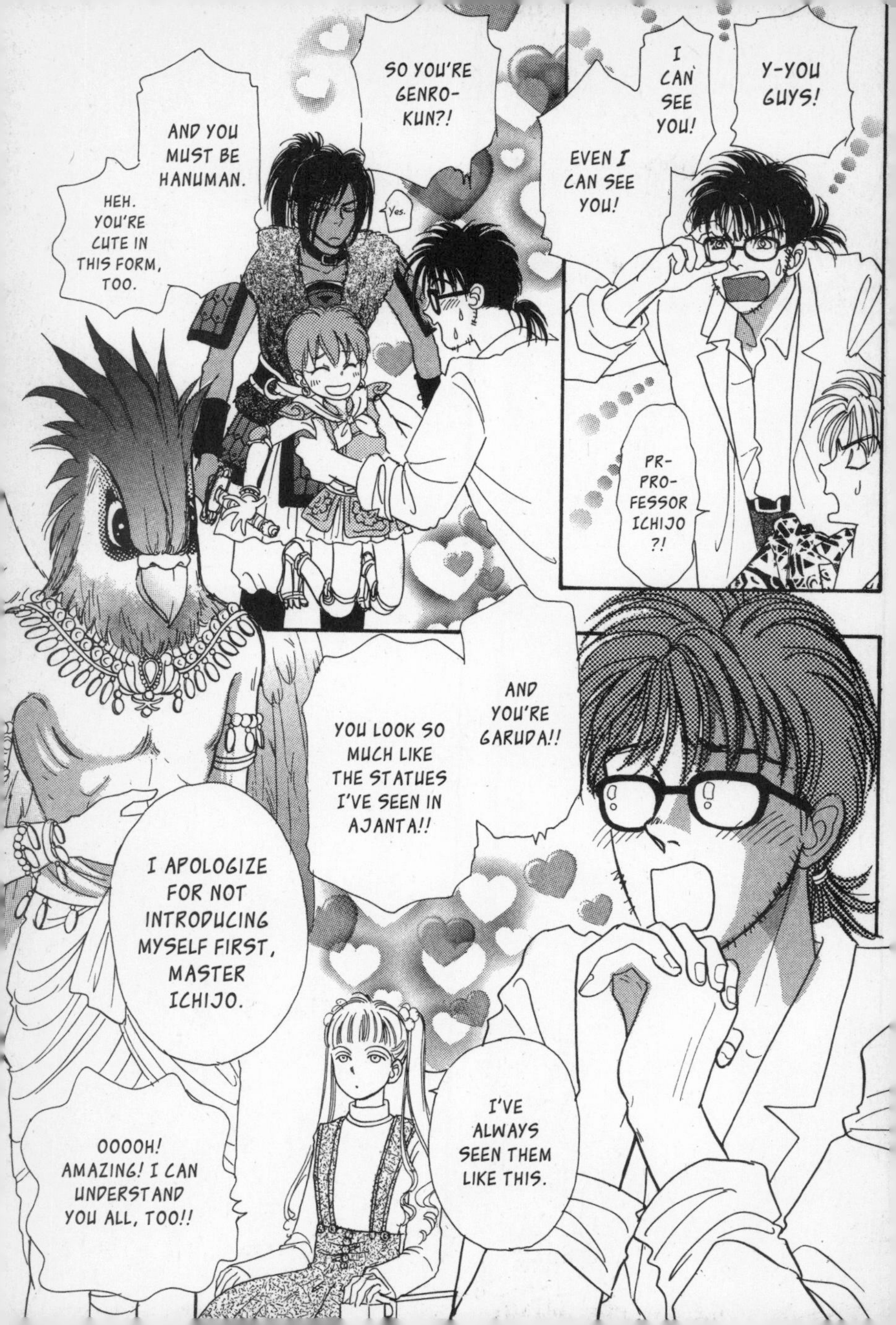
Y-YOU GUYS!
I CAN SEE YOU!
EVEN I CAN SEE YOU!
PR-PRO-FESSOR ICHIJO ?!
SO YOU'RE GENRO-KUN?!
Yes.
AND YOU MUST BE HANUMAN.
HEH. YOU'RE CUTE IN THIS FORM, TOO.
AND YOU'RE GARUDA!!
YOU LOOK SO MUCH LIKE THE STATUES I'VE SEEN IN AJANTA!!
I APOLOGIZE FOR NOT INTRODUCING MYSELF FIRST, MASTER ICHIJO.
I'VE ALWAYS SEEN THEM LIKE THIS.
OOOOH! AMAZING! I CAN UNDERSTAND YOU ALL, TOO!!

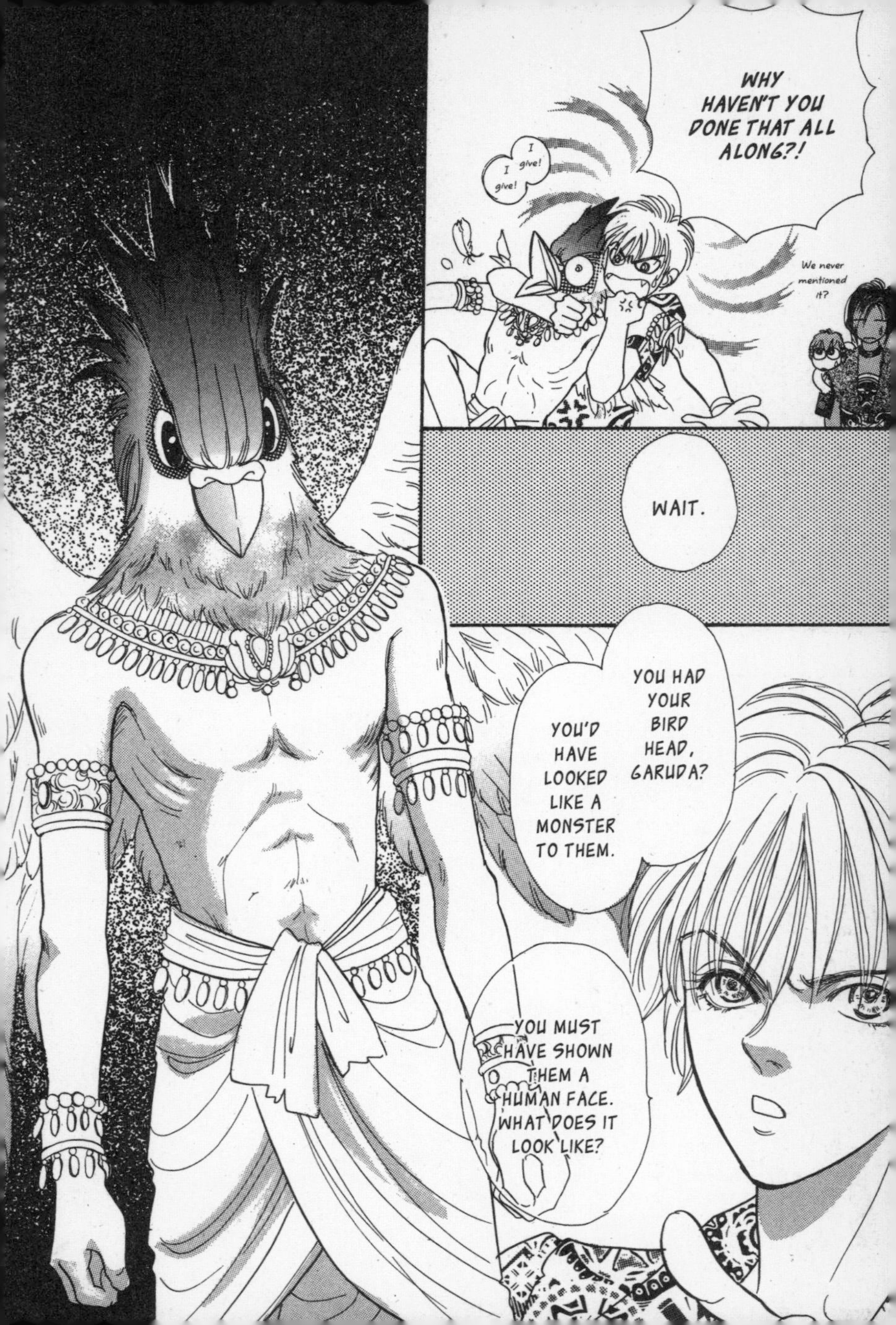
WHY HAVEN'T YOU DONE THAT ALL ALONG?!
I give! I give!
We never mentioned it?
WAIT.
YOU HAD YOUR BIRD HEAD, GARUDA?
YOU'D HAVE LOOKED LIKE A MONSTER TO THEM.
YOU MUST HAVE SHOWN THEM A HUMAN FACE. WHAT DOES IT LOOK LIKE?

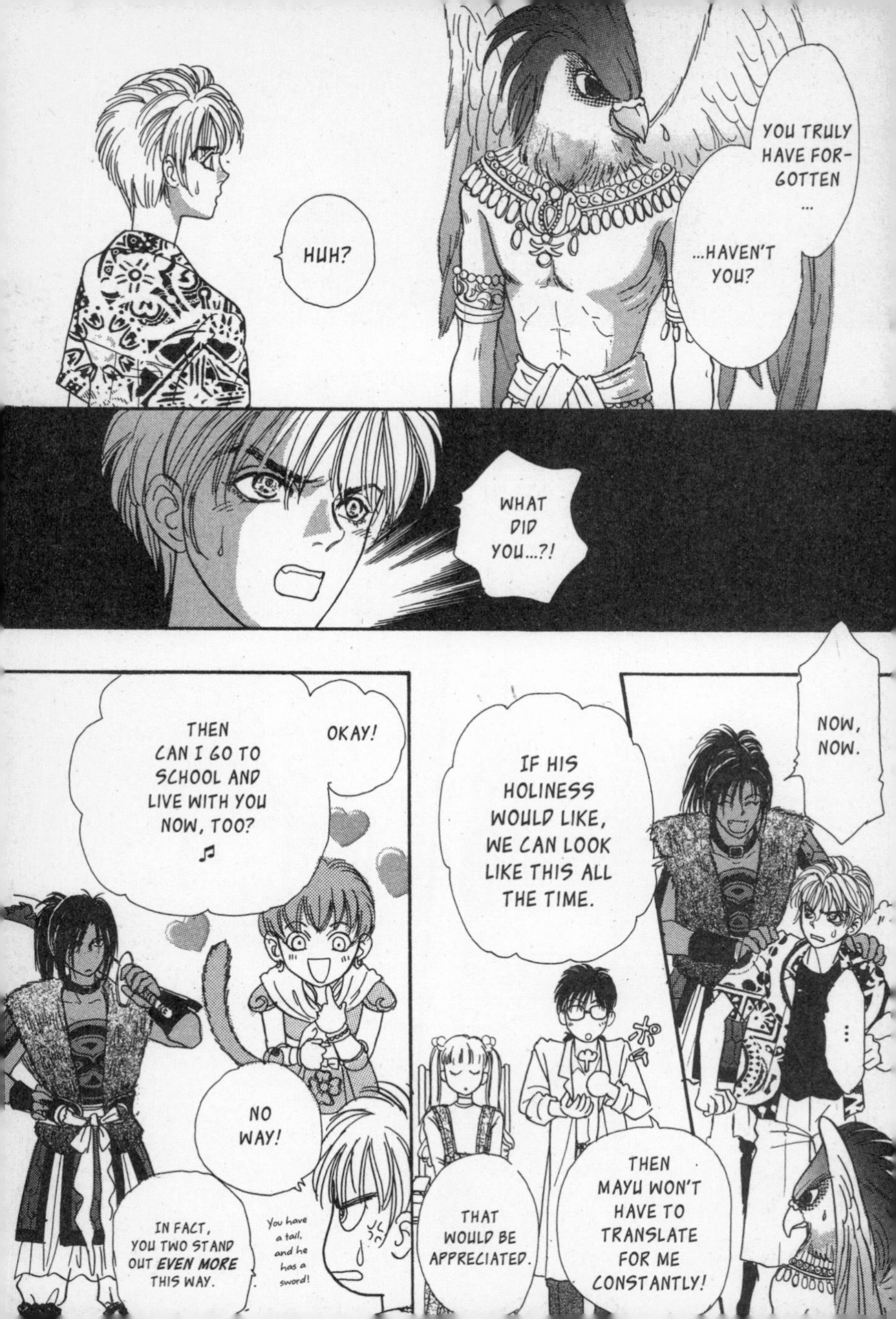

YOU TRULY HAVE FOR- GOTTEN ...
...HAVEN'T YOU?
HUH?
WHAT DID YOU...?!
NOW, NOW.
IF HIS HOLINESS WOULD LIKE, WE CAN LOOK LIKE THIS ALL THE TIME.
...
THEN MAYU WON'T HAVE TO TRANSLATE FOR ME CONSTANTLY!
THAT WOULD BE APPRECIATED.
OKAY!
THEN CAN I GO TO SCHOOL AND LIVE WITH YOU NOW, TOO? ♪
NO WAY!
You have a tail, and he has a sword!
IN FACT, YOU TWO STAND OUT EVEN MORE THIS WAY.

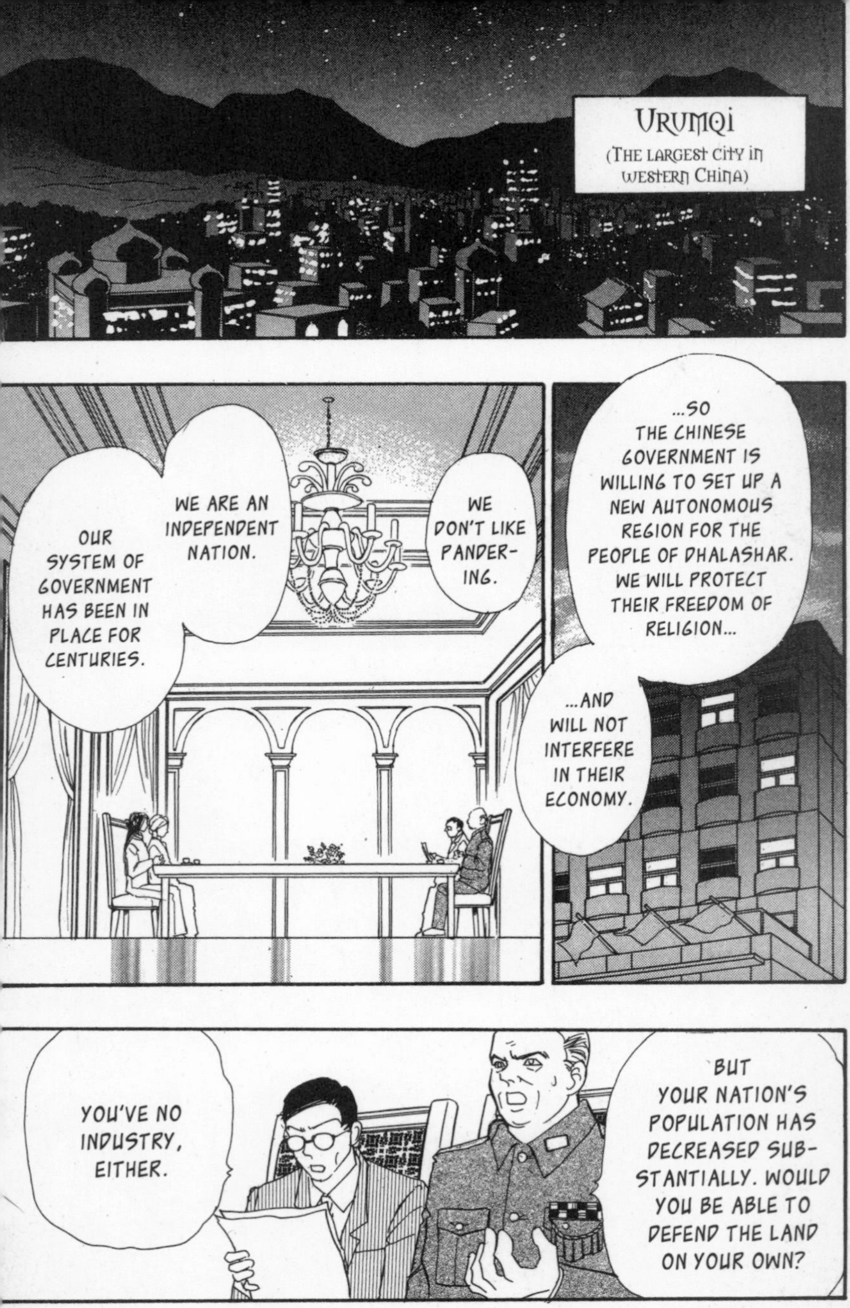
Urumqi
(The largest city in western China)
...SO THE CHINESE GOVERNMENT IS WILLING TO SET UP A NEW AUTONOMOUS REGION FOR THE PEOPLE OF DHALASHAR. WE WILL PROTECT THEIR FREEDOM OF RELIGION...
...AND WILL NOT INTERFERE IN THEIR ECONOMY.
WE DON'T LIKE PANDER-ING.
WE ARE AN INDEPENDENT NATION.
OUR SYSTEM OF GOVERNMENT HAS BEEN IN PLACE FOR CENTURIES.
BUT YOUR NATION'S POPULATION HAS DECREASED SUB-STANTIALLY. WOULD YOU BE ABLE TO DEFEND THE LAND ON YOUR OWN?
YOU'VE NO INDUSTRY, EITHER.

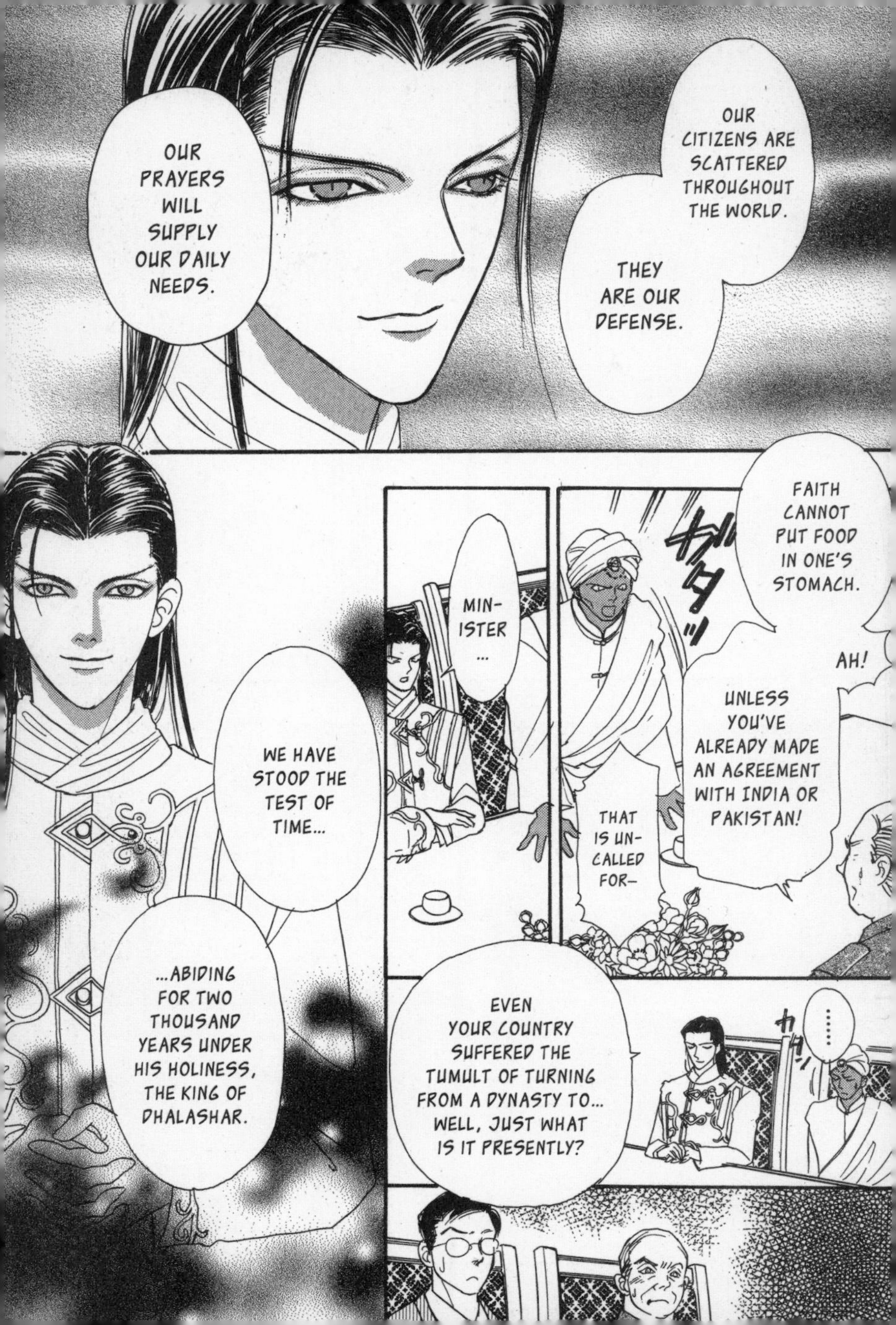
OUR CITIZENS ARE SCATTERED THROUGHOUT THE WORLD.
THEY ARE OUR DEFENSE.
OUR PRAYERS WILL SUPPLY OUR DAILY NEEDS.
FAITH CANNOT PUT FOOD IN ONE'S STOMACH.
AH!
UNLESS YOU'VE ALREADY MADE AN AGREEMENT WITH INDIA OR PAKISTAN!
THAT IS UN-CALLED FOR—
MIN-ISTER...
......
EVEN YOUR COUNTRY SUFFERED THE TUMULT OF TURNING FROM A DYNASTY TO... WELL, JUST WHAT IS IT PRESENTLY?
WE HAVE STOOD THE TEST OF TIME...
...ABIDING FOR TWO THOUSAND YEARS UNDER HIS HOLINESS, THE KING OF DHALASHAR.

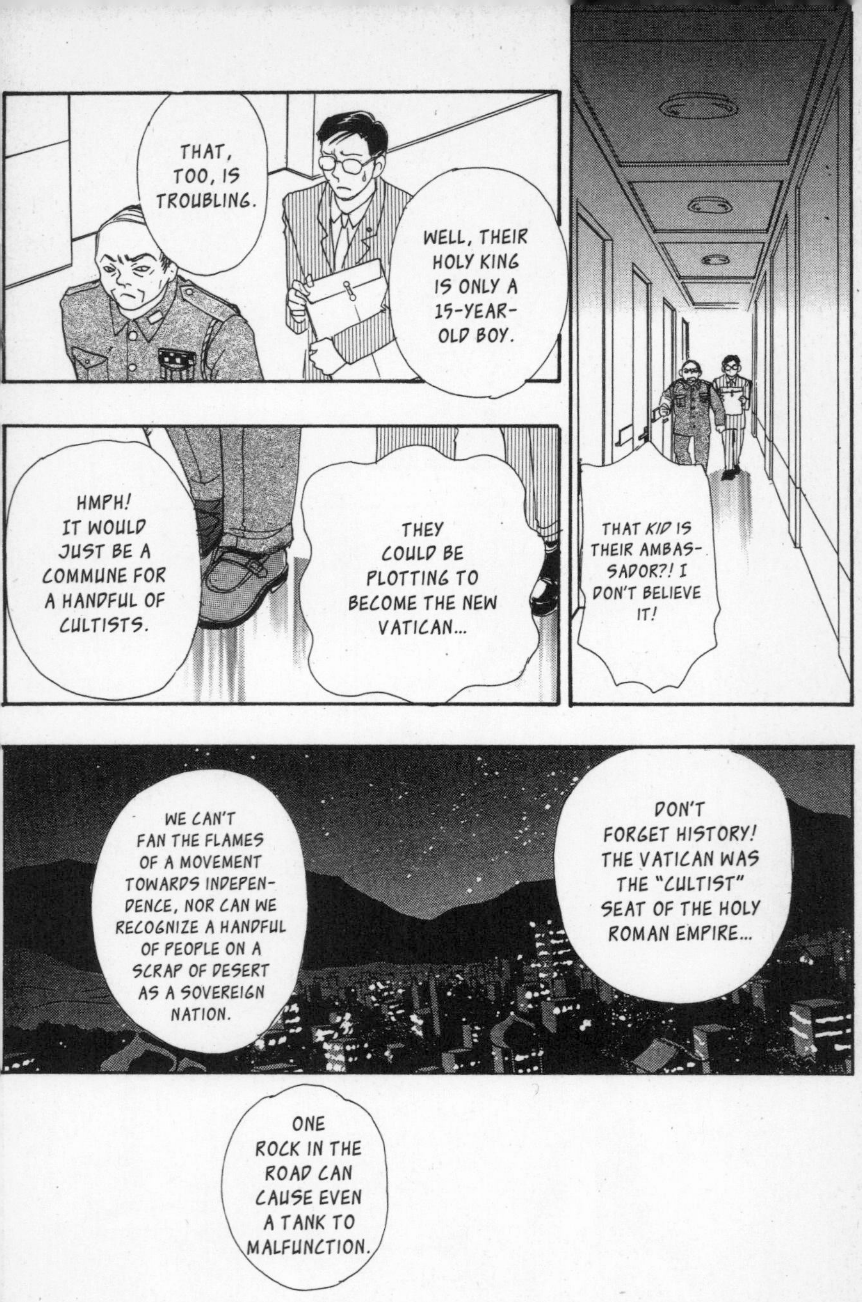

THAT *KID* IS THEIR AMBAS-SADOR?! I DON'T BELIEVE IT!
WELL, THEIR HOLY KING IS ONLY A 15-YEAR-OLD BOY.
THAT, TOO, IS TROUBLING.
THEY COULD BE PLOTTING TO BECOME THE NEW VATICAN...
HMPH! IT WOULD JUST BE A COMMUNE FOR A HANDFUL OF CULTISTS.
DON'T FORGET HISTORY! THE VATICAN WAS THE "CULTIST" SEAT OF THE HOLY ROMAN EMPIRE...
WE CAN'T FAN THE FLAMES OF A MOVEMENT TOWARDS INDEPEN-DENCE, NOR CAN WE RECOGNIZE A HANDFUL OF PEOPLE ON A SCRAP OF DESERT AS A SOVEREIGN NATION.
ONE ROCK IN THE ROAD CAN CAUSE EVEN A TANK TO MALFUNCTION.

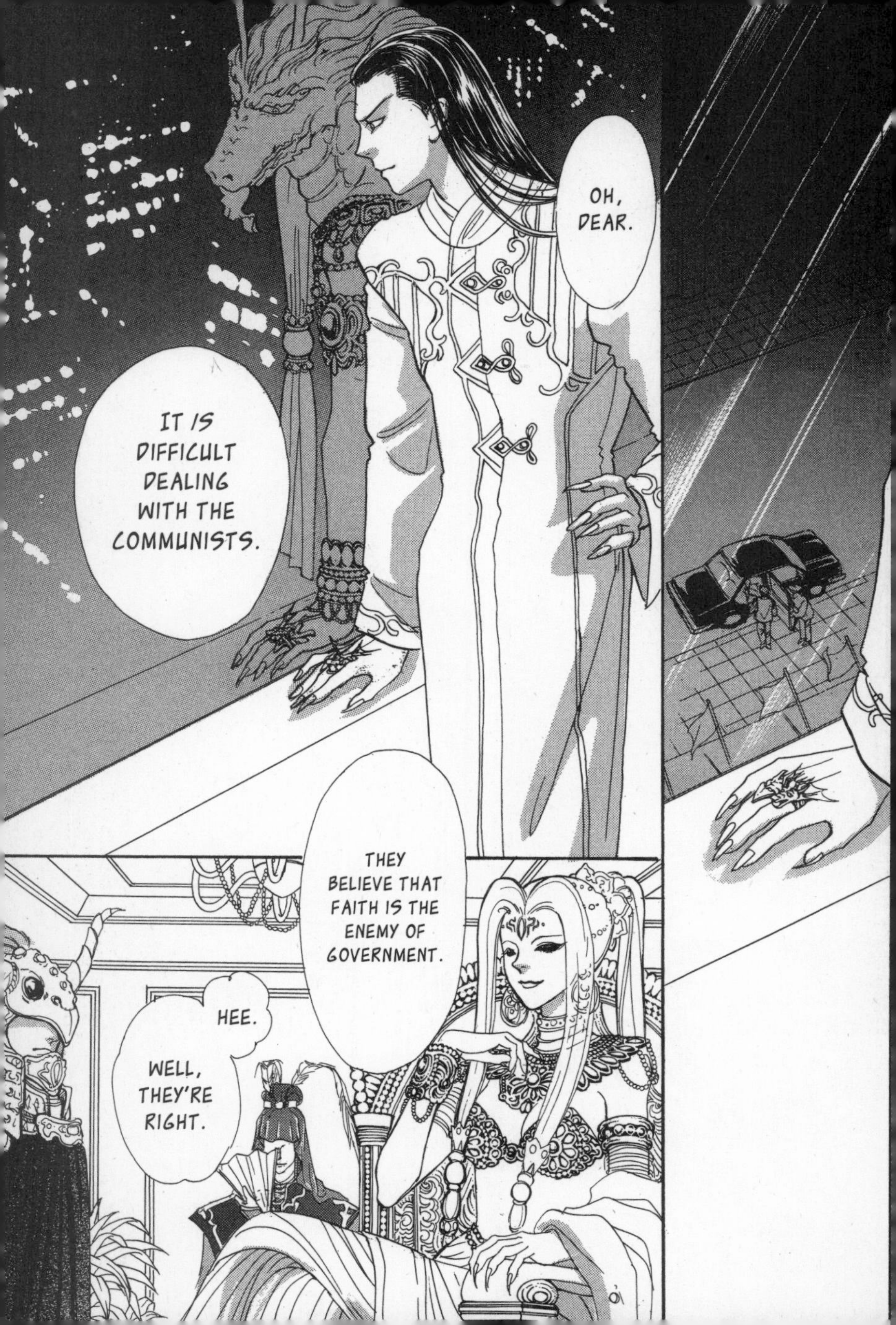
OH, DEAR.
IT IS DIFFICULT DEALING WITH THE COMMUNISTS.
THEY BELIEVE THAT FAITH IS THE ENEMY OF GOVERNMENT.
HEE.
WELL, THEY'RE RIGHT.

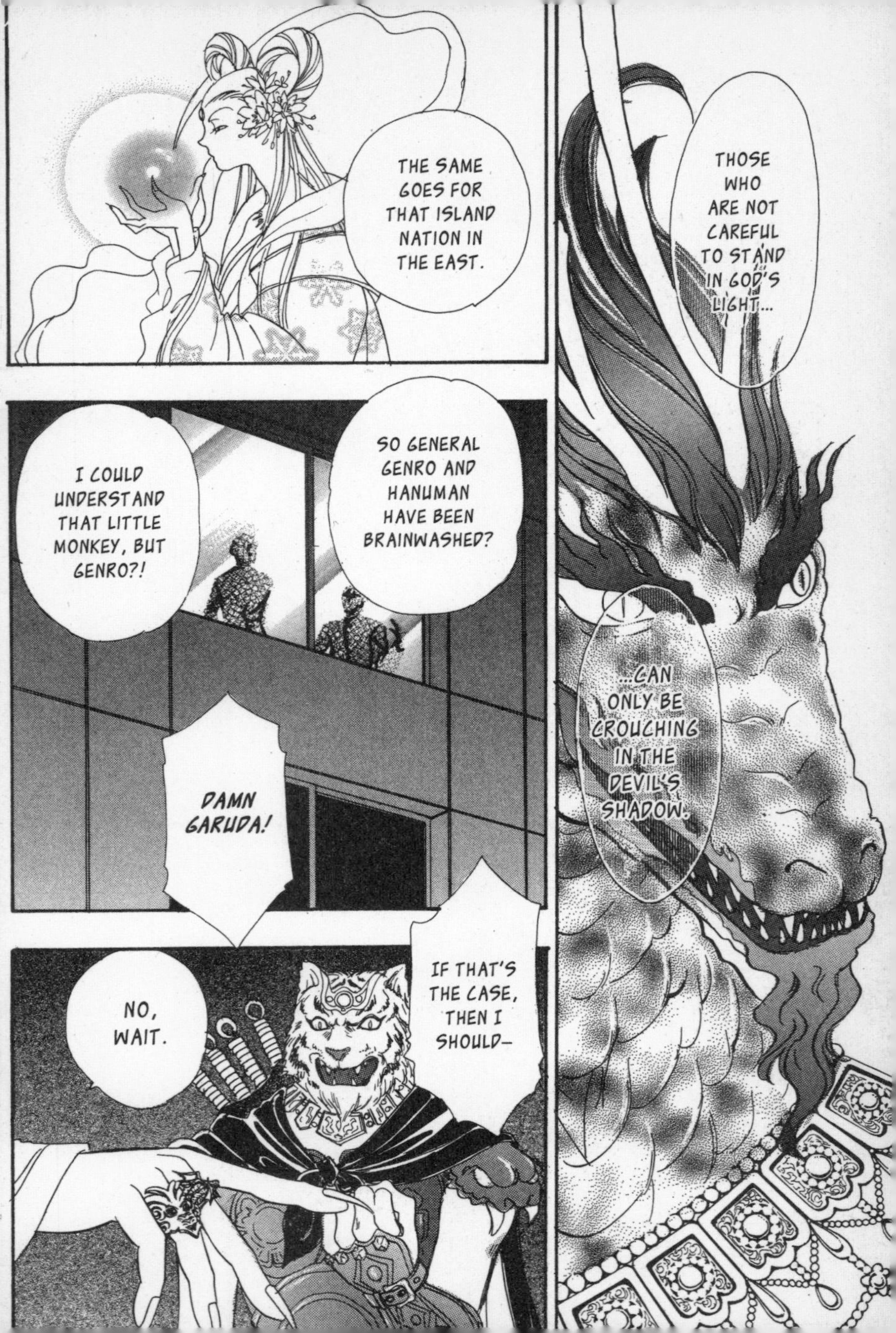
THOSE WHO ARE NOT CAREFUL TO STAND IN GOD'S LIGHT...
...CAN ONLY BE CROUCHING IN THE DEVIL'S SHADOW.
THE SAME GOES FOR THAT ISLAND NATION IN THE EAST.
SO GENERAL GENRO AND HANUMAN HAVE BEEN BRAINWASHED?
I COULD UNDERSTAND THAT LITTLE MONKEY, BUT GENRO?!
DAMN GARUDA!
IF THAT'S THE CASE, THEN I SHOULD–
NO, WAIT.

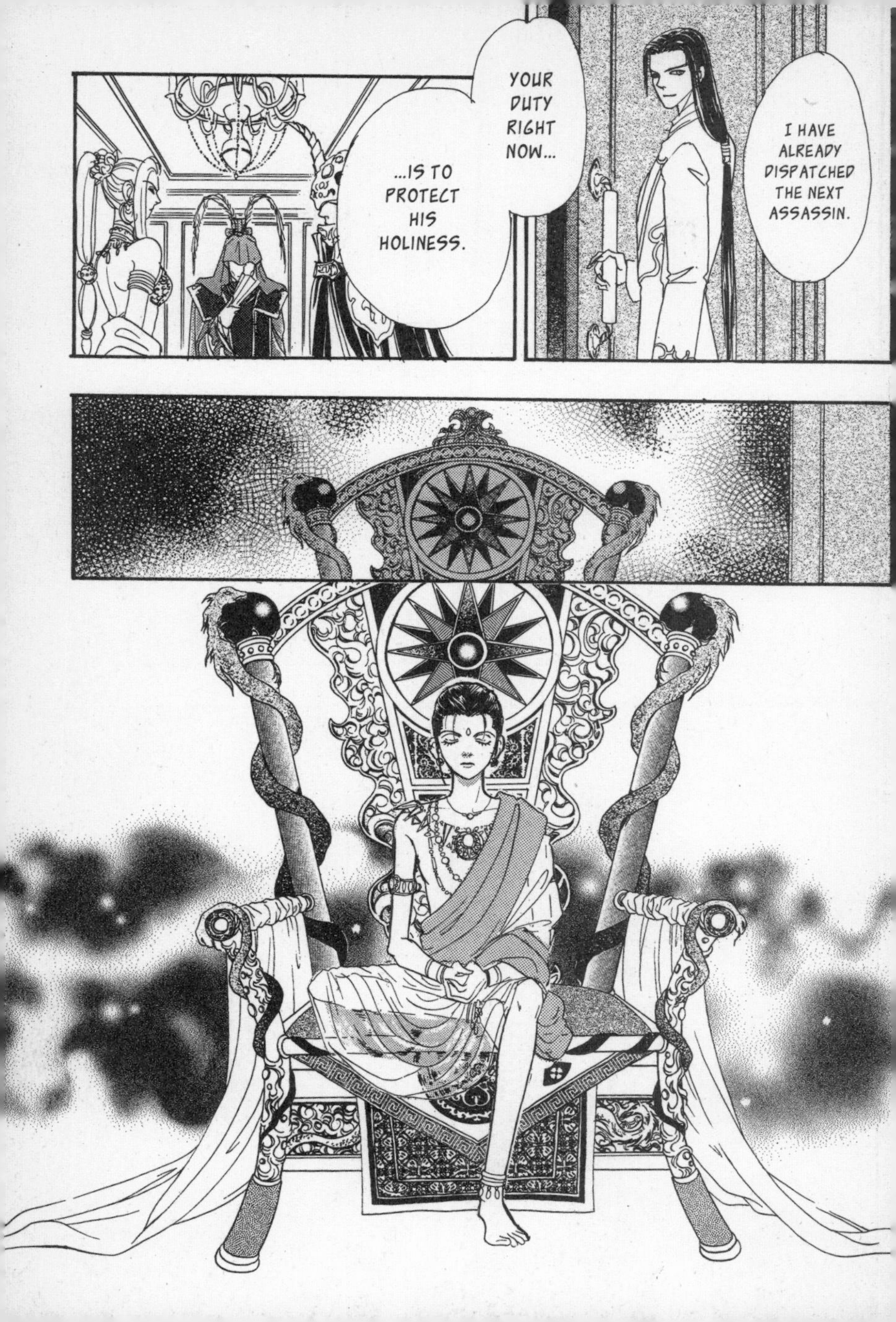
I HAVE ALREADY DISPATCHED THE NEXT ASSASSIN.
YOUR DUTY RIGHT NOW...
...IS TO PROTECT HIS HOLINESS.

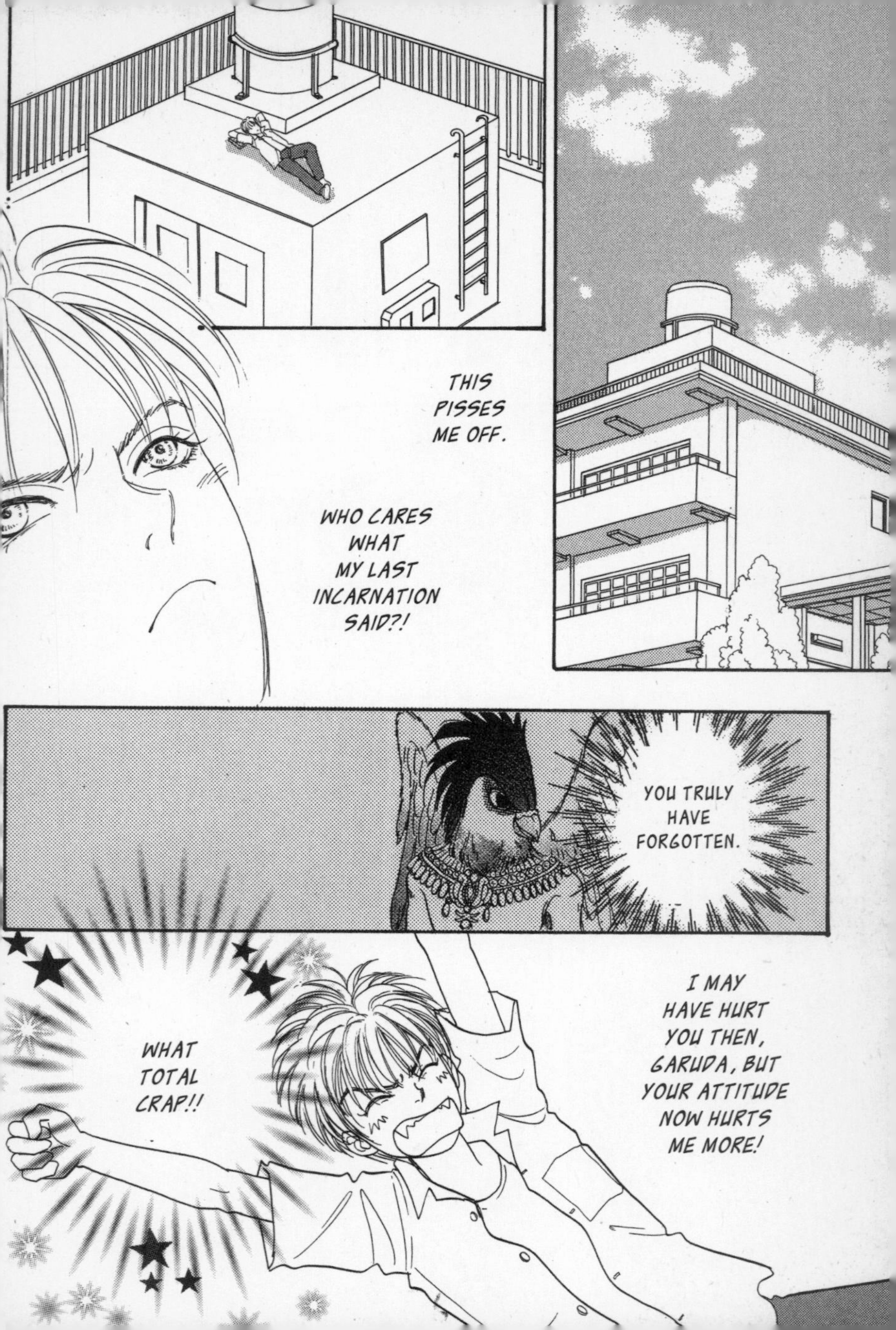
THIS PISSES ME OFF.
WHO CARES WHAT MY LAST INCARNATION SAID?!
YOU TRULY HAVE FORGOTTEN.
I MAY HAVE HURT YOU THEN, GARUDA, BUT YOUR ATTITUDE NOW HURTS ME MORE!
WHAT TOTAL CRAP!!

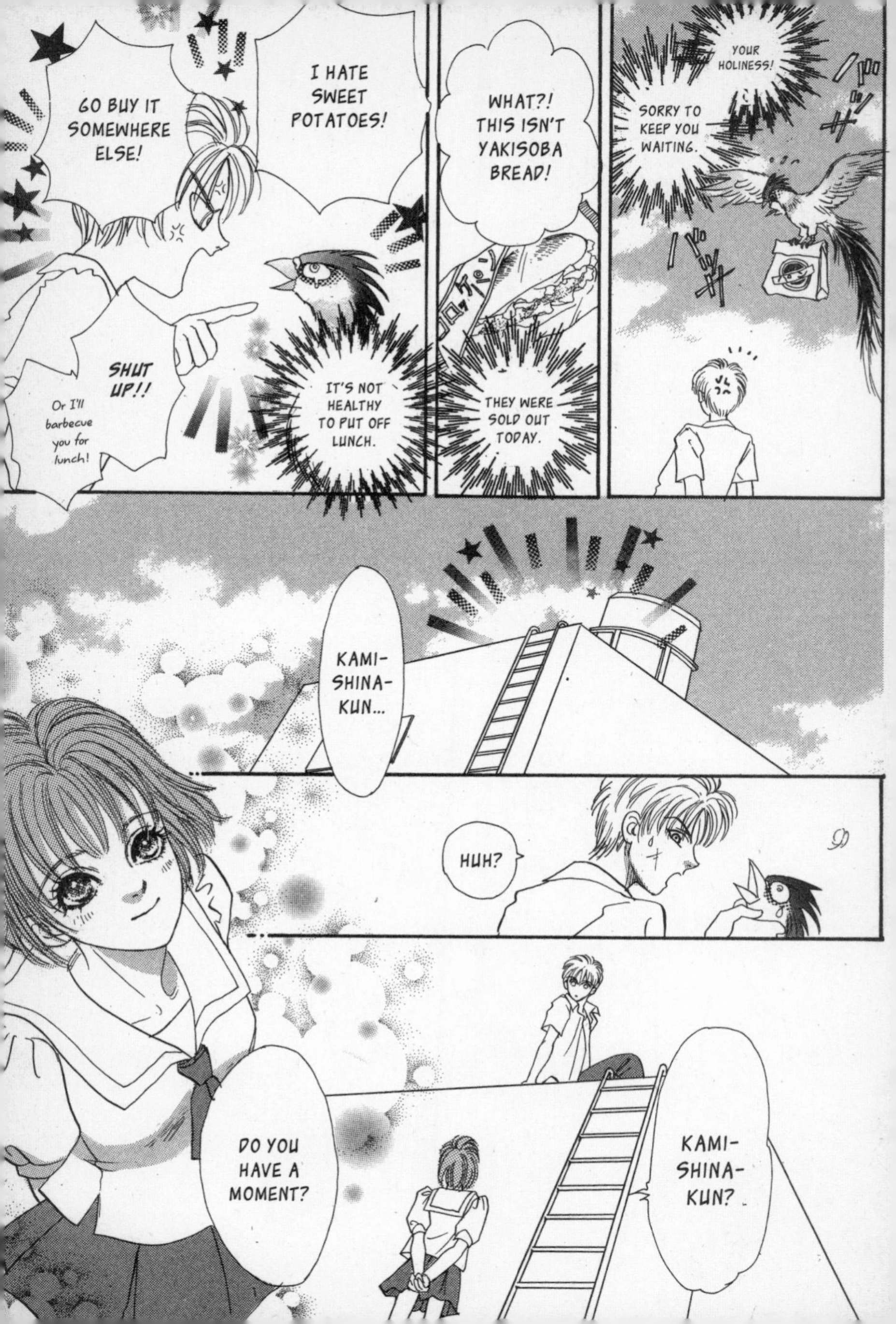
YOUR HOLINESS!
SORRY TO KEEP YOU WAITING.
WHAT?! THIS ISN'T YAKISOBA BREAD!
THEY WERE SOLD OUT TODAY.
I HATE SWEET POTATOES!
IT'S NOT HEALTHY TO PUT OFF LUNCH.
GO BUY IT SOMEWHERE ELSE!
SHUT UP!!
Or I'll barbecue you for lunch!
KAMI-SHINA-KUN...
HUH?
KAMI-SHINA-KUN?
DO YOU HAVE A MOMENT?

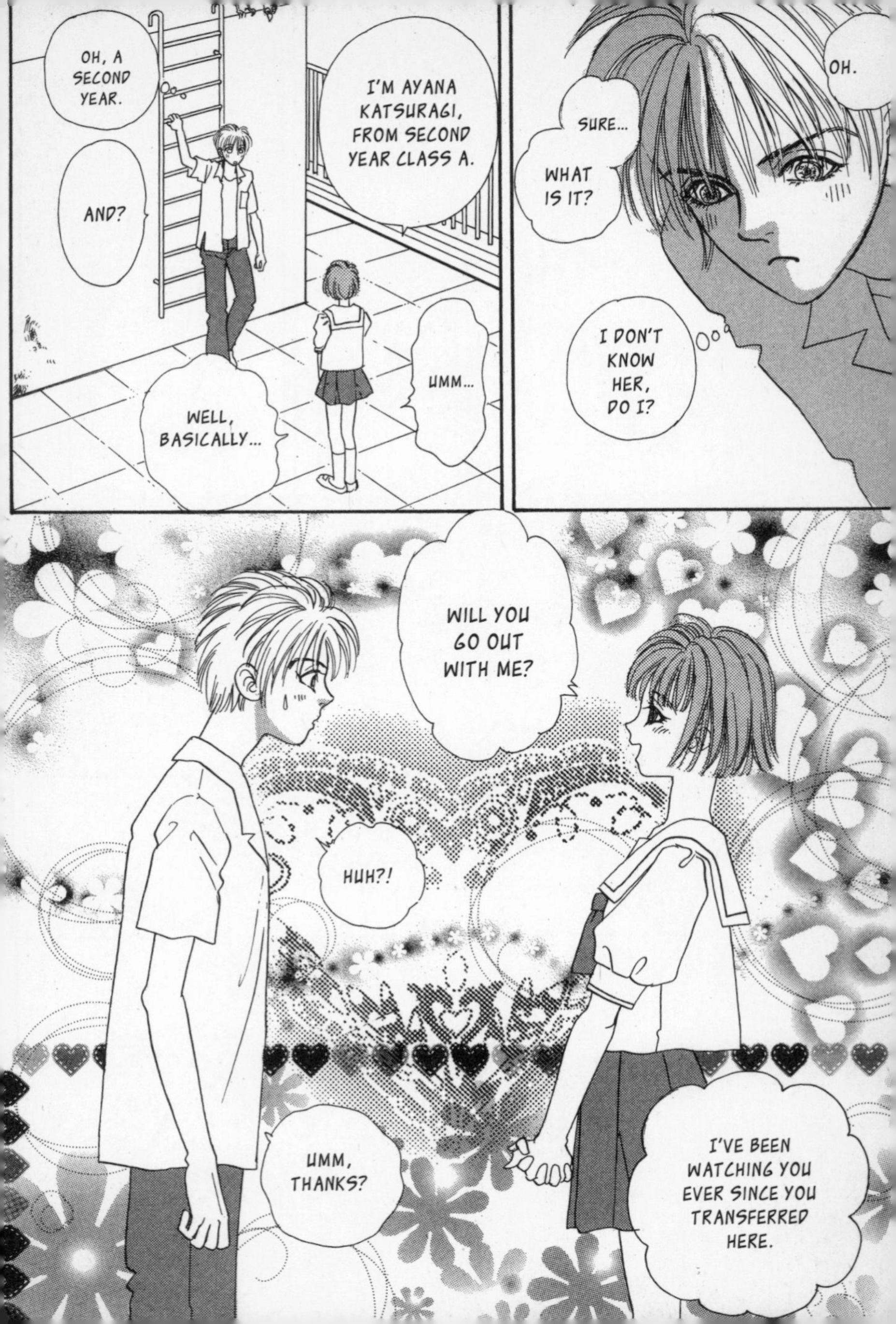
OH.
SURE...
WHAT IS IT?
I DON'T KNOW HER, DO I?
I'M AYANA KATSURAGI, FROM SECOND YEAR CLASS A.
OH, A SECOND YEAR.
AND?
UMM...
WELL, BASICALLY...
WILL YOU GO OUT WITH ME?
HUH?!
I'VE BEEN WATCHING YOU EVER SINCE YOU TRANSFERRED HERE.
UMM, THANKS?

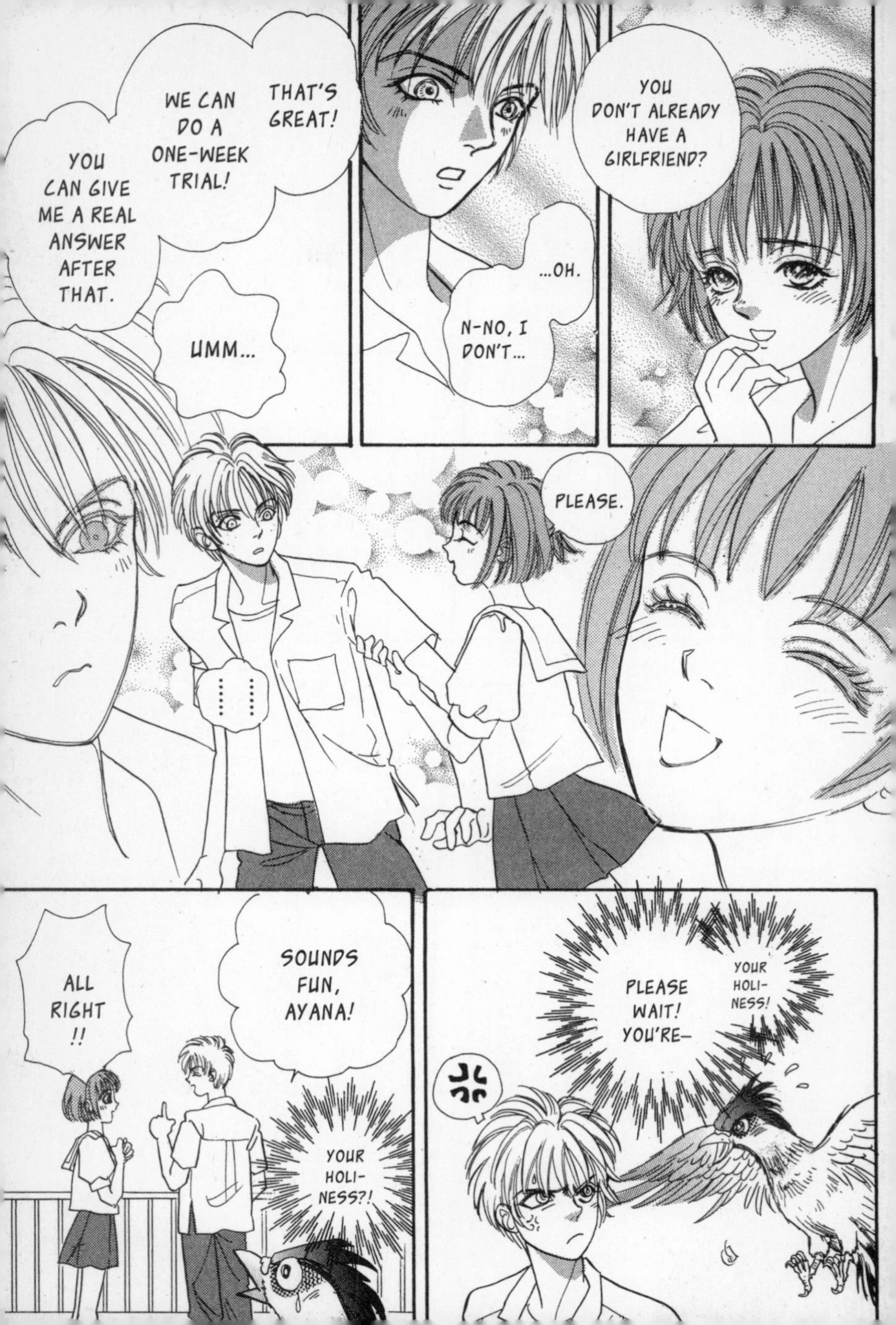
YOU DON'T ALREADY HAVE A GIRLFRIEND?
...OH.
N-NO, I DON'T...
THAT'S GREAT!
WE CAN DO A ONE-WEEK TRIAL!
YOU CAN GIVE ME A REAL ANSWER AFTER THAT.
UMM...
PLEASE.
......
PLEASE WAIT! YOU'RE—
YOUR HOLI-NESS!
SOUNDS FUN, AYANA!
ALL RIGHT !!
YOUR HOLI-NESS?!

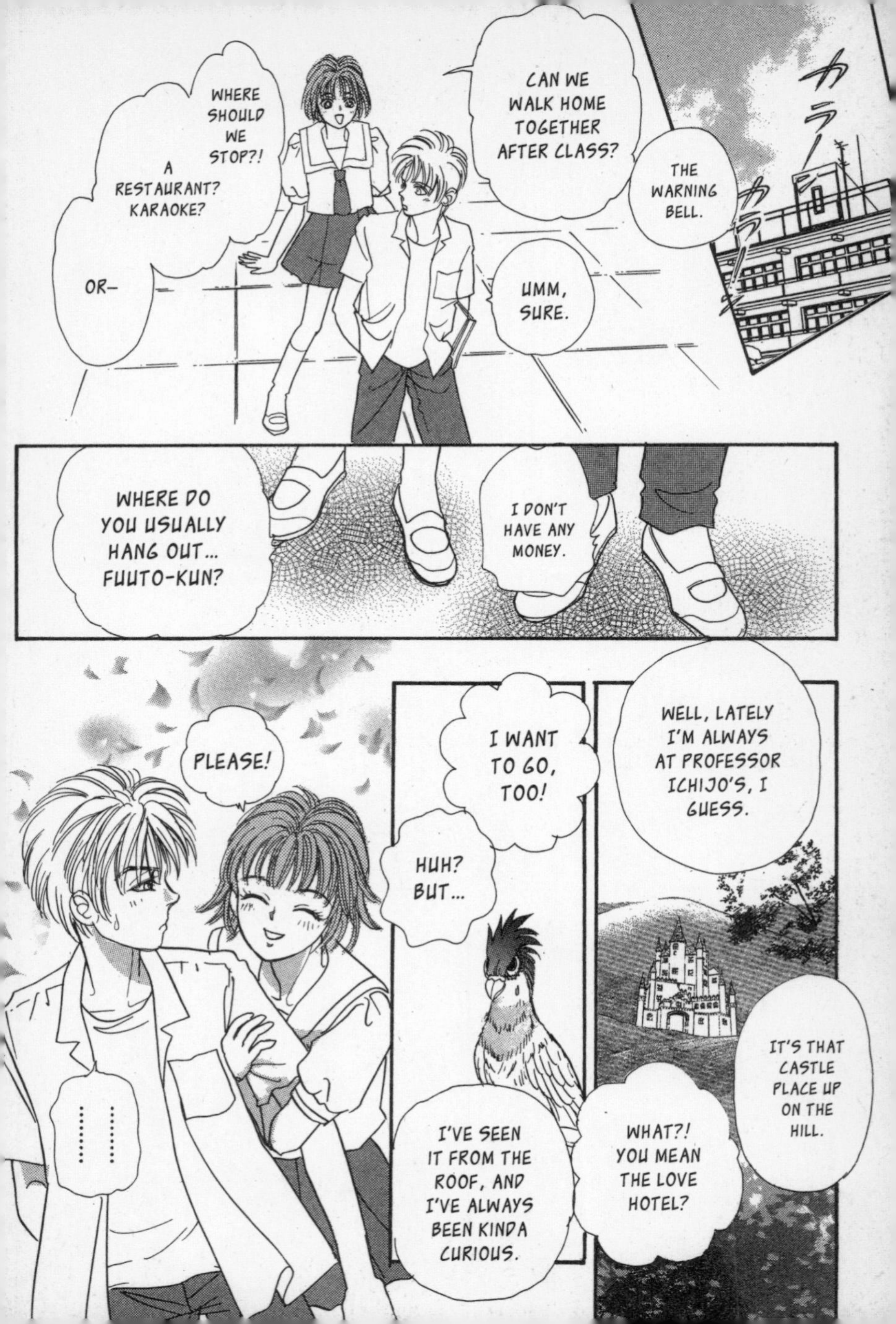

カラーン
カラーン
THE WARNING BELL.
CAN WE WALK HOME TOGETHER AFTER CLASS?
UMM, SURE.
WHERE SHOULD WE STOP?!
A RESTAURANT? KARAOKE?
OR–
I DON'T HAVE ANY MONEY.
WHERE DO YOU USUALLY HANG OUT... FUUTO-KUN?
WELL, LATELY I'M ALWAYS AT PROFESSOR ICHIJO'S, I GUESS.
IT'S THAT CASTLE PLACE UP ON THE HILL.
WHAT?! YOU MEAN THE LOVE HOTEL?
I WANT TO GO, TOO!
HUH? BUT...
I'VE SEEN IT FROM THE ROOF, AND I'VE ALWAYS BEEN KINDA CURIOUS.
PLEASE!
......

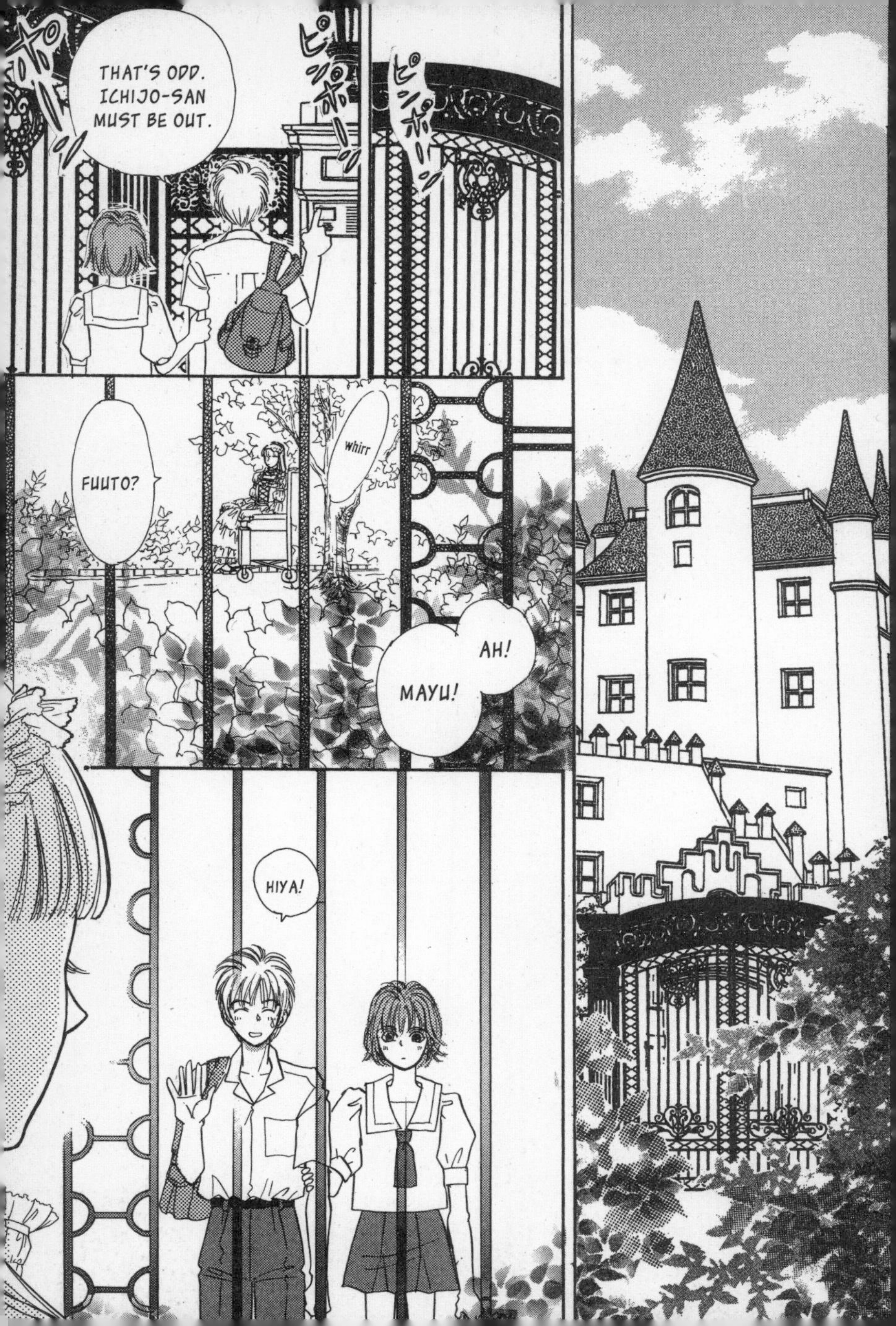
THAT'S ODD. ICHIJO-SAN MUST BE OUT.
AH!
MAYU!
whirr
FUUTO?
HIYA!

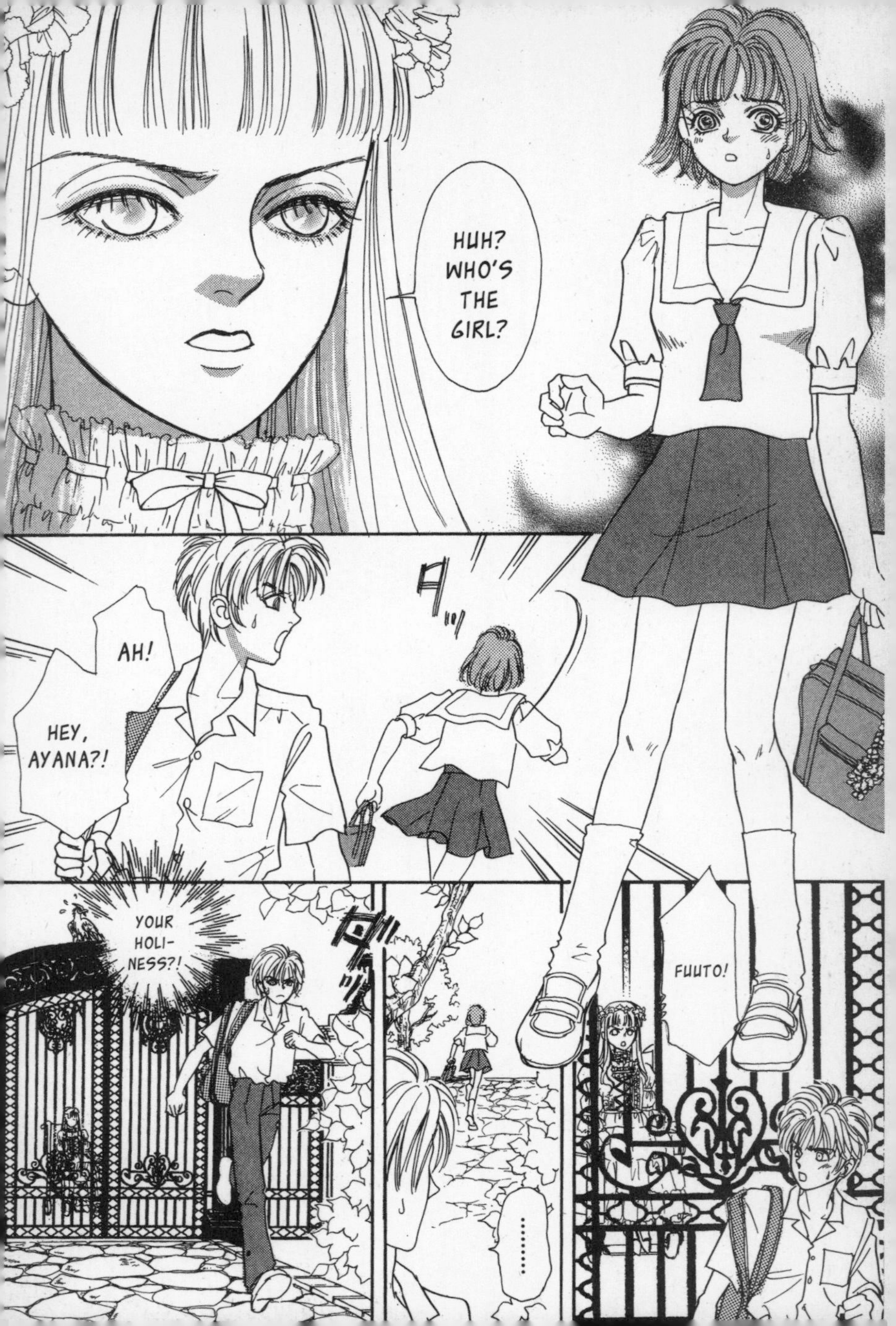
HUH? WHO'S THE GIRL?
AH!
HEY, AYANA?!
FUUTO!
......
YOUR HOLI-NESS?!

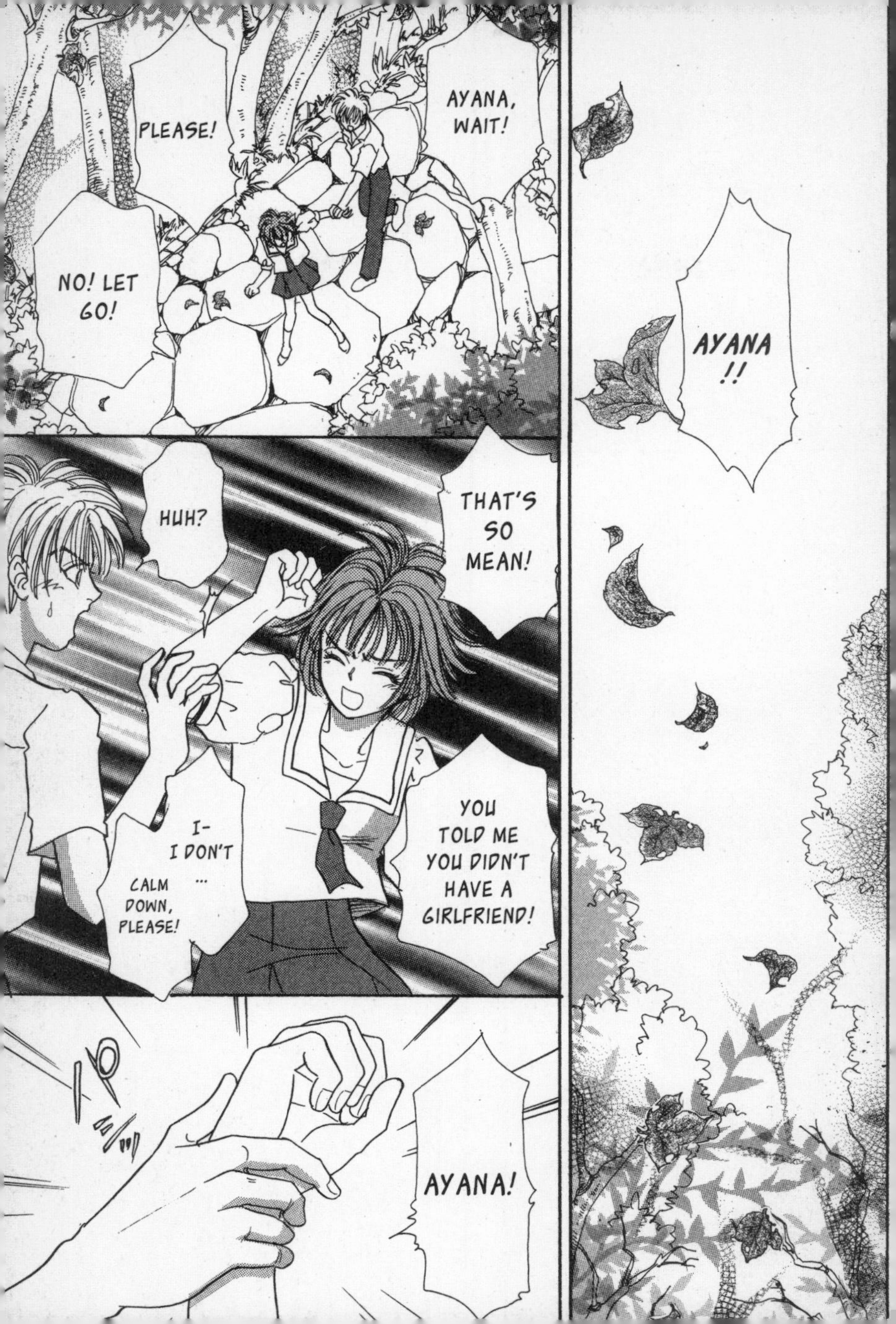
AYANA !!
AYANA, WAIT!
PLEASE!
NO! LET GO!
THAT'S SO MEAN!
HUH?
YOU TOLD ME YOU DIDN'T HAVE A GIRLFRIEND!
I- I DON'T ...
CALM DOWN, PLEASE!
AYANA!

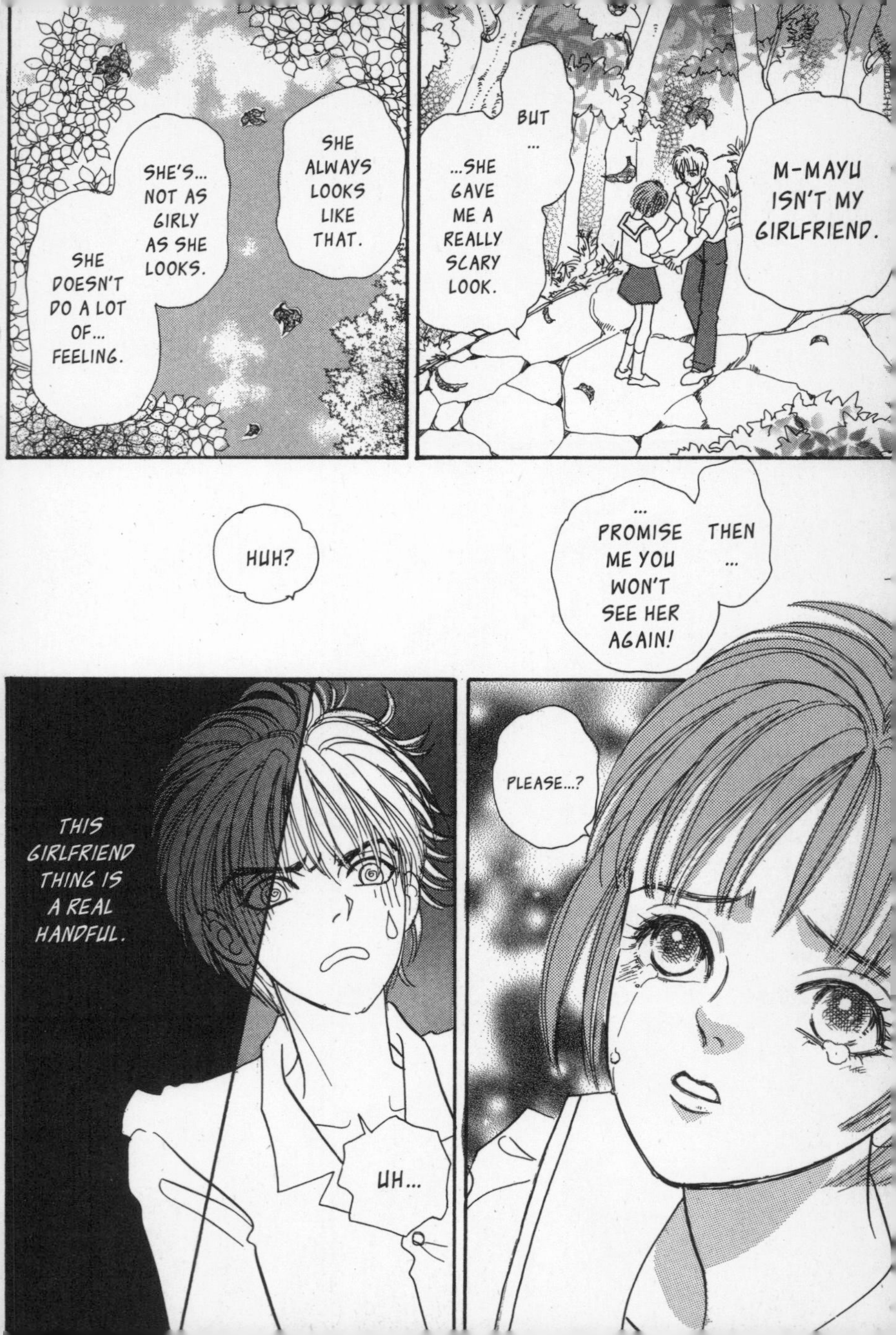
M-MAYU ISN'T MY GIRLFRIEND.
BUT ... ...SHE GAVE ME A REALLY SCARY LOOK.
SHE ALWAYS LOOKS LIKE THAT.
SHE'S... NOT AS GIRLY AS SHE LOOKS. SHE DOESN'T DO A LOT OF... FEELING.
THEN ... ... PROMISE ME YOU WON'T SEE HER AGAIN!
HUH?
PLEASE...?
UH...
THIS GIRLFRIEND THING IS A REAL HANDFUL.

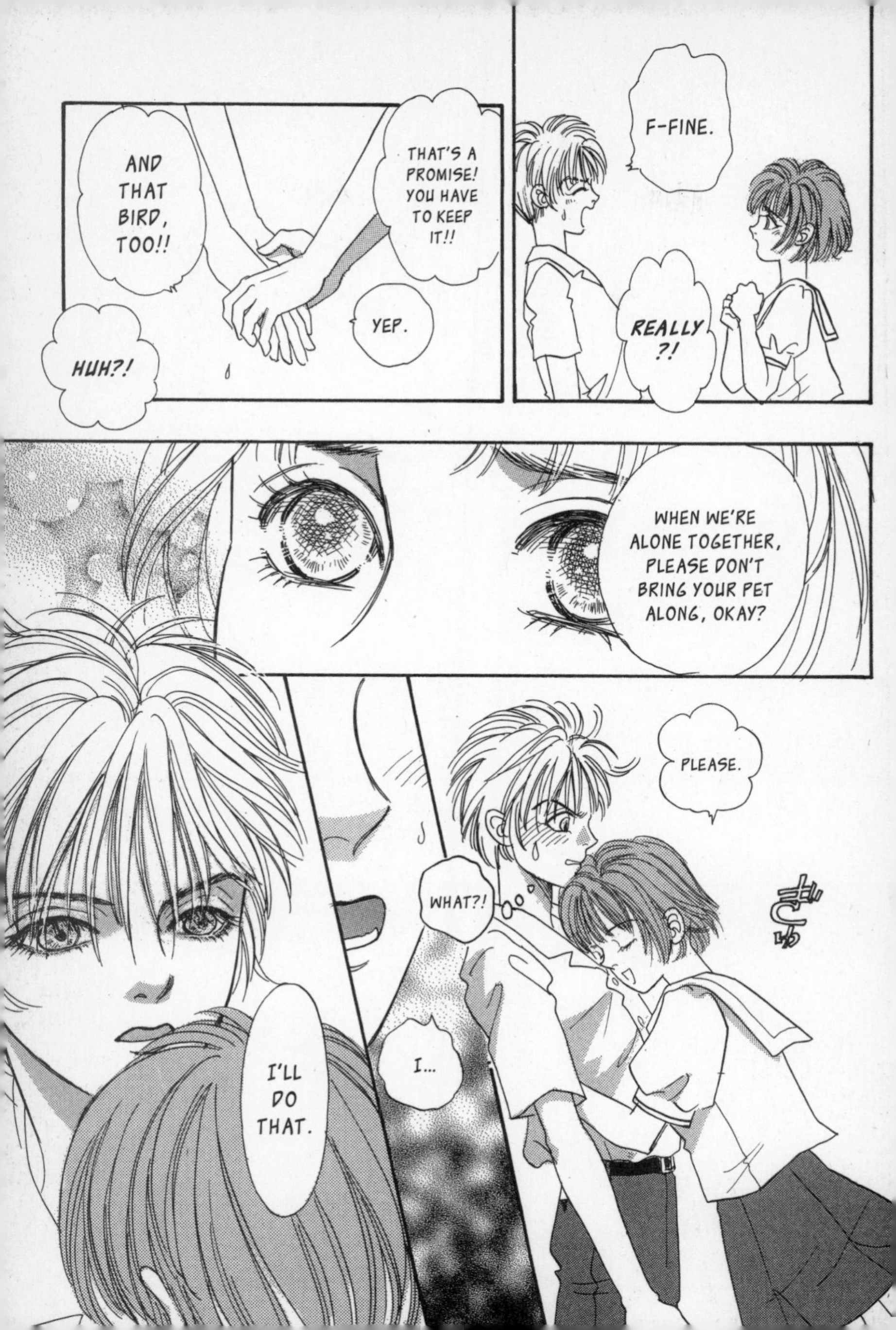
F-FINE.
REALLY ?!
THAT'S A PROMISE! YOU HAVE TO KEEP IT!!
AND THAT BIRD, TOO!!
YEP.
HUH?!
WHEN WE'RE ALONE TOGETHER, PLEASE DON'T BRING YOUR PET ALONG, OKAY?
PLEASE.
WHAT?!
I...
I'LL DO THAT.

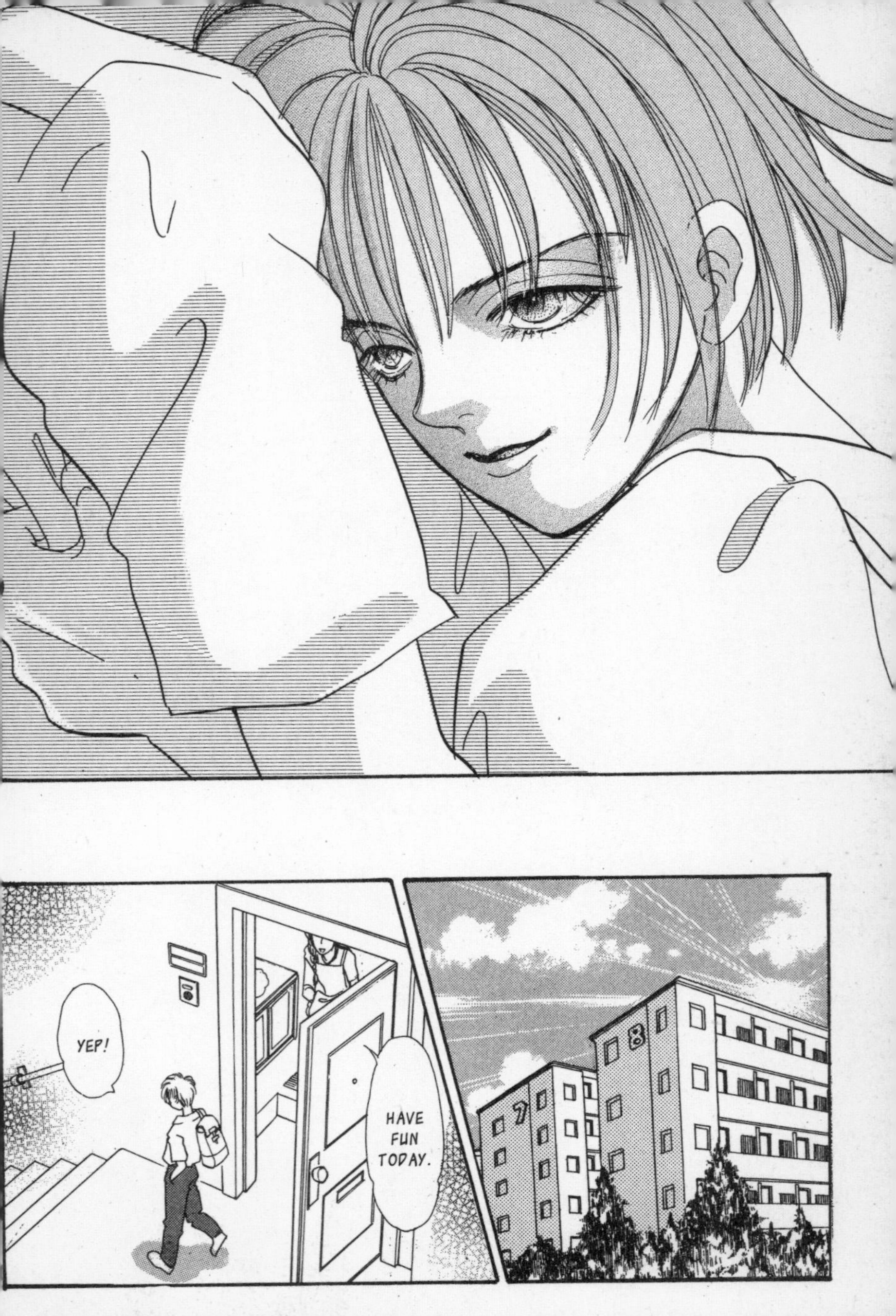
HAVE FUN TODAY.
YEP!

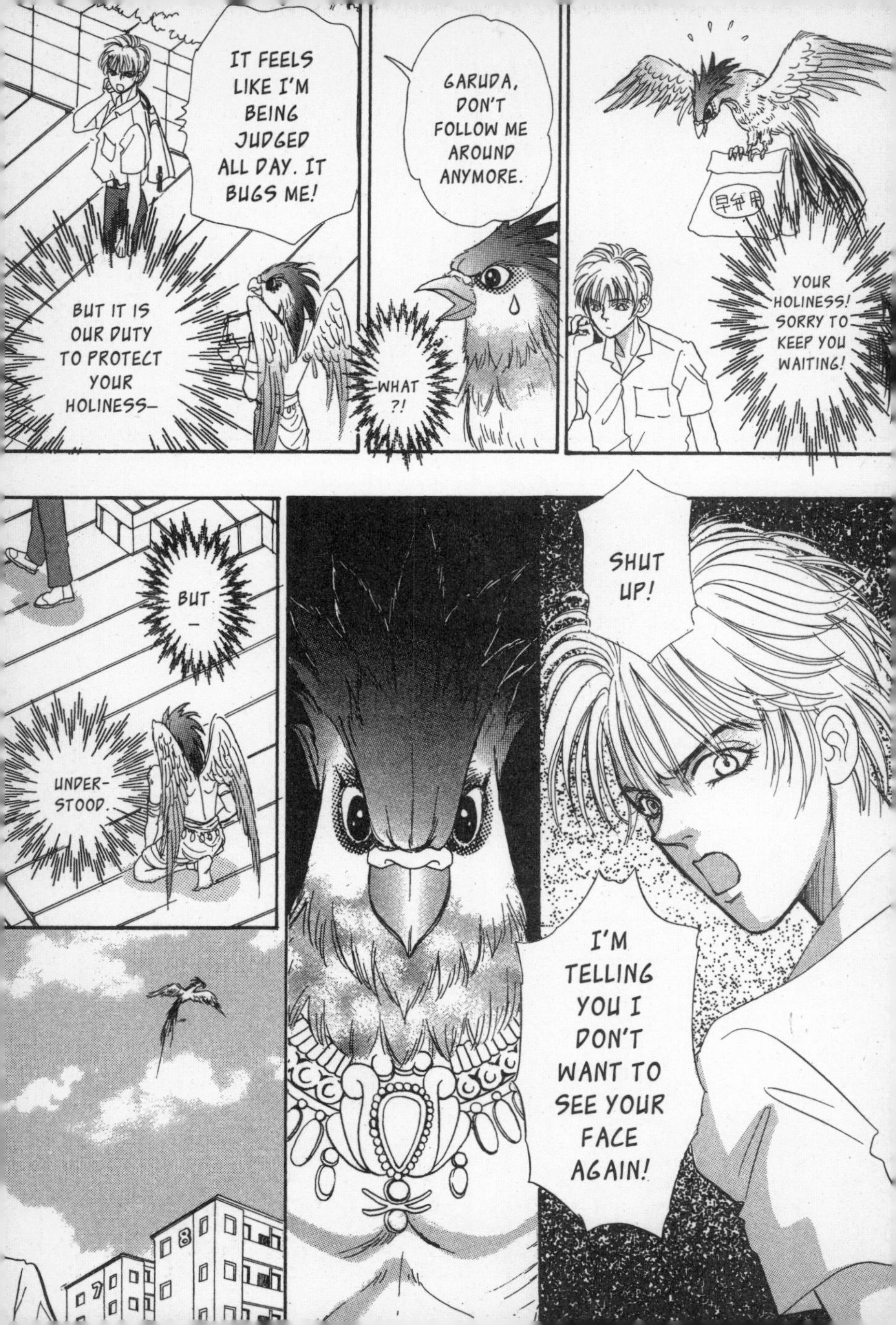
早弁用
YOUR HOLINESS! SORRY TO KEEP YOU WAITING!
GARUDA, DON'T FOLLOW ME AROUND ANYMORE.
WHAT?!
IT FEELS LIKE I'M BEING JUDGED ALL DAY. IT BUGS ME!
BUT IT IS OUR DUTY TO PROTECT YOUR HOLINESS—
SHUT UP!
I'M TELLING YOU I DON'T WANT TO SEE YOUR FACE AGAIN!
BUT—
UNDER-STOOD.

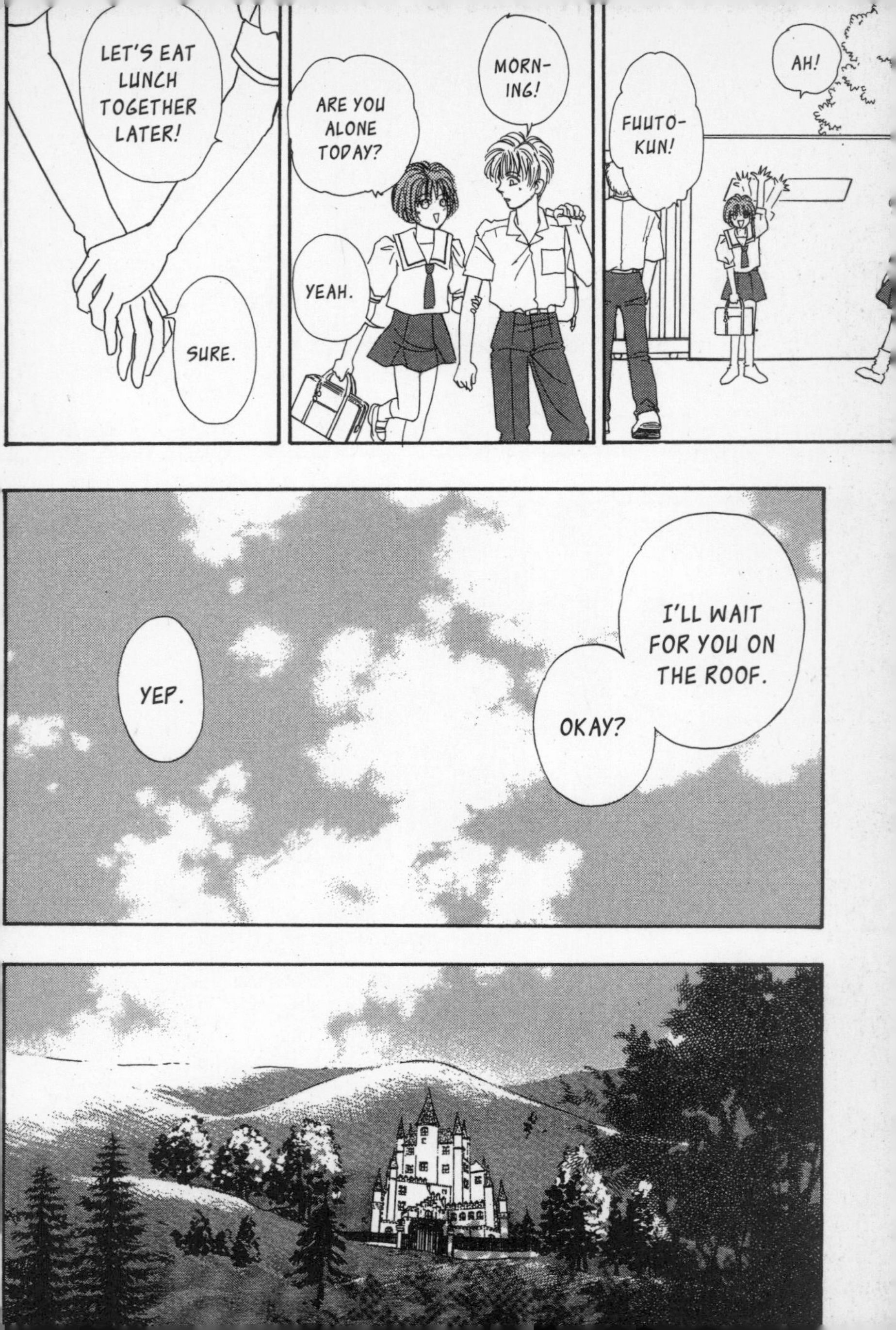
AH!
FUUTO-KUN!
MORN-ING!
ARE YOU ALONE TODAY?
YEAH.
LET'S EAT LUNCH TOGETHER LATER!
SURE.
I'LL WAIT FOR YOU ON THE ROOF.
OKAY?
YEP.

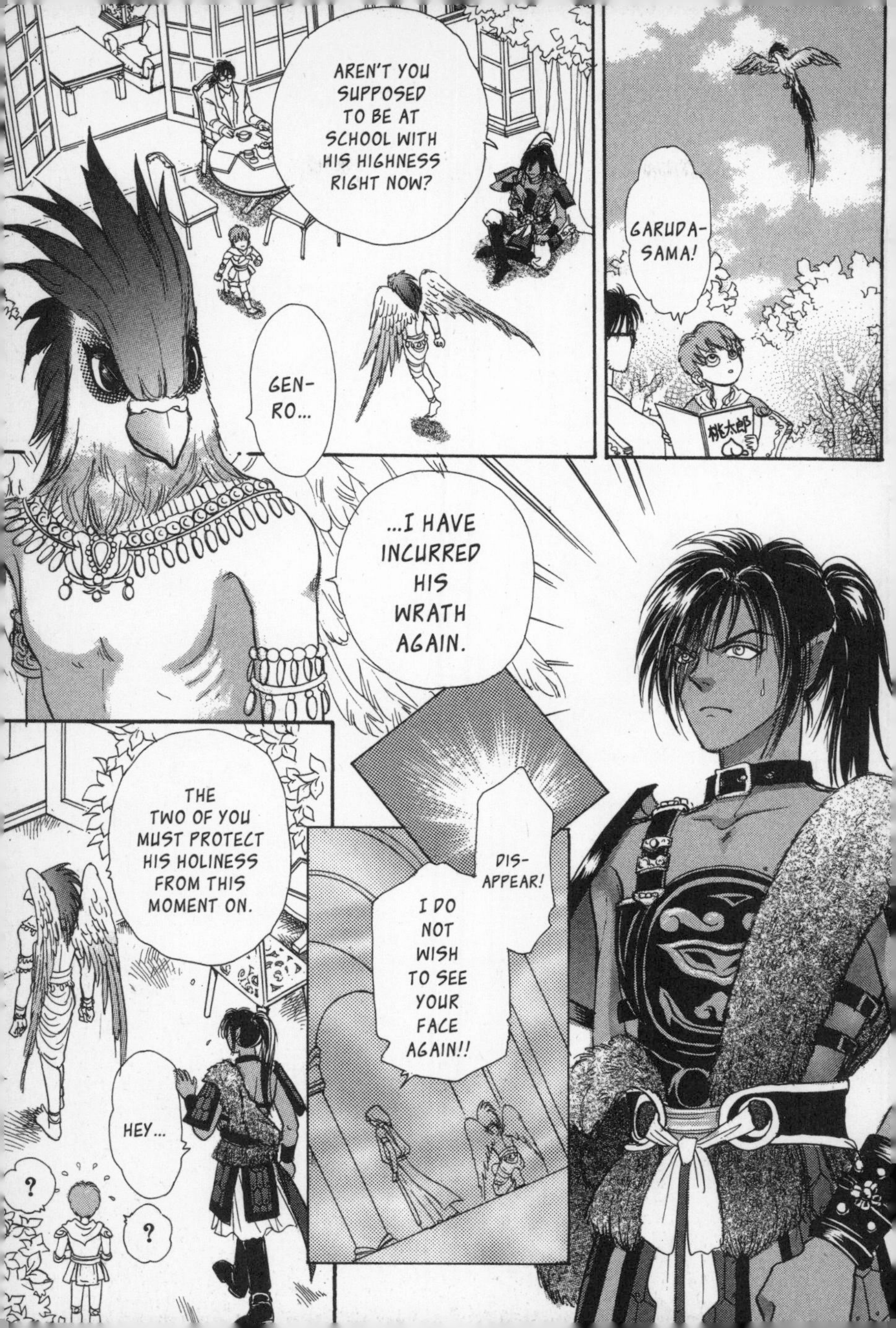
GARUDA-SAMA!
AREN'T YOU SUPPOSED TO BE AT SCHOOL WITH HIS HIGHNESS RIGHT NOW?
GEN-RO...
...I HAVE INCURRED HIS WRATH AGAIN.
DIS-APPEAR!
I DO NOT WISH TO SEE YOUR FACE AGAIN!!
THE TWO OF YOU MUST PROTECT HIS HOLINESS FROM THIS MOMENT ON.
HEY...
?
?

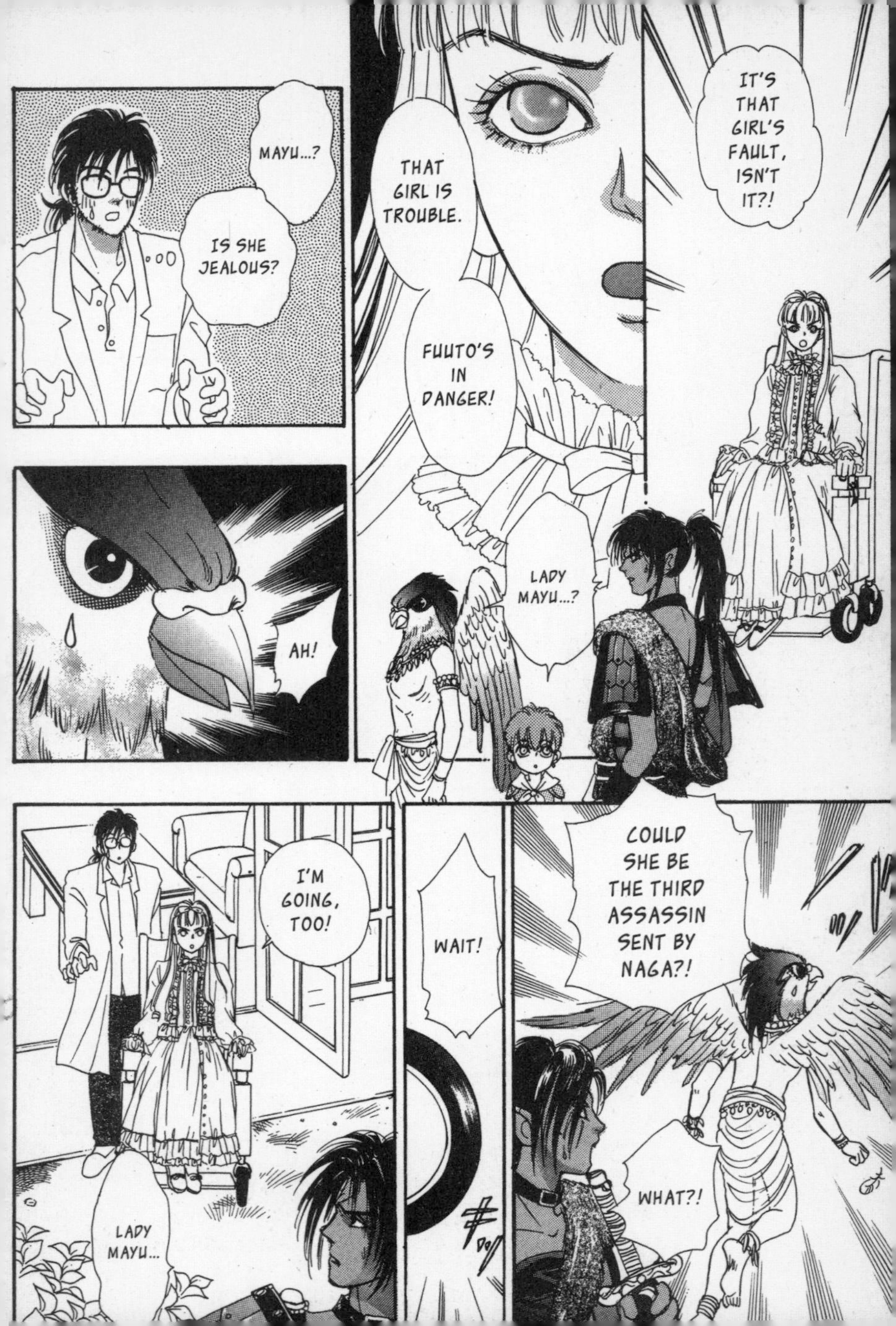
IT'S THAT GIRL'S FAULT, ISN'T IT?!
THAT GIRL IS TROUBLE.
FUUTO'S IN DANGER!
LADY MAYU...?
MAYU...?
IS SHE JEALOUS?
AH!
COULD SHE BE THE THIRD ASSASSIN SENT BY NAGA?!
WHAT?!
WAIT!
I'M GOING, TOO!
LADY MAYU...

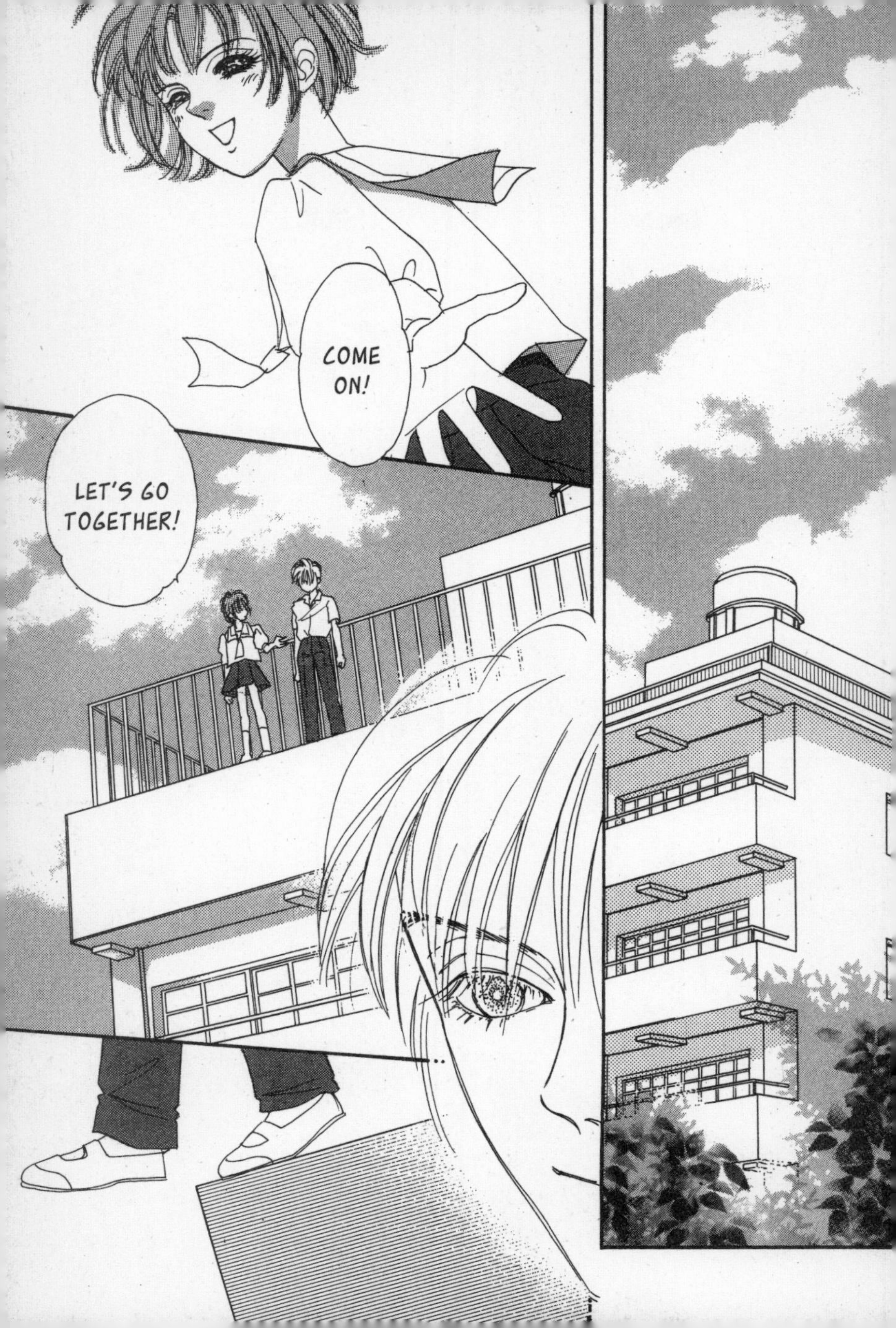
COME ON!
LET'S GO TOGETHER!

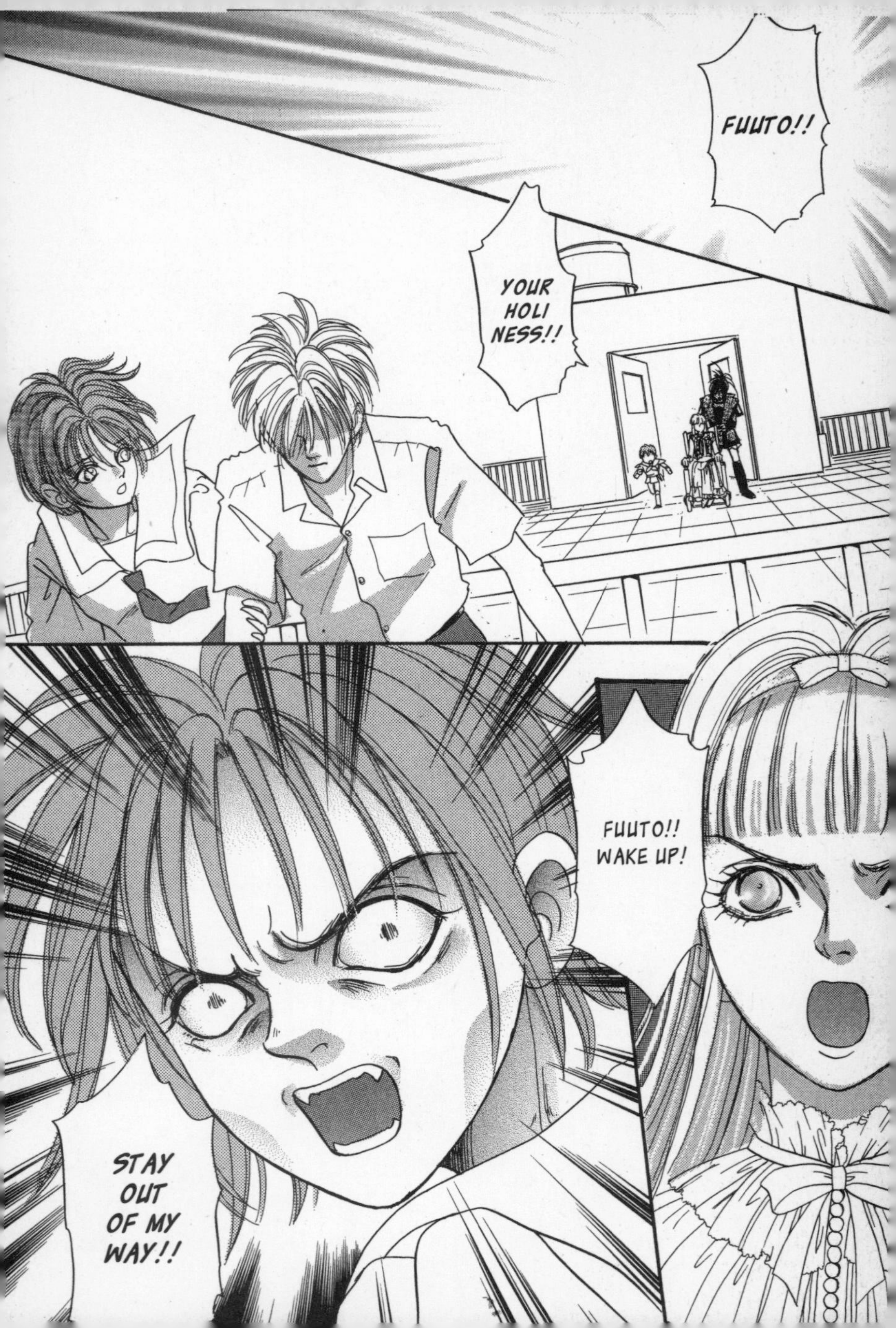
FUUTO!!
YOUR HOLINESS!!
FUUTO!! WAKE UP!
STAY OUT OF MY WAY!!

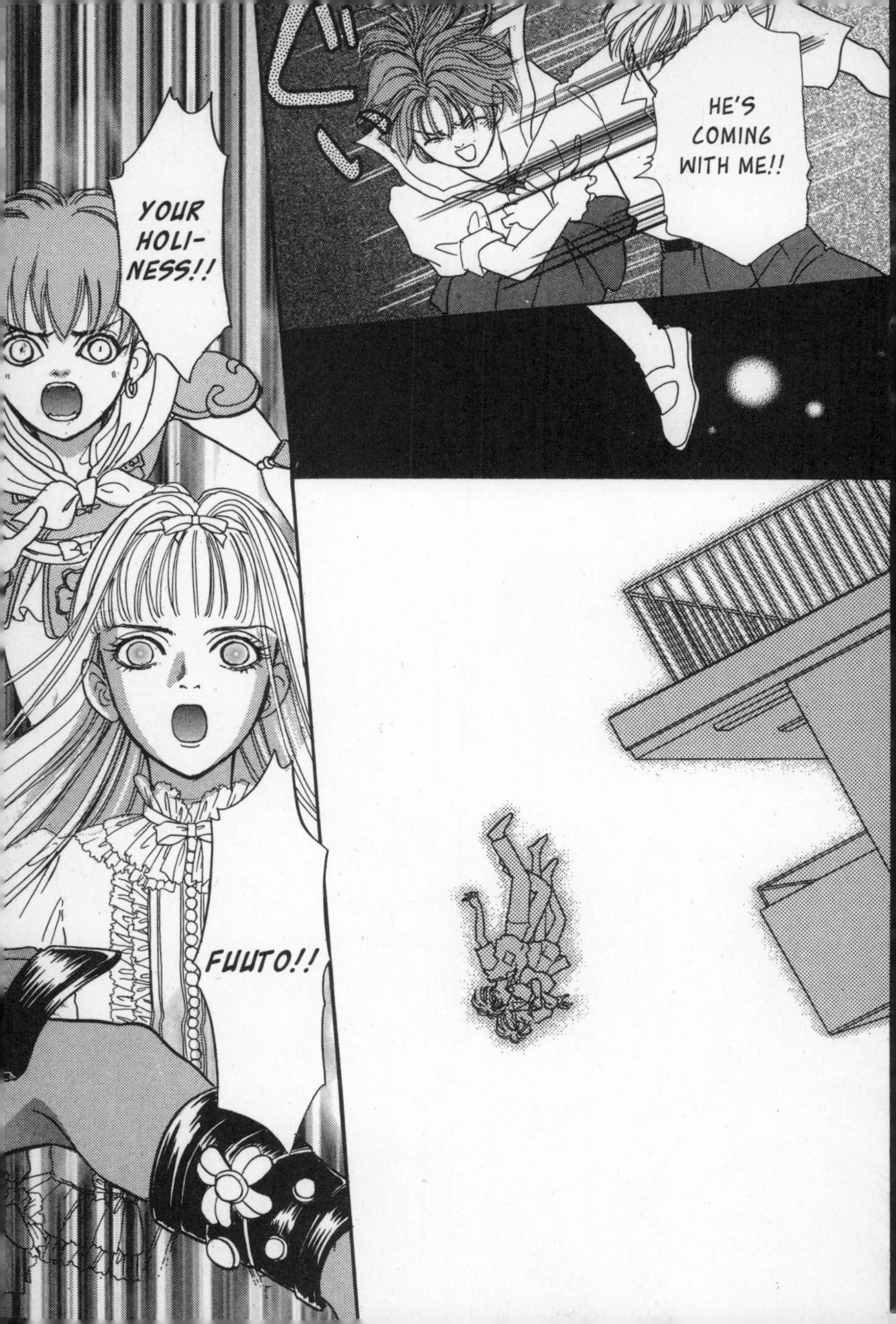
HE'S COMING WITH ME!!
YOUR HOLI-NESS!!
FUUTO!!

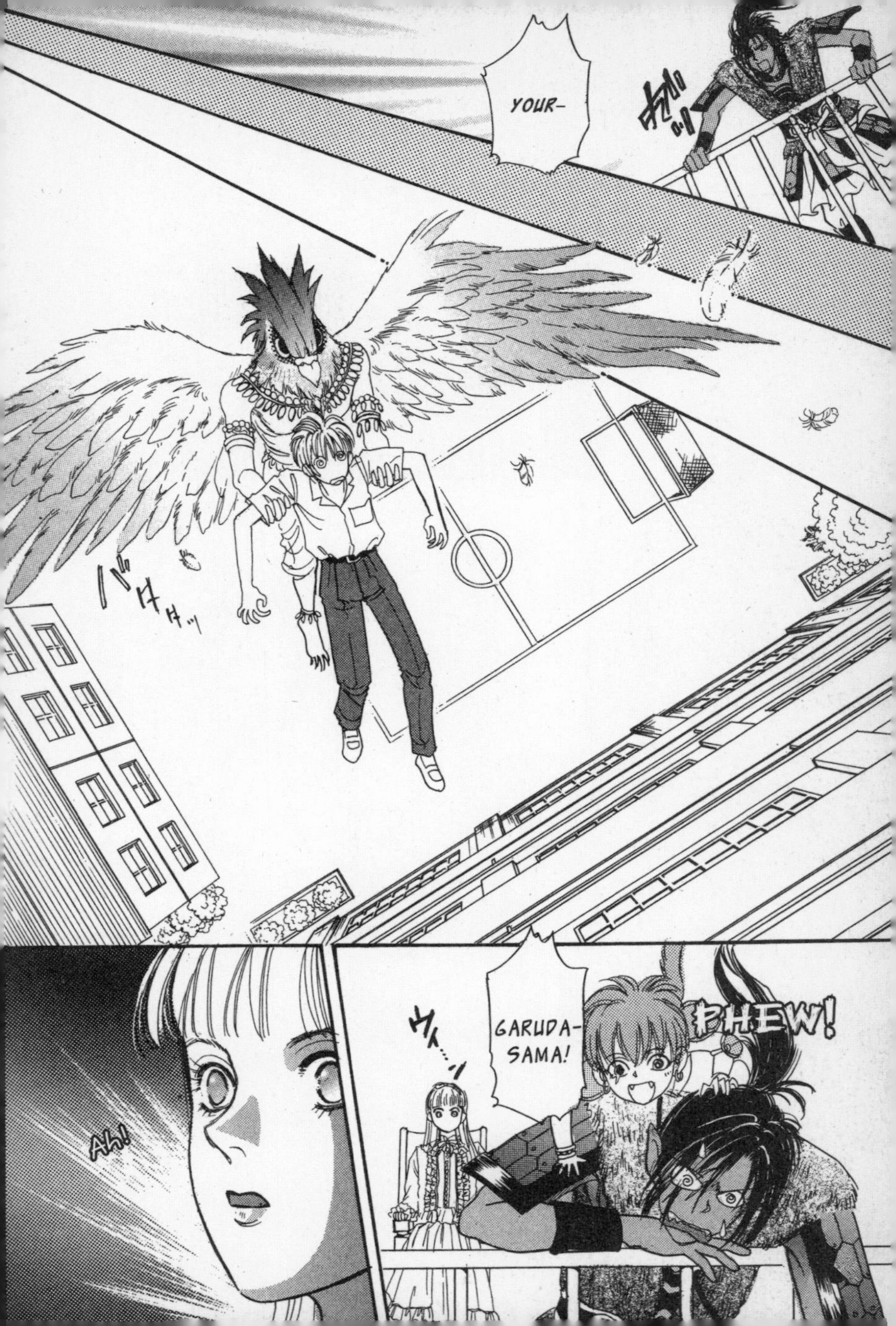
YOUR-
PHEW!
GARUDA-SAMA!
Ah!

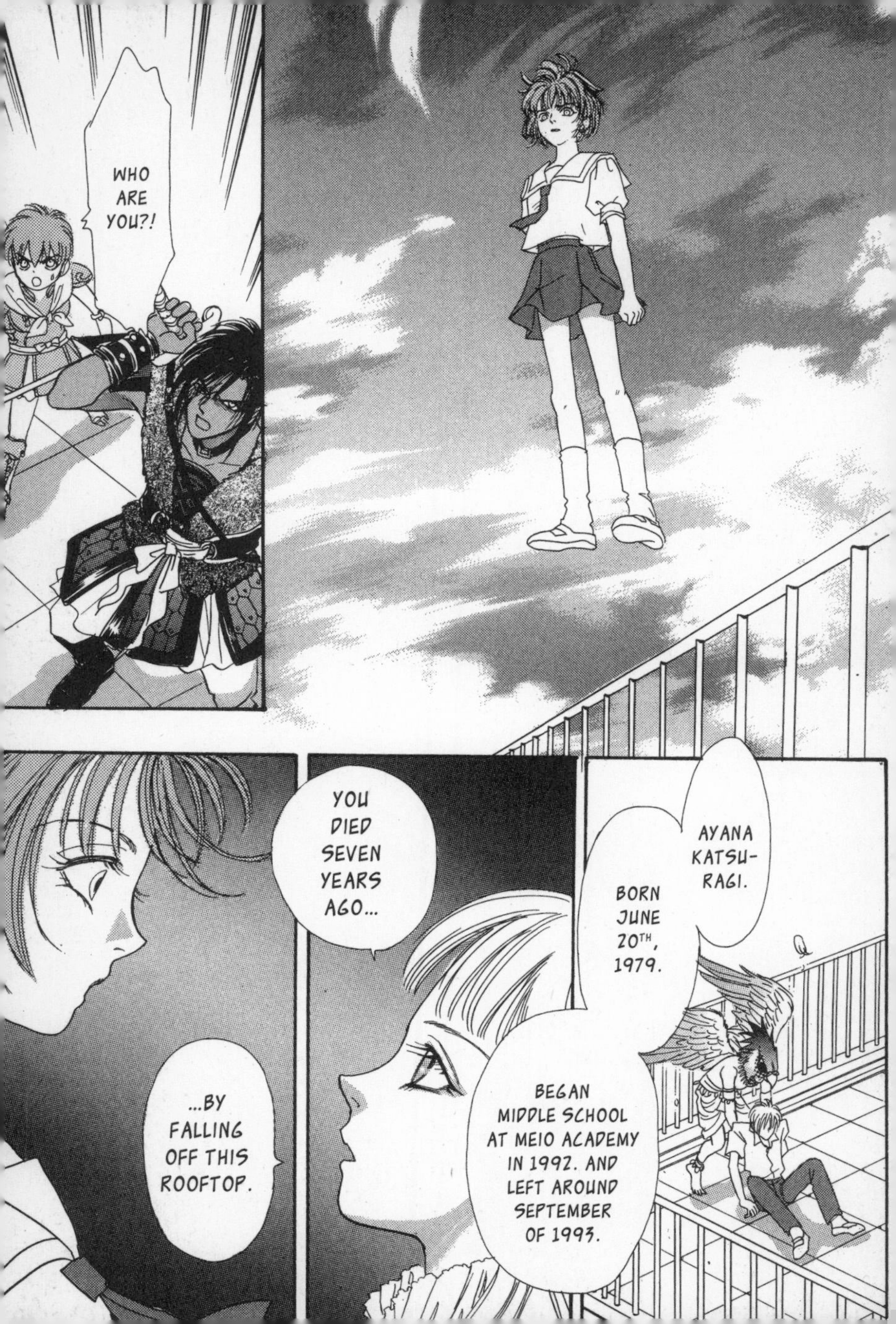
WHO ARE YOU?!
AYANA KATSU-RAGI.
BORN JUNE 20TH, 1979.
BEGAN MIDDLE SCHOOL AT MEIO ACADEMY IN 1992. AND LEFT AROUND SEPTEMBER OF 1993.
YOU DIED SEVEN YEARS AGO...
...BY FALLING OFF THIS ROOFTOP.

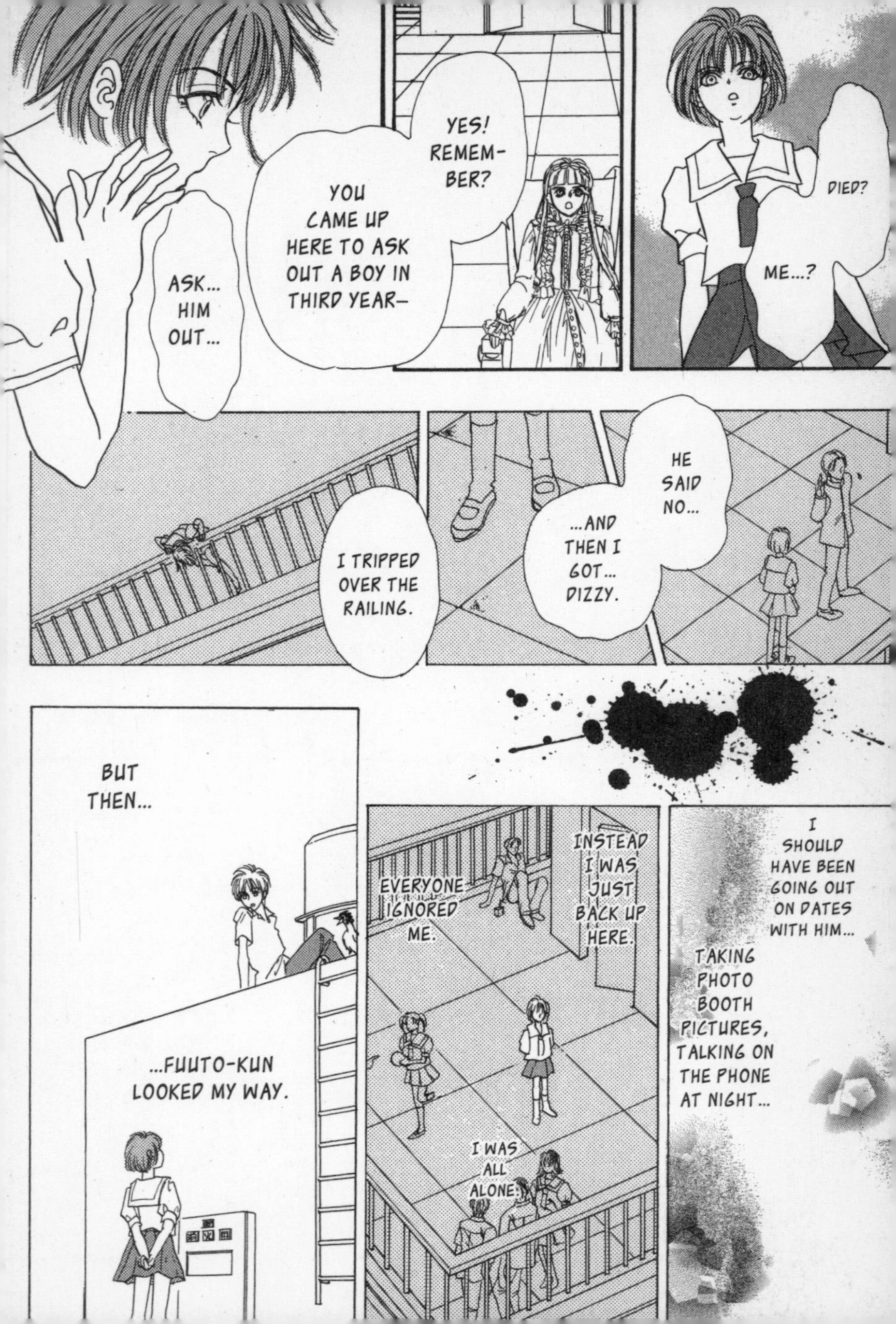
DIED?
ME...?
YES! REMEM-BER?
YOU CAME UP HERE TO ASK OUT A BOY IN THIRD YEAR—
ASK... HIM OUT...
HE SAID NO...
...AND THEN I GOT... DIZZY.
I TRIPPED OVER THE RAILING.
I SHOULD HAVE BEEN GOING OUT ON DATES WITH HIM...
TAKING PHOTO BOOTH PICTURES, TALKING ON THE PHONE AT NIGHT...
INSTEAD I WAS JUST BACK UP HERE.
EVERYONE IGNORED ME.
I WAS ALL ALONE.
BUT THEN...
...FUUTO-KUN LOOKED MY WAY.

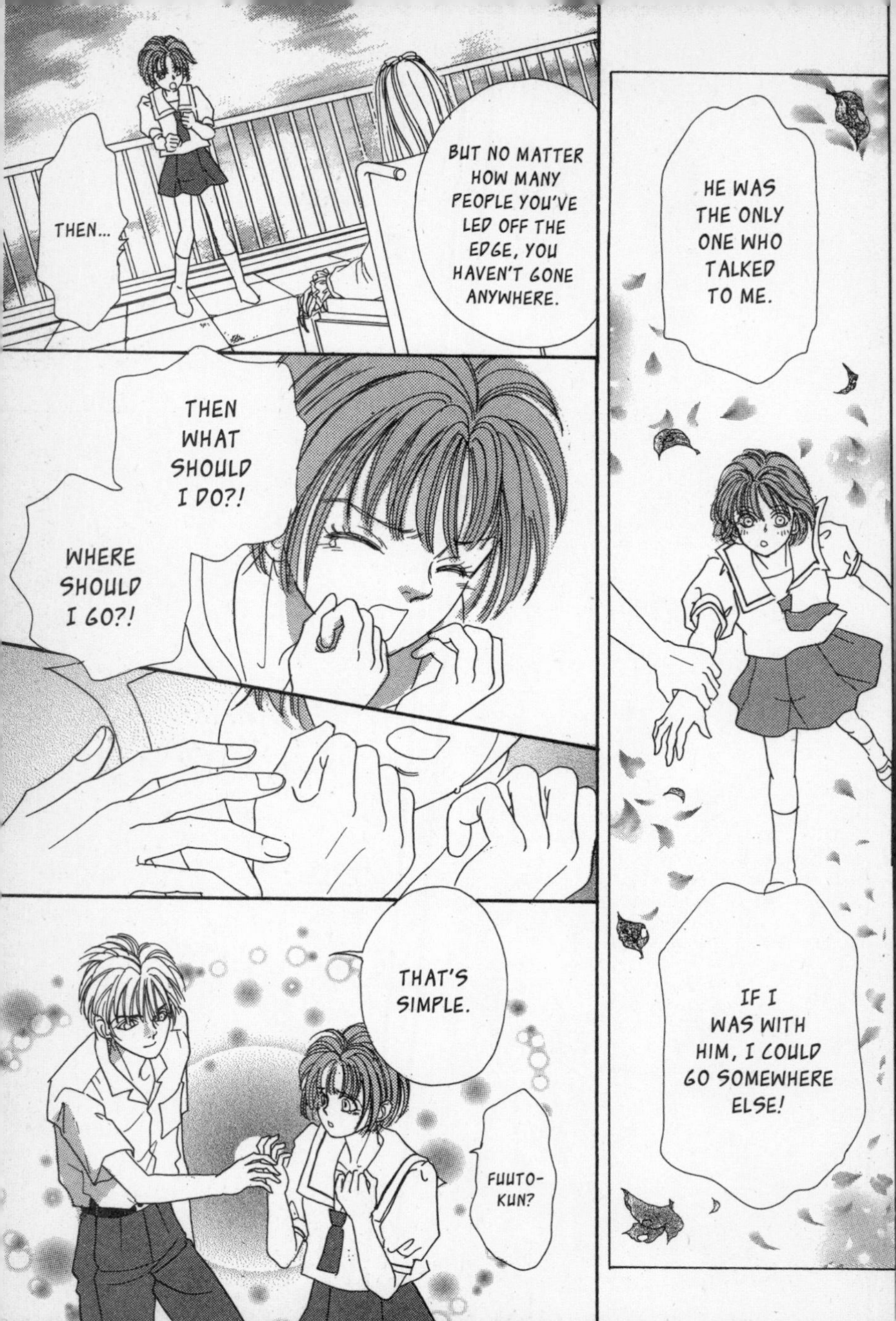
HE WAS THE ONLY ONE WHO TALKED TO ME.
IF I WAS WITH HIM, I COULD GO SOMEWHERE ELSE!
BUT NO MATTER HOW MANY PEOPLE YOU'VE LED OFF THE EDGE, YOU HAVEN'T GONE ANYWHERE.
THEN...
THEN WHAT SHOULD I DO?!
WHERE SHOULD I GO?!
THAT'S SIMPLE.
FUUTO-KUN?

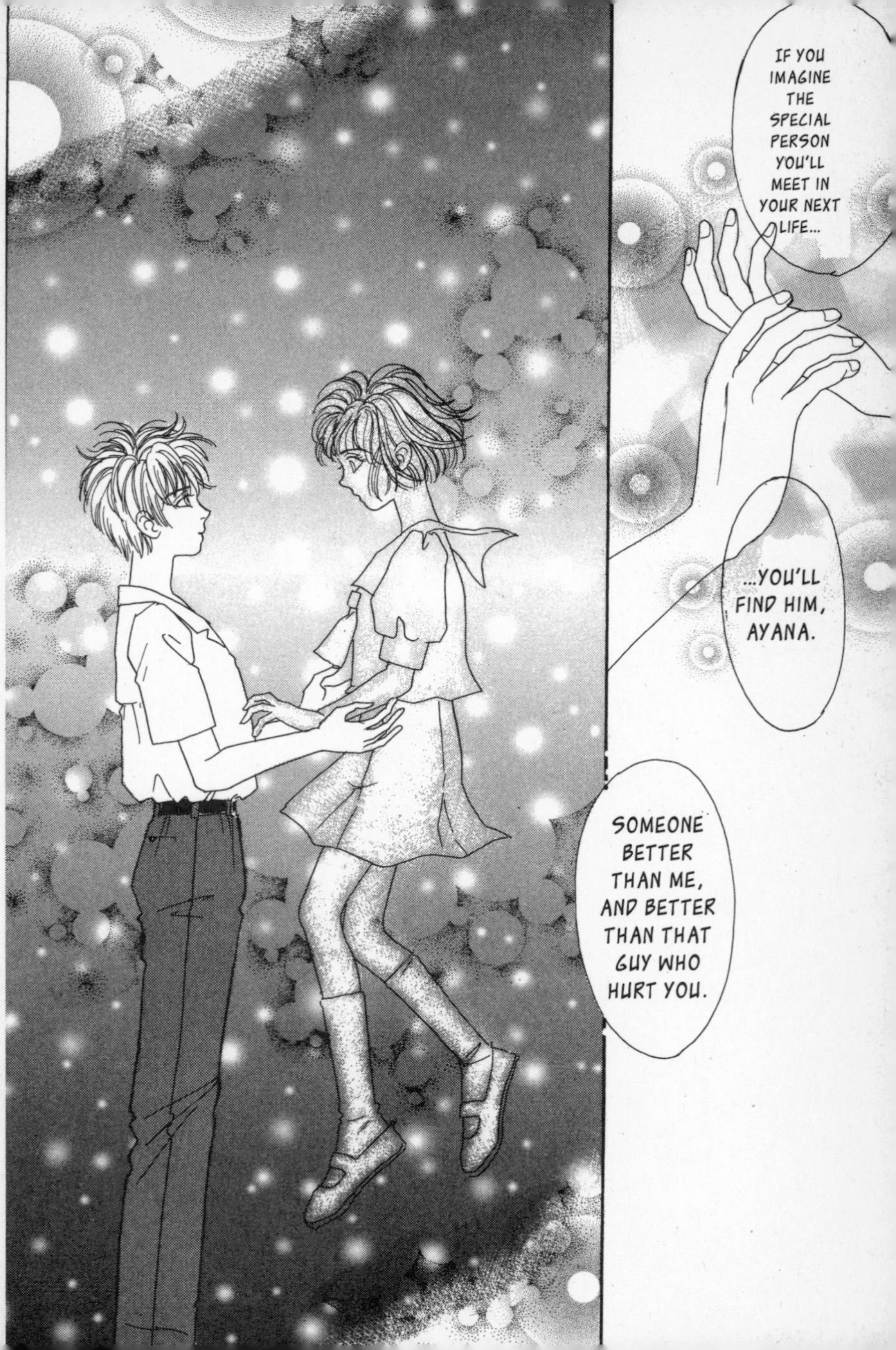
IF YOU IMAGINE THE SPECIAL PERSON YOU'LL MEET IN YOUR NEXT LIFE...
...YOU'LL FIND HIM, AYANA.
SOMEONE BETTER THAN ME, AND BETTER THAN THAT GUY WHO HURT YOU.

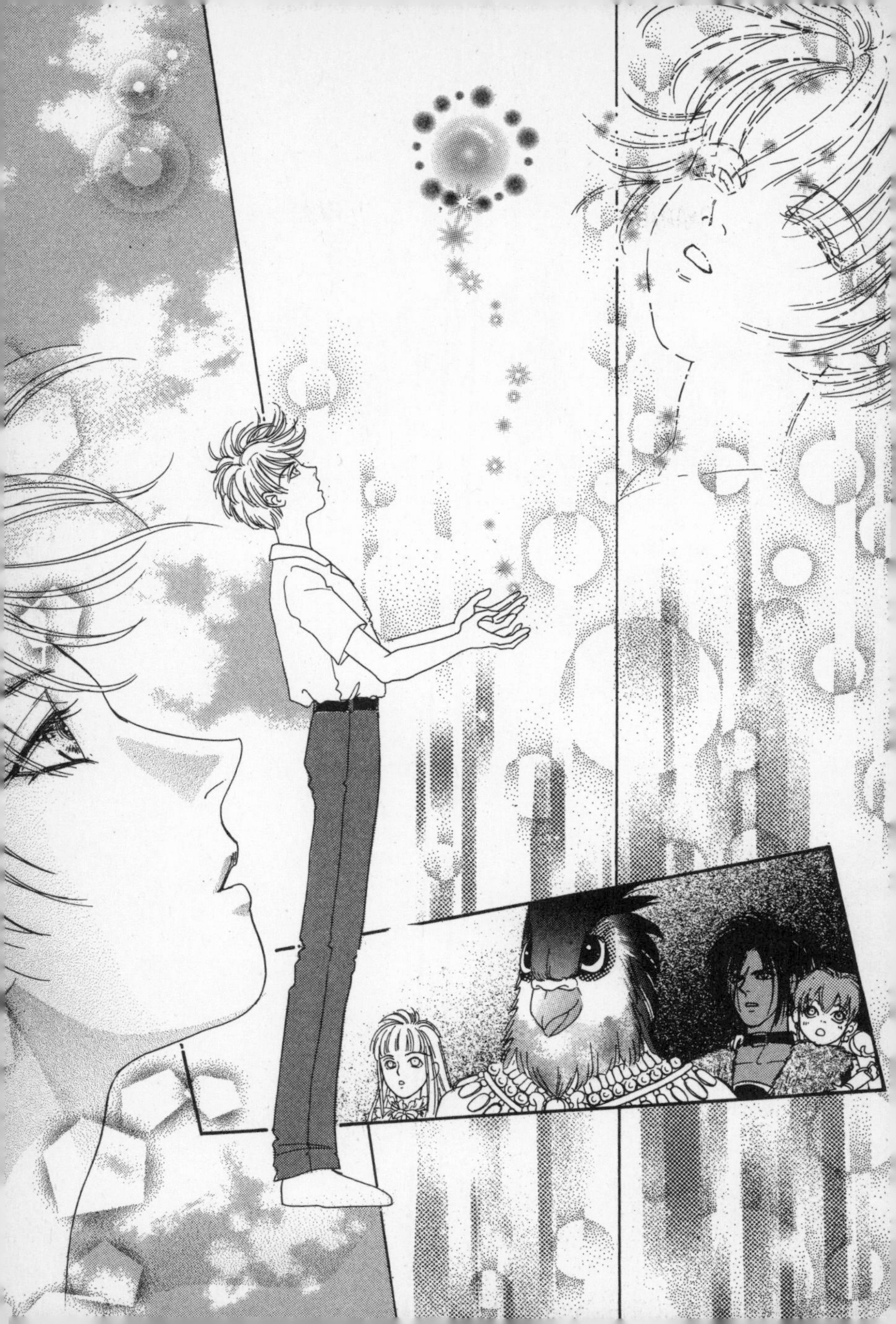

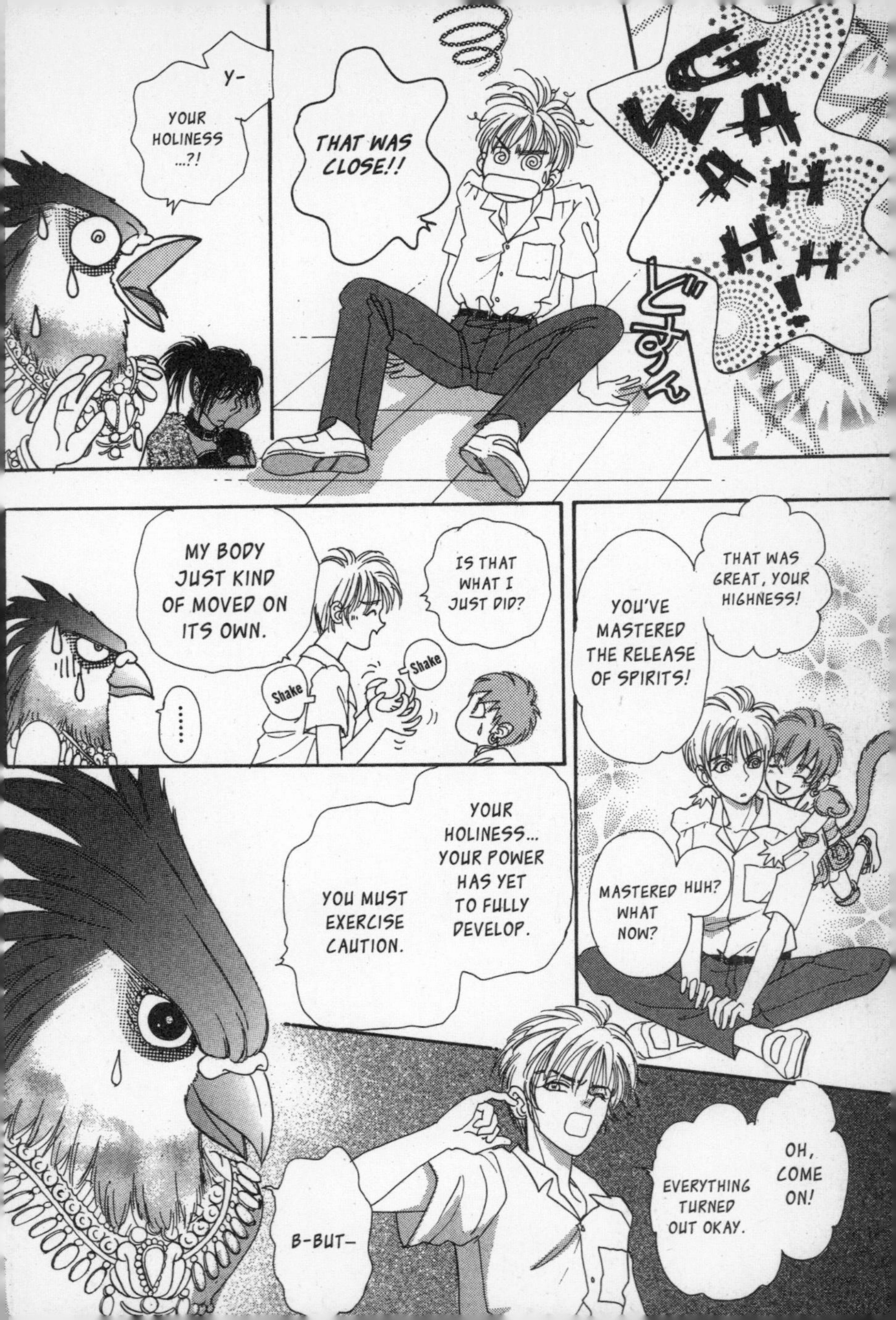
GWAAHHH!!
どすん
THAT WAS CLOSE!!
Y-
YOUR HOLINESS ...?!
THAT WAS GREAT, YOUR HIGHNESS!
YOU'VE MASTERED THE RELEASE OF SPIRITS!
HUH?
MASTERED WHAT NOW?
IS THAT WHAT I JUST DID?
Shake
Shake
MY BODY JUST KIND OF MOVED ON ITS OWN.
......
YOUR HOLINESS... YOUR POWER HAS YET TO FULLY DEVELOP.
YOU MUST EXERCISE CAUTION.
OH, COME ON!
EVERYTHING TURNED OUT OKAY.
B-BUT-

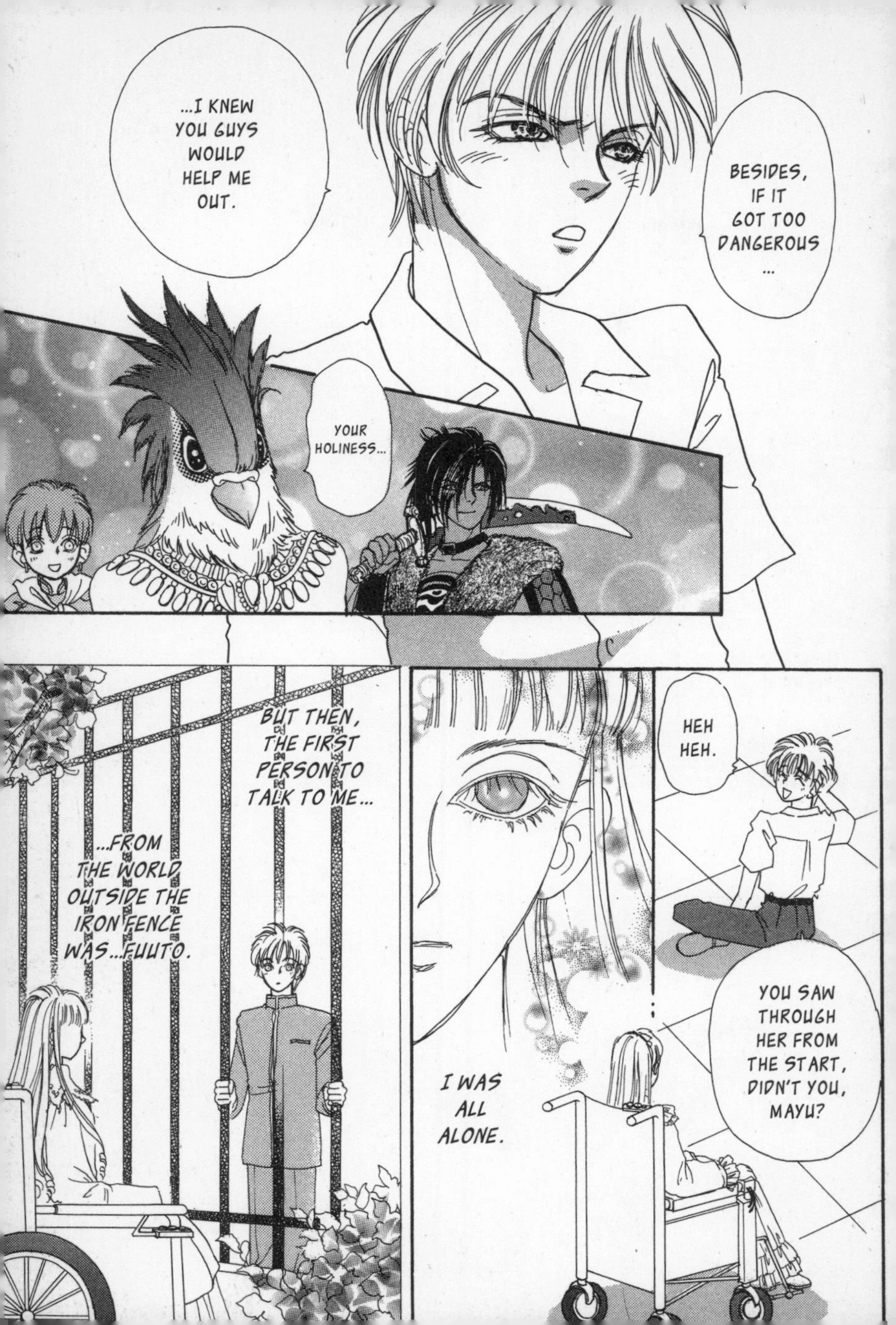
BESIDES, IF IT GOT TOO DANGEROUS...
...I KNEW YOU GUYS WOULD HELP ME OUT.
YOUR HOLINESS...
HEH HEH.
YOU SAW THROUGH HER FROM THE START, DIDN'T YOU, MAYU?
...
I WAS ALL ALONE.
BUT THEN, THE FIRST PERSON TO TALK TO ME...
...FROM THE WORLD OUTSIDE THE IRON FENCE WAS...FUUTO.

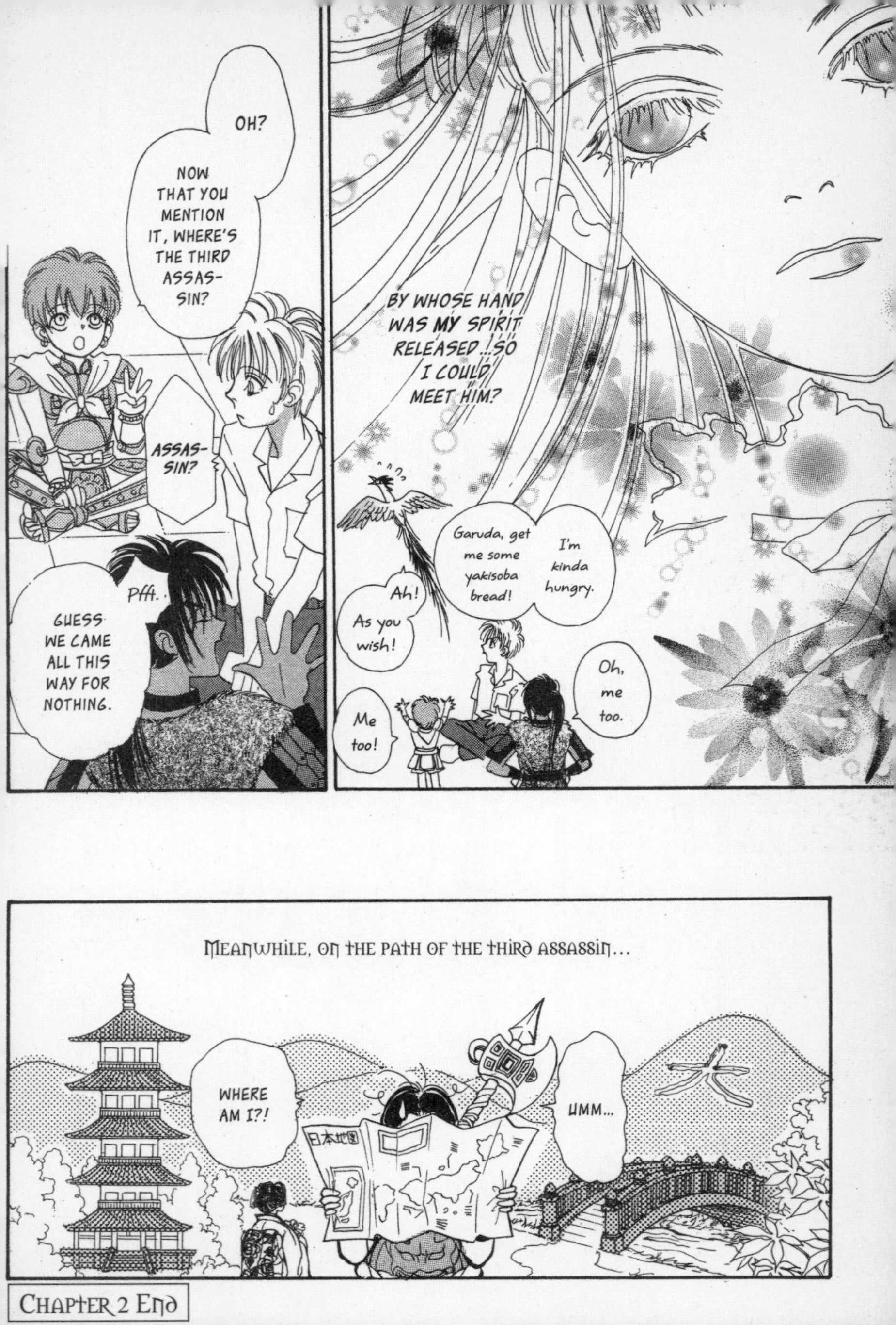
BY WHOSE HAND WAS MY SPIRIT RELEASED...SO I COULD MEET HIM?
I'm kinda hungry.
Garuda, get me some yakisoba bread!
Ah! As you wish!
Oh, me too.
Me too!
OH?
NOW THAT YOU MENTION IT, WHERE'S THE THIRD ASSAS-SIN?
ASSAS-SIN?
Pff.
GUESS WE CAME ALL THIS WAY FOR NOTHING.
MEANWHILE, ON THE PATH OF THE THIRD ASSASSIN...
UMM...
WHERE AM I?!
日本地図

CHAPTER 2 END

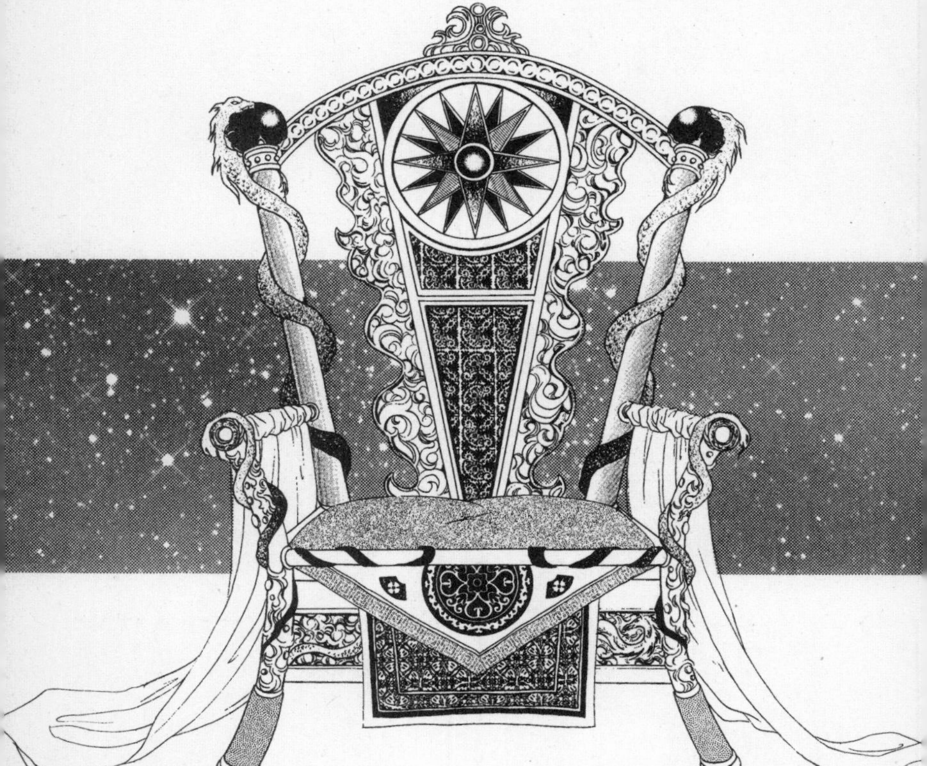

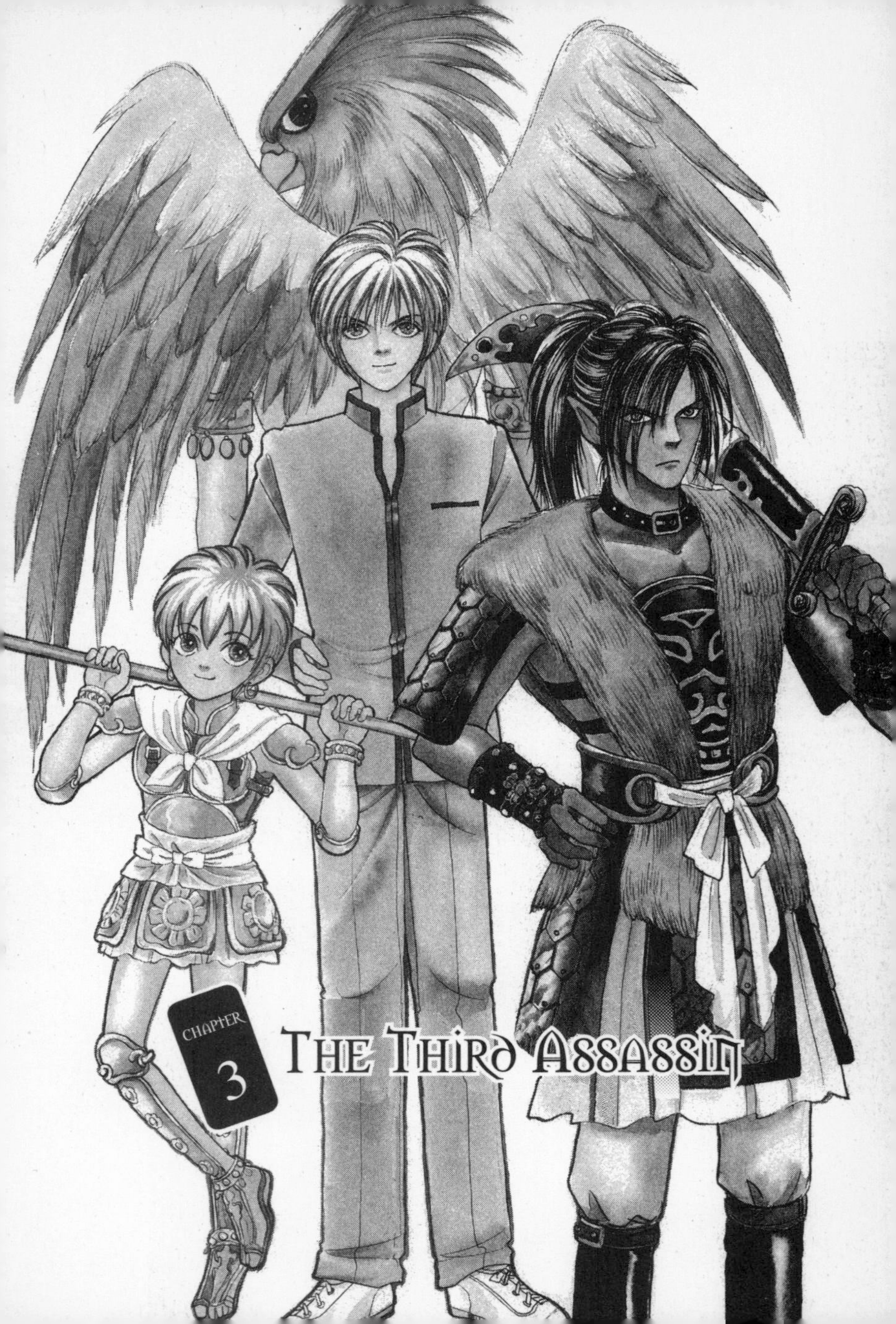
CHAPTER
3
THE THIRD ASSASSIN

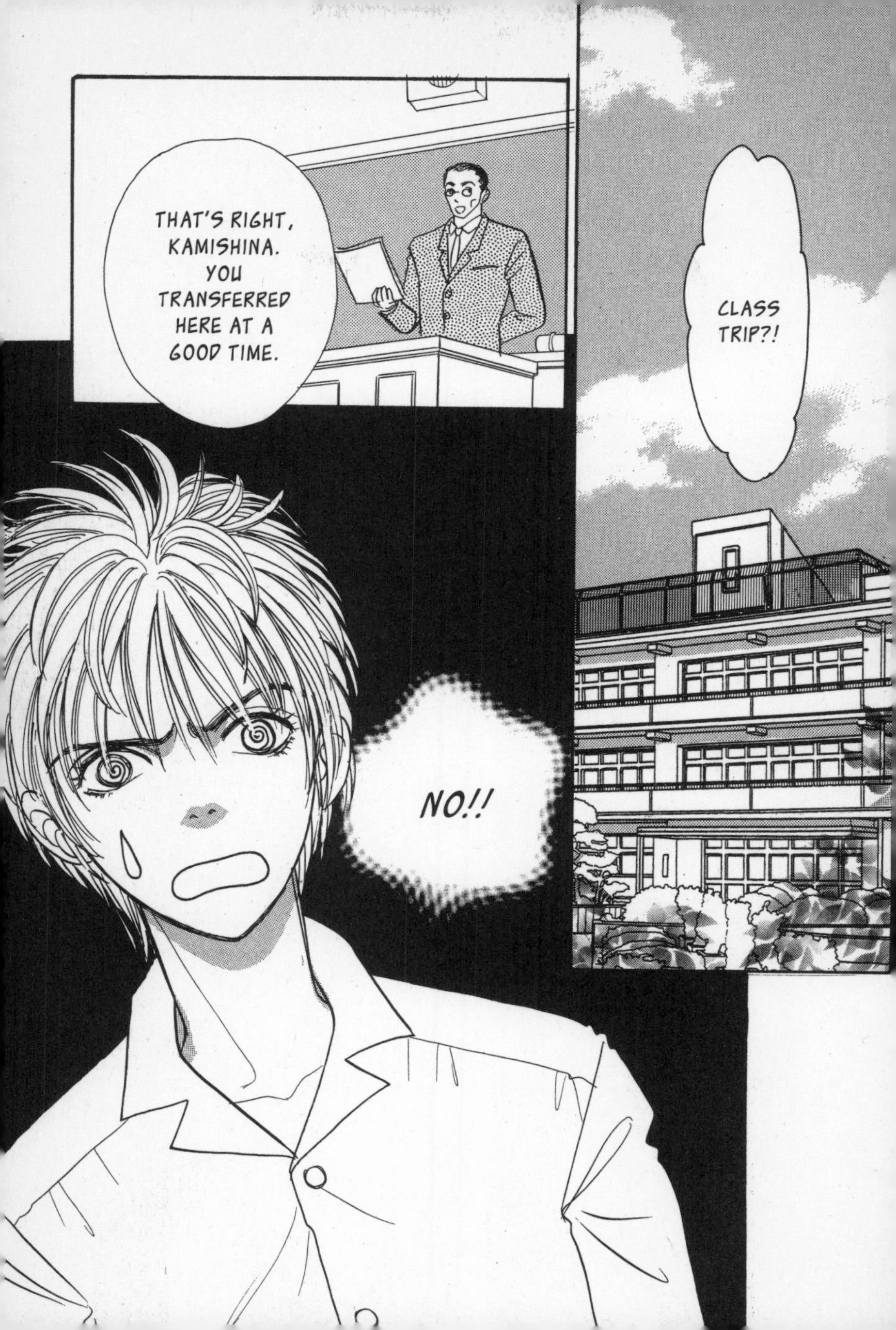

CLASS TRIP?!
THAT'S RIGHT, KAMISHINA. YOU TRANSFERRED HERE AT A GOOD TIME.
NO!!

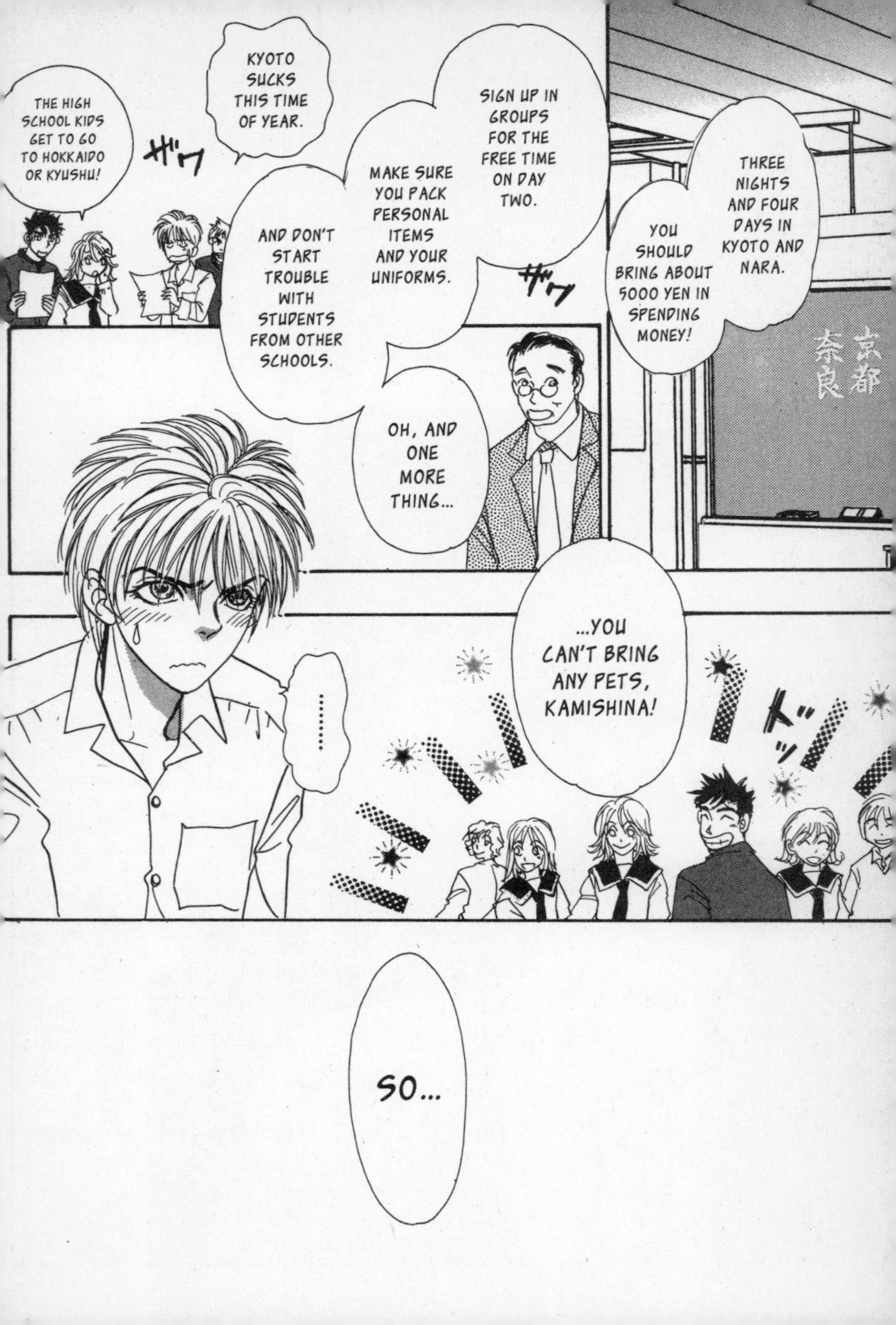
京都
奈良
THREE NIGHTS AND FOUR DAYS IN KYOTO AND NARA.
YOU SHOULD BRING ABOUT 5000 YEN IN SPENDING MONEY!
ザワ
SIGN UP IN GROUPS FOR THE FREE TIME ON DAY TWO.
MAKE SURE YOU PACK PERSONAL ITEMS AND YOUR UNIFORMS.
AND DON'T START TROUBLE WITH STUDENTS FROM OTHER SCHOOLS.
KYOTO SUCKS THIS TIME OF YEAR.
ザワ
THE HIGH SCHOOL KIDS GET TO GO TO HOKKAIDO OR KYUSHU!
OH, AND ONE MORE THING...
...YOU CAN'T BRING ANY PETS, KAMISHINA!
ドッ
......
SO...

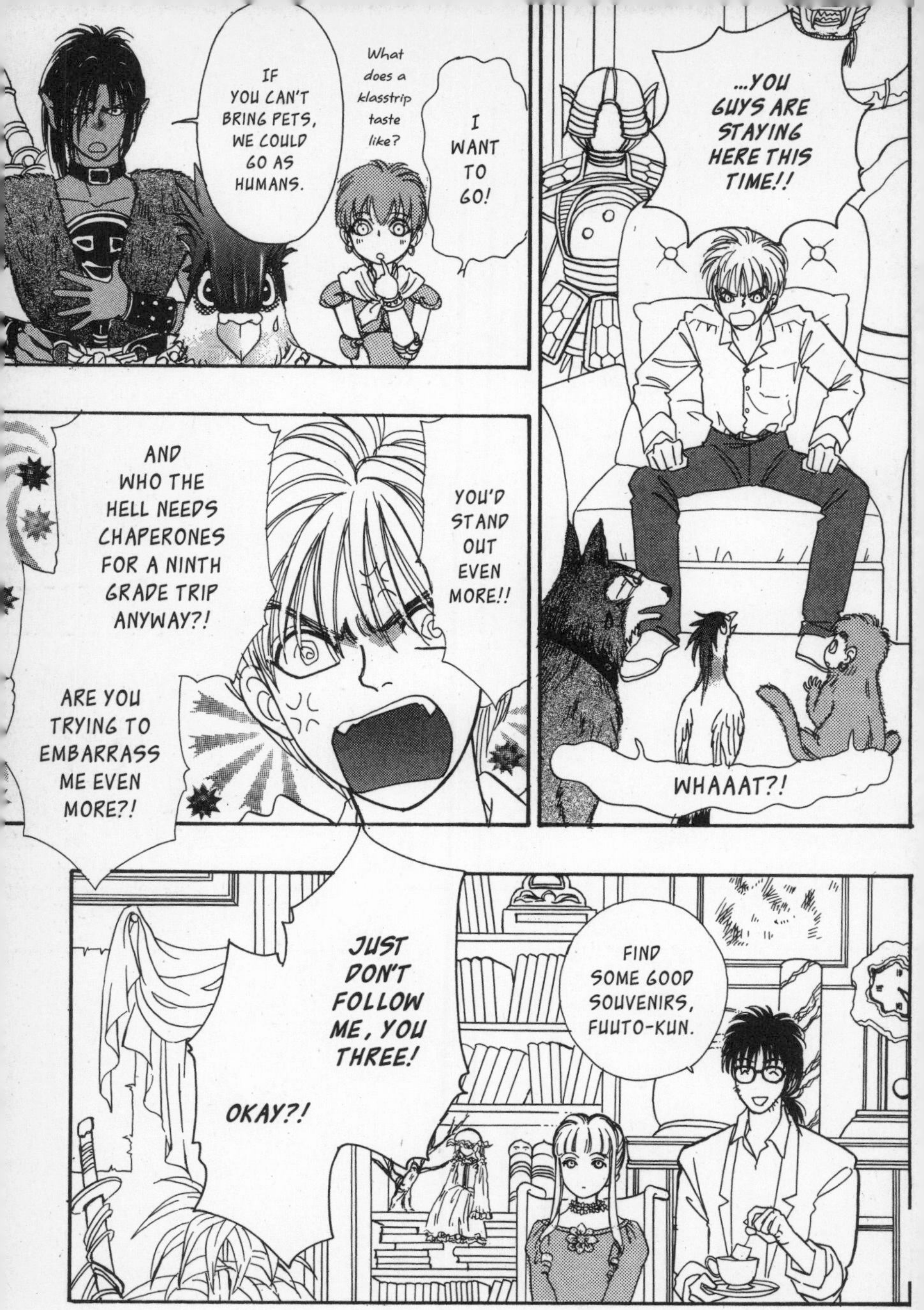
...YOU GUYS ARE STAYING HERE THIS TIME!!
WHAAAT?!
I WANT TO GO!
What does a klasstrip taste like?
IF YOU CAN'T BRING PETS, WE COULD GO AS HUMANS.
YOU'D STAND OUT EVEN MORE!!
AND WHO THE HELL NEEDS CHAPERONES FOR A NINTH GRADE TRIP ANYWAY?!
ARE YOU TRYING TO EMBARRASS ME EVEN MORE?!
FIND SOME GOOD SOUVENIRS, FUUTO-KUN.
JUST DON'T FOLLOW ME, YOU THREE!
OKAY?!

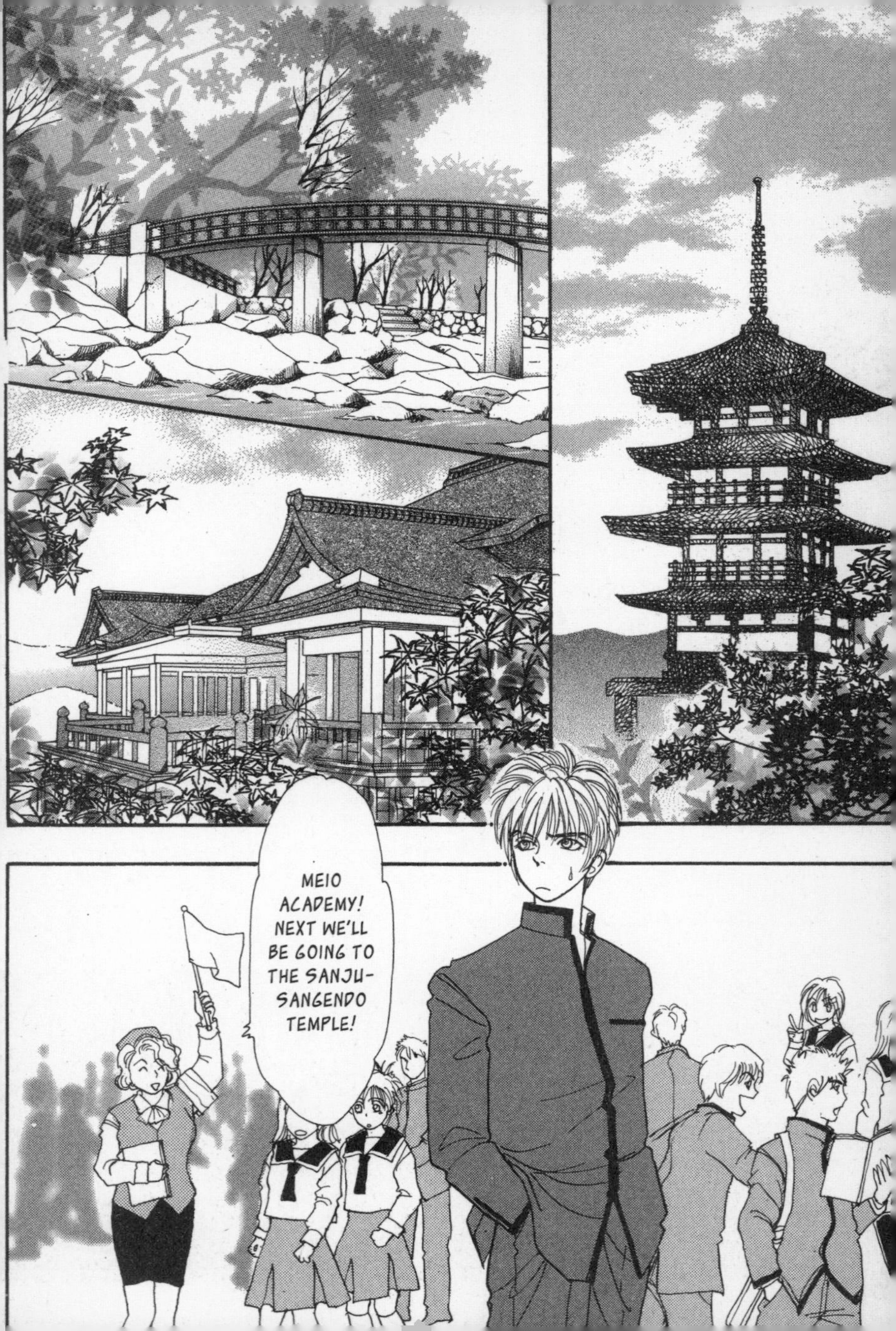
MEIO ACADEMY! NEXT WE'LL BE GOING TO THE SANJU-SANGENDO TEMPLE!

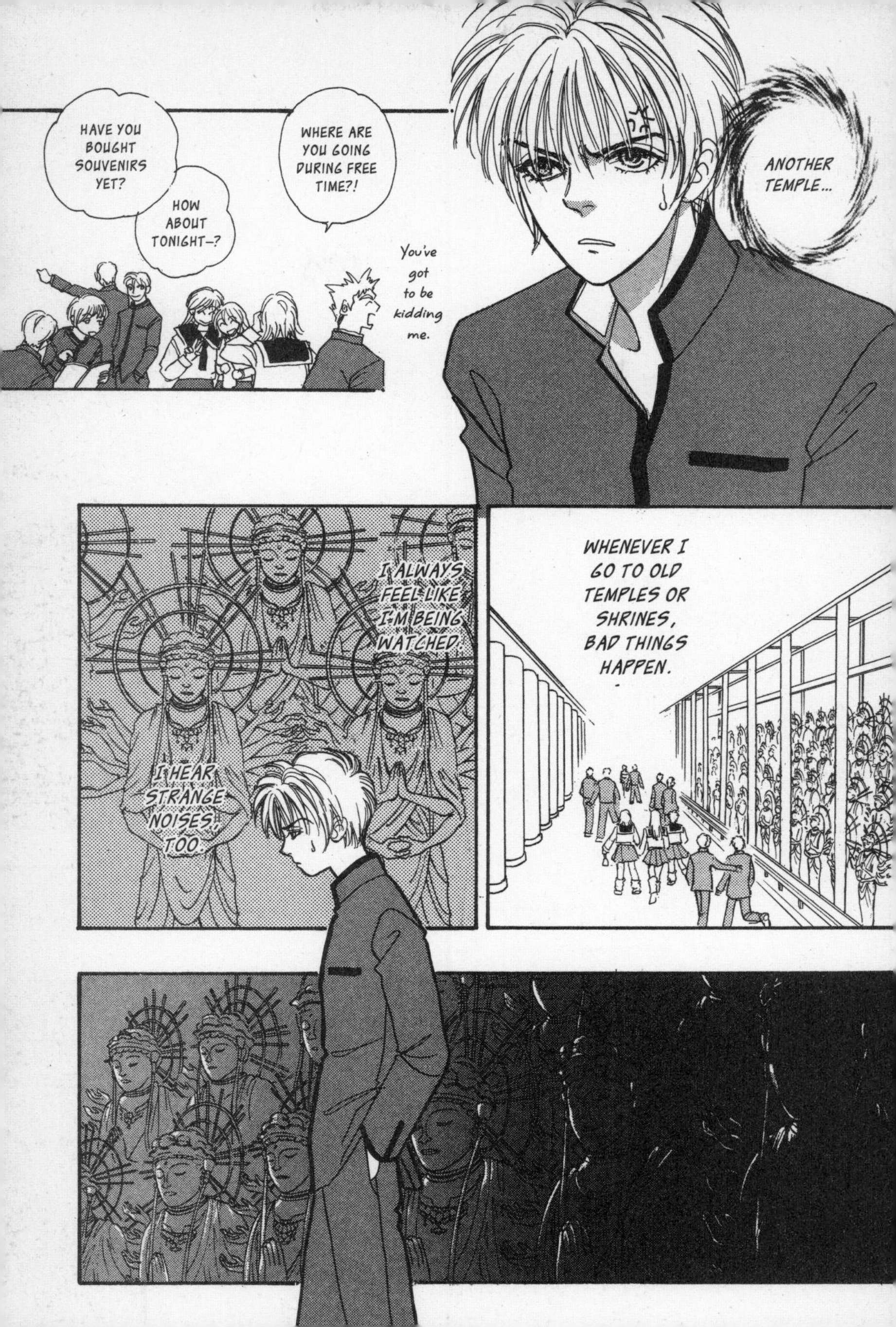
ANOTHER TEMPLE...
WHERE ARE YOU GOING DURING FREE TIME?!
HAVE YOU BOUGHT SOUVENIRS YET?
HOW ABOUT TONIGHT–?
You've got to be kidding me.
WHENEVER I GO TO OLD TEMPLES OR SHRINES, BAD THINGS HAPPEN.
I ALWAYS FEEL LIKE I'M BEING WATCHED.
I HEAR STRANGE NOISES, TOO.

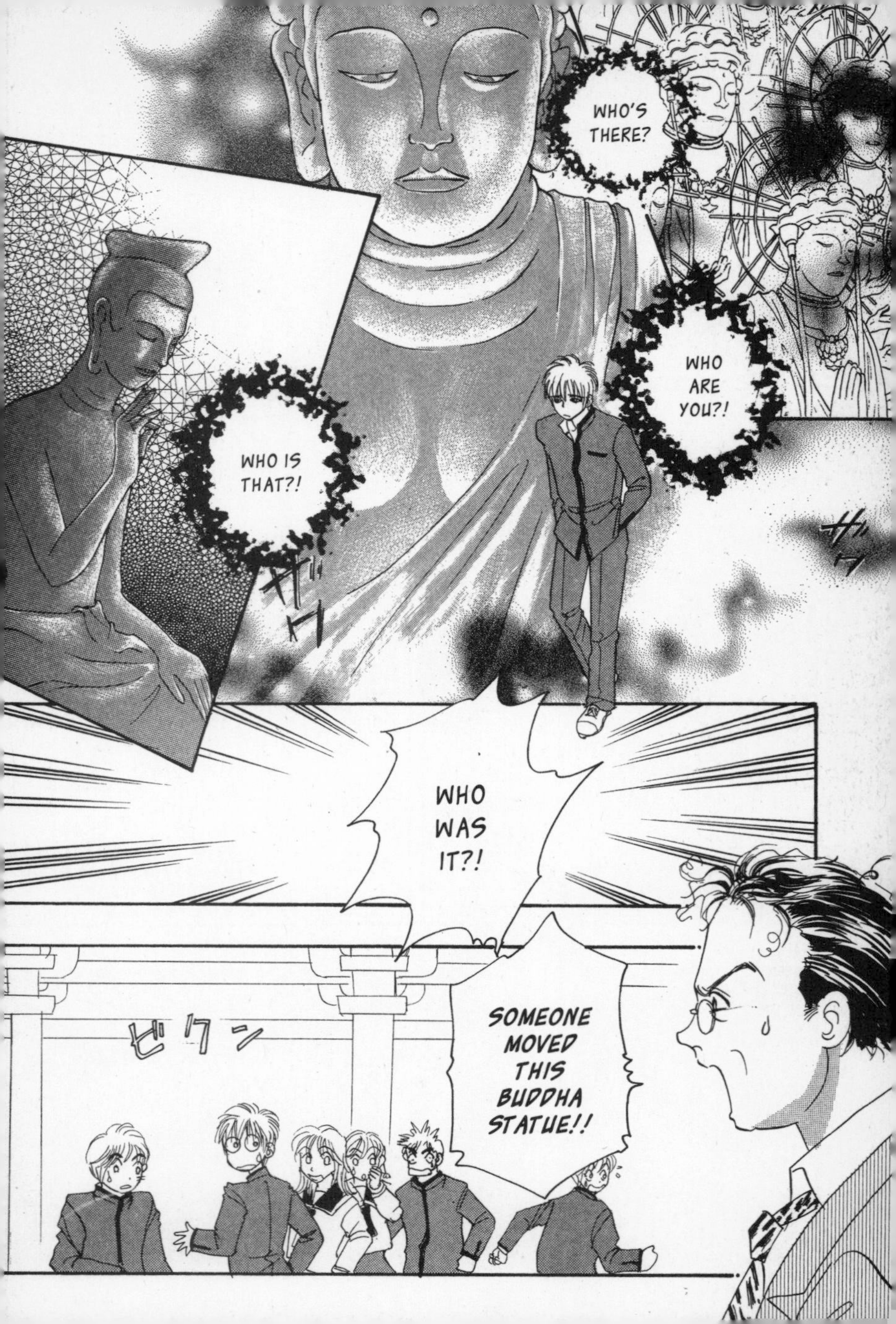
WHO'S THERE?
WHO ARE YOU?!
WHO IS THAT?!
WHO WAS IT?!
SOMEONE MOVED THIS BUDDHA STATUE!!
ビクン

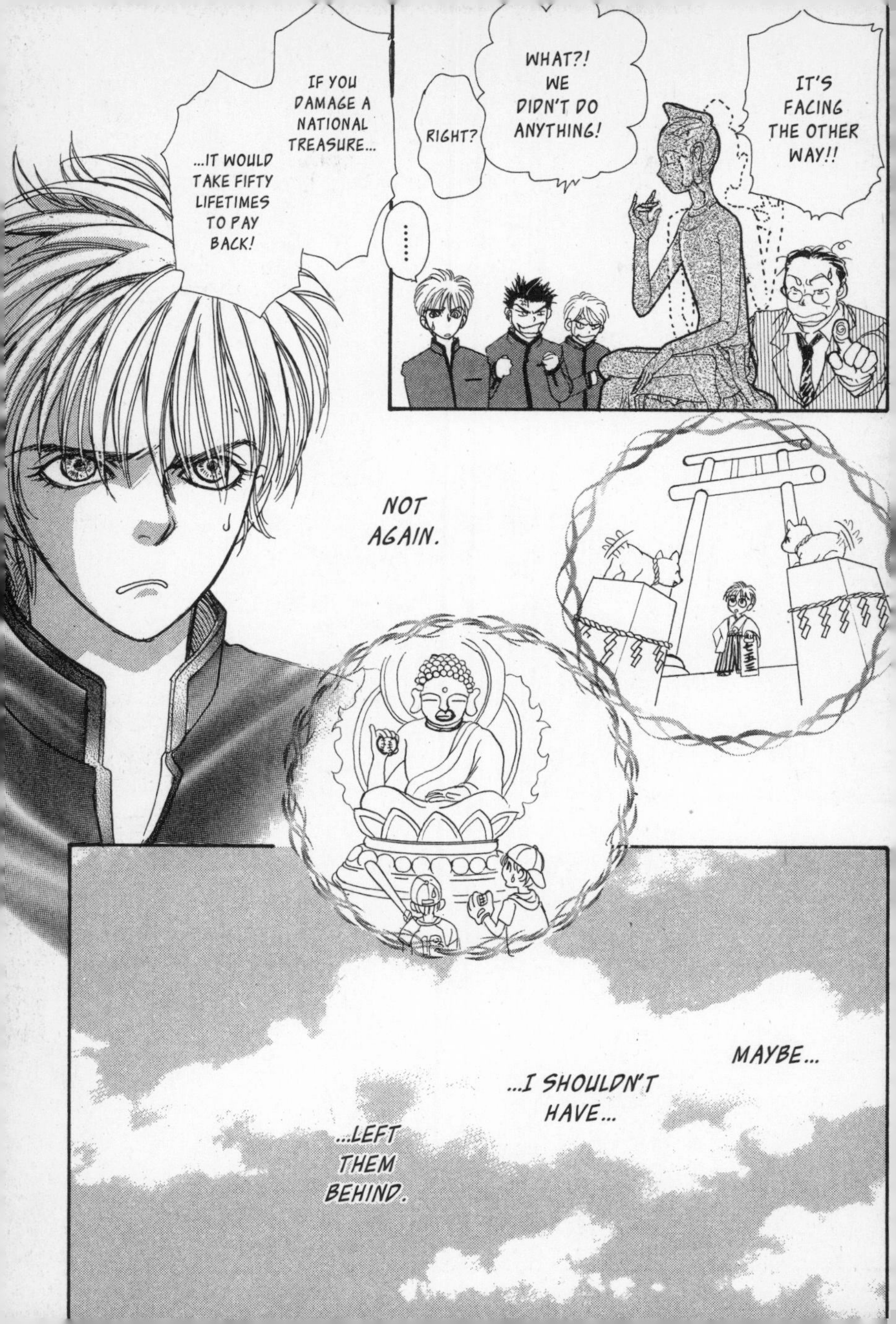
IT'S FACING THE OTHER WAY!!
WHAT?! WE DIDN'T DO ANYTHING!
RIGHT?
......
IF YOU DAMAGE A NATIONAL TREASURE...
...IT WOULD TAKE FIFTY LIFETIMES TO PAY BACK!
NOT AGAIN.
MAYBE...
...I SHOULDN'T HAVE...
...LEFT THEM BEHIND.

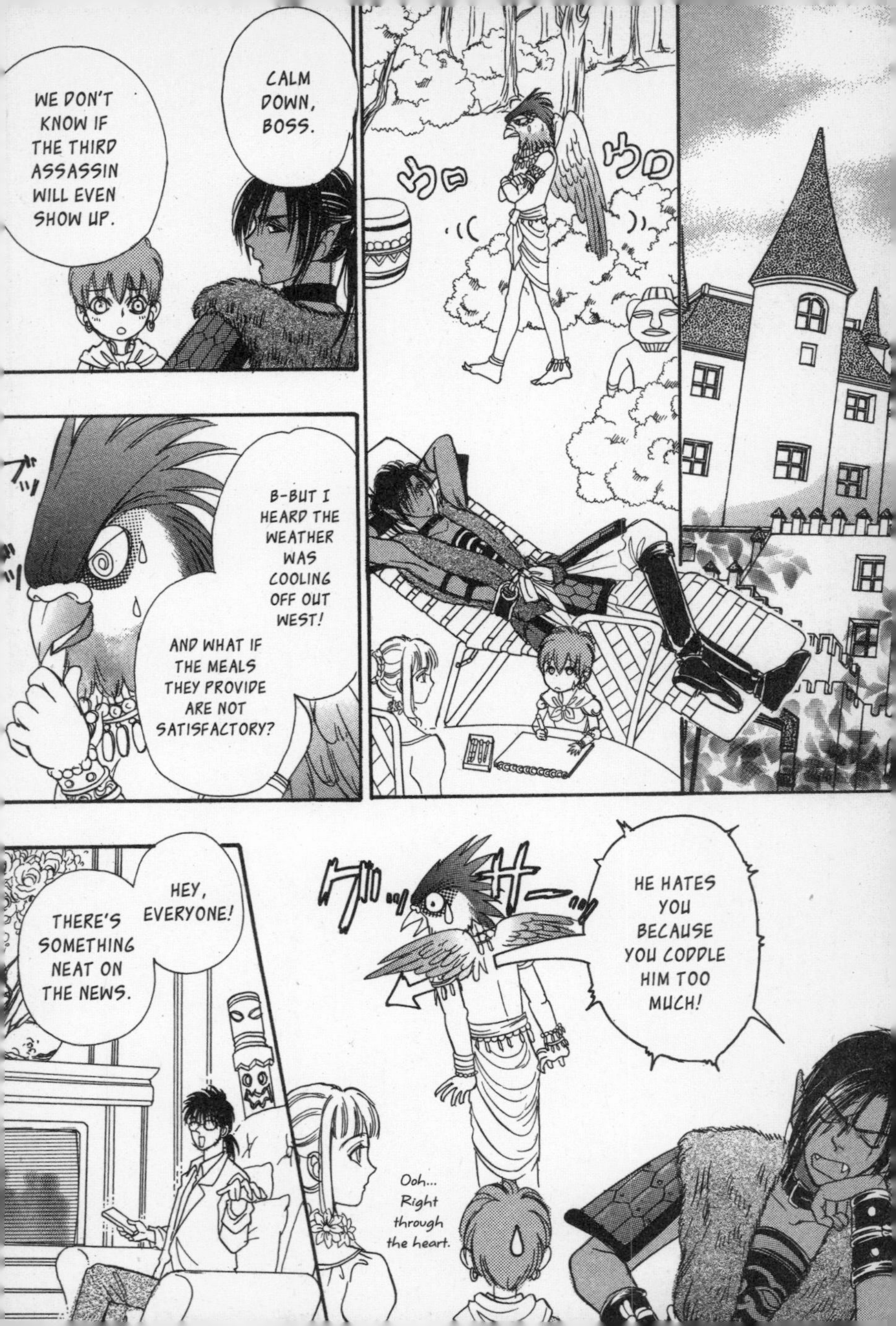
ウロ
ウロ
CALM DOWN, BOSS.
WE DON'T KNOW IF THE THIRD ASSASSIN WILL EVEN SHOW UP.
B-BUT I HEARD THE WEATHER WAS COOLING OFF OUT WEST!
AND WHAT IF THE MEALS THEY PROVIDE ARE NOT SATISFACTORY?
HE HATES YOU BECAUSE YOU CODDLE HIM TOO MUCH!
Ooh... Right through the heart.
HEY, EVERYONE!
THERE'S SOMETHING NEAT ON THE NEWS.

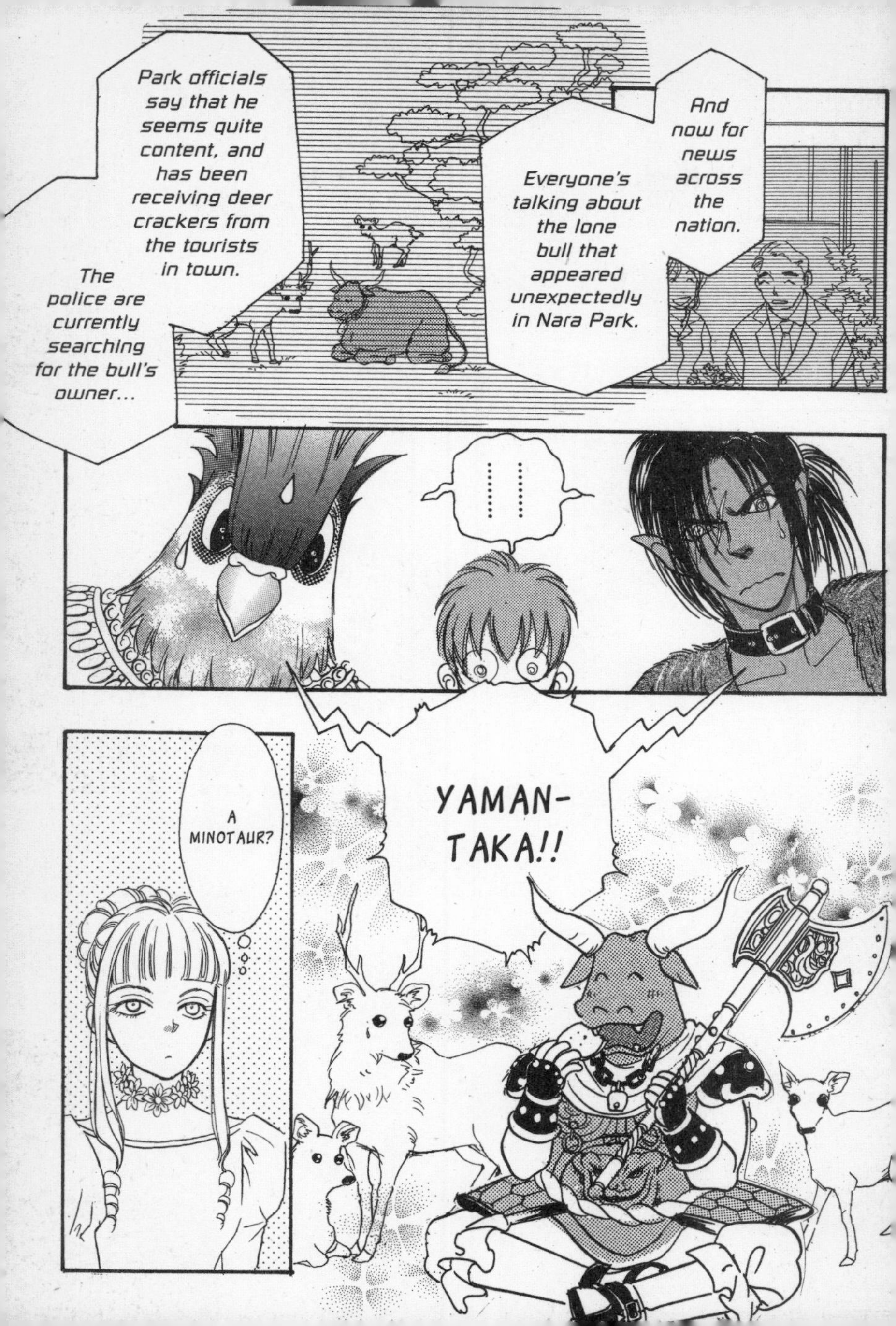
And now for news across the nation.
Everyone's talking about the lone bull that appeared unexpectedly in Nara Park.
Park officials say that he seems quite content, and has been receiving deer crackers from the tourists in town.
The police are currently searching for the bull's owner...
......
YAMAN-TAKA!!
A MINOTAUR?

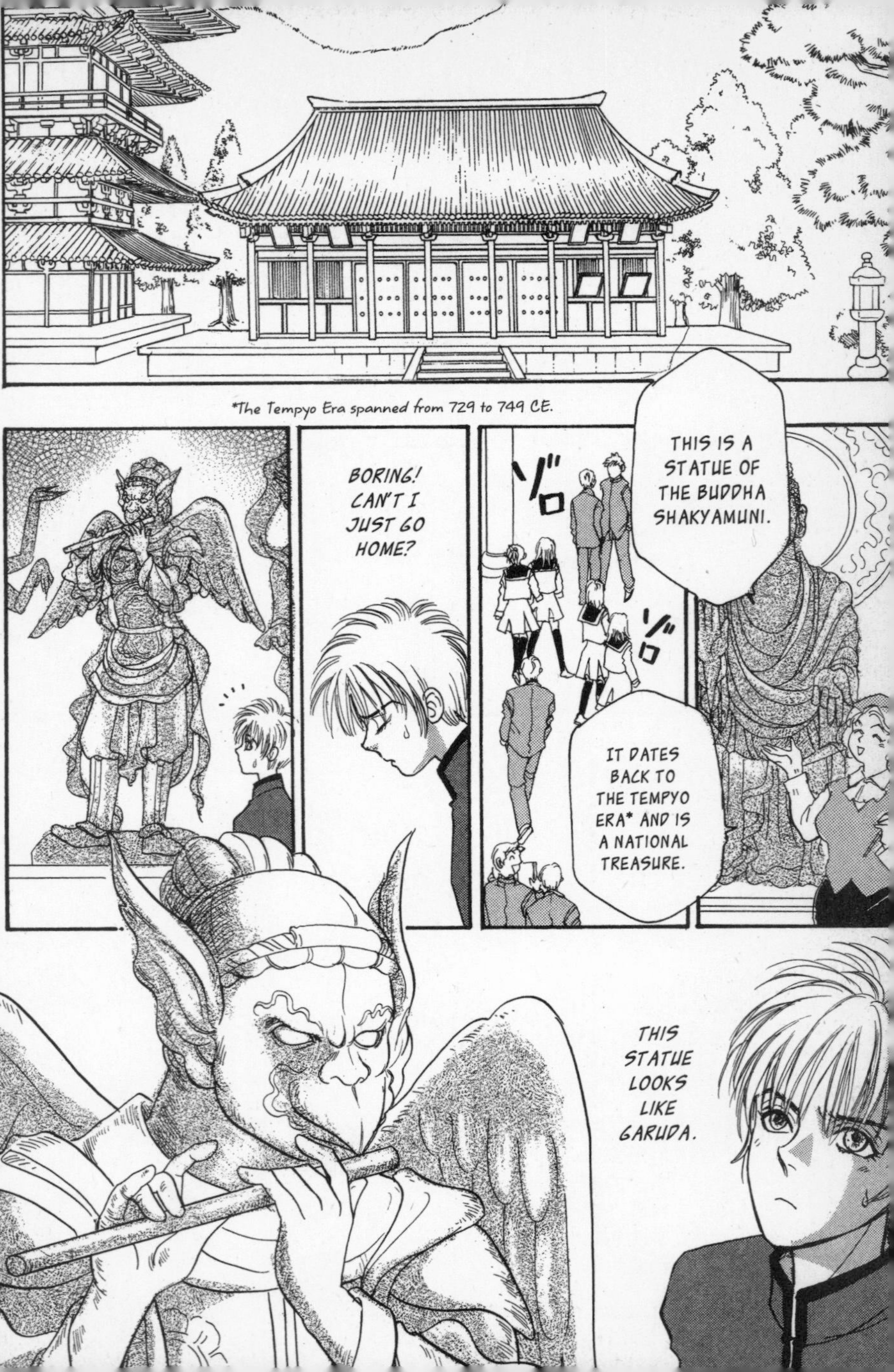
THIS IS A STATUE OF THE BUDDHA SHAKYAMUNI.
IT DATES BACK TO THE TEMPYO ERA* AND IS A NATIONAL TREASURE.
ゾロ
ゾロ
BORING! CAN'T I JUST GO HOME?
THIS STATUE LOOKS LIKE GARUDA.

*The Tempyo Era spanned from 729 to 749 CE.

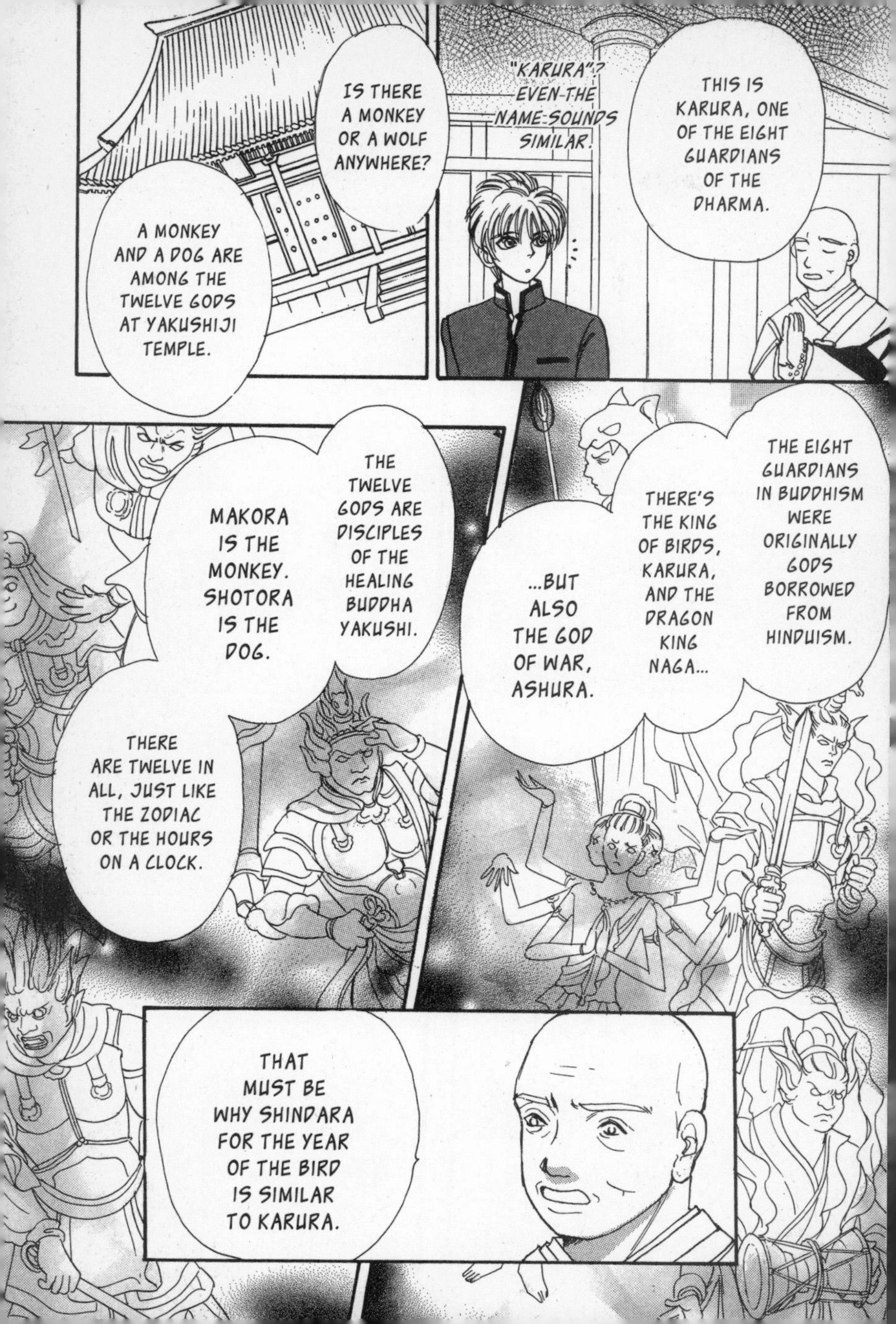
THIS IS KARURA, ONE OF THE EIGHT GUARDIANS OF THE DHARMA.
"KARURA"? EVEN THE NAME SOUNDS SIMILAR.
IS THERE A MONKEY OR A WOLF ANYWHERE?
A MONKEY AND A DOG ARE AMONG THE TWELVE GODS AT YAKUSHIJI TEMPLE.
THE EIGHT GUARDIANS IN BUDDHISM WERE ORIGINALLY GODS BORROWED FROM HINDUISM.
THERE'S THE KING OF BIRDS, KARURA, AND THE DRAGON KING NAGA...
...BUT ALSO THE GOD OF WAR, ASHURA.
THE TWELVE GODS ARE DISCIPLES OF THE HEALING BUDDHA YAKUSHI.
MAKORA IS THE MONKEY. SHOTORA IS THE DOG.
THERE ARE TWELVE IN ALL, JUST LIKE THE ZODIAC OR THE HOURS ON A CLOCK.
THAT MUST BE WHY SHINDARA FOR THE YEAR OF THE BIRD IS SIMILAR TO KARURA.

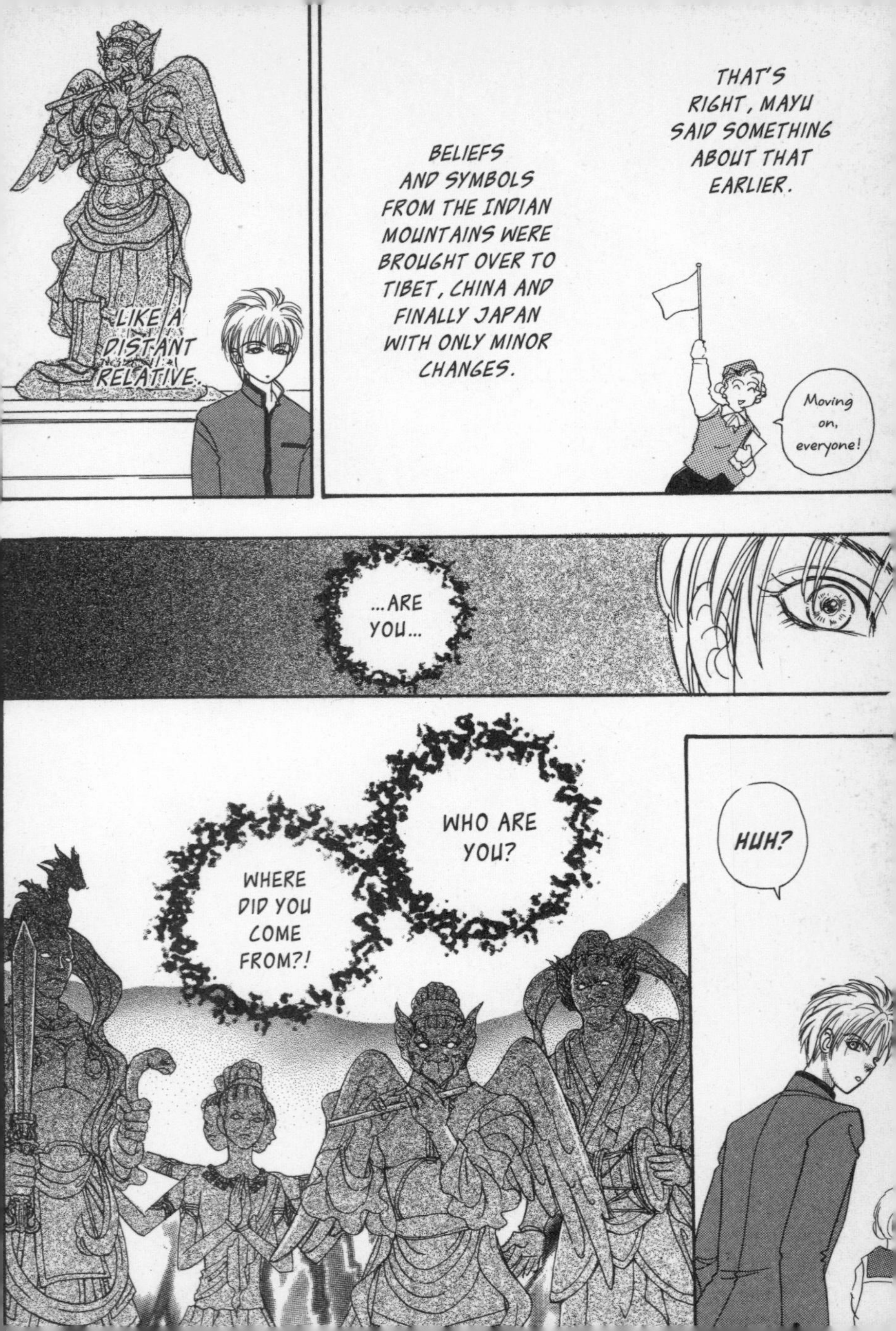
THAT'S RIGHT, MAYU SAID SOMETHING ABOUT THAT EARLIER.
BELIEFS AND SYMBOLS FROM THE INDIAN MOUNTAINS WERE BROUGHT OVER TO TIBET, CHINA AND FINALLY JAPAN WITH ONLY MINOR CHANGES.
Moving on, everyone!
LIKE A DISTANT RELATIVE.
...ARE YOU...
HUH?
WHO ARE YOU?
WHERE DID YOU COME FROM?!

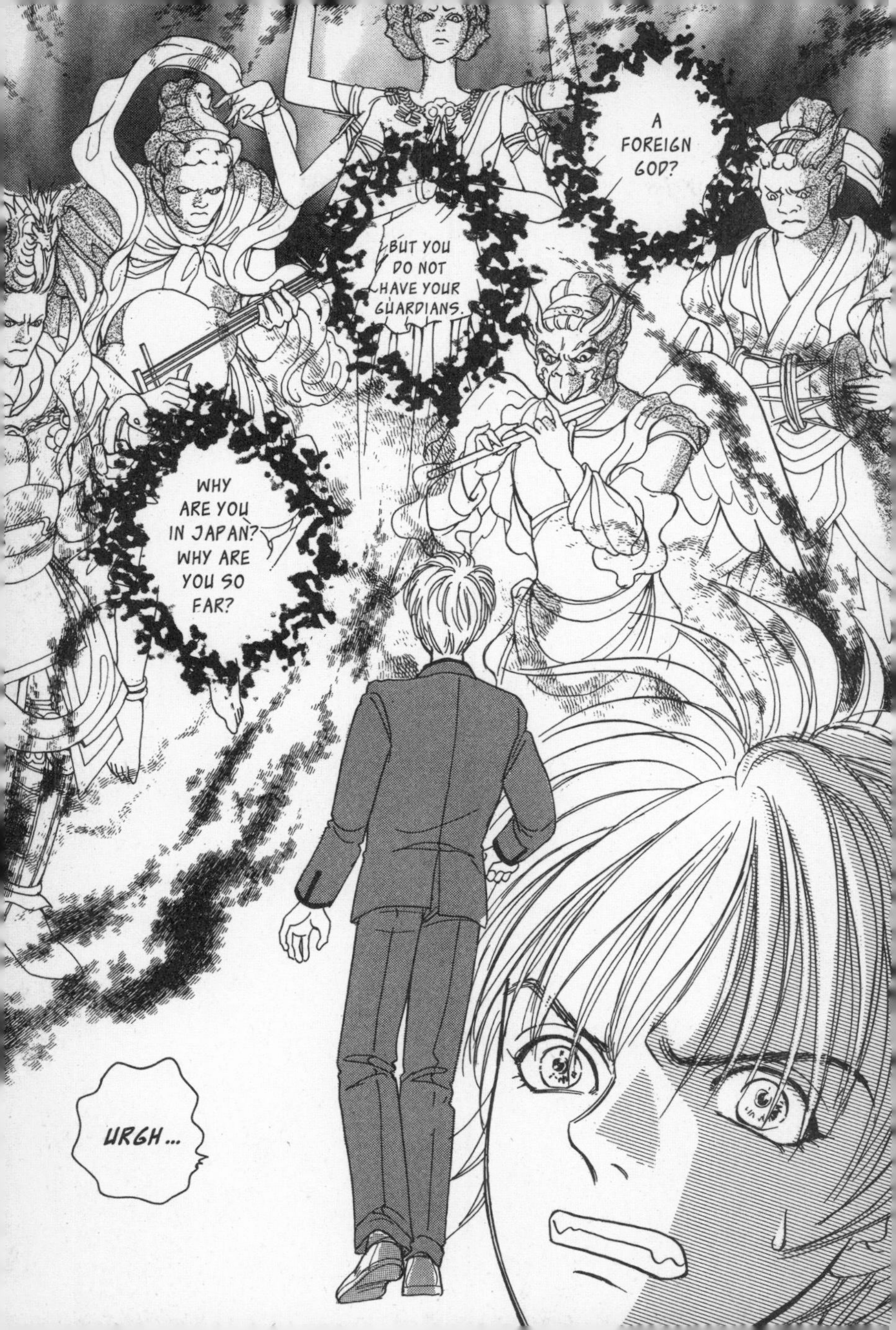
A FOREIGN GOD?
BUT YOU DO NOT HAVE YOUR GUARDIANS.
WHY ARE YOU IN JAPAN? WHY ARE YOU SO FAR?
URGH...

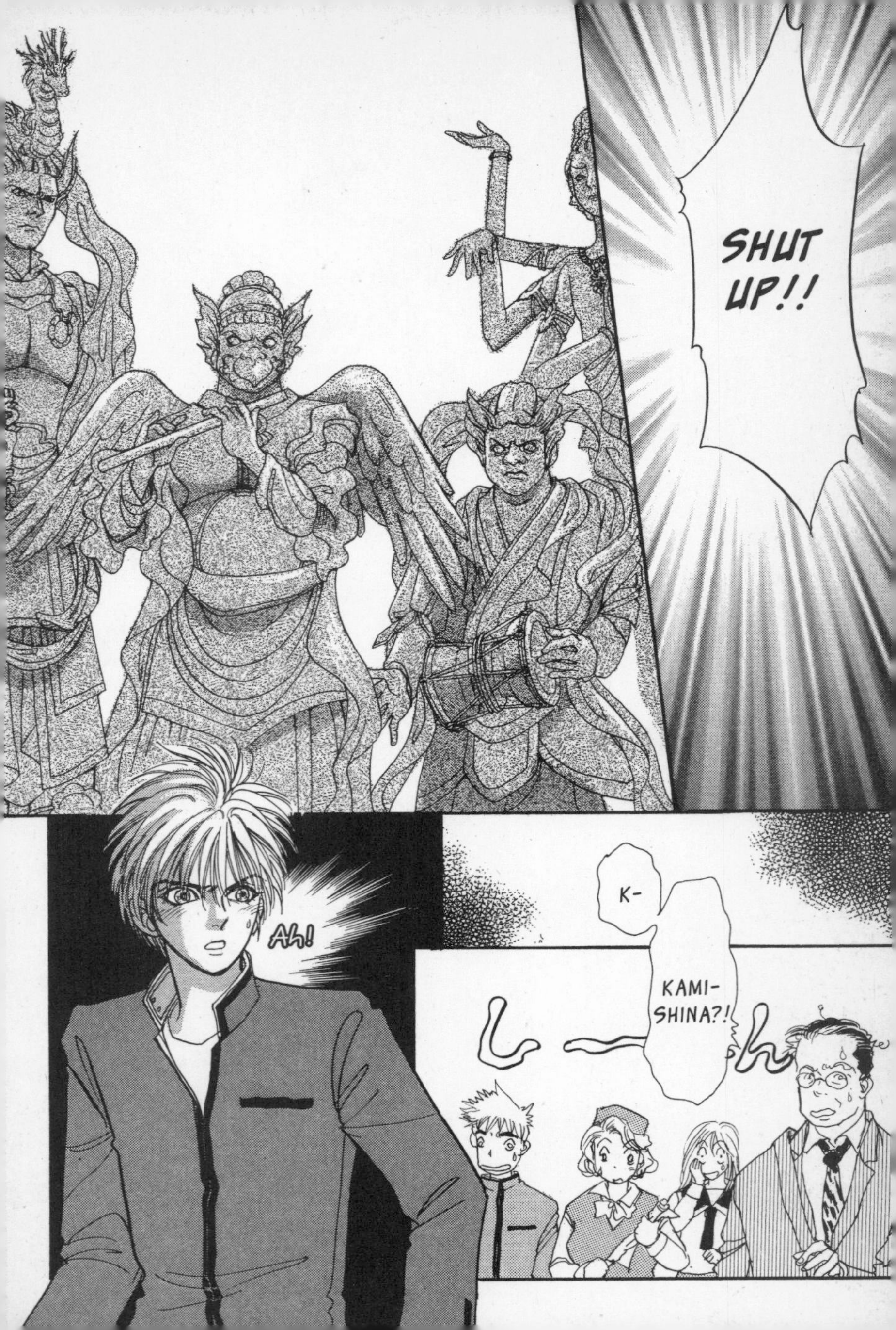
SHUT UP!!
K-
KAMI-SHINA?!
Ah!

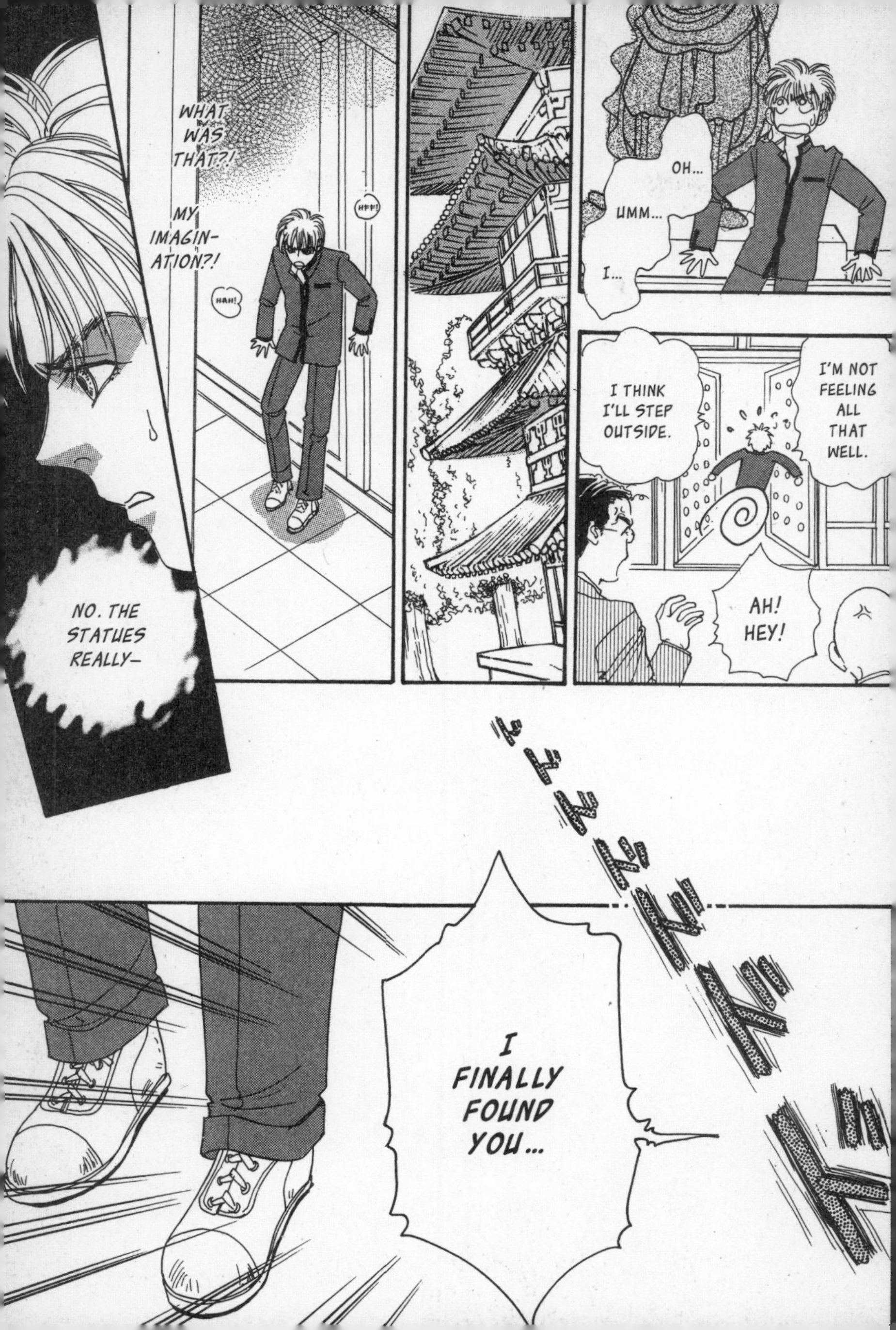
OH...
UMM...
I...
I'M NOT FEELING ALL THAT WELL.
I THINK I'LL STEP OUTSIDE.
AH! HEY!
WHAT WAS THAT?!
MY IMAGINATION?!
HFF!
HAH!
NO. THE STATUES REALLY–
I FINALLY FOUND YOU...

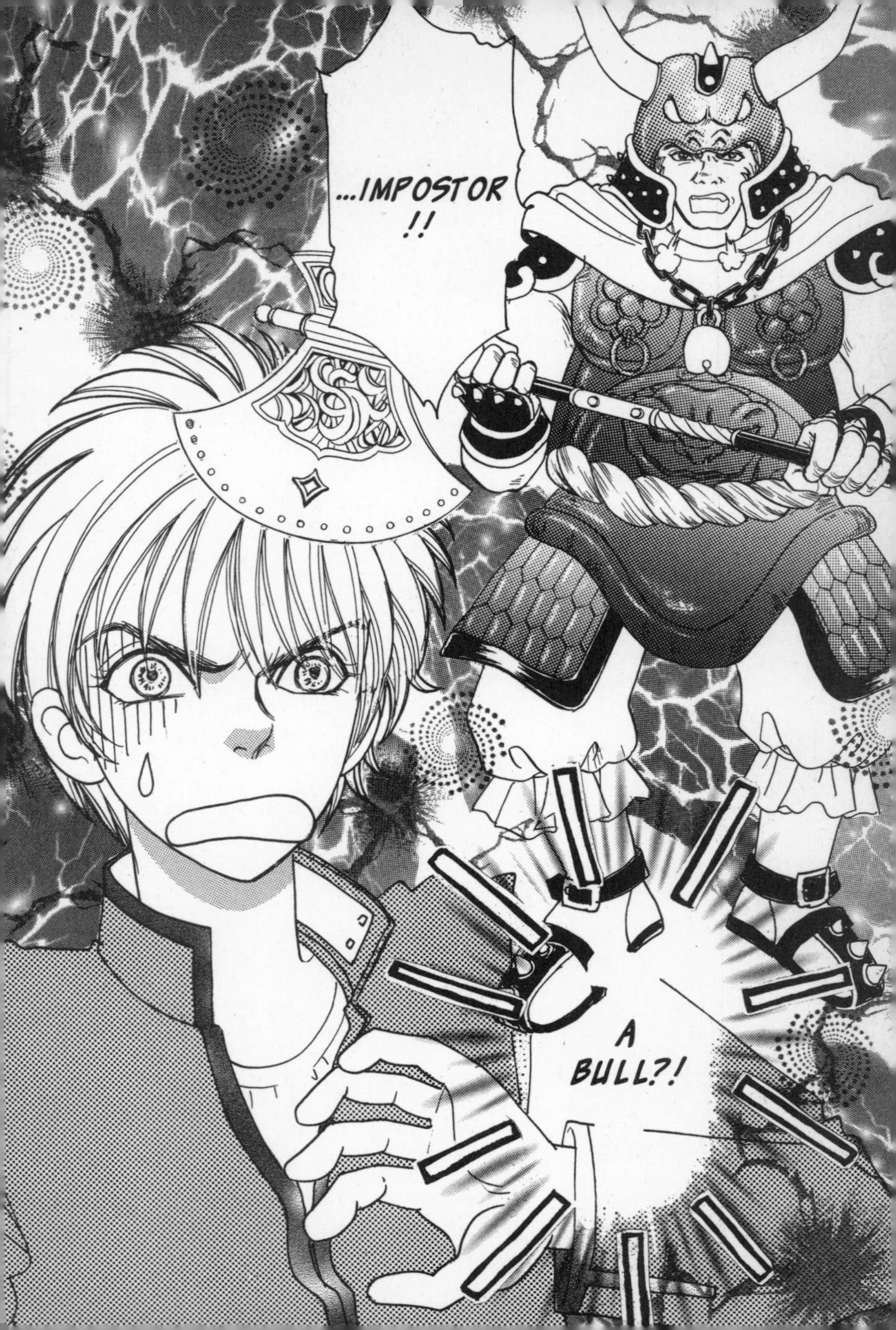
...IMPOSTOR !!
A BULL?!

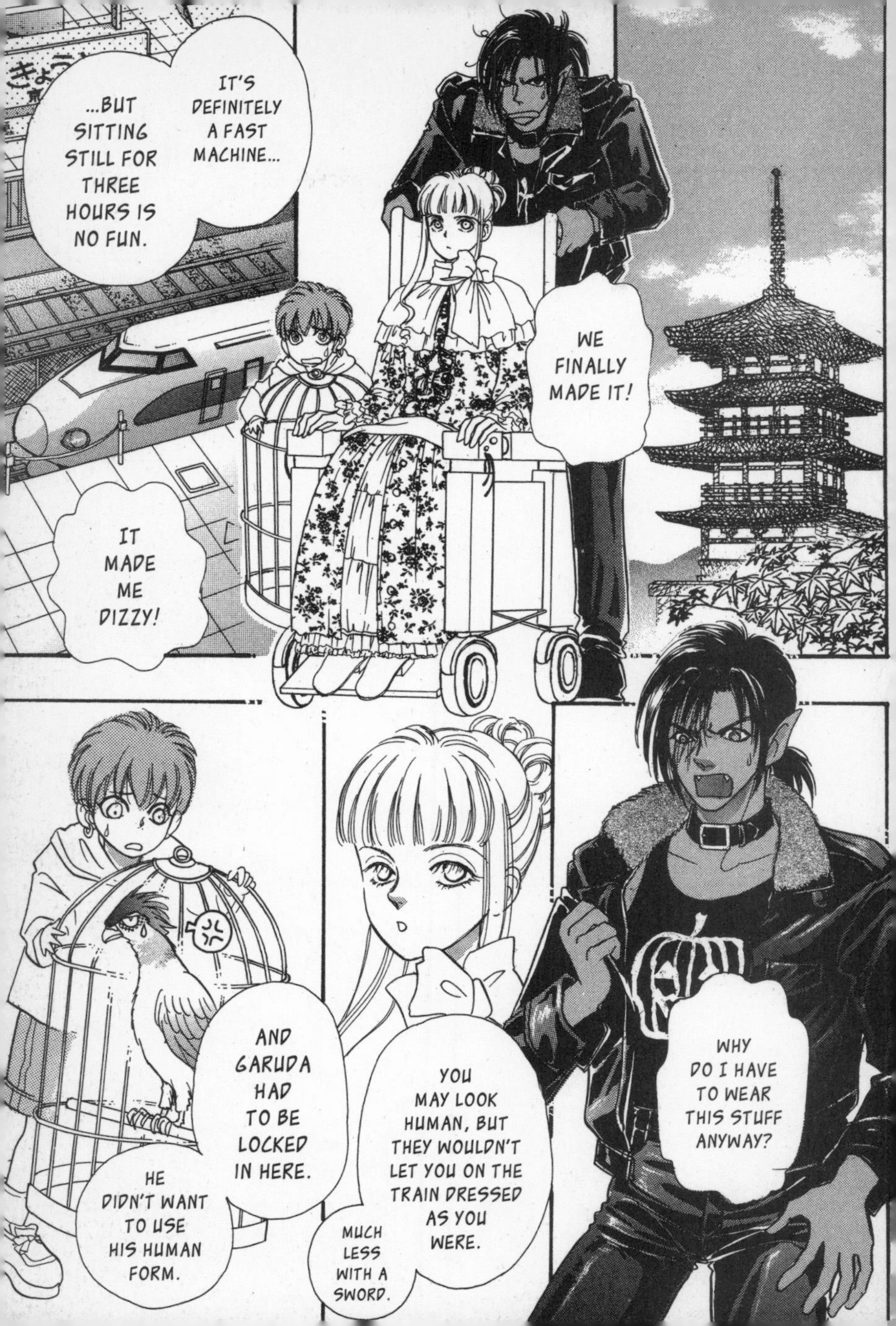
WE FINALLY MADE IT!
IT'S DEFINITELY A FAST MACHINE...
...BUT SITTING STILL FOR THREE HOURS IS NO FUN.
IT MADE ME DIZZY!
WHY DO I HAVE TO WEAR THIS STUFF ANYWAY?
YOU MAY LOOK HUMAN, BUT THEY WOULDN'T LET YOU ON THE TRAIN DRESSED AS YOU WERE.
MUCH LESS WITH A SWORD.
AND GARUDA HAD TO BE LOCKED IN HERE.
HE DIDN'T WANT TO USE HIS HUMAN FORM.

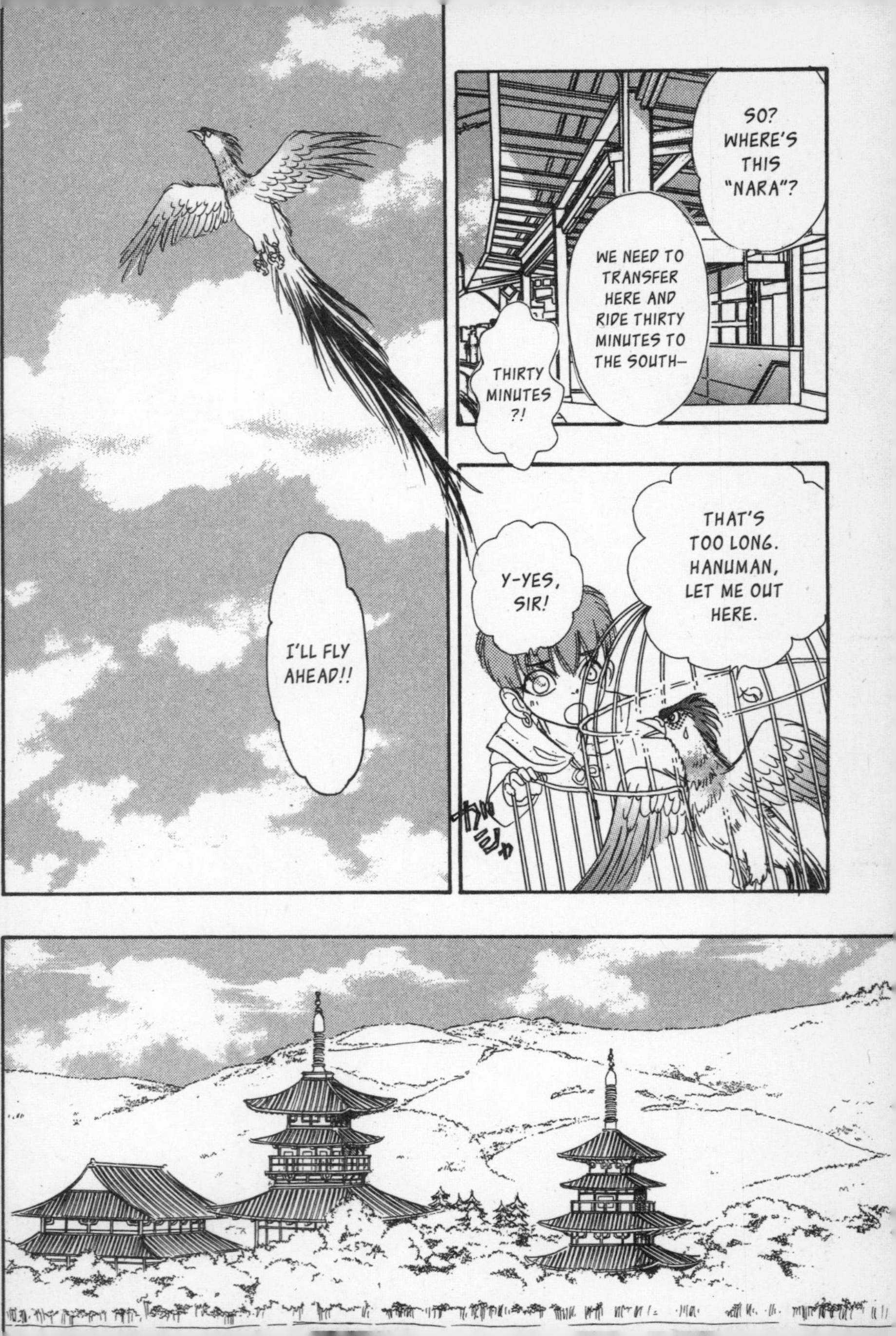
SO? WHERE'S THIS "NARA"?
WE NEED TO TRANSFER HERE AND RIDE THIRTY MINUTES TO THE SOUTH–
THIRTY MINUTES ?!
THAT'S TOO LONG. HANUMAN, LET ME OUT HERE.
Y-YES, SIR!
I'LL FLY AHEAD!!

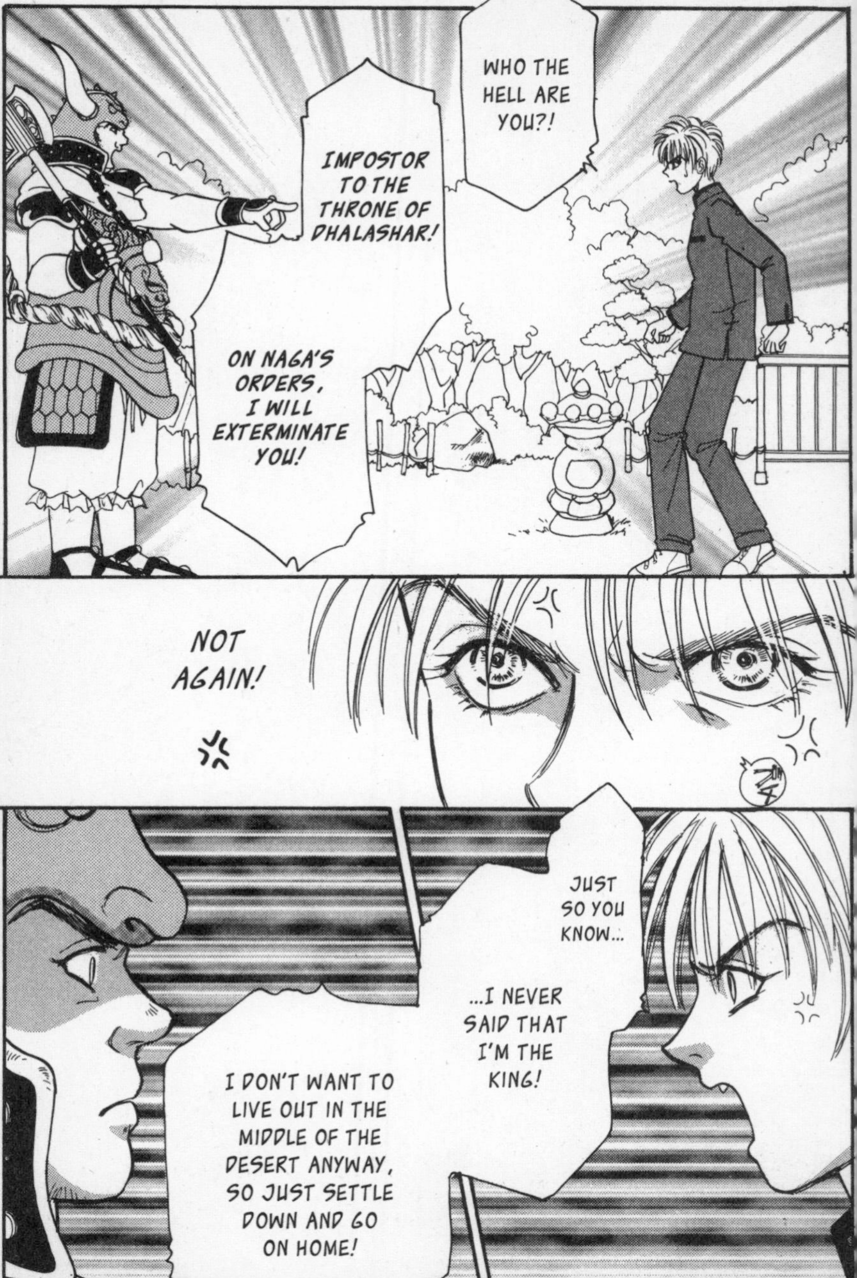
WHO THE HELL ARE YOU?!
IMPOSTOR TO THE THRONE OF DHALASHAR!
ON NAGA'S ORDERS, I WILL EXTERMINATE YOU!
NOT AGAIN!
JUST SO YOU KNOW...
...I NEVER SAID THAT I'M THE KING!
I DON'T WANT TO LIVE OUT IN THE MIDDLE OF THE DESERT ANYWAY, SO JUST SETTLE DOWN AND GO ON HOME!

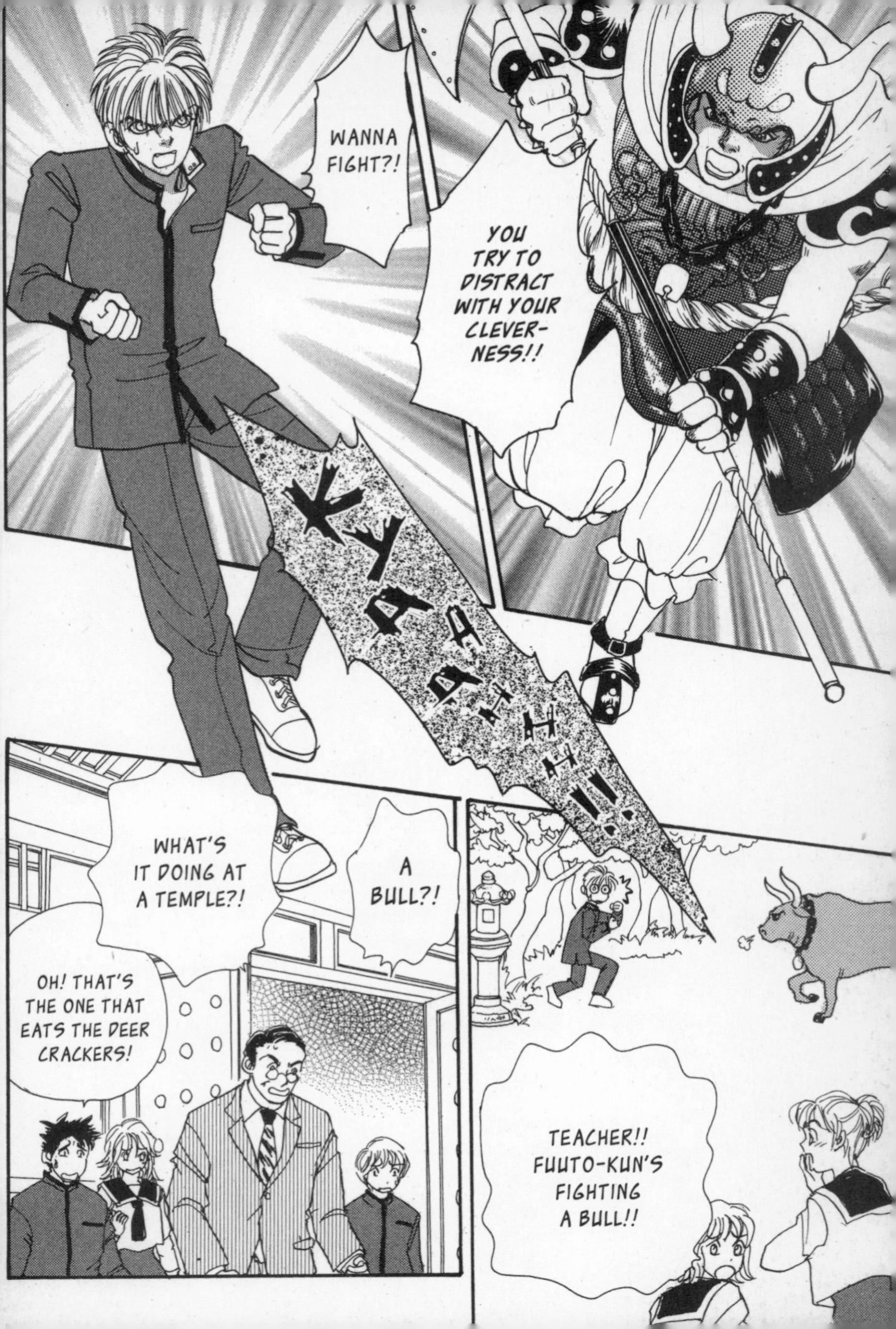
WANNA FIGHT?!
YOU TRY TO DISTRACT WITH YOUR CLEVER-NESS!!
KYAAAHHH!!
TEACHER!! FUUTO-KUN'S FIGHTING A BULL!!
A BULL?!
WHAT'S IT DOING AT A TEMPLE?!
OH! THAT'S THE ONE THAT EATS THE DEER CRACKERS!

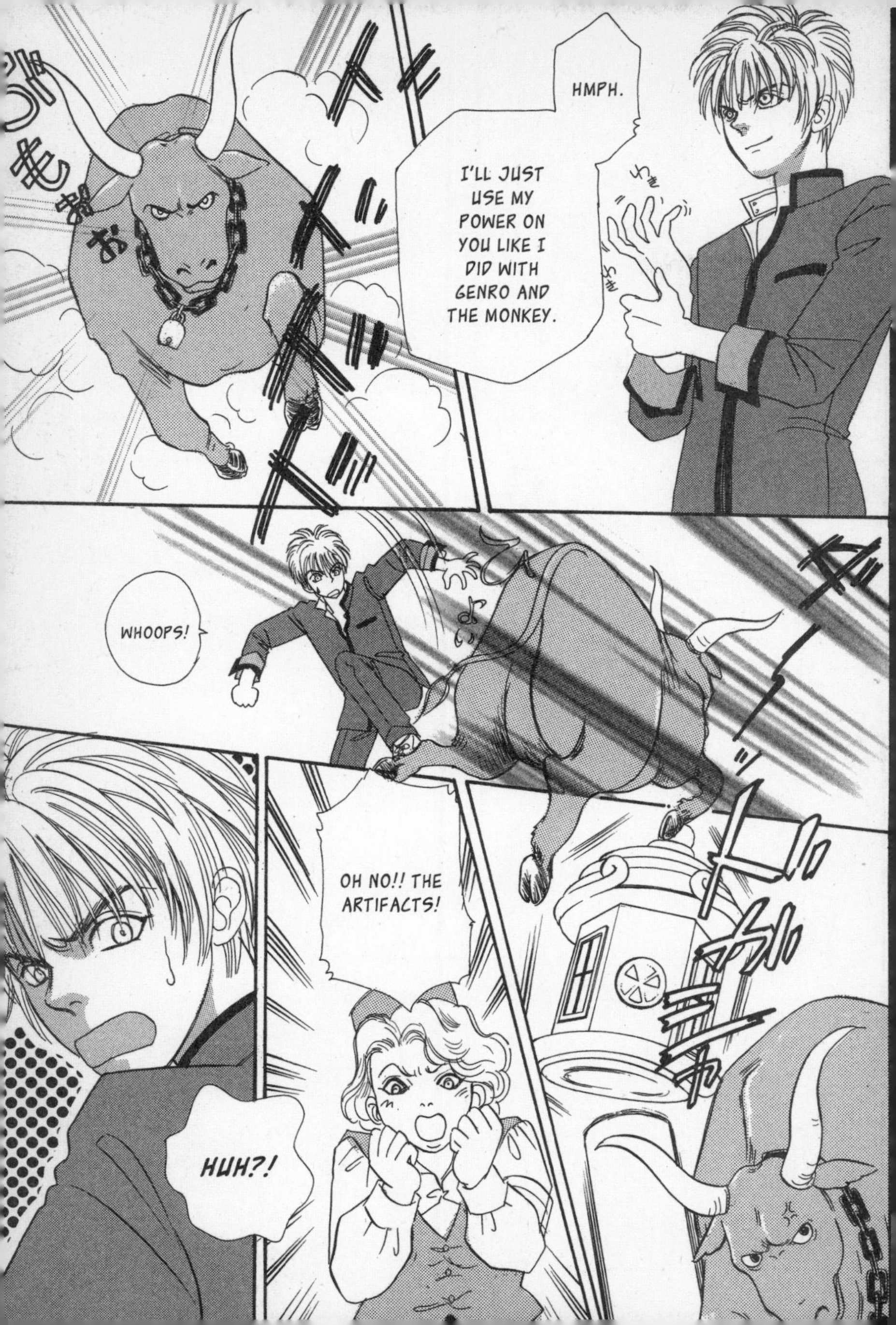
HMPH.
I'LL JUST USE MY POWER ON YOU LIKE I DID WITH GENRO AND THE MONKEY.
WHOOPS!
OH NO!! THE ARTIFACTS!
HUH?!

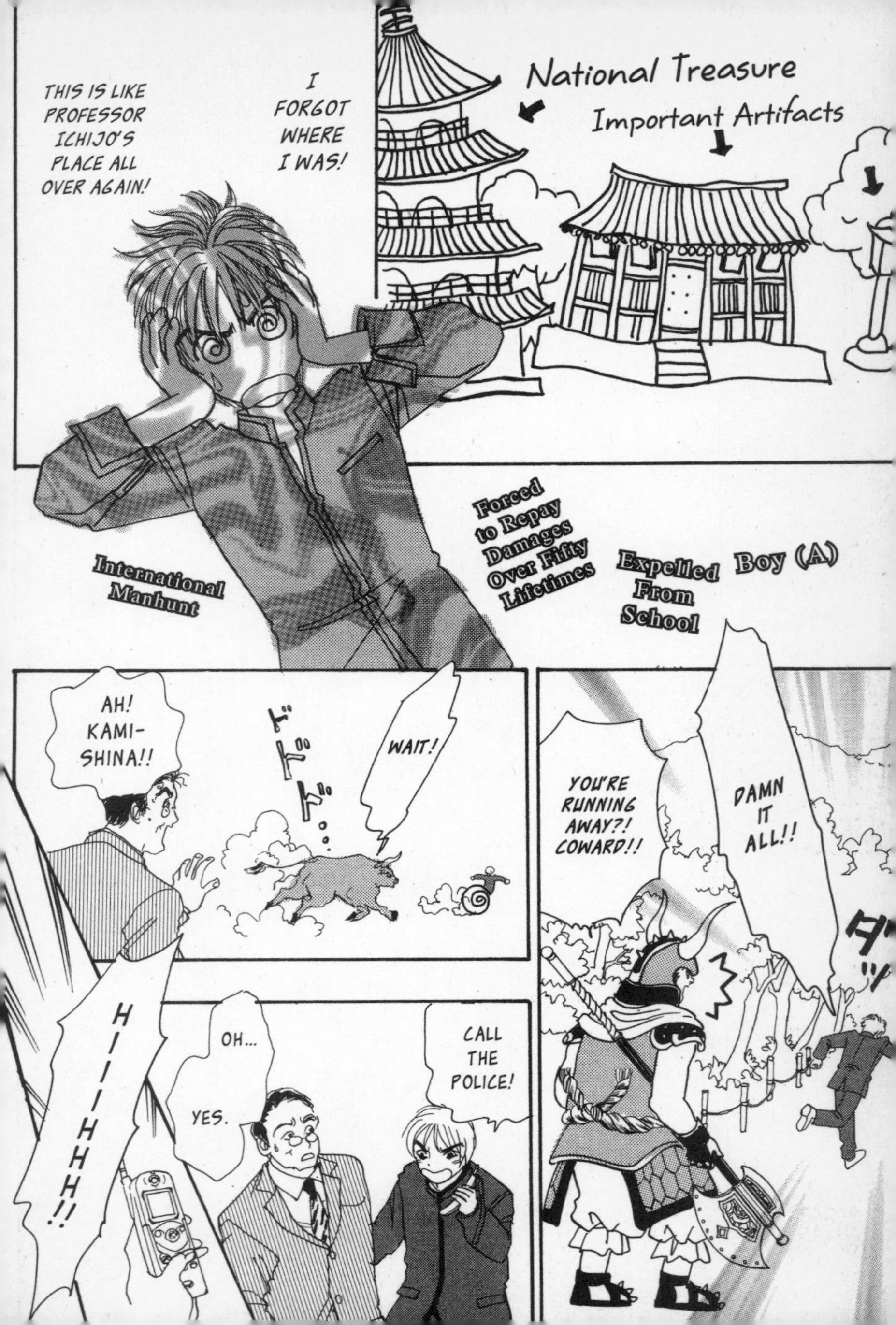
National Treasure
Important Artifacts
I FORGOT WHERE I WAS!
THIS IS LIKE PROFESSOR ICHIJO'S PLACE ALL OVER AGAIN!
Boy (A)
Expelled From School
Forced to Repay Damages Over Fifty Lifetimes
International Manhunt
DAMN IT ALL!!
YOU'RE RUNNING AWAY?! COWARD!!
ダッ
WAIT!
ドドド
AH! KAMI-SHINA!!
CALL THE POLICE!
OH...
YES.
HIIIHHHH!!

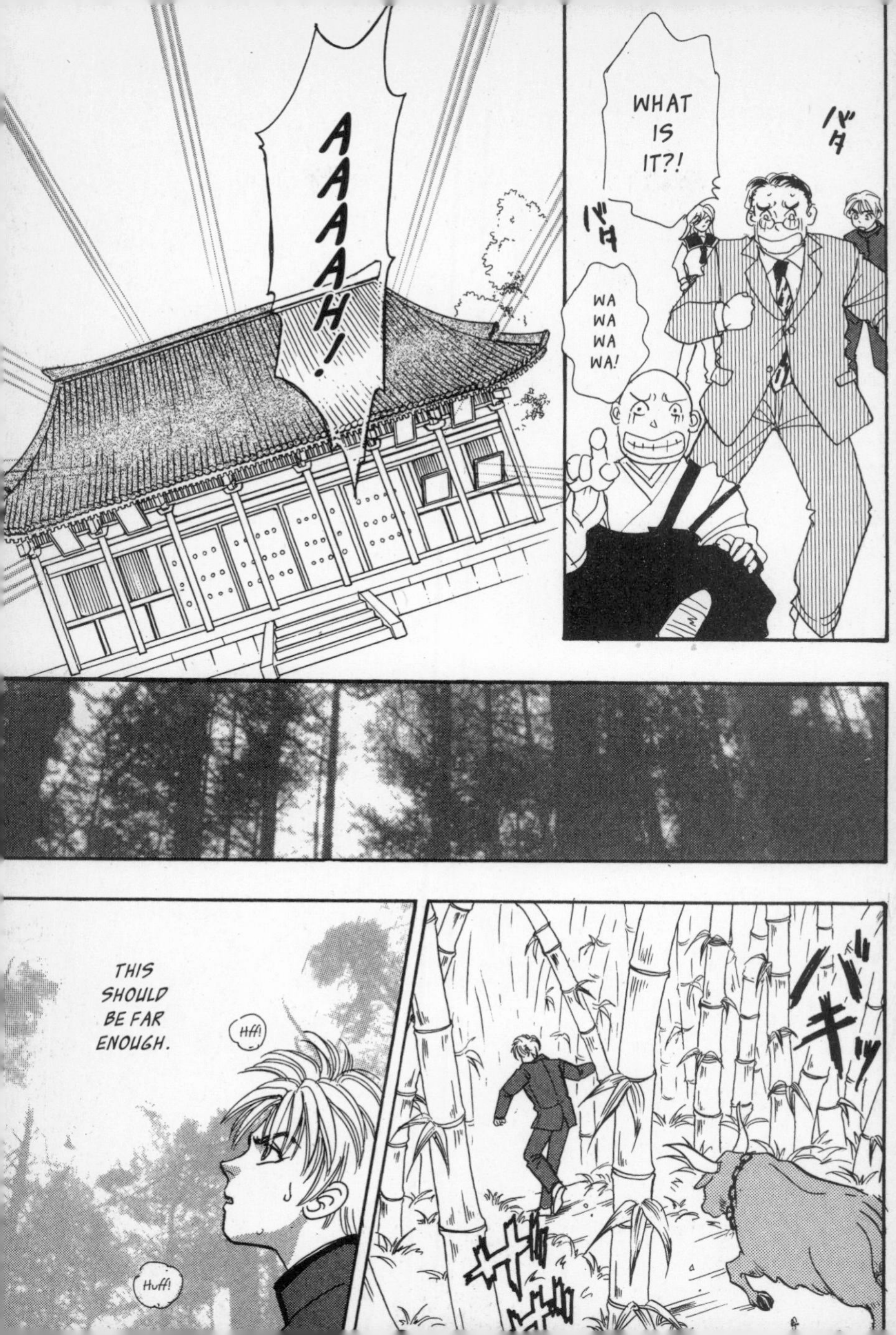
WHAT IS IT?!
バタ
バタ
WA WA WA WA WA!
AAAAAH!
バキッ
THIS SHOULD BE FAR ENOUGH.
Hff!
Huff!

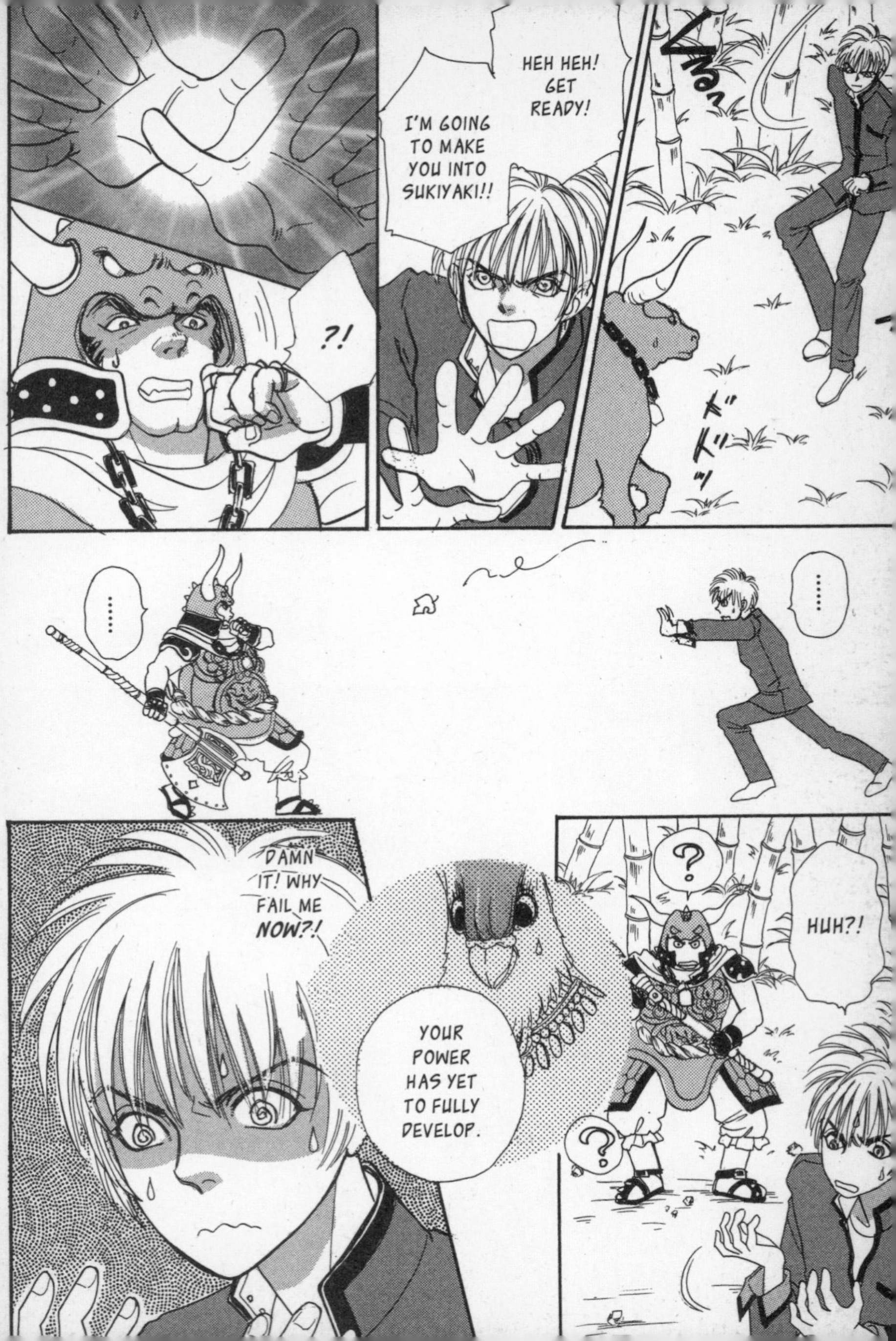
HEH HEH! GET READY!
I'M GOING TO MAKE YOU INTO SUKIYAKI!!
?!
......
......
HUH?!
?
?
DAMN IT! WHY FAIL ME NOW?!
YOUR POWER HAS YET TO FULLY DEVELOP.

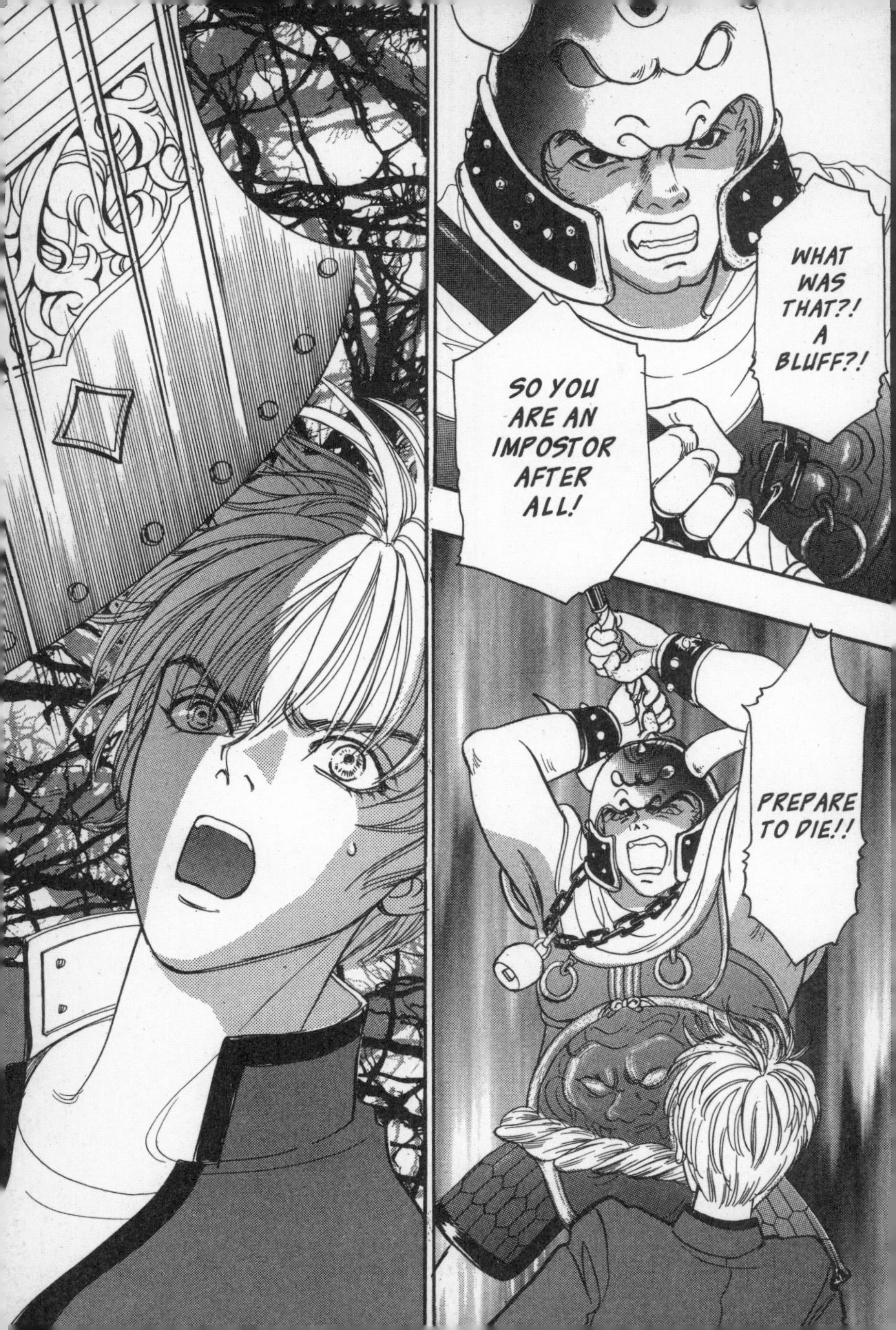
WHAT WAS THAT?! A BLUFF?!
SO YOU ARE AN IMPOSTOR AFTER ALL!
PREPARE TO DIE!!

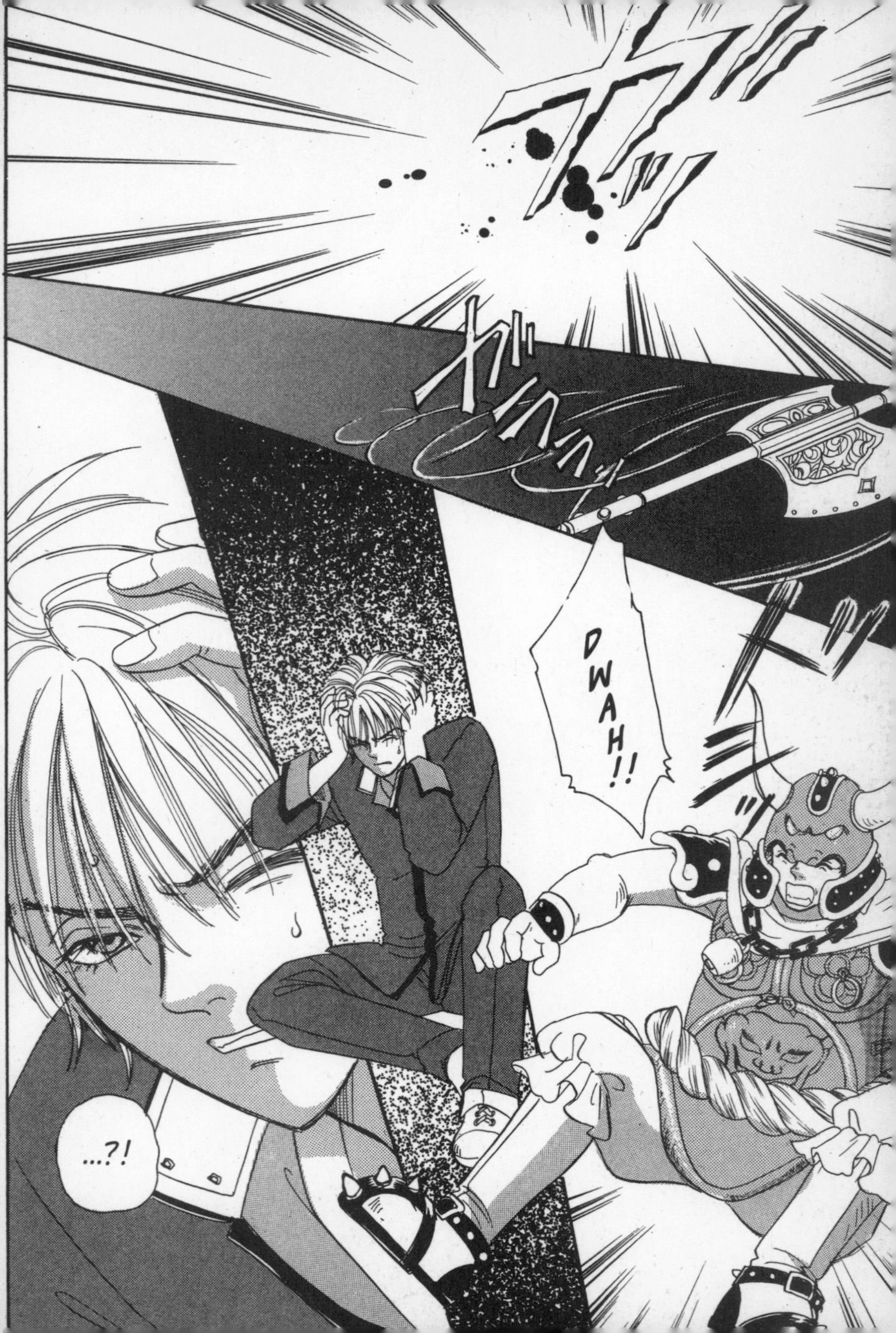
DWAH!!
...?!

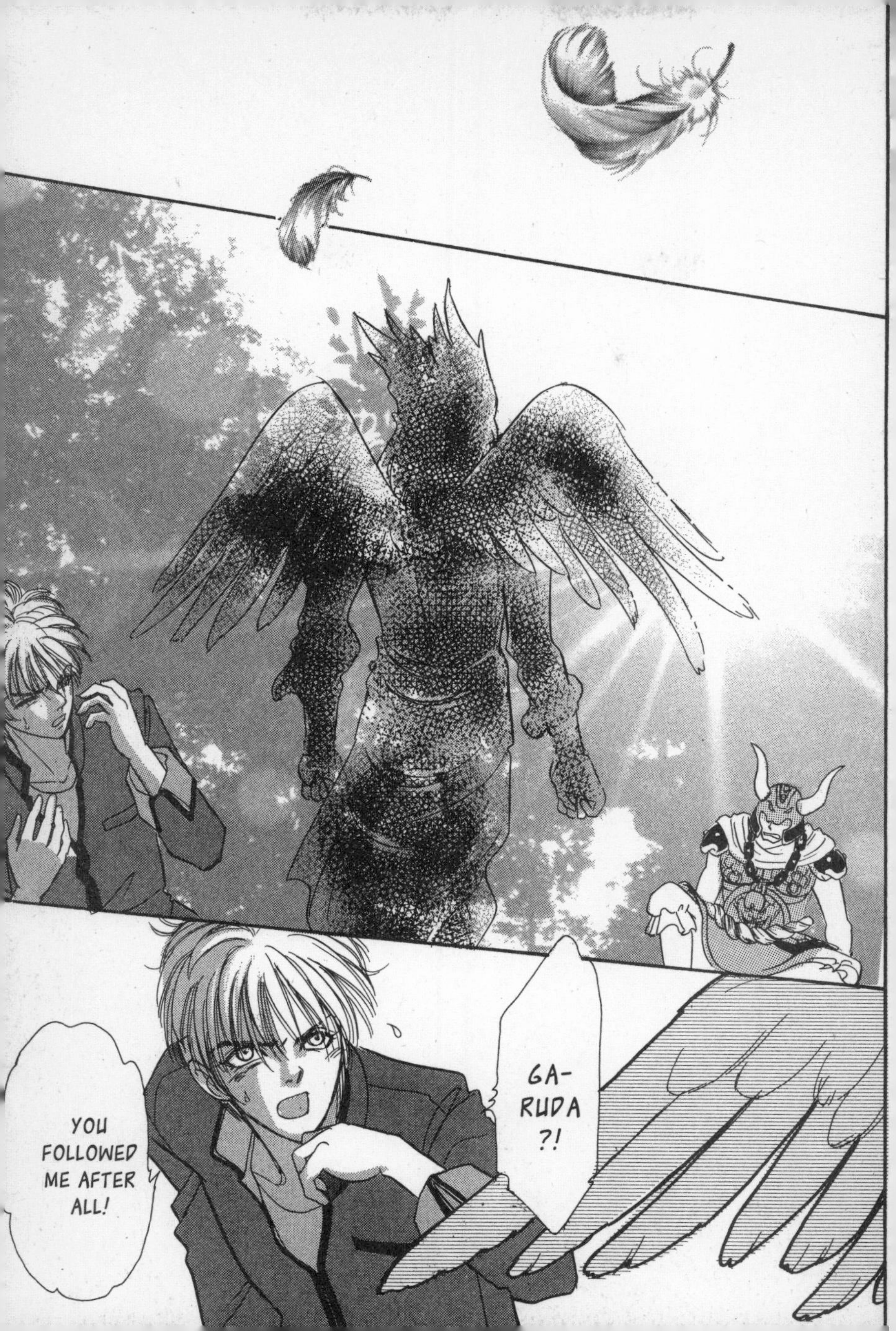
GA-RUDA ?!
YOU FOLLOWED ME AFTER ALL!

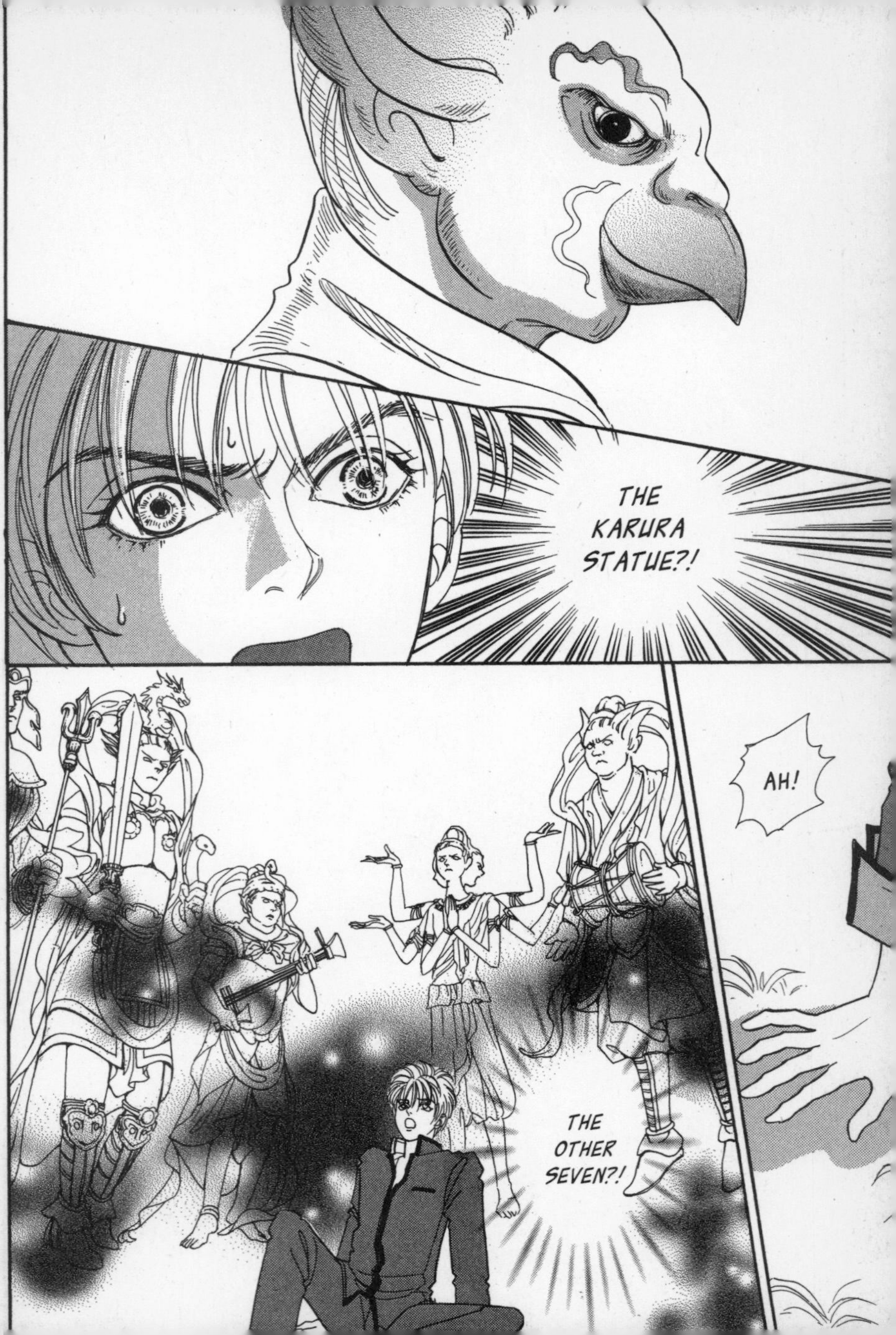
THE KARURA STATUE?!
AH!
THE OTHER SEVEN?!

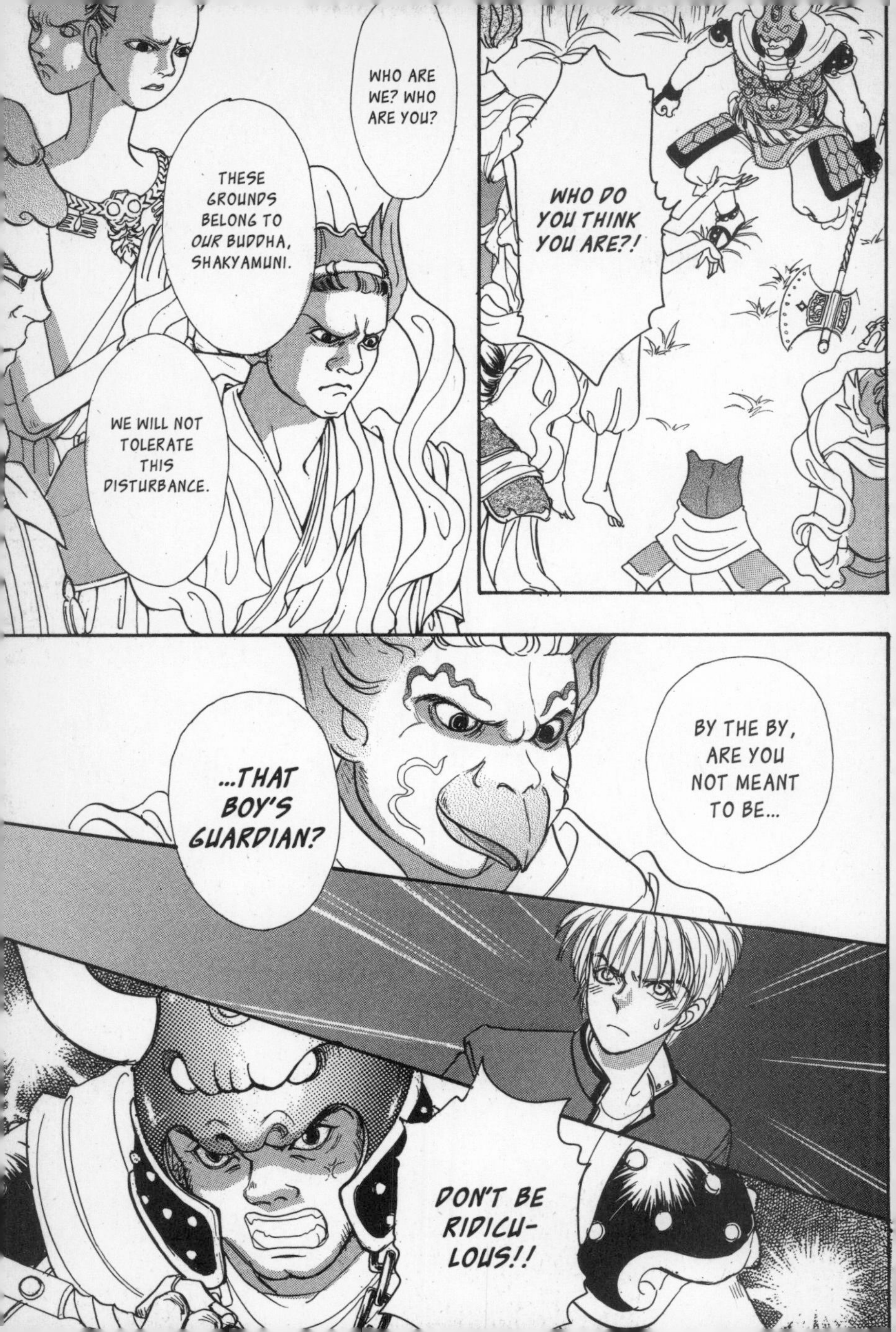
WHO DO YOU THINK YOU ARE?!
WHO ARE WE? WHO ARE YOU?
THESE GROUNDS BELONG TO OUR BUDDHA, SHAKYAMUNI.
WE WILL NOT TOLERATE THIS DISTURBANCE.
BY THE BY, ARE YOU NOT MEANT TO BE...
...THAT BOY'S GUARDIAN?
DON'T BE RIDICULOUS!!

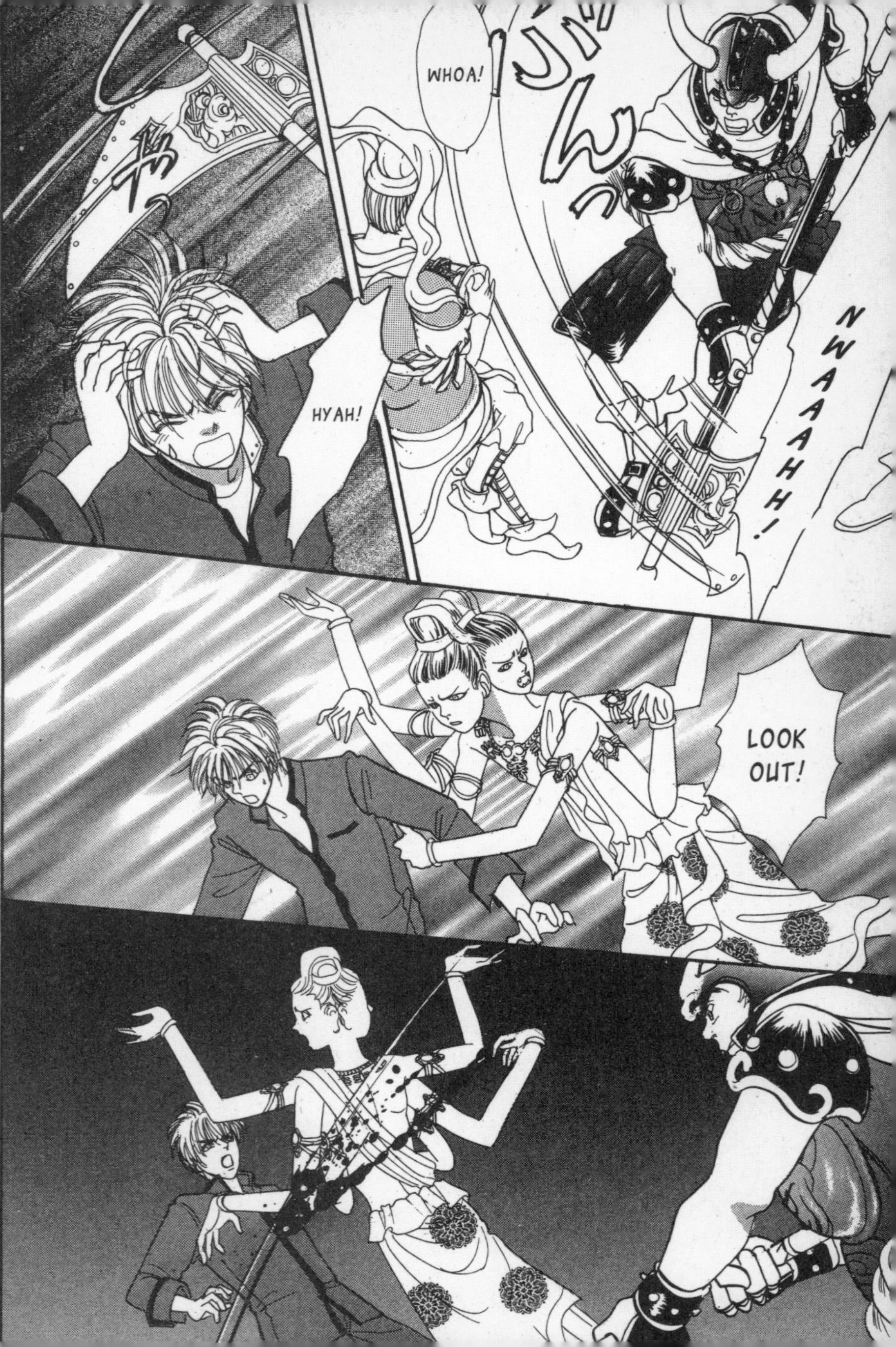
ぶんっ
WHOA!
NWAAAAHH!
HYAH!
LOOK OUT!

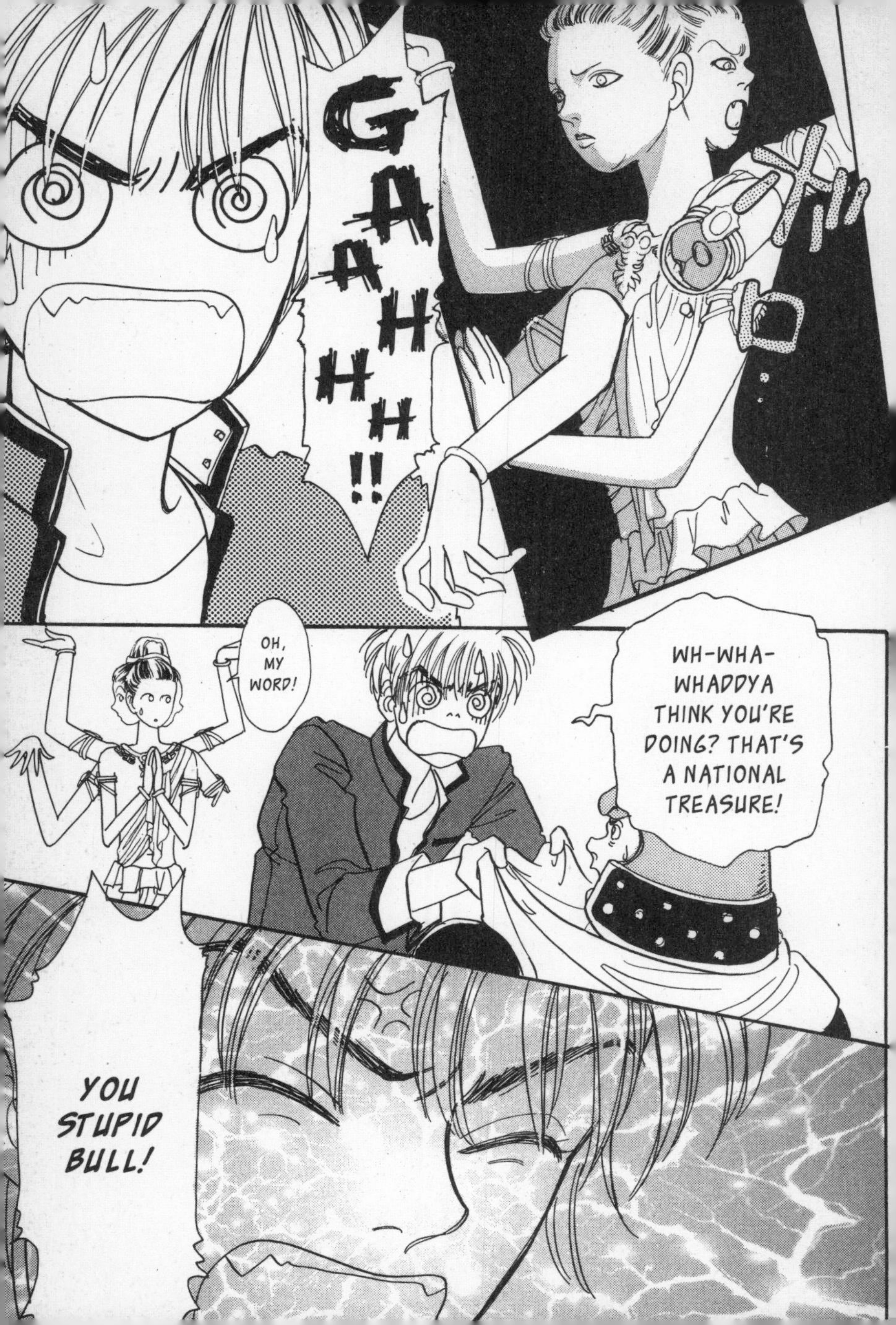
GAHHHH!!
WH-WHA-WHADDYA THINK YOU'RE DOING? THAT'S A NATIONAL TREASURE!
OH, MY WORD!
YOU STUPID BULL!

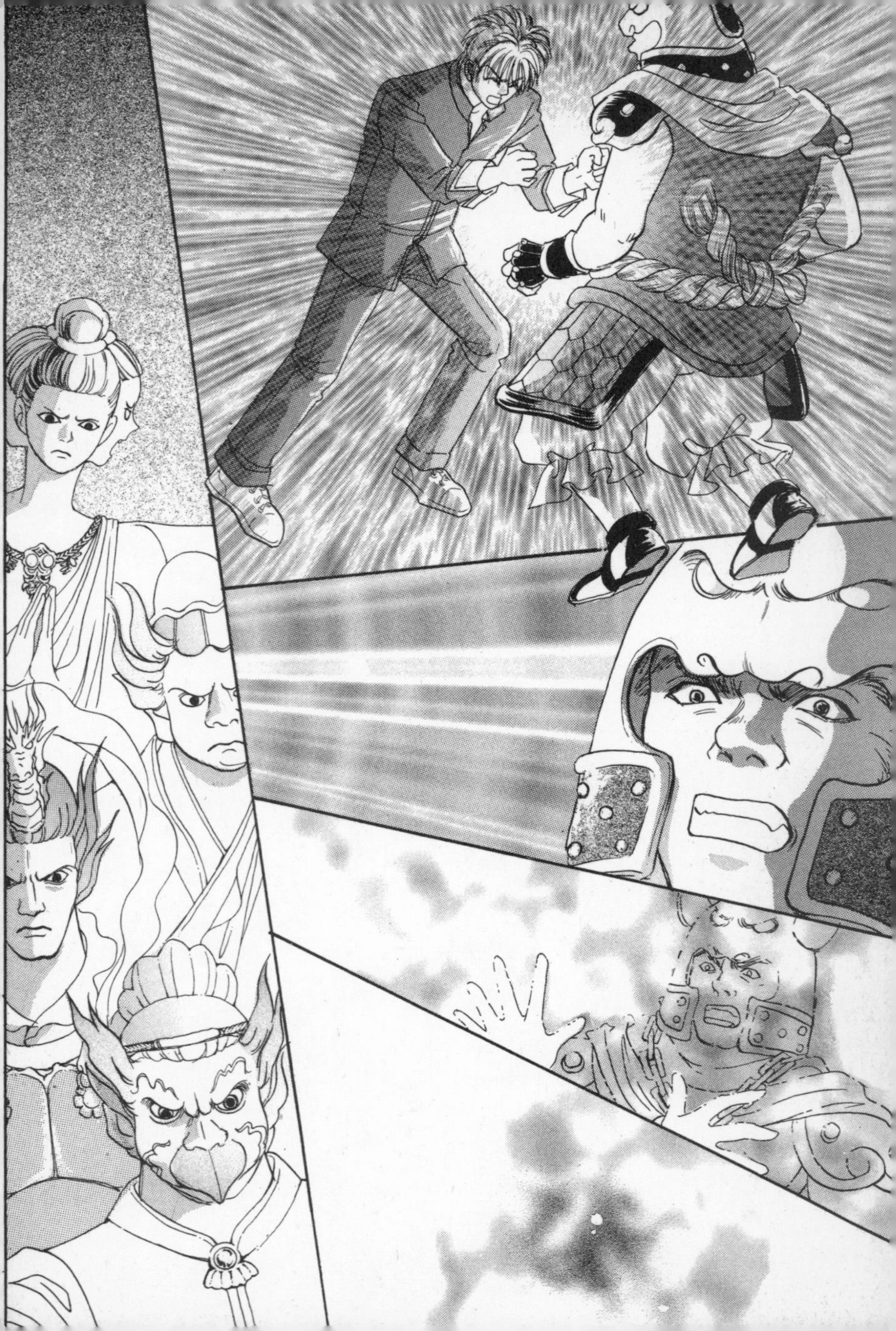

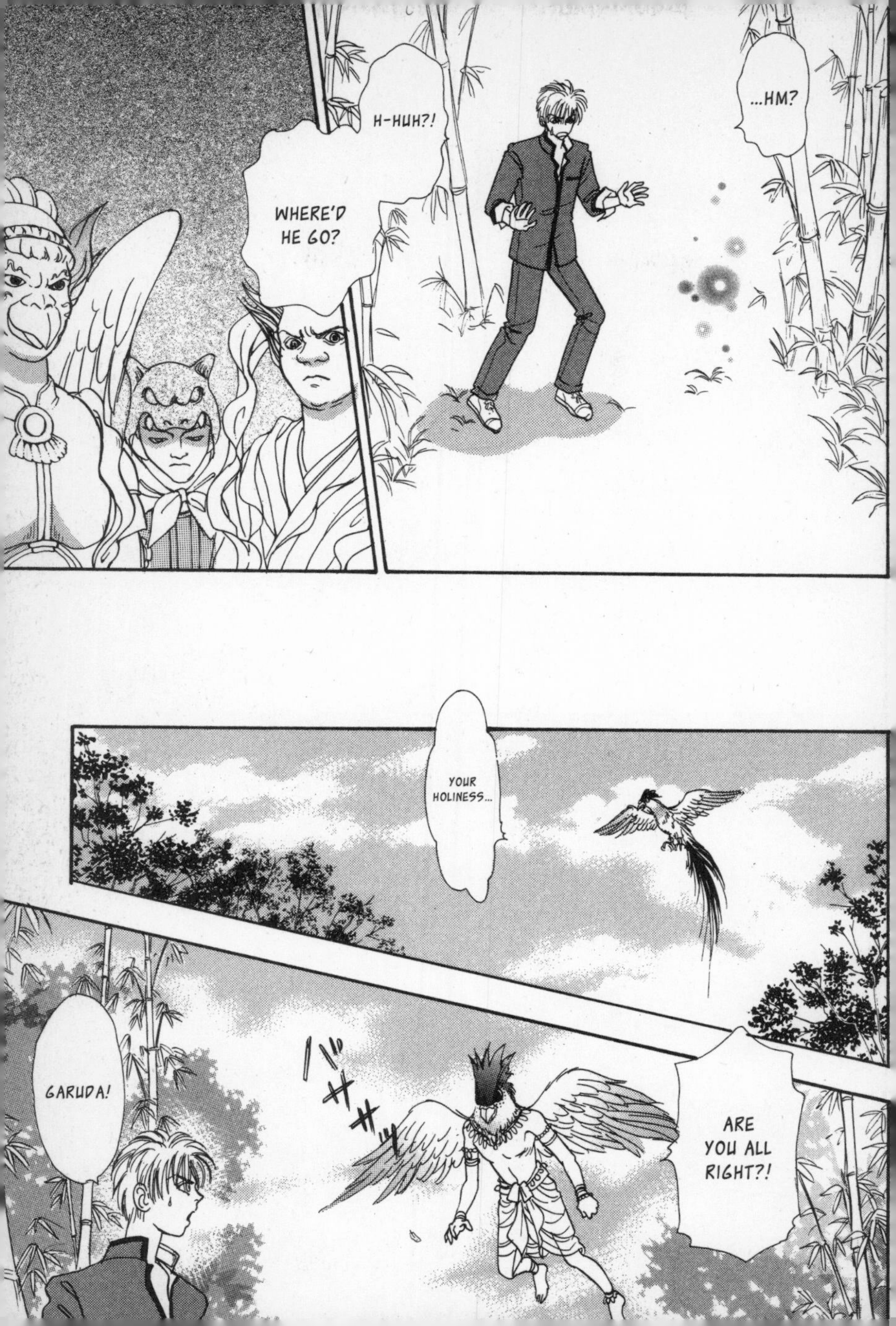
...HM?
H-HUH?!
WHERE'D HE GO?
YOUR HOLINESS...
ARE YOU ALL RIGHT?!
GARUDA!

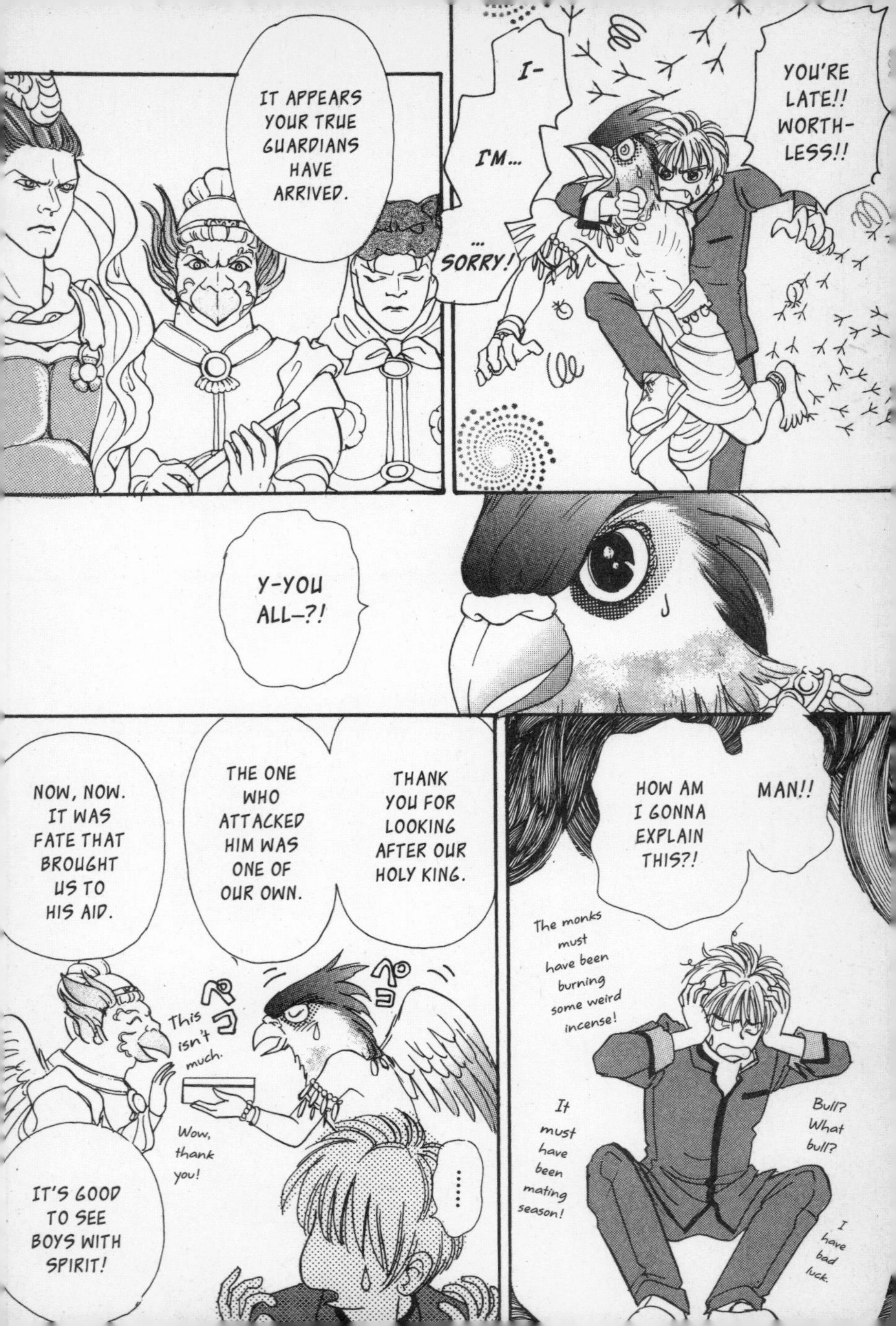
YOU'RE LATE!! WORTHLESS!!
I- I'M... ...SORRY!
IT APPEARS YOUR TRUE GUARDIANS HAVE ARRIVED.
Y-YOU ALL-?!
MAN!!
HOW AM I GONNA EXPLAIN THIS?!
The monks must have been burning some weird incense!
Bull? What bull?
It must have been mating season!
I have bad luck.
THANK YOU FOR LOOKING AFTER OUR HOLY KING.
THE ONE WHO ATTACKED HIM WAS ONE OF OUR OWN.
NOW, NOW. IT WAS FATE THAT BROUGHT US TO HIS AID.
This isn't much.
Wow, thank you!
......
IT'S GOOD TO SEE BOYS WITH SPIRIT!

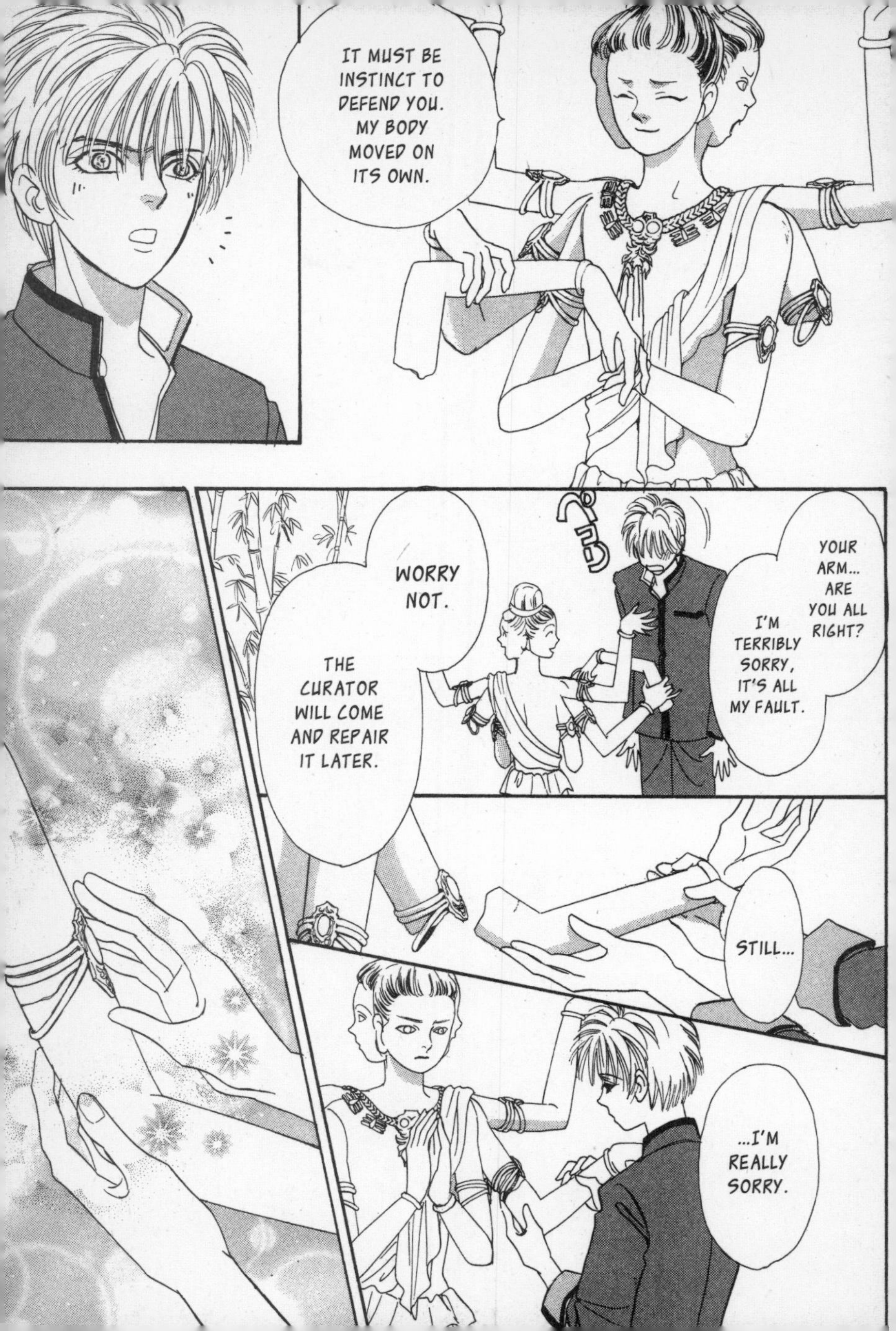
IT MUST BE INSTINCT TO DEFEND YOU. MY BODY MOVED ON ITS OWN.
YOUR ARM... ARE YOU ALL RIGHT?
I'M TERRIBLY SORRY, IT'S ALL MY FAULT.
WORRY NOT.
THE CURATOR WILL COME AND REPAIR IT LATER.
STILL...
...I'M REALLY SORRY.

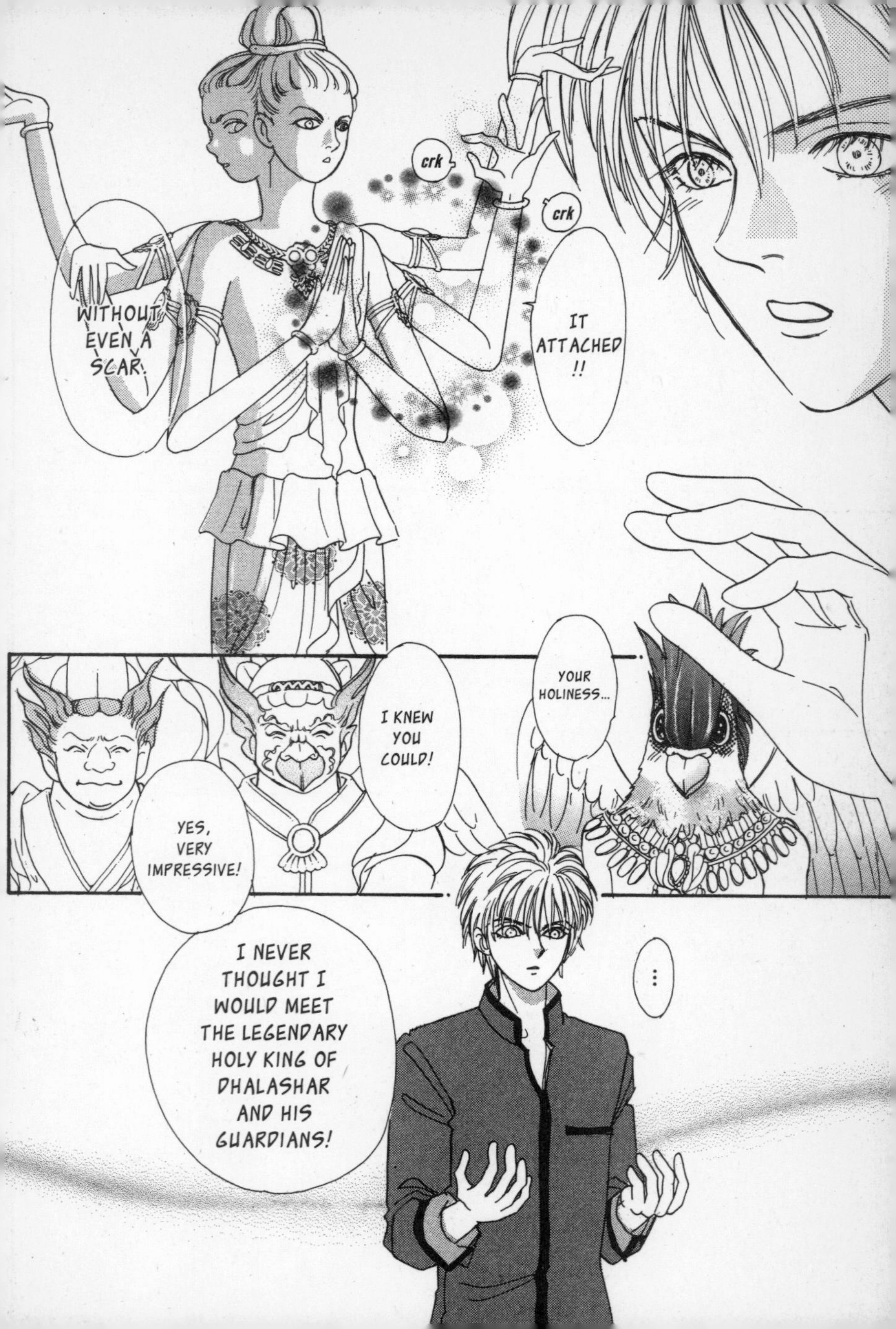
crk
IT ATTACHED !!
crk
WITHOUT EVEN A SCAR.
YOUR HOLINESS...
I KNEW YOU COULD!
YES, VERY IMPRESSIVE!
I NEVER THOUGHT I WOULD MEET THE LEGENDARY HOLY KING OF DHALASHAR AND HIS GUARDIANS!
...

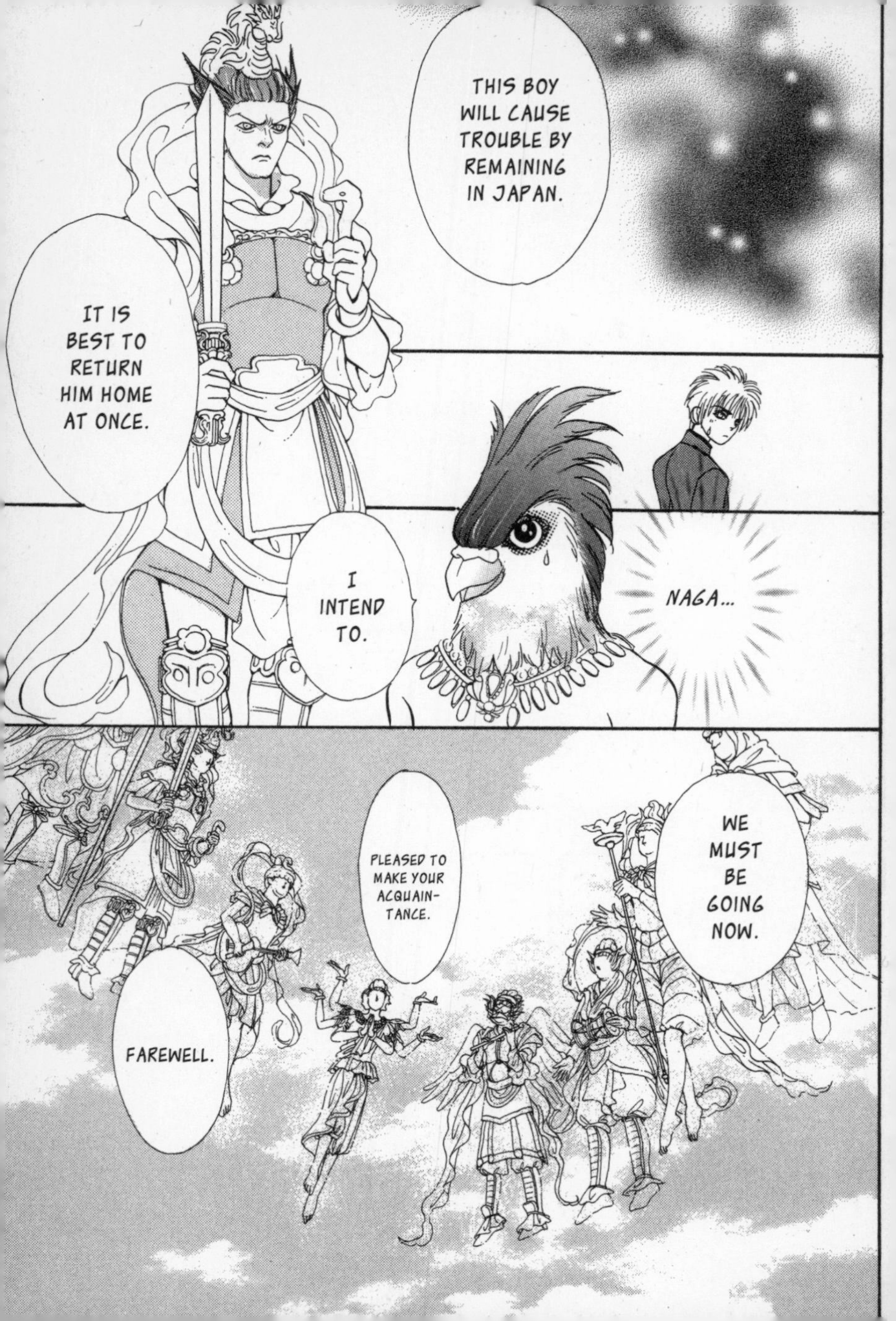
THIS BOY WILL CAUSE TROUBLE BY REMAINING IN JAPAN.
IT IS BEST TO RETURN HIM HOME AT ONCE.
I INTEND TO.
NAGA...
WE MUST BE GOING NOW.
PLEASED TO MAKE YOUR ACQUAIN-TANCE.
FAREWELL.

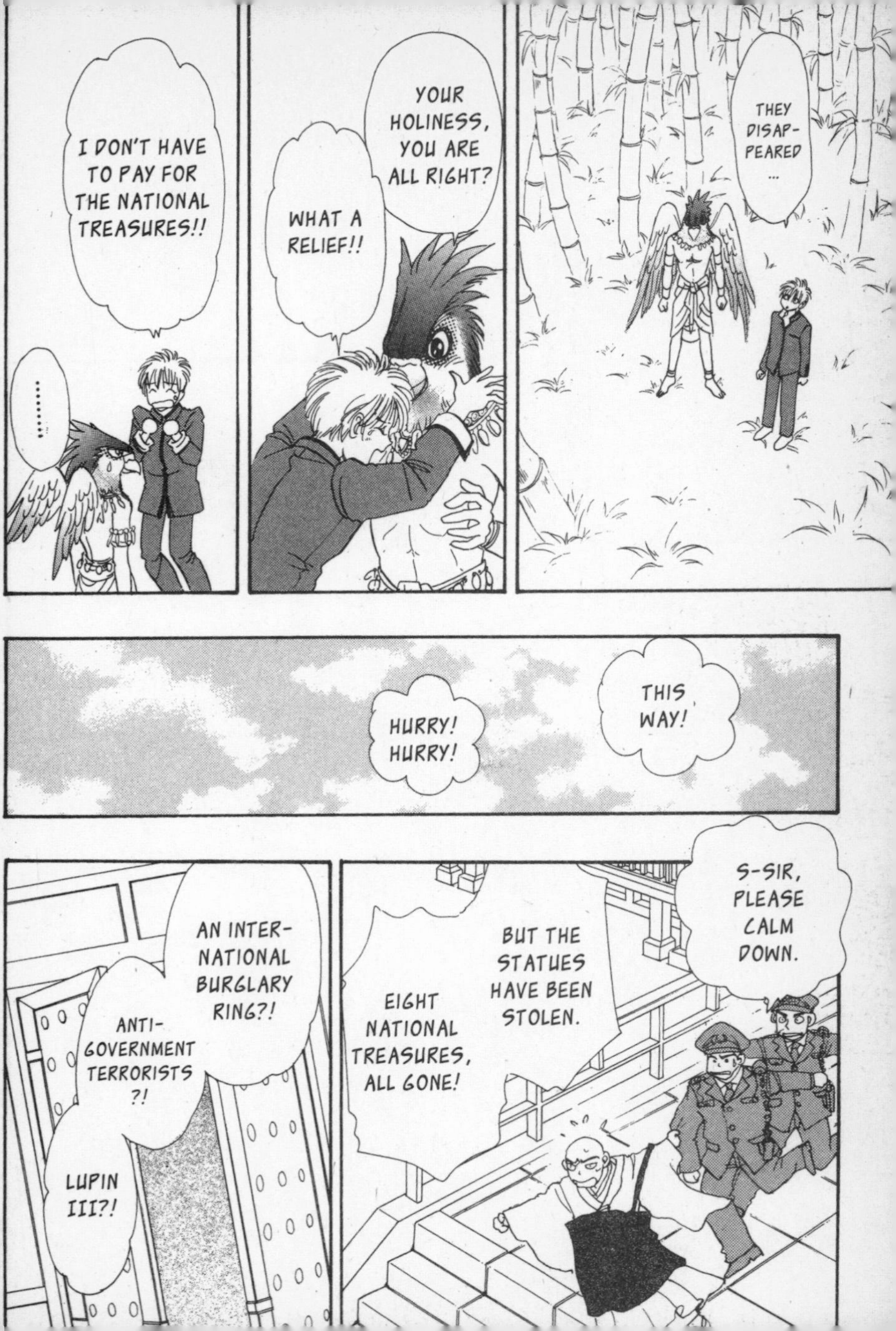
THEY DISAP-PEARED ...
YOUR HOLINESS, YOU ARE ALL RIGHT?
WHAT A RELIEF!!
I DON'T HAVE TO PAY FOR THE NATIONAL TREASURES!!
......
THIS WAY!
HURRY! HURRY!
S-SIR, PLEASE CALM DOWN.
BUT THE STATUES HAVE BEEN STOLEN.
EIGHT NATIONAL TREASURES, ALL GONE!
AN INTER-NATIONAL BURGLARY RING?!
ANTI-GOVERNMENT TERRORISTS ?!
LUPIN III?!

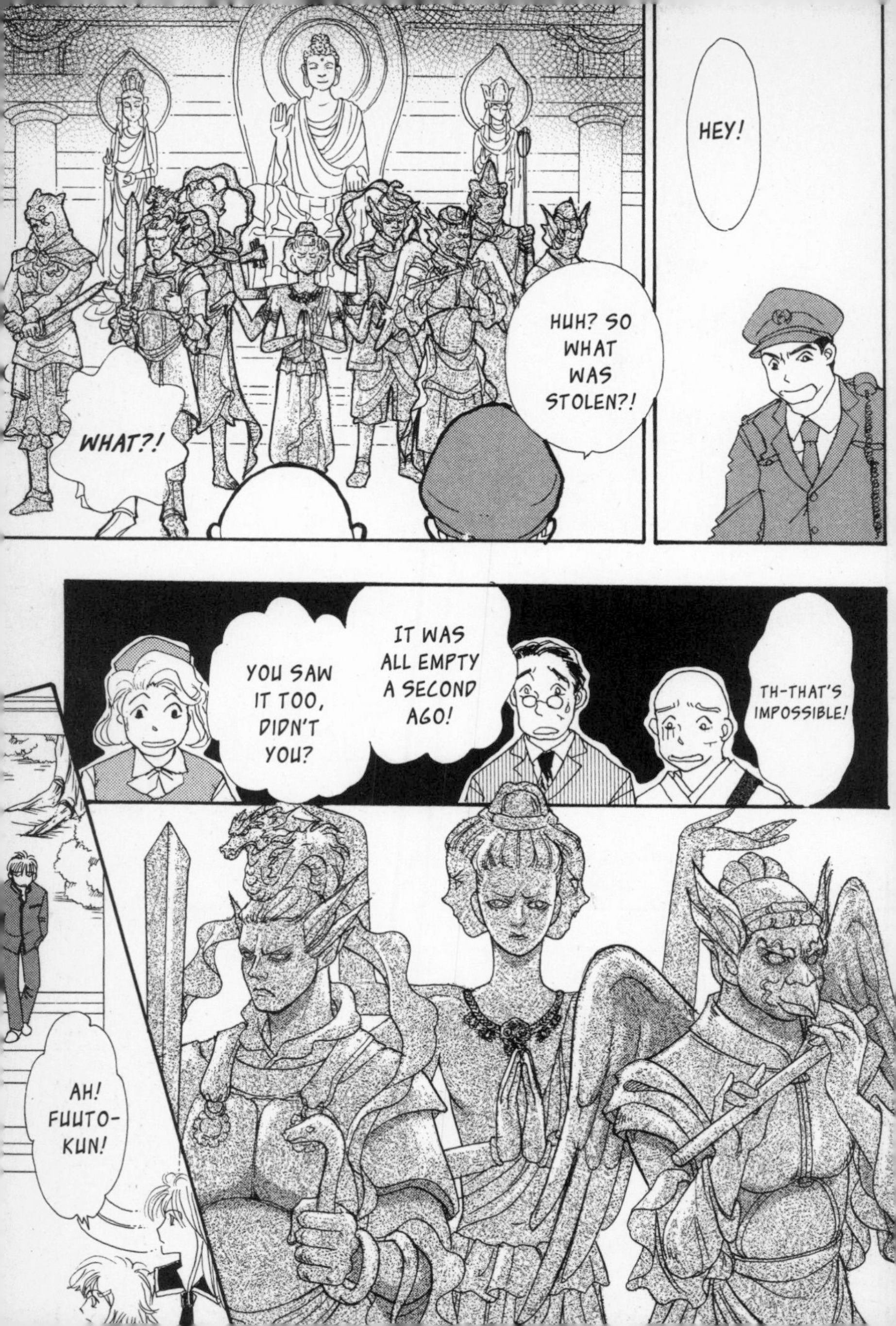
HEY!
HUH? SO WHAT WAS STOLEN?!
WHAT?!
TH-THAT'S IMPOSSIBLE!
IT WAS ALL EMPTY A SECOND AGO!
YOU SAW IT TOO, DIDN'T YOU?
AH! FUUTO-KUN!

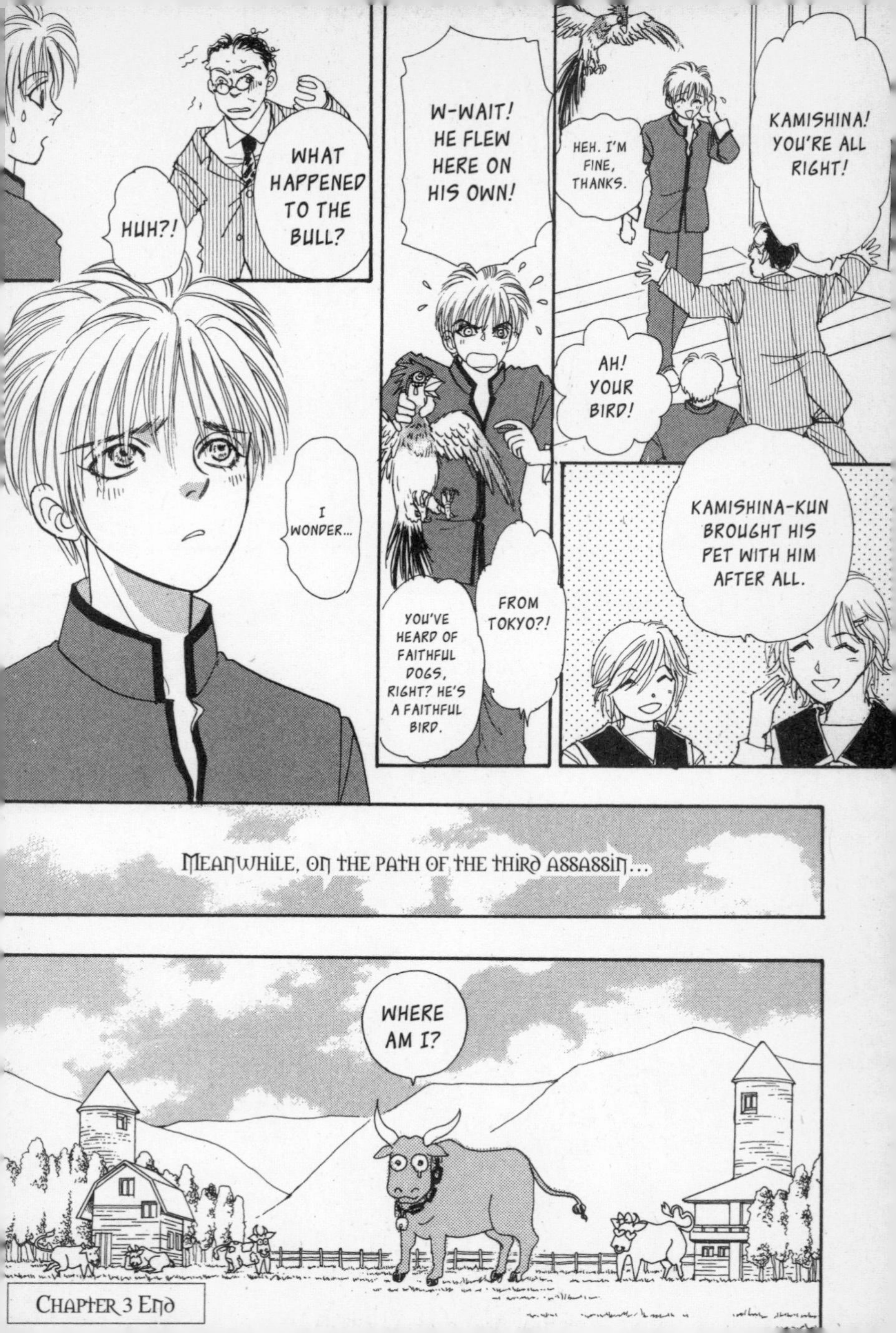
KAMISHINA! YOU'RE ALL RIGHT!
HEH. I'M FINE, THANKS.
AH! YOUR BIRD!
KAMISHINA-KUN BROUGHT HIS PET WITH HIM AFTER ALL.
W-WAIT! HE FLEW HERE ON HIS OWN!
FROM TOKYO?!
YOU'VE HEARD OF FAITHFUL DOGS, RIGHT? HE'S A FAITHFUL BIRD.
WHAT HAPPENED TO THE BULL?
HUH?!
I WONDER...
MEANWHILE, ON THE PATH OF THE THIRD ASSASSIN...
WHERE AM I?
CHAPTER 3 END

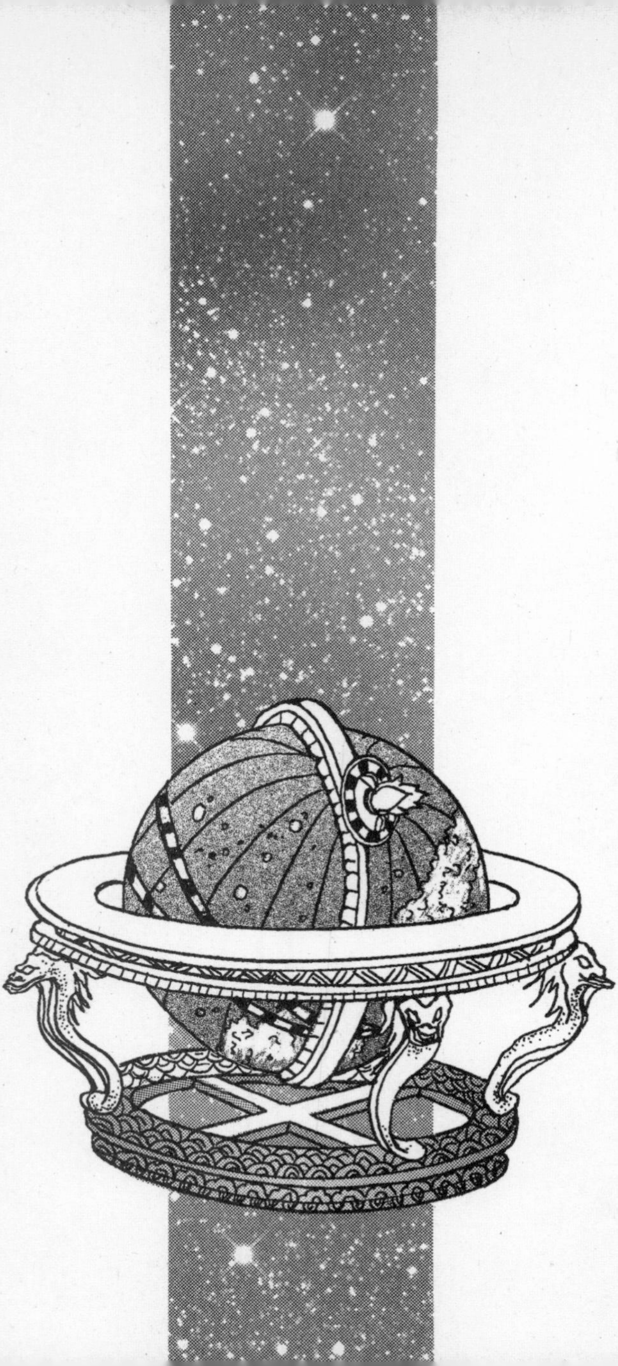

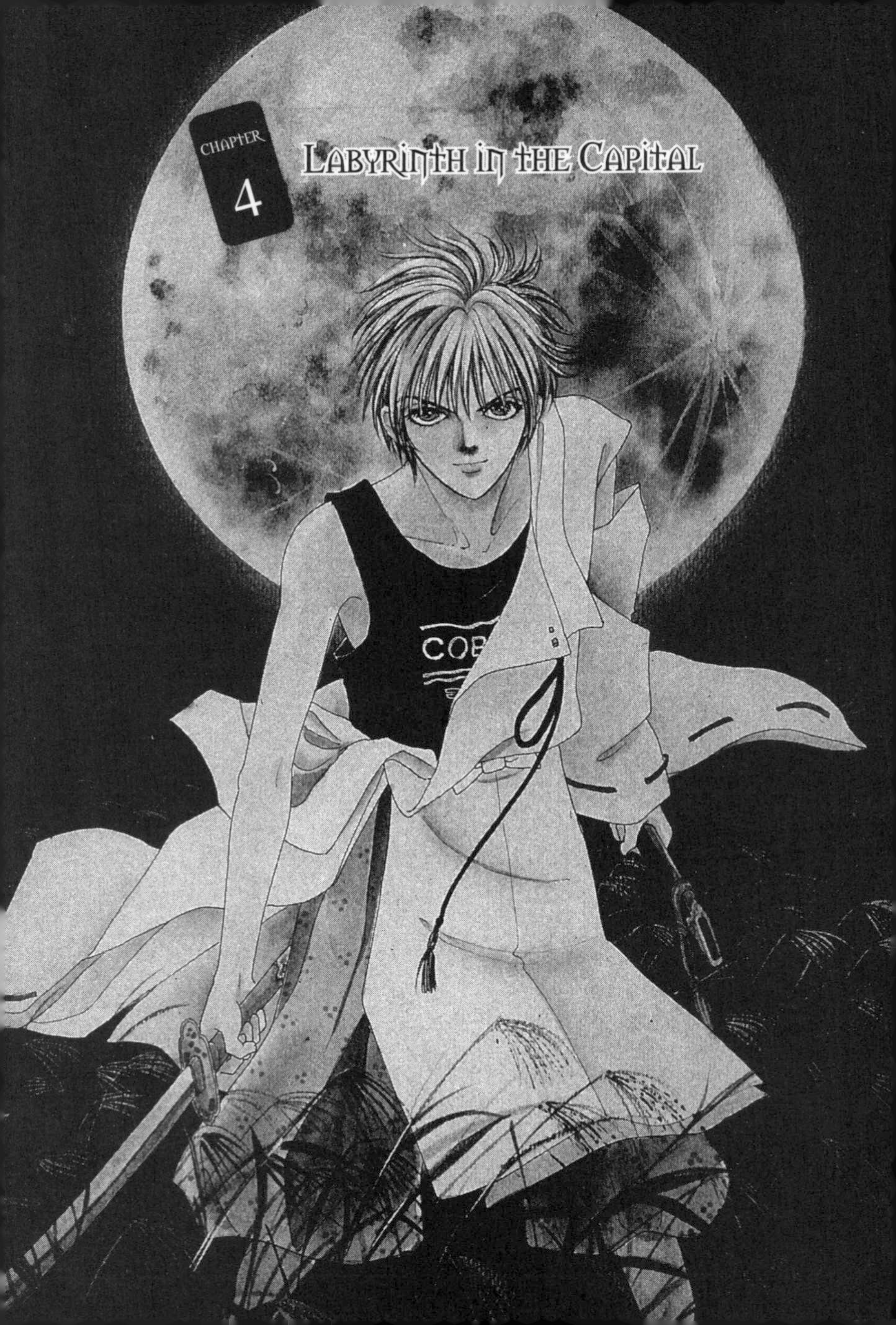
CHAPTER
4
LABYRINTH IN THE CAPITAL

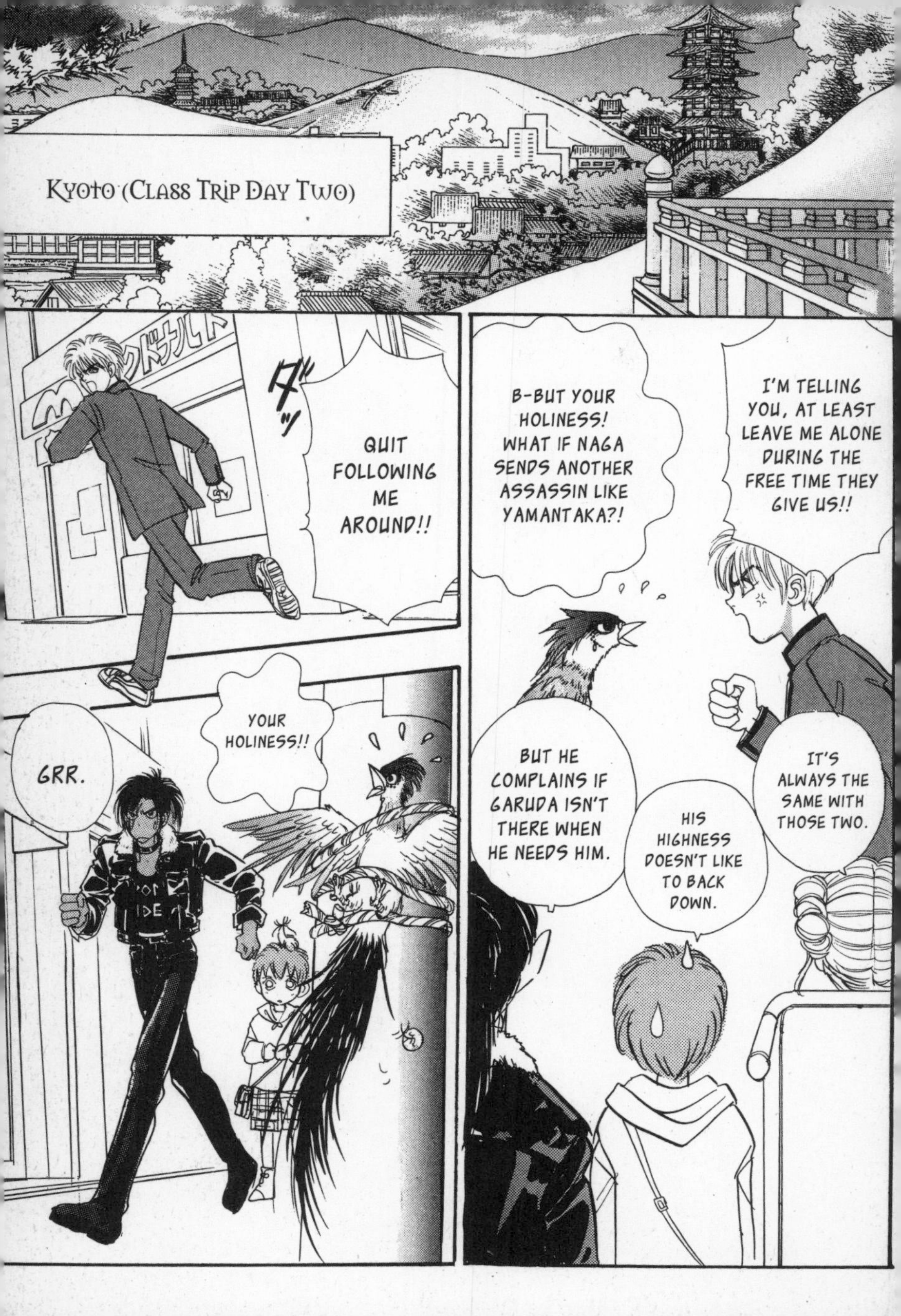
Kyoto (Class Trip Day Two)
I'M TELLING YOU, AT LEAST LEAVE ME ALONE DURING THE FREE TIME THEY GIVE US!!
B-BUT YOUR HOLINESS! WHAT IF NAGA SENDS ANOTHER ASSASSIN LIKE YAMANTAKA?!
IT'S ALWAYS THE SAME WITH THOSE TWO.
HIS HIGHNESS DOESN'T LIKE TO BACK DOWN.
BUT HE COMPLAINS IF GARUDA ISN'T THERE WHEN HE NEEDS HIM.
ダッ
QUIT FOLLOWING ME AROUND!!
YOUR HOLINESS!!
GRR.

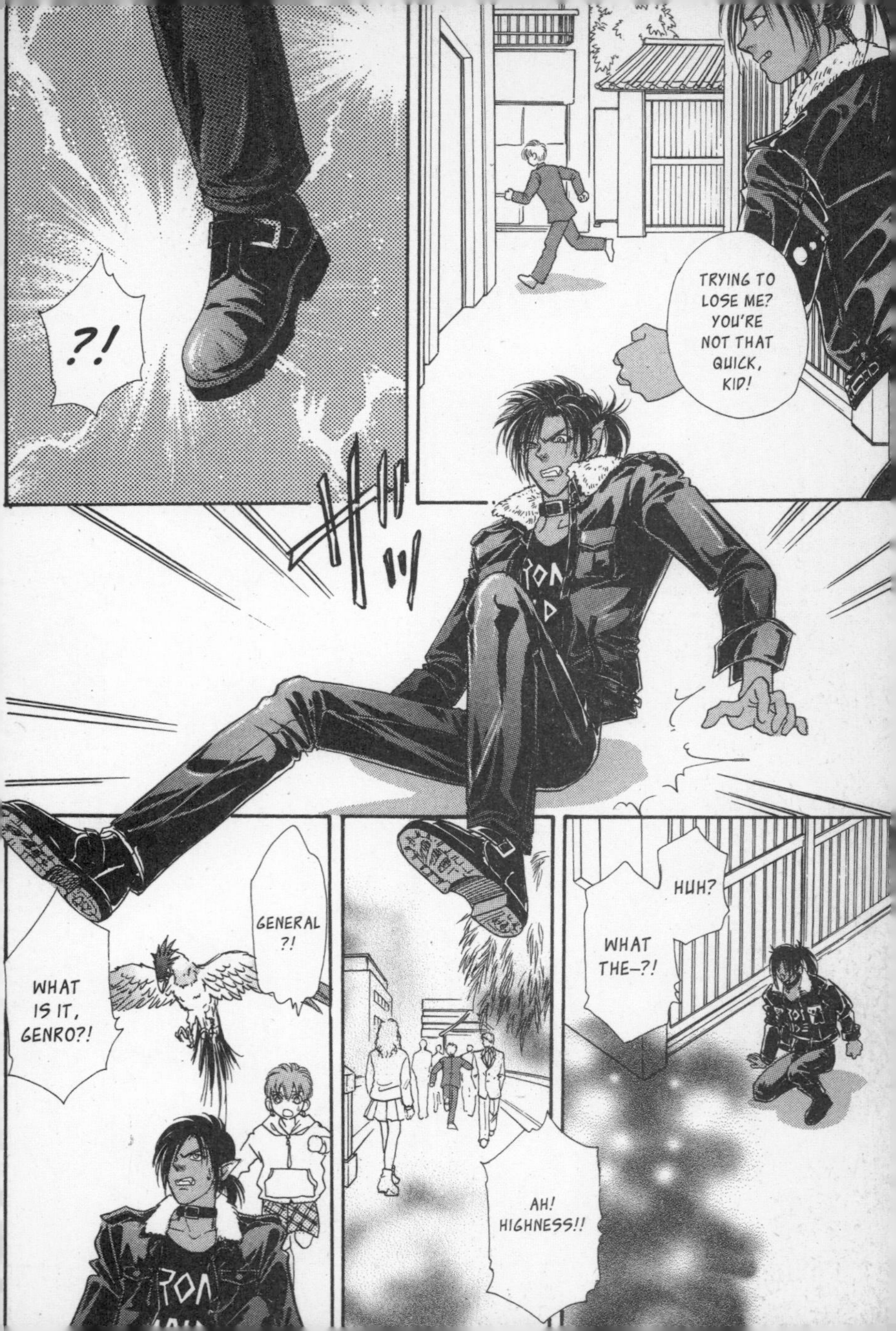
TRYING TO LOSE ME? YOU'RE NOT THAT QUICK, KID!
?!
HUH?
WHAT THE–?!
AH! HIGHNESS!!
GENERAL ?!
WHAT IS IT, GENRO?!

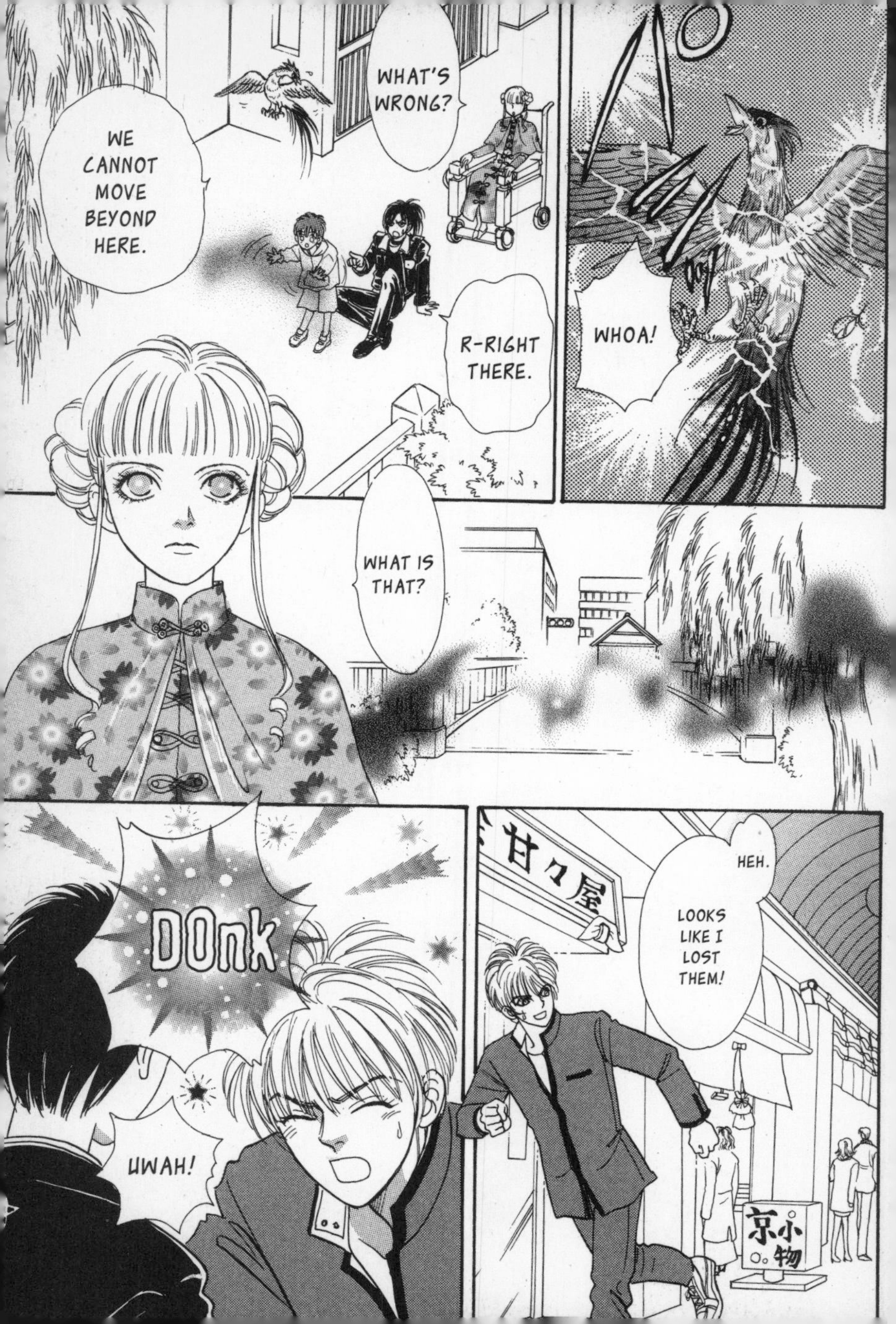
WHOA!
WHAT'S WRONG?
WE CANNOT MOVE BEYOND HERE.
R-RIGHT THERE.
WHAT IS THAT?
甘々屋
HEH.
LOOKS LIKE I LOST THEM!
京小物
DOnk
UWAH!

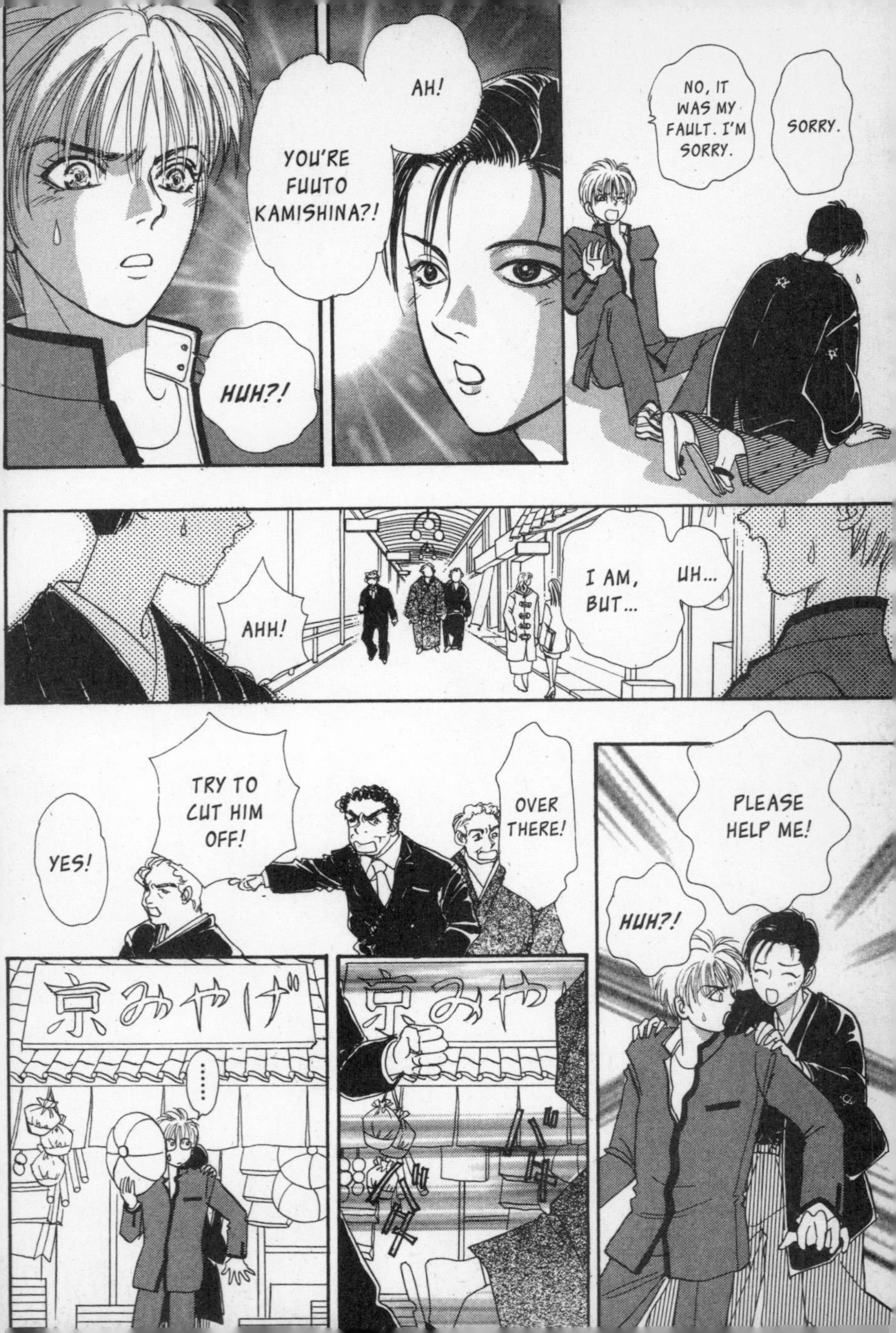
SORRY.
NO, IT WAS MY FAULT. I'M SORRY.
AH!
YOU'RE FUUTO KAMISHINA?!
HUH?!
UH...
I AM, BUT...
AHH!
PLEASE HELP ME!
HUH?!
OVER THERE!
TRY TO CUT HIM OFF!
YES!
京みや
京みやげ
......

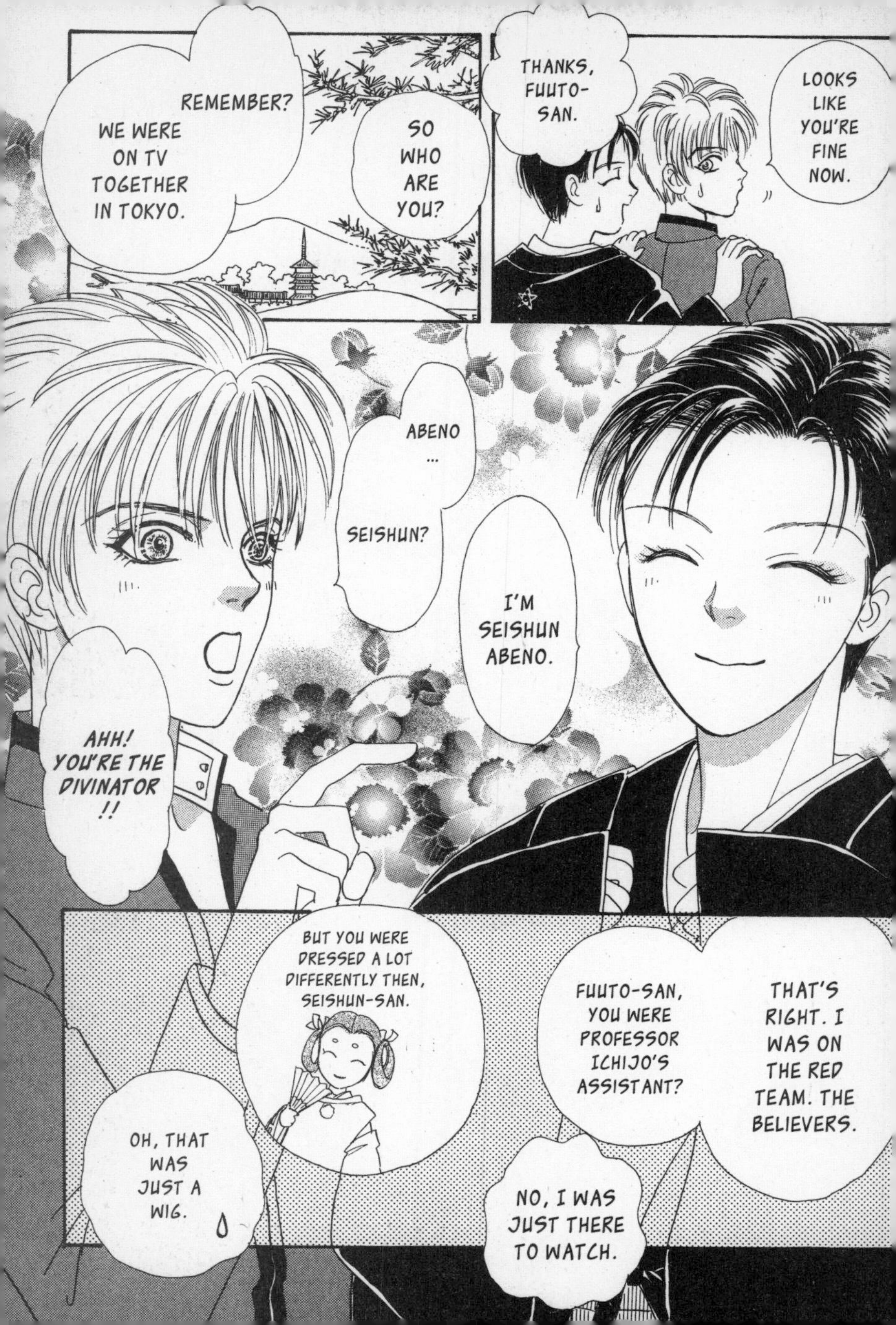
LOOKS LIKE YOU'RE FINE NOW.
THANKS, FUUTO-SAN.
SO WHO ARE YOU?
REMEMBER? WE WERE ON TV TOGETHER IN TOKYO.
I'M SEISHUN ABENO.
ABENO ... SEISHUN?
AHH! YOU'RE THE DIVINATOR !!
THAT'S RIGHT. I WAS ON THE RED TEAM. THE BELIEVERS.
FUUTO-SAN, YOU WERE PROFESSOR ICHIJO'S ASSISTANT?
NO, I WAS JUST THERE TO WATCH.
BUT YOU WERE DRESSED A LOT DIFFERENTLY THEN, SEISHUN-SAN.
OH, THAT WAS JUST A WIG.

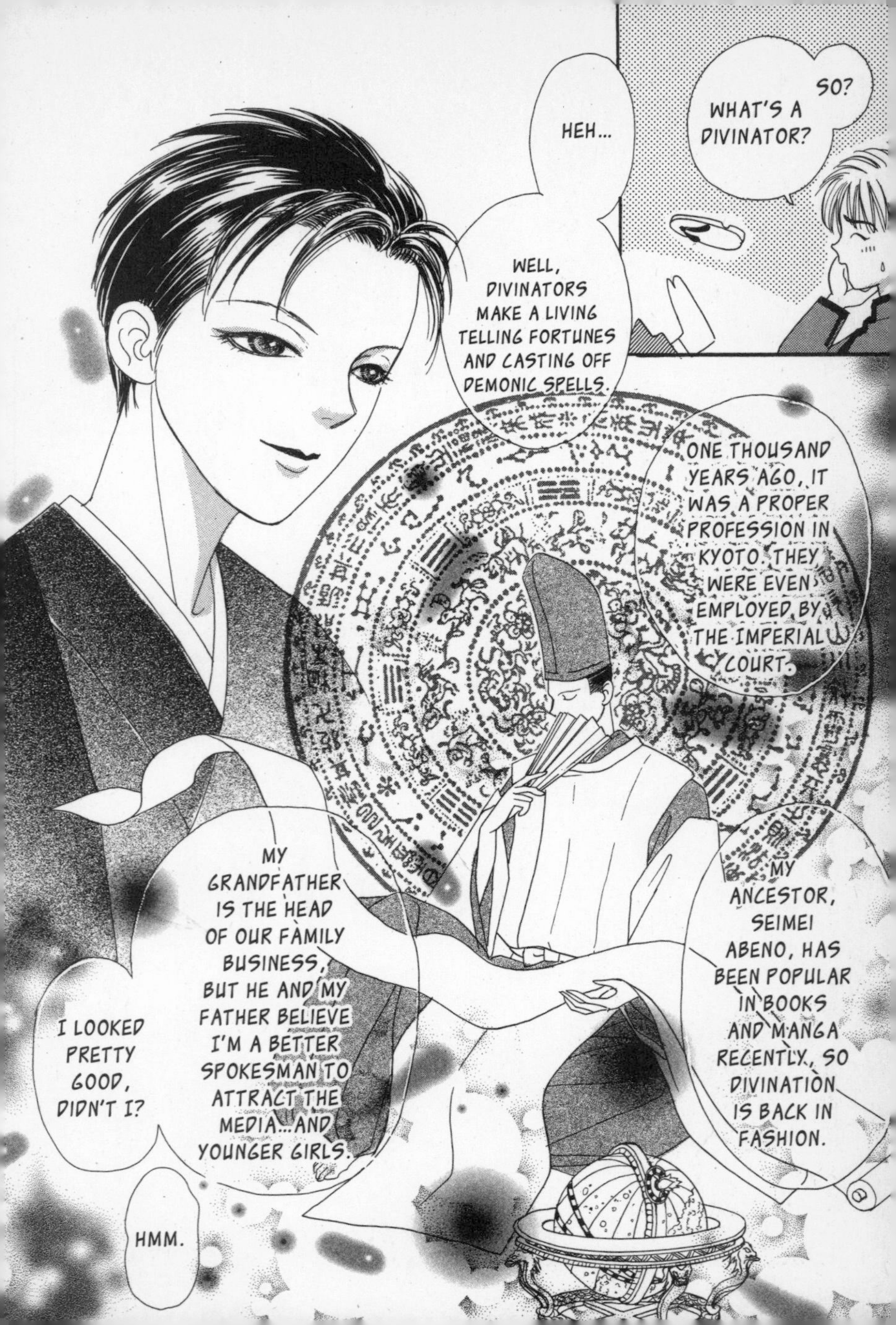
SO? WHAT'S A DIVINATOR?
HEH...
WELL, DIVINATORS MAKE A LIVING TELLING FORTUNES AND CASTING OFF DEMONIC SPELLS.
ONE THOUSAND YEARS AGO, IT WAS A PROPER PROFESSION IN KYOTO. THEY WERE EVEN EMPLOYED BY THE IMPERIAL COURT.
MY ANCESTOR, SEIMEI ABENO, HAS BEEN POPULAR IN BOOKS AND MANGA RECENTLY, SO DIVINATION IS BACK IN FASHION.
MY GRANDFATHER IS THE HEAD OF OUR FAMILY BUSINESS, BUT HE AND MY FATHER BELIEVE I'M A BETTER SPOKESMAN TO ATTRACT THE MEDIA...AND YOUNGER GIRLS.
I LOOKED PRETTY GOOD, DIDN'T I?
HMM.

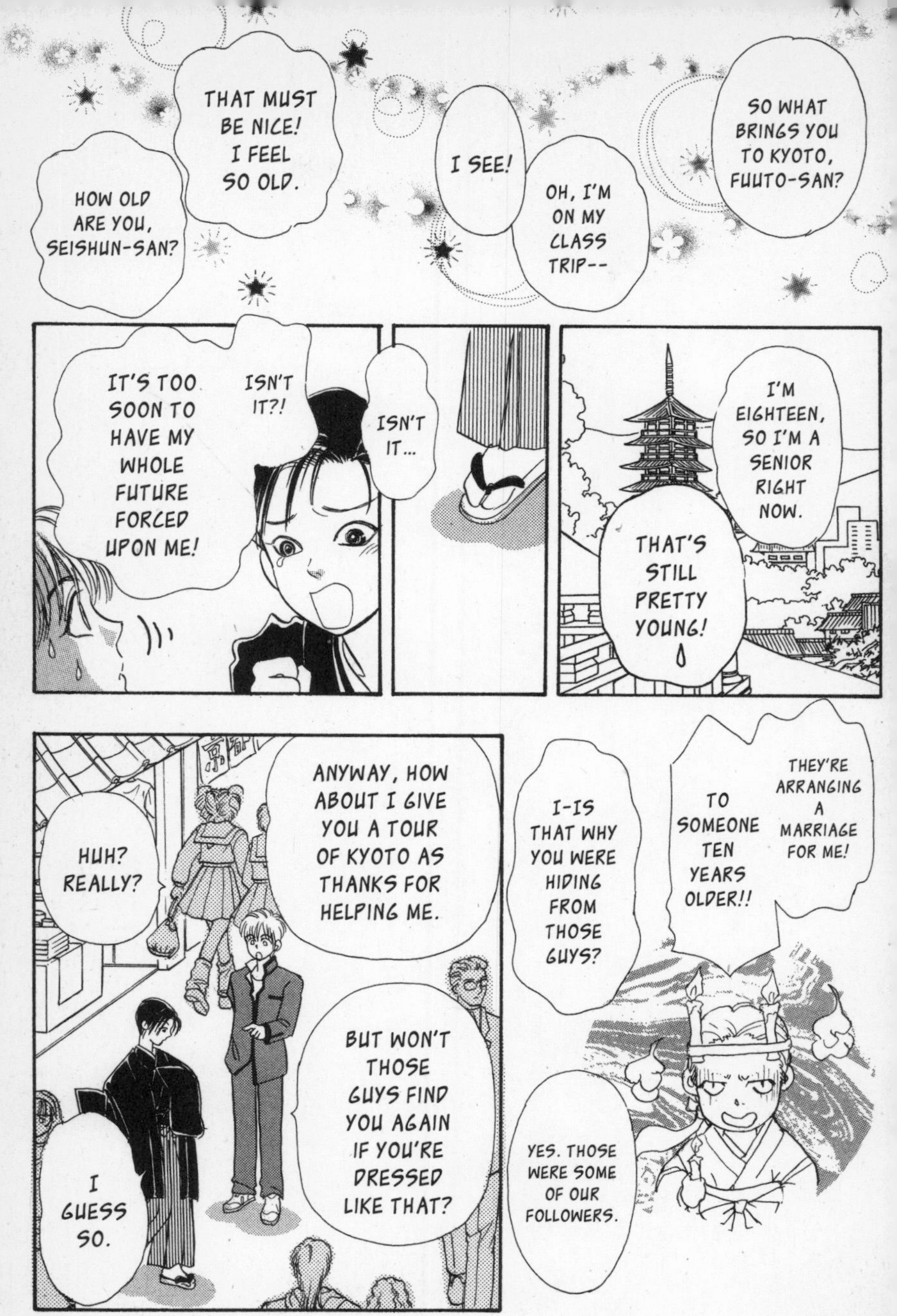
SO WHAT BRINGS YOU TO KYOTO, FUUTO-SAN?
OH, I'M ON MY CLASS TRIP--
I SEE!
THAT MUST BE NICE! I FEEL SO OLD.
HOW OLD ARE YOU, SEISHUN-SAN?
I'M EIGHTEEN, SO I'M A SENIOR RIGHT NOW.
THAT'S STILL PRETTY YOUNG!
ISN'T IT...
ISN'T IT?!
IT'S TOO SOON TO HAVE MY WHOLE FUTURE FORCED UPON ME!
THEY'RE ARRANGING A MARRIAGE FOR ME!
TO SOMEONE TEN YEARS OLDER!!
I-IS THAT WHY YOU WERE HIDING FROM THOSE GUYS?
YES. THOSE WERE SOME OF OUR FOLLOWERS.
ANYWAY, HOW ABOUT I GIVE YOU A TOUR OF KYOTO AS THANKS FOR HELPING ME.
HUH? REALLY?
BUT WON'T THOSE GUYS FIND YOU AGAIN IF YOU'RE DRESSED LIKE THAT?
I GUESS SO.

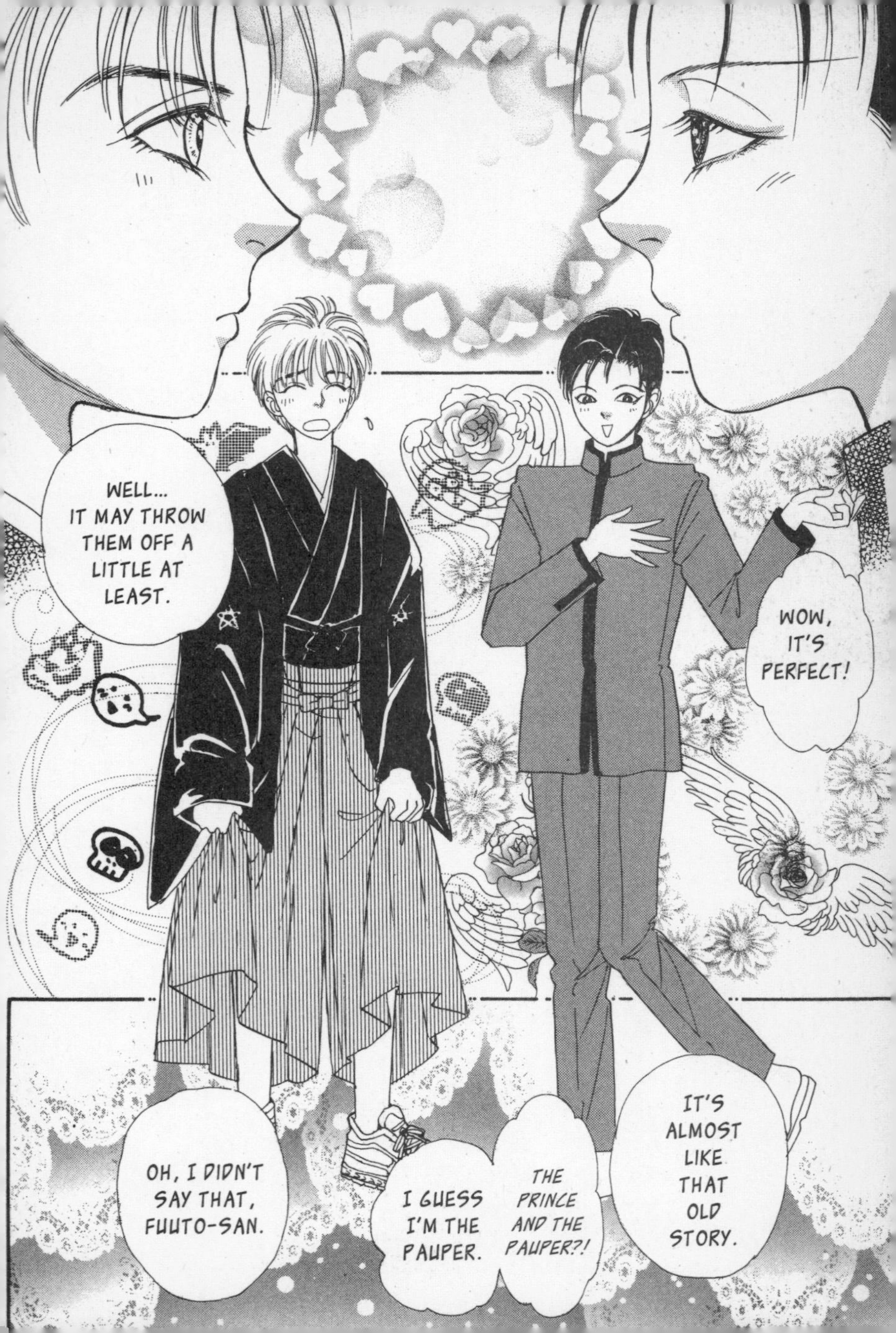
WOW, IT'S PERFECT!
WELL... IT MAY THROW THEM OFF A LITTLE AT LEAST.
IT'S ALMOST LIKE THAT OLD STORY.
THE PRINCE AND THE PAUPER?!
I GUESS I'M THE PAUPER.
OH, I DIDN'T SAY THAT, FUUTO-SAN.

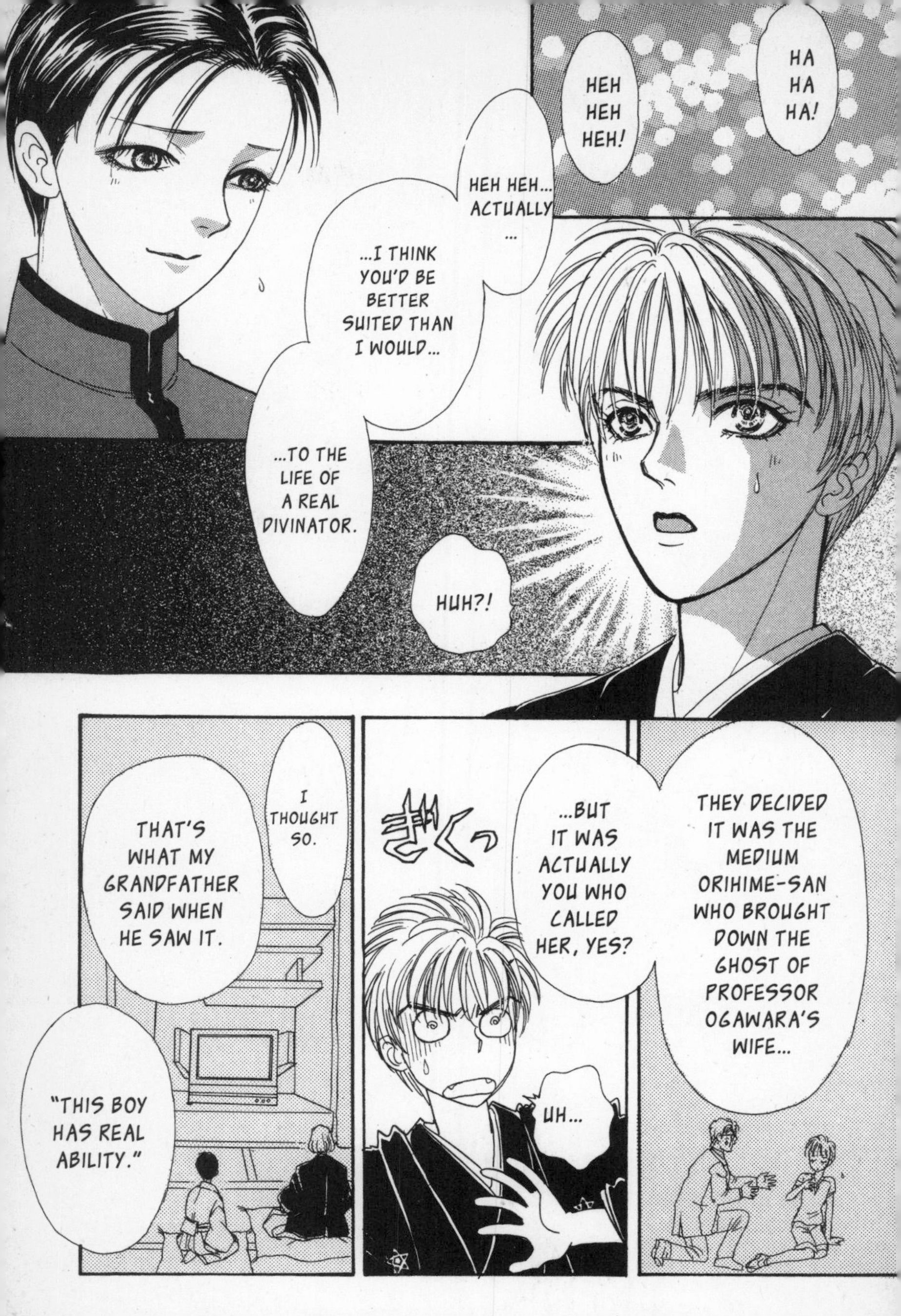
HA HA HA!
HEH HEH HEH!
HEH HEH... ACTUALLY ...
...I THINK YOU'D BE BETTER SUITED THAN I WOULD...
...TO THE LIFE OF A REAL DIVINATOR.
HUH?!
THEY DECIDED IT WAS THE MEDIUM ORIHIME-SAN WHO BROUGHT DOWN THE GHOST OF PROFESSOR OGAWARA'S WIFE...
...BUT IT WAS ACTUALLY YOU WHO CALLED HER, YES?
ぎくっ
UH...
I THOUGHT SO.
THAT'S WHAT MY GRANDFATHER SAID WHEN HE SAW IT.
"THIS BOY HAS REAL ABILITY."

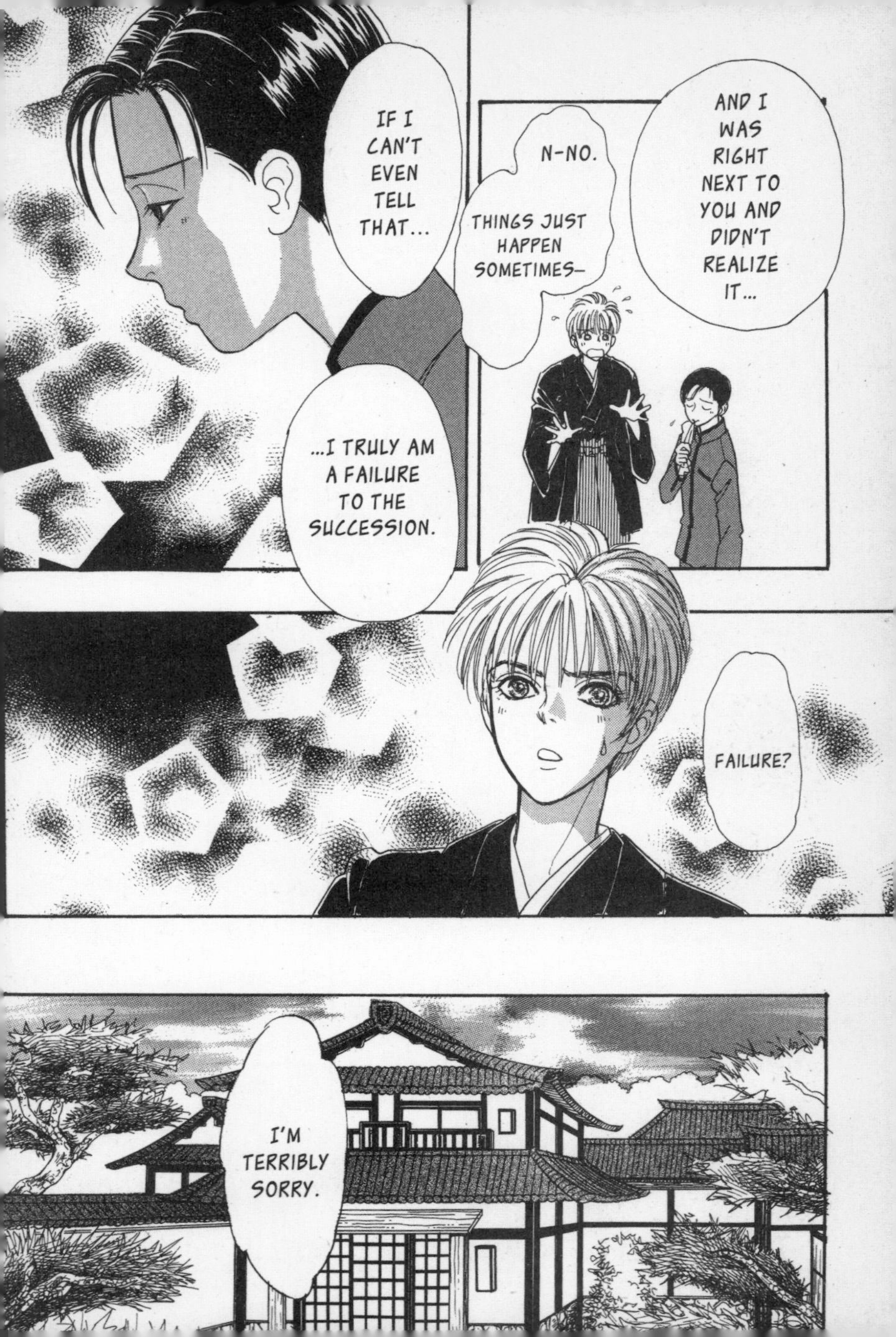
AND I WAS RIGHT NEXT TO YOU AND DIDN'T REALIZE IT...
N-NO.
THINGS JUST HAPPEN SOMETIMES—
IF I CAN'T EVEN TELL THAT...
...I TRULY AM A FAILURE TO THE SUCCESSION.
FAILURE?
I'M TERRIBLY SORRY.

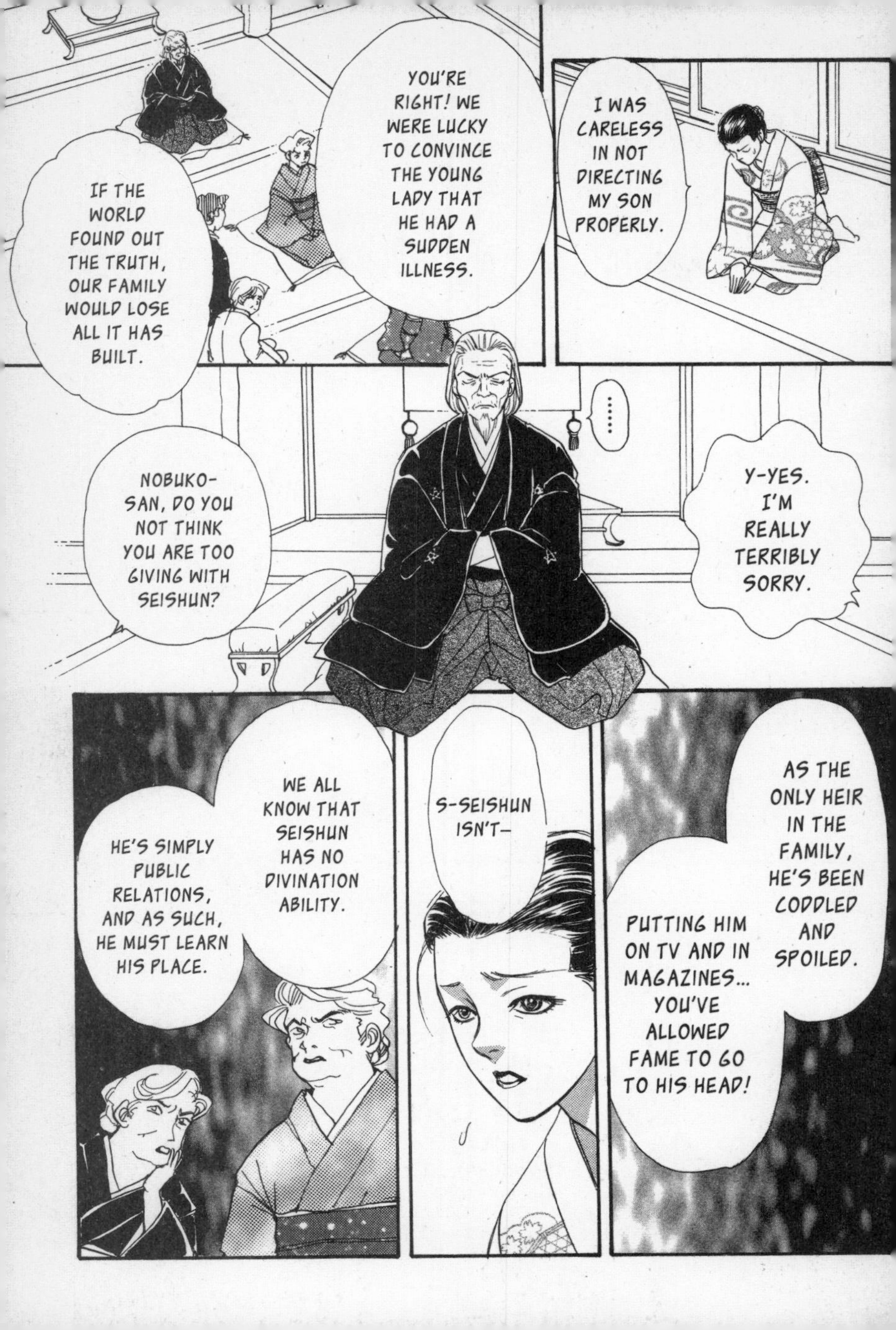
I WAS CARELESS IN NOT DIRECTING MY SON PROPERLY.
YOU'RE RIGHT! WE WERE LUCKY TO CONVINCE THE YOUNG LADY THAT HE HAD A SUDDEN ILLNESS.
IF THE WORLD FOUND OUT THE TRUTH, OUR FAMILY WOULD LOSE ALL IT HAS BUILT.
......
NOBUKO-SAN, DO YOU NOT THINK YOU ARE TOO GIVING WITH SEISHUN?
Y-YES. I'M REALLY TERRIBLY SORRY.
AS THE ONLY HEIR IN THE FAMILY, HE'S BEEN CODDLED AND SPOILED.
PUTTING HIM ON TV AND IN MAGAZINES... YOU'VE ALLOWED FAME TO GO TO HIS HEAD!
S-SEISHUN ISN'T—
WE ALL KNOW THAT SEISHUN HAS NO DIVINATION ABILITY.
HE'S SIMPLY PUBLIC RELATIONS, AND AS SUCH, HE MUST LEARN HIS PLACE.

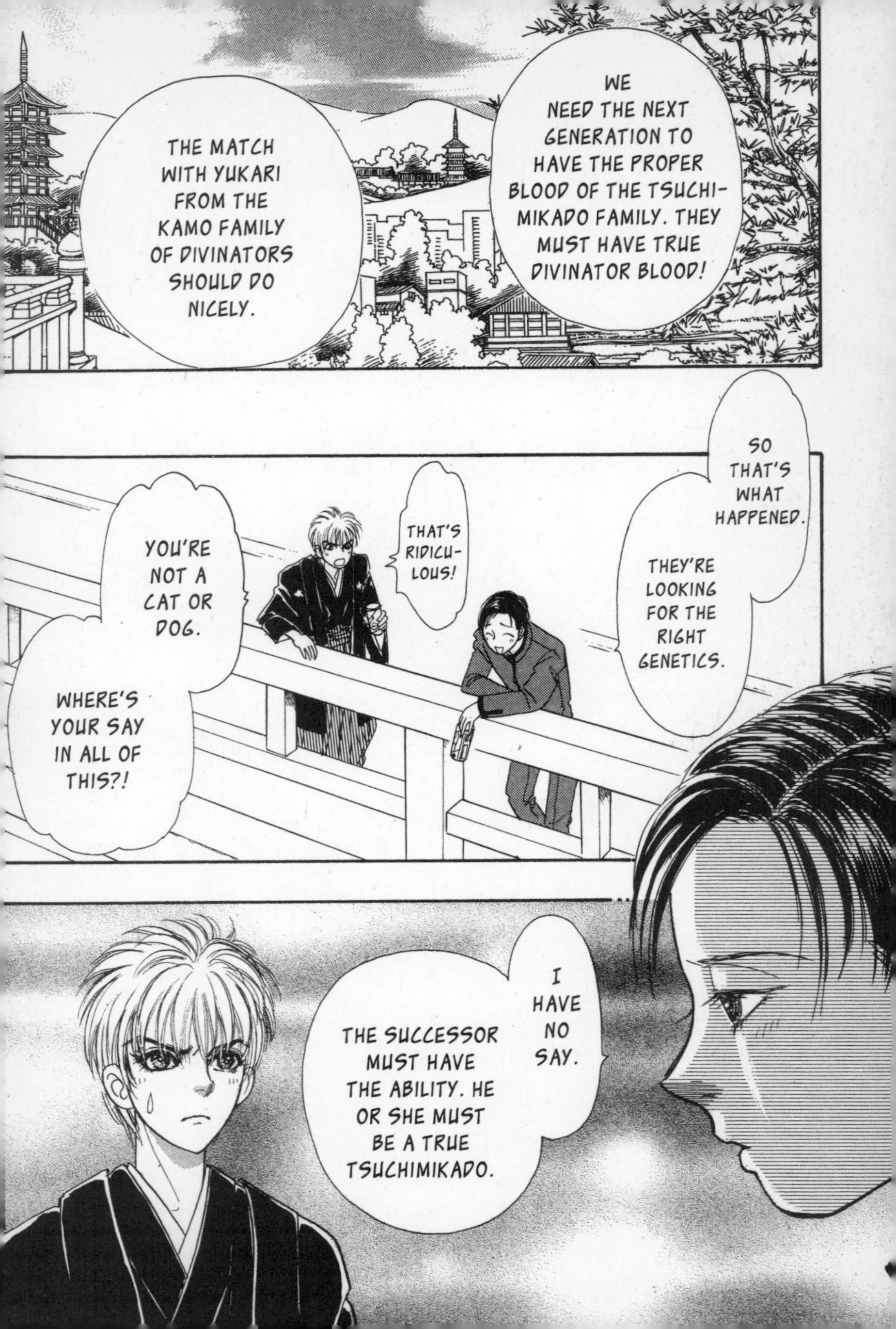
WE NEED THE NEXT GENERATION TO HAVE THE PROPER BLOOD OF THE TSUCHI-MIKADO FAMILY. THEY MUST HAVE TRUE DIVINATOR BLOOD!
THE MATCH WITH YUKARI FROM THE KAMO FAMILY OF DIVINATORS SHOULD DO NICELY.
SO THAT'S WHAT HAPPENED.
THEY'RE LOOKING FOR THE RIGHT GENETICS.
THAT'S RIDICU-LOUS!
YOU'RE NOT A CAT OR DOG.
WHERE'S YOUR SAY IN ALL OF THIS?!
I HAVE NO SAY.
THE SUCCESSOR MUST HAVE THE ABILITY. HE OR SHE MUST BE A TRUE TSUCHIMIKADO.

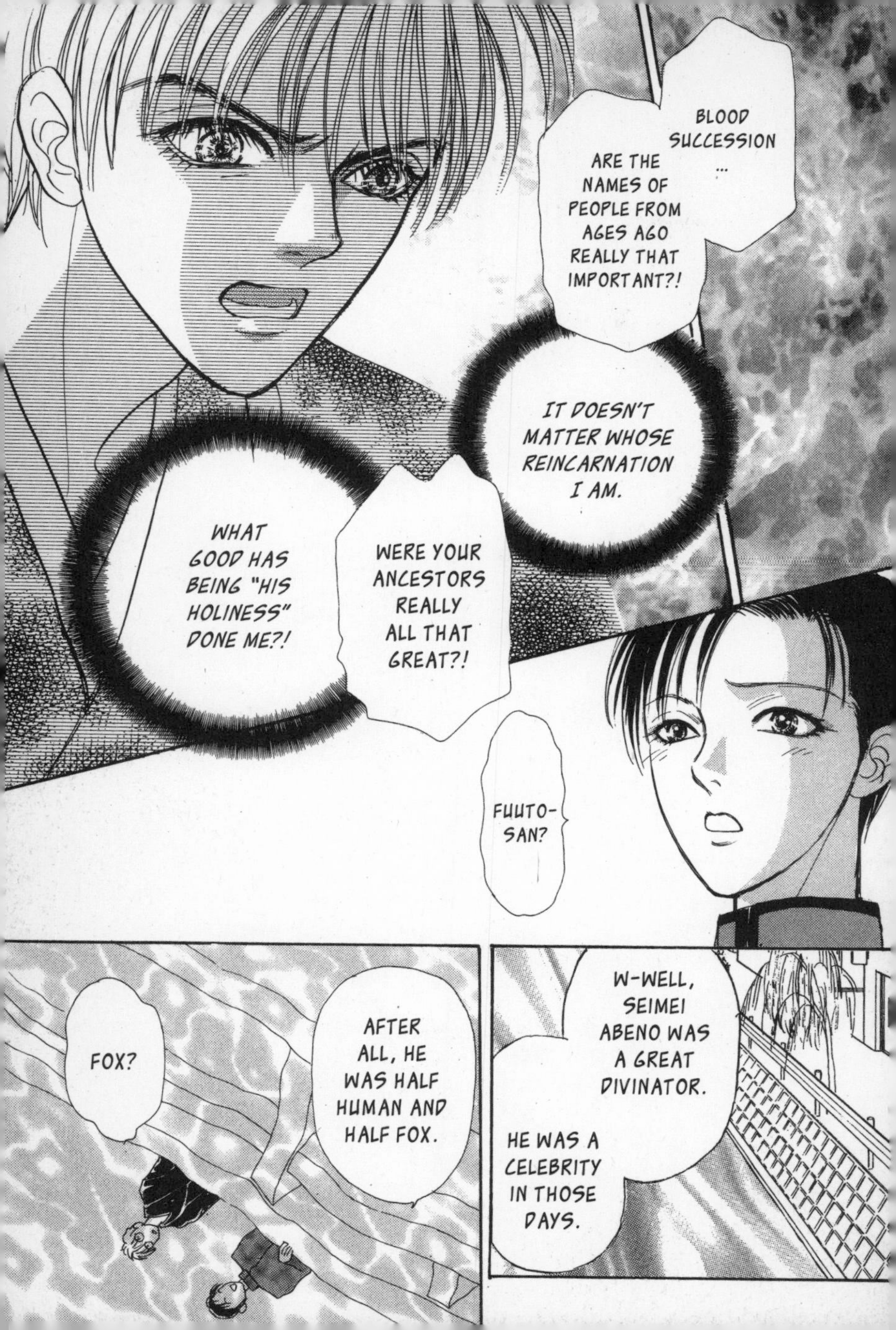
BLOOD SUCCESSION ...
ARE THE NAMES OF PEOPLE FROM AGES AGO REALLY THAT IMPORTANT?!
IT DOESN'T MATTER WHOSE REINCARNATION I AM.
WERE YOUR ANCESTORS REALLY ALL THAT GREAT?!
WHAT GOOD HAS BEING "HIS HOLINESS" DONE ME?!
FUUTO-SAN?
W-WELL, SEIMEI ABENO WAS A GREAT DIVINATOR.
HE WAS A CELEBRITY IN THOSE DAYS.
AFTER ALL, HE WAS HALF HUMAN AND HALF FOX.
FOX?

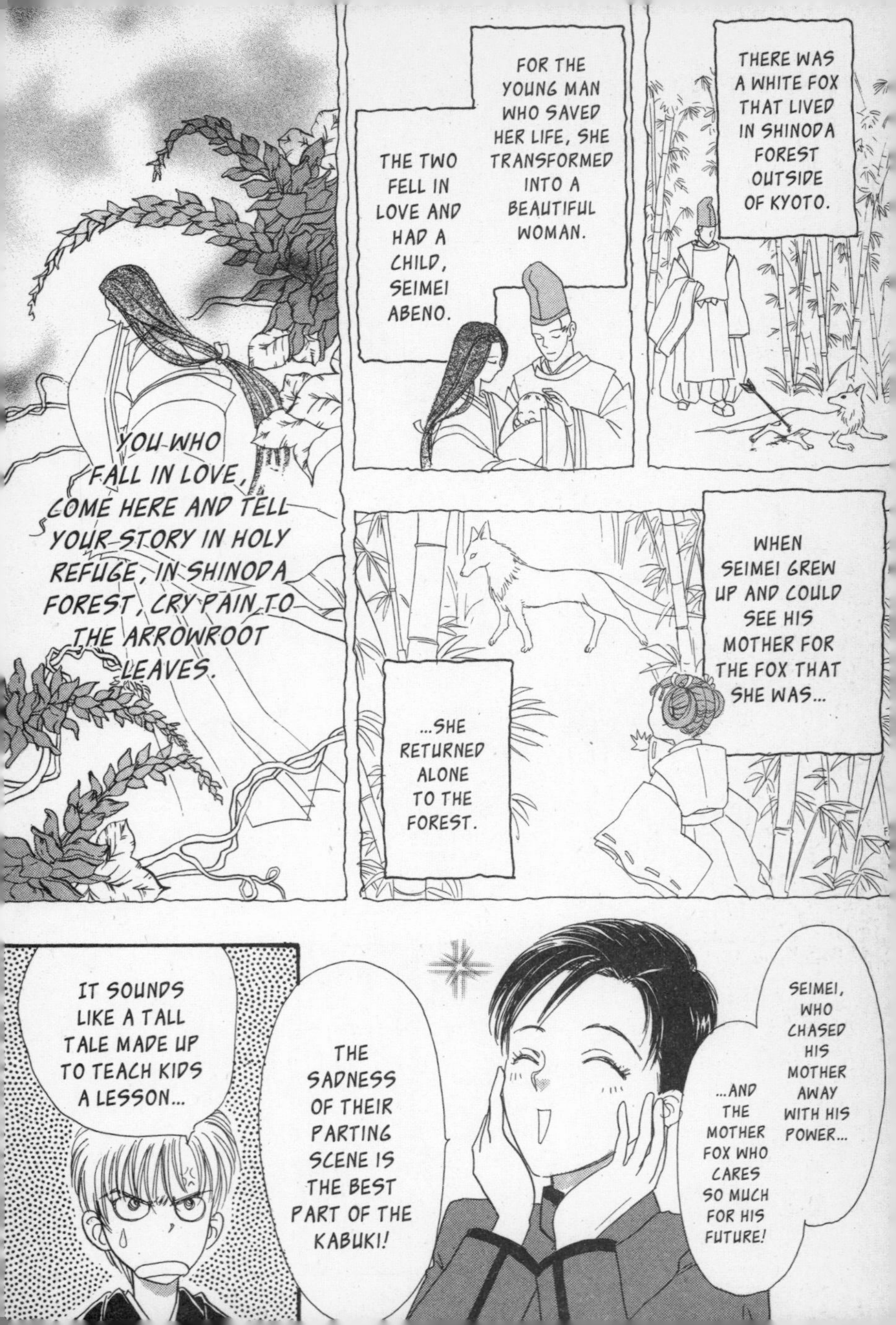
THERE WAS A WHITE FOX THAT LIVED IN SHINODA FOREST OUTSIDE OF KYOTO.
FOR THE YOUNG MAN WHO SAVED HER LIFE, SHE TRANSFORMED INTO A BEAUTIFUL WOMAN.
THE TWO FELL IN LOVE AND HAD A CHILD, SEIMEI ABENO.
WHEN SEIMEI GREW UP AND COULD SEE HIS MOTHER FOR THE FOX THAT SHE WAS...
...SHE RETURNED ALONE TO THE FOREST.
YOU WHO FALL IN LOVE, COME HERE AND TELL YOUR STORY IN HOLY REFUGE, IN SHINODA FOREST, CRY PAIN TO THE ARROWROOT LEAVES.
SEIMEI, WHO CHASED HIS MOTHER AWAY WITH HIS POWER...
...AND THE MOTHER FOX WHO CARES SO MUCH FOR HIS FUTURE!
THE SADNESS OF THEIR PARTING SCENE IS THE BEST PART OF THE KABUKI!
IT SOUNDS LIKE A TALL TALE MADE UP TO TEACH KIDS A LESSON...

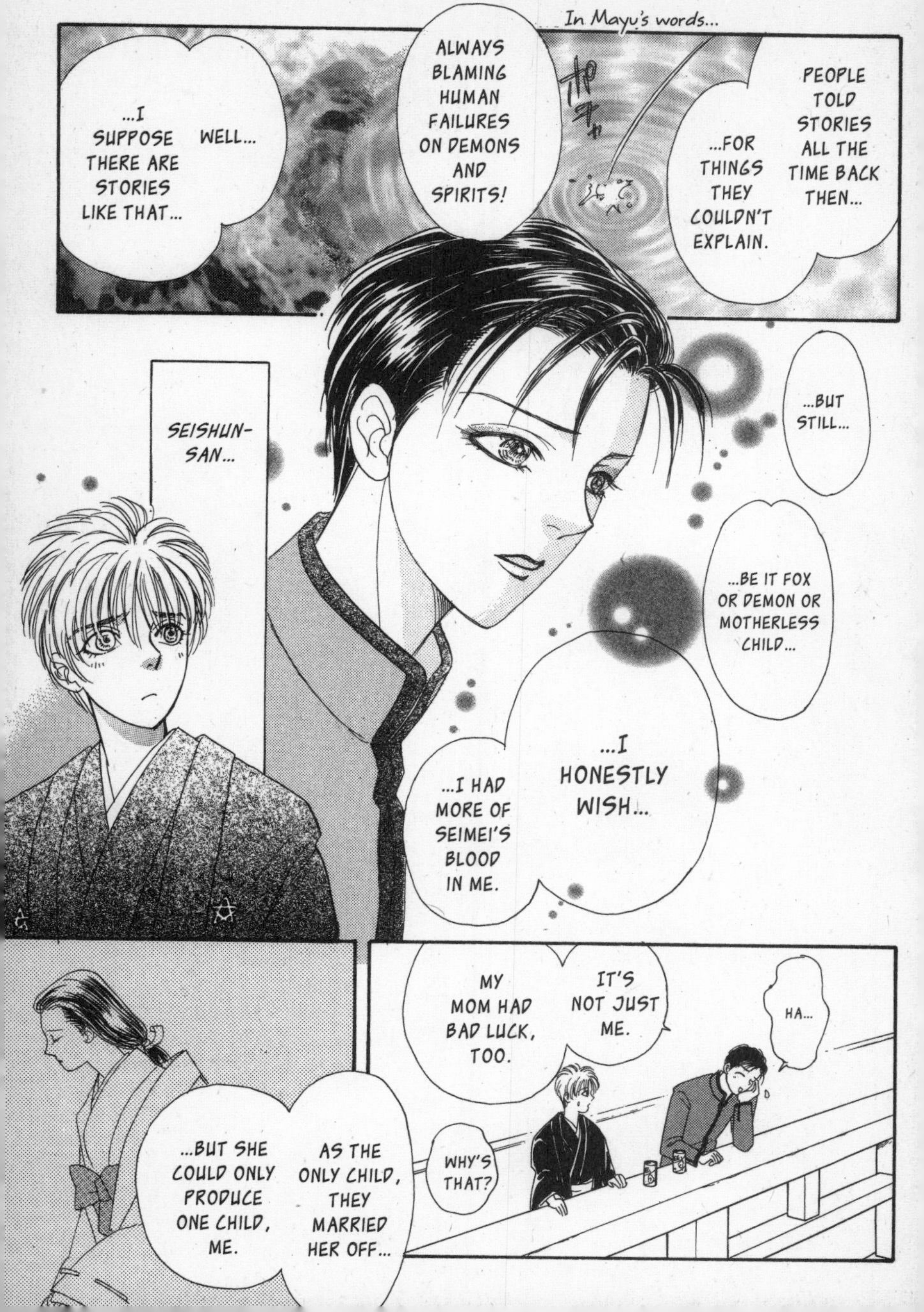
In Mayu's words...
PEOPLE TOLD STORIES ALL THE TIME BACK THEN...
...FOR THINGS THEY COULDN'T EXPLAIN.
ポチャ
ALWAYS BLAMING HUMAN FAILURES ON DEMONS AND SPIRITS!
WELL...
...I SUPPOSE THERE ARE STORIES LIKE THAT...
...BUT STILL...
...BE IT FOX OR DEMON OR MOTHERLESS CHILD...
...I HONESTLY WISH...
...I HAD MORE OF SEIMEI'S BLOOD IN ME.
SEISHUN-SAN...
HA...
IT'S NOT JUST ME.
MY MOM HAD BAD LUCK, TOO.
WHY'S THAT?
AS THE ONLY CHILD, THEY MARRIED HER OFF...
...BUT SHE COULD ONLY PRODUCE ONE CHILD, ME.

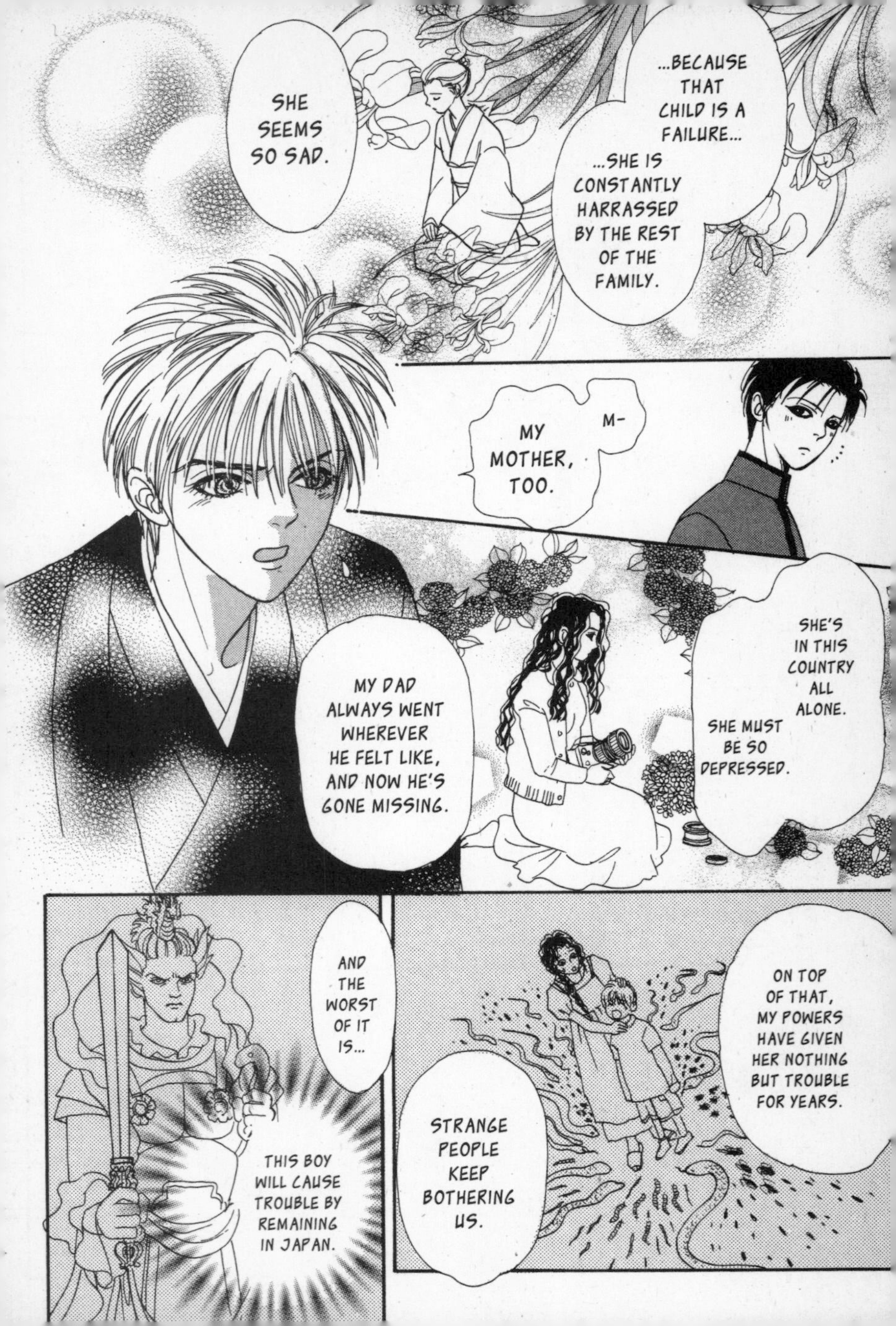
...BECAUSE THAT CHILD IS A FAILURE...
...SHE IS CONSTANTLY HARRASSED BY THE REST OF THE FAMILY.
SHE SEEMS SO SAD.
M-
MY MOTHER, TOO.
SHE'S IN THIS COUNTRY ALL ALONE.
SHE MUST BE SO DEPRESSED.
MY DAD ALWAYS WENT WHEREVER HE FELT LIKE, AND NOW HE'S GONE MISSING.
ON TOP OF THAT, MY POWERS HAVE GIVEN HER NOTHING BUT TROUBLE FOR YEARS.
STRANGE PEOPLE KEEP BOTHERING US.
AND THE WORST OF IT IS...
THIS BOY WILL CAUSE TROUBLE BY REMAINING IN JAPAN.

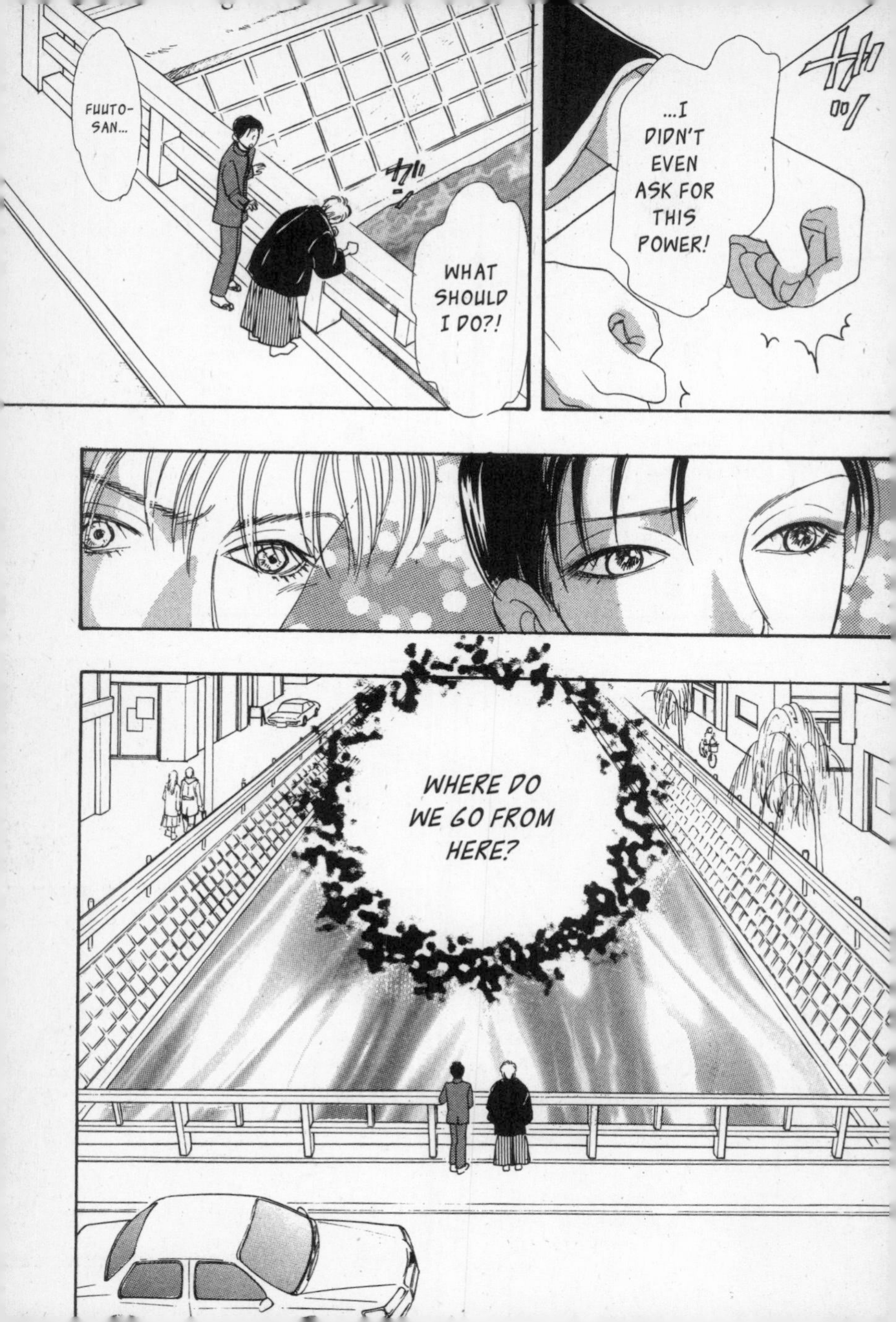
...I DIDN'T EVEN ASK FOR THIS POWER!
WHAT SHOULD I DO?!
FUUTO-SAN...
WHERE DO WE GO FROM HERE?

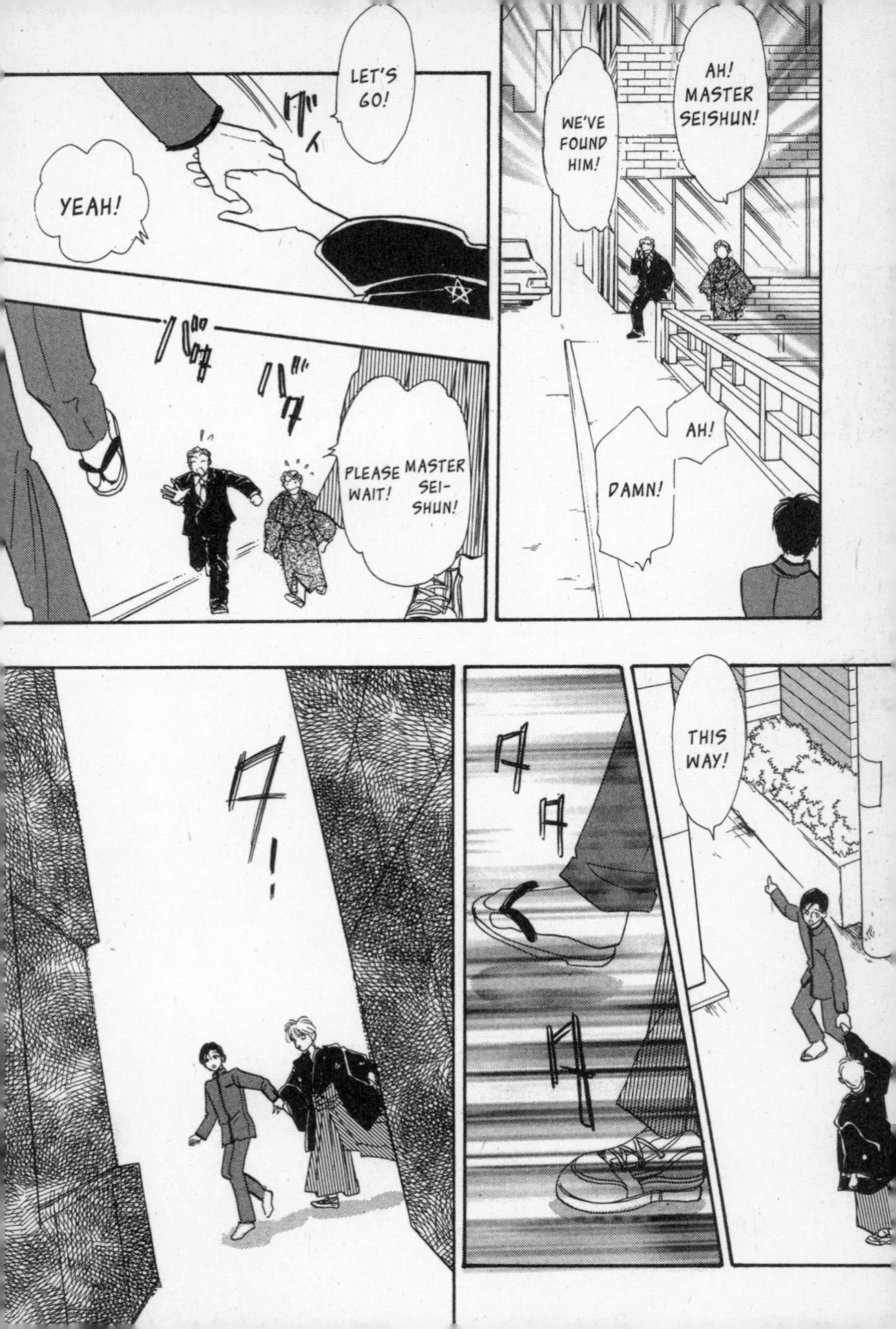
AH! MASTER SEISHUN!
WE'VE FOUND HIM!
AH!
DAMN!
LET'S GO!
YEAH!
PLEASE WAIT! MASTER SEI-SHUN!
THIS WAY!

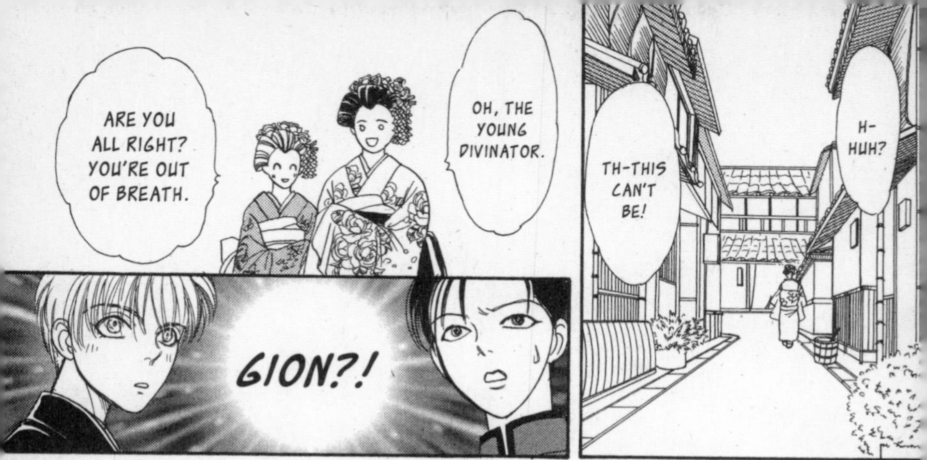
H-HUH?
TH-THIS CAN'T BE!
OH, THE YOUNG DIVINATOR.
ARE YOU ALL RIGHT? YOU'RE OUT OF BREATH.
GION?!

Gion is the historic Geisha district in Kyoto.

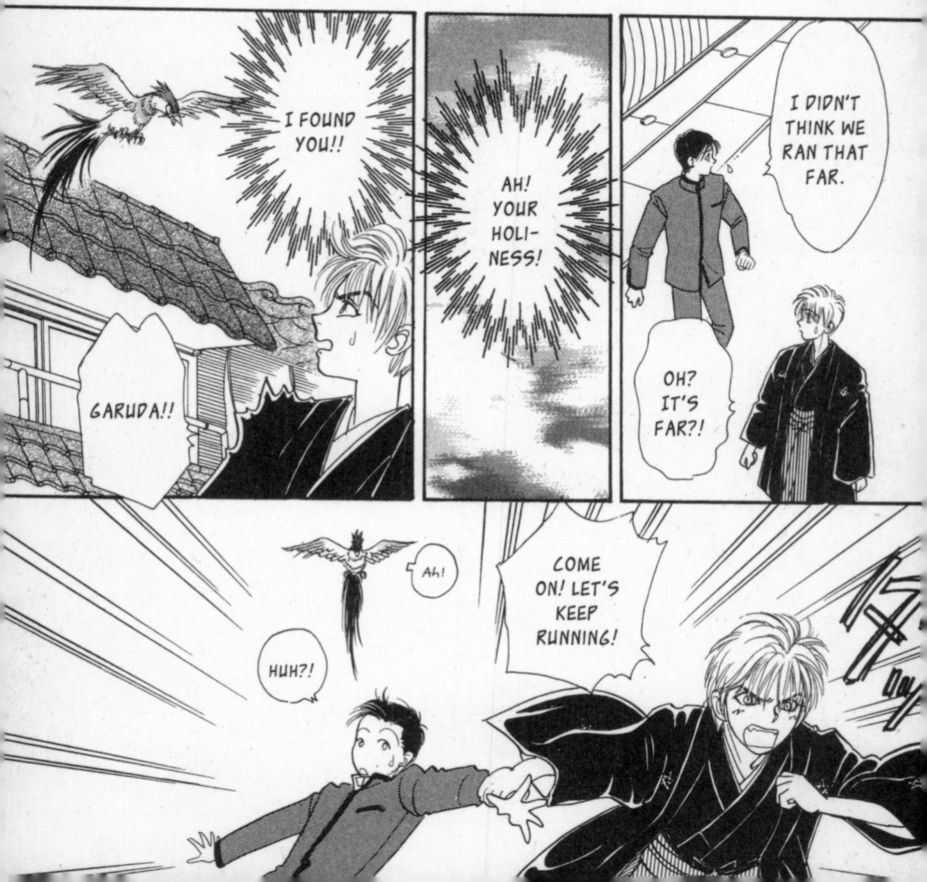
I DIDN'T THINK WE RAN THAT FAR.
OH? IT'S FAR?!
AH! YOUR HOLINESS!
I FOUND YOU!!
GARUDA!!
COME ON! LET'S KEEP RUNNING!
Ah!
HUH?!

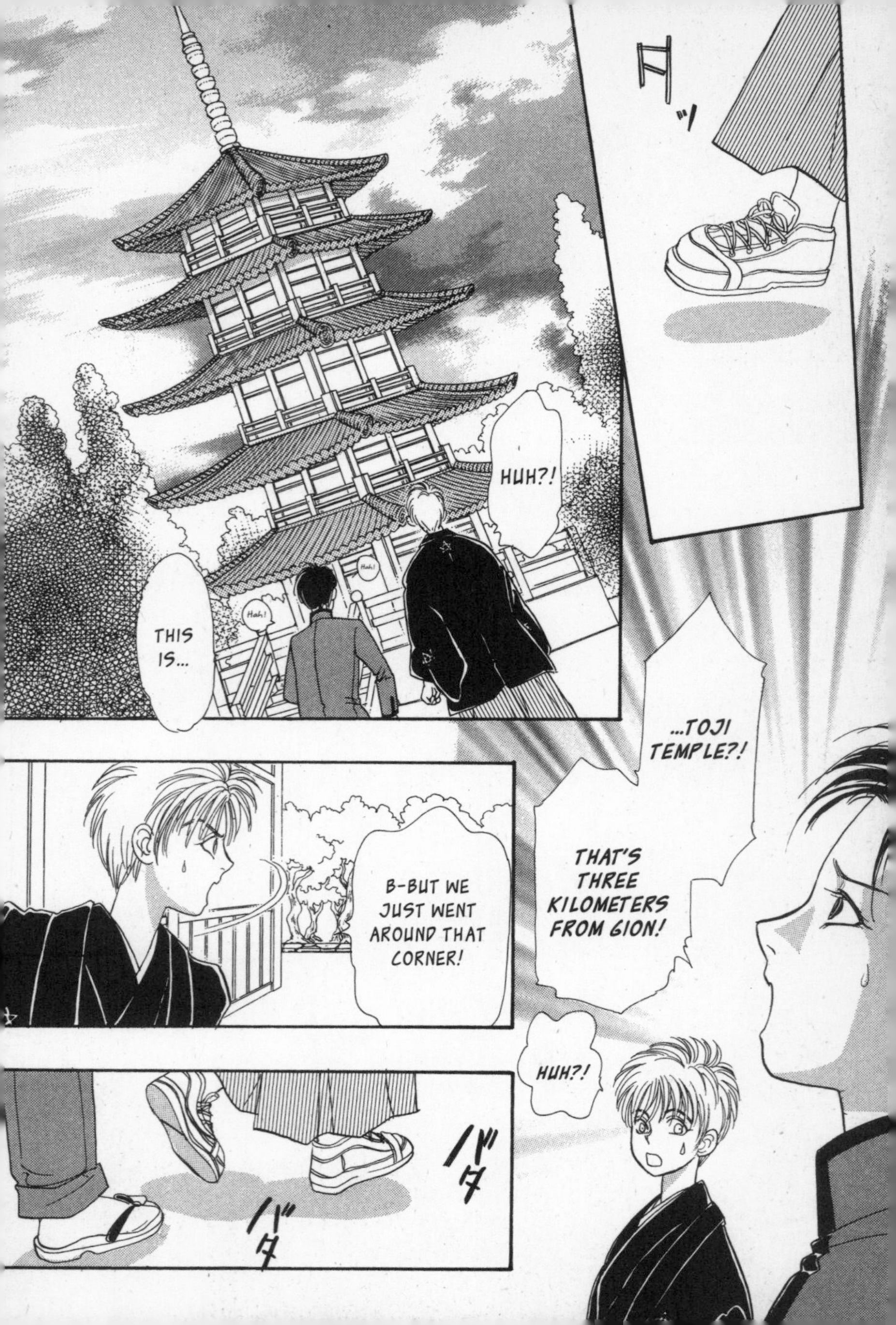
ガッ
HUH?!
Hah!
Hah!
THIS IS...
...TOJI TEMPLE?!
THAT'S THREE KILOMETERS FROM GION!
HUH?!
B-BUT WE JUST WENT AROUND THAT CORNER!
バタ
バタ

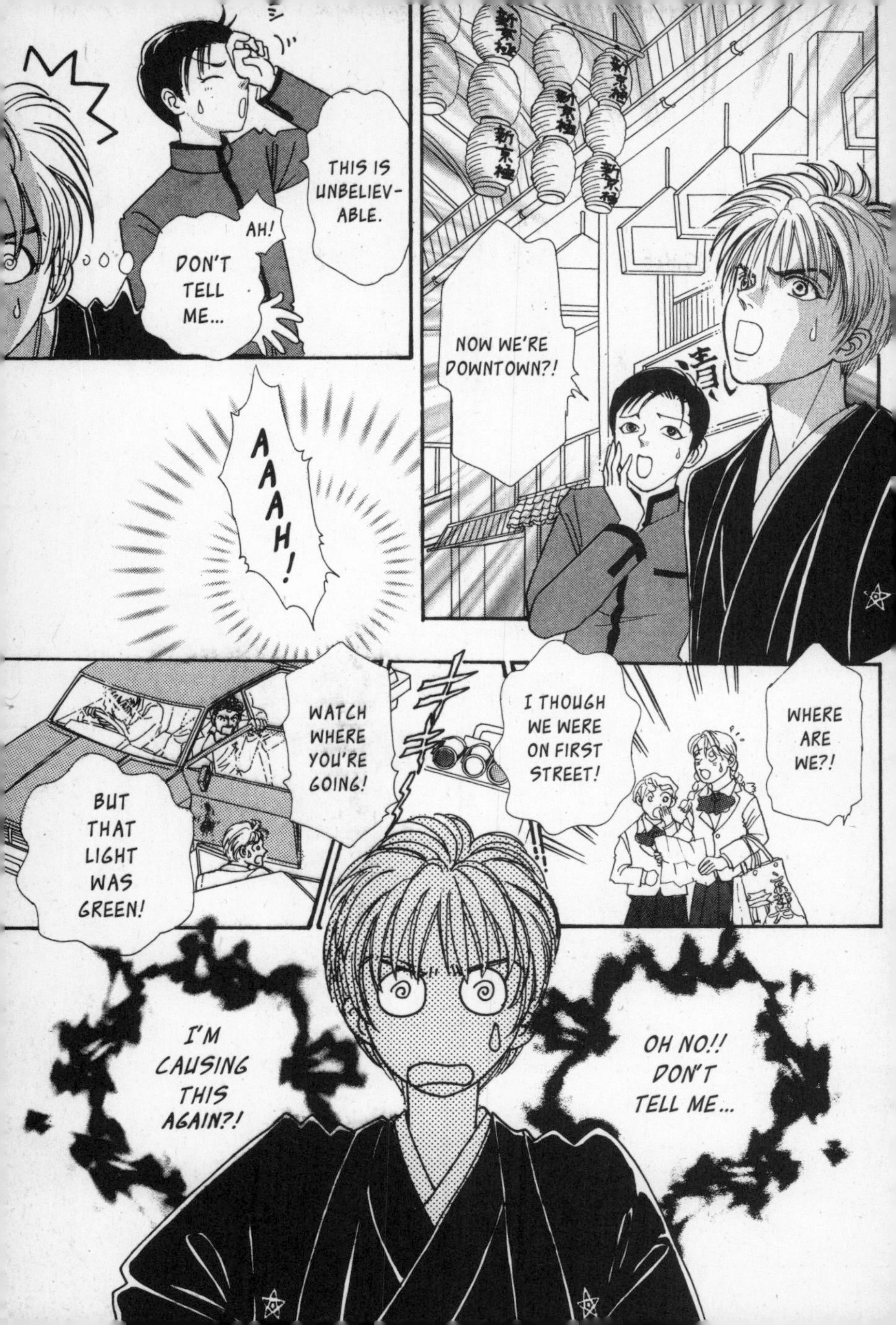
NOW WE'RE DOWNTOWN?!
THIS IS UNBELIEV-ABLE.
AH!
DON'T TELL ME...
AAAAH!
WHERE ARE WE?!
I THOUGH WE WERE ON FIRST STREET!
WATCH WHERE YOU'RE GOING!
BUT THAT LIGHT WAS GREEN!
OH NO!! DON'T TELL ME...
I'M CAUSING THIS AGAIN?!

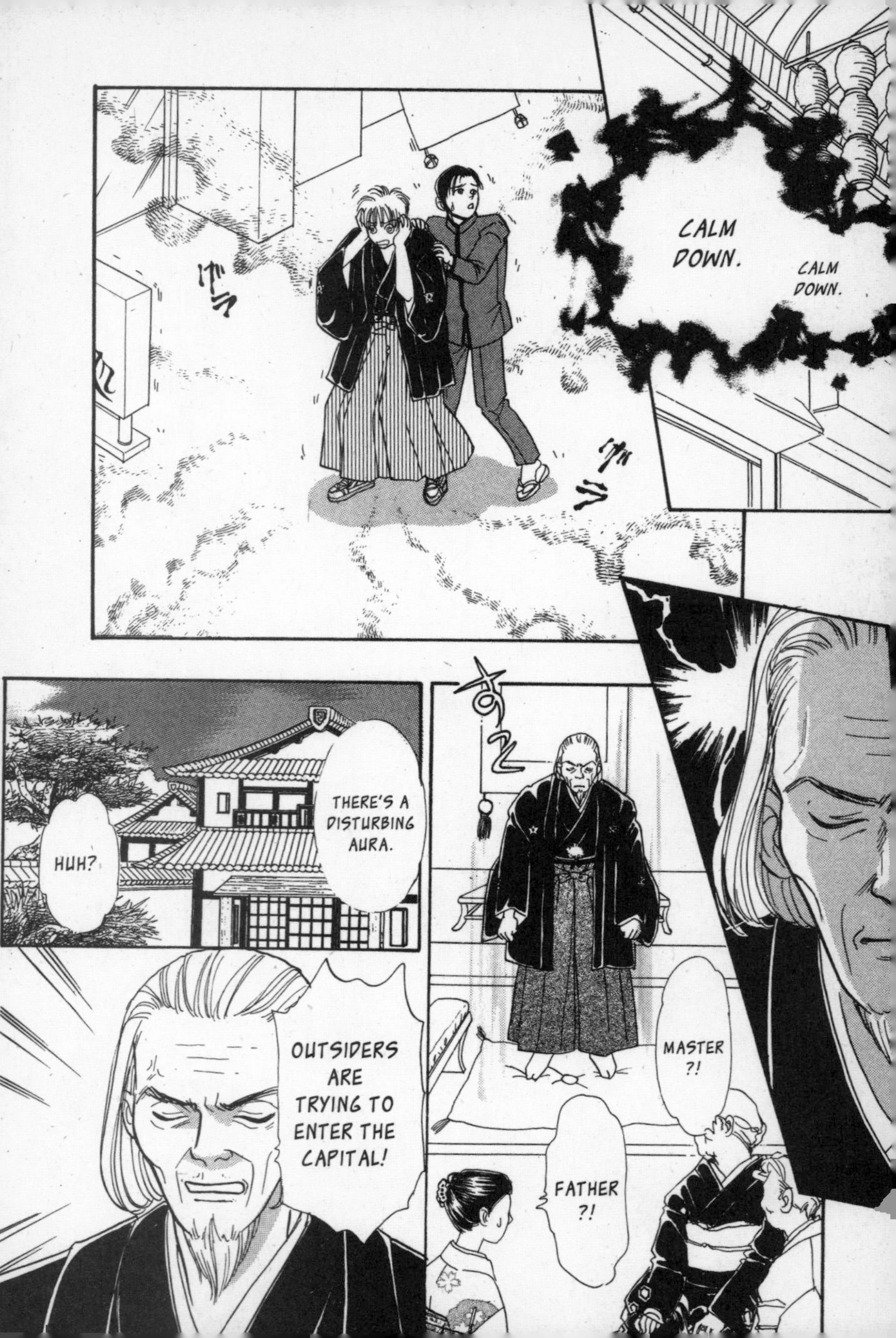
CALM DOWN.
CALM DOWN.
MASTER?!
FATHER?!
THERE'S A DISTURBING AURA.
HUH?
OUTSIDERS ARE TRYING TO ENTER THE CAPITAL!

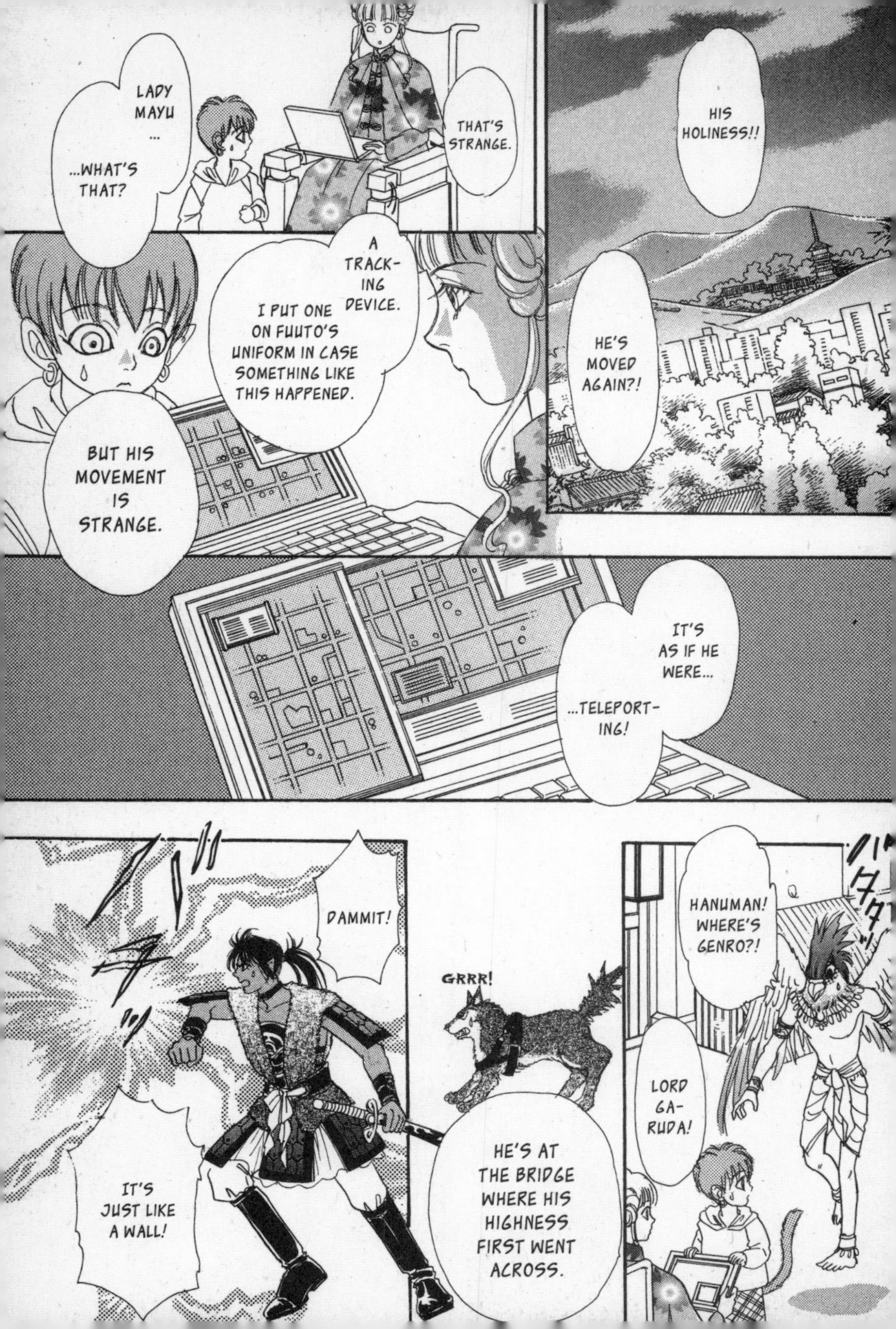
HIS HOLINESS!!
HE'S MOVED AGAIN?!
THAT'S STRANGE.
LADY MAYU ... ...WHAT'S THAT?
A TRACKING DEVICE.
I PUT ONE ON FUUTO'S UNIFORM IN CASE SOMETHING LIKE THIS HAPPENED.
BUT HIS MOVEMENT IS STRANGE.
IT'S AS IF HE WERE...
...TELEPORTING!
HANUMAN! WHERE'S GENRO?!
LORD GARUDA!
HE'S AT THE BRIDGE WHERE HIS HIGHNESS FIRST WENT ACROSS.
DAMMIT!
GRRR!
IT'S JUST LIKE A WALL!

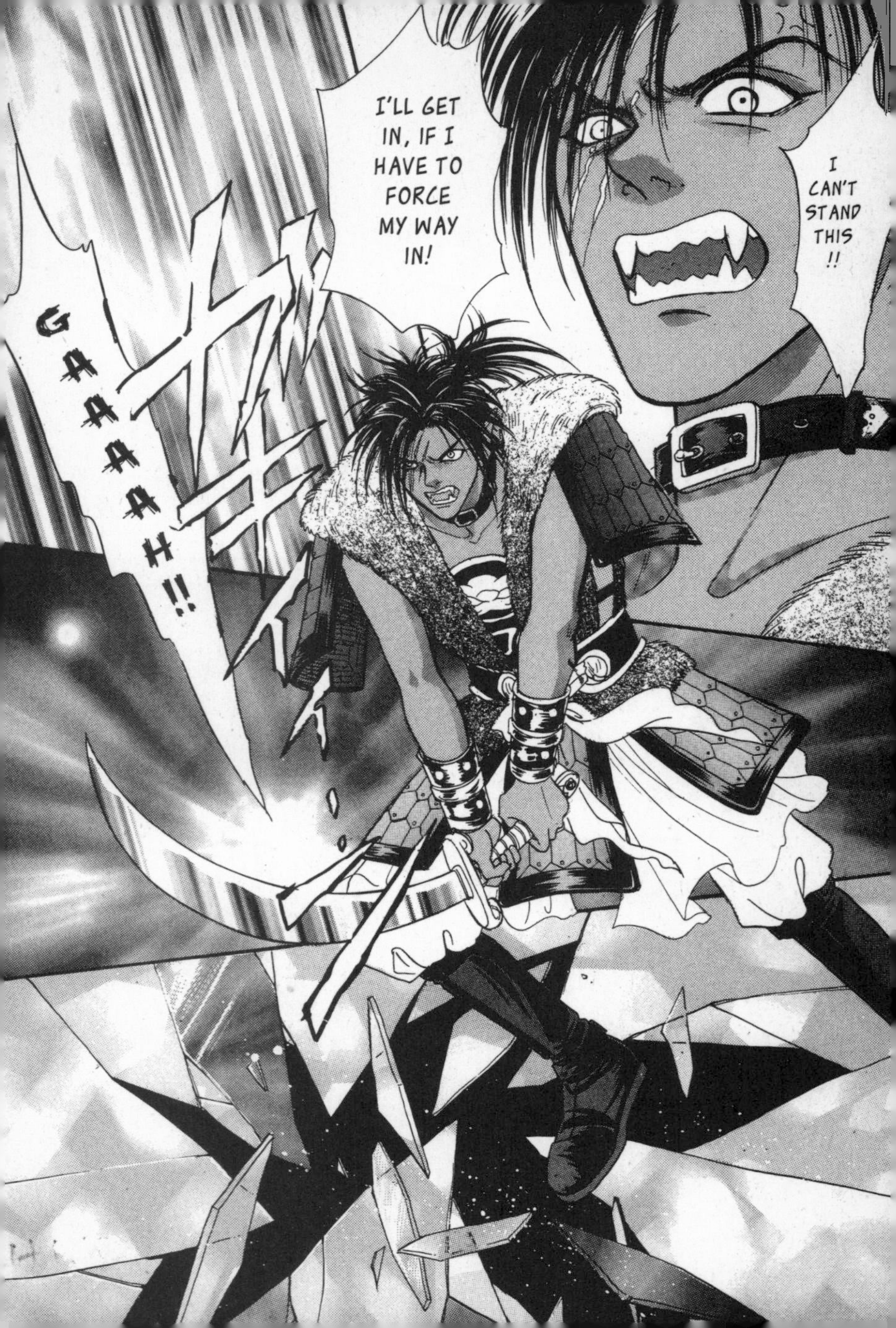
I CAN'T STAND THIS !!
I'LL GET IN, IF I HAVE TO FORCE MY WAY IN!
GAAAAAH!!

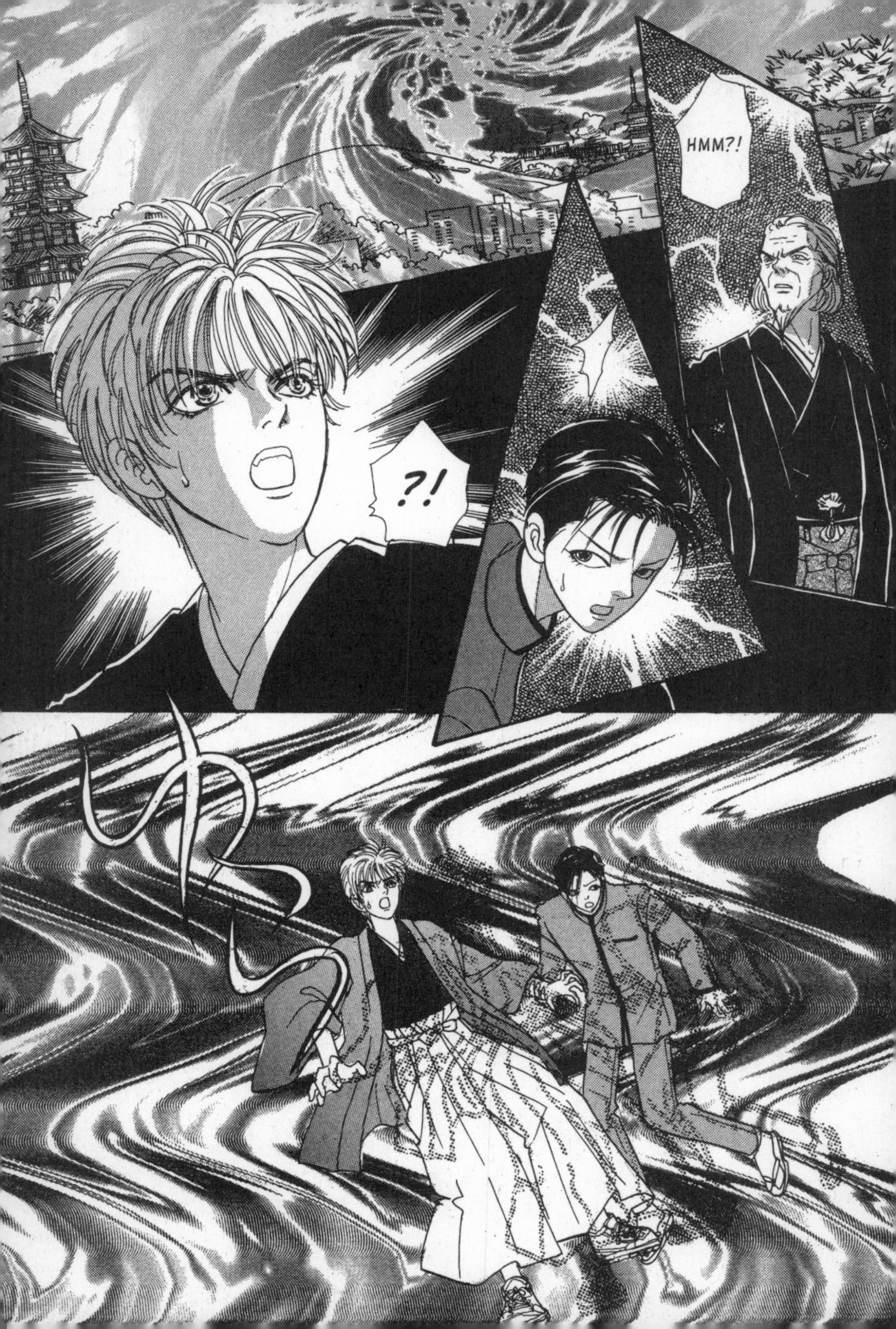
HMM?!
?!

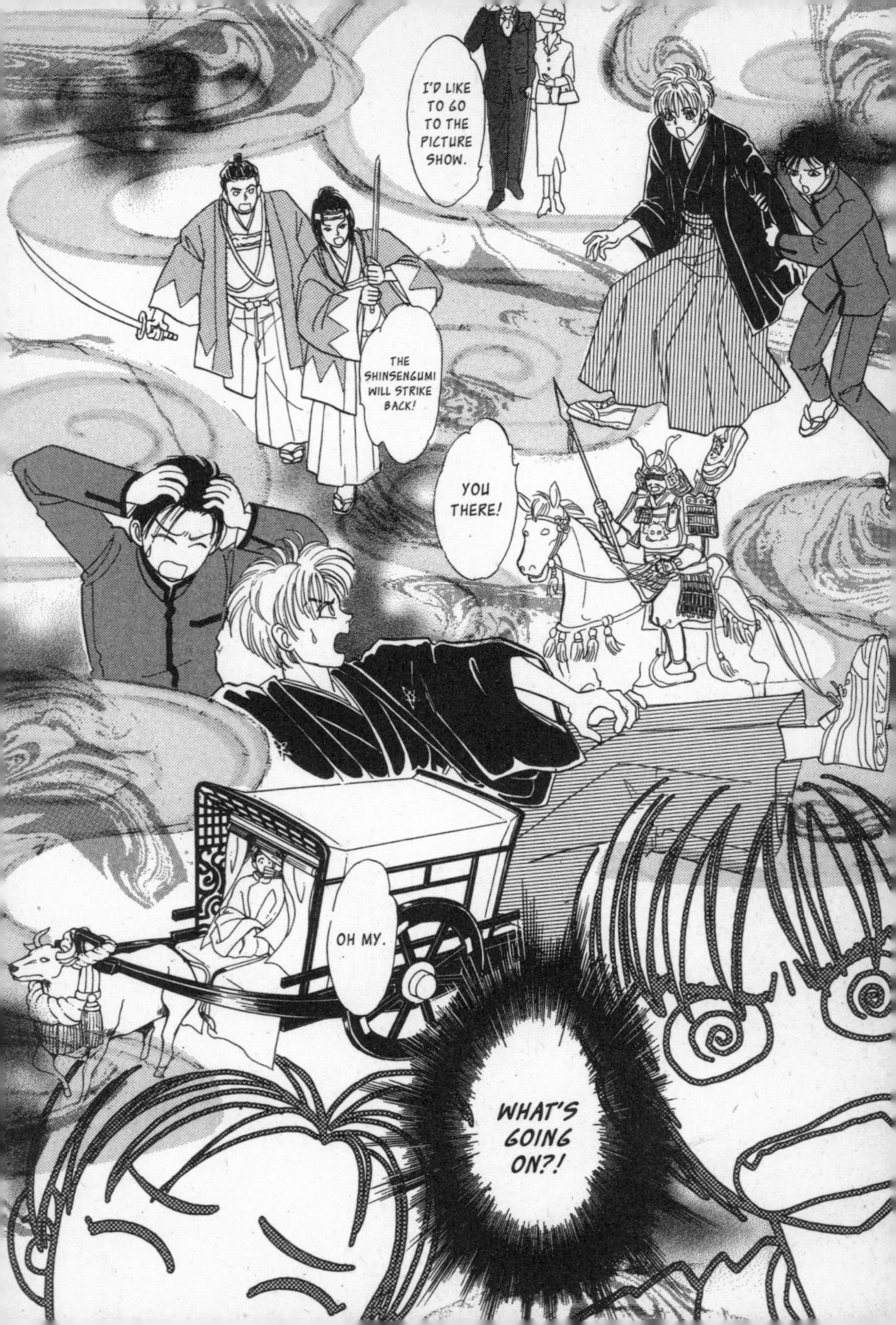
I'D LIKE TO GO TO THE PICTURE SHOW.
THE SHINSENGUMI WILL STRIKE BACK!
YOU THERE!
OH MY.
WHAT'S GOING ON?!

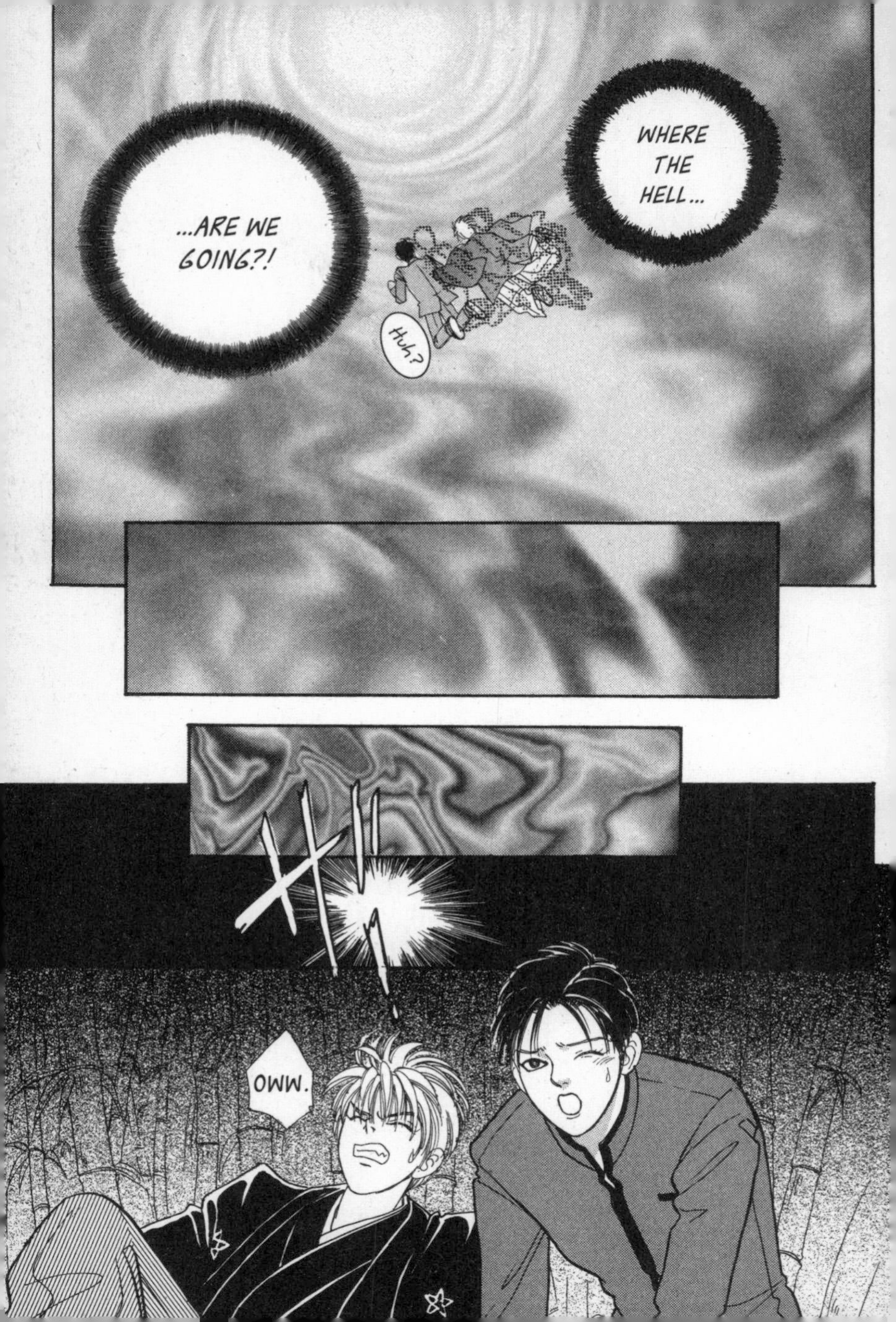
WHERE THE HELL...
...ARE WE GOING?!
Huh?
OWW.

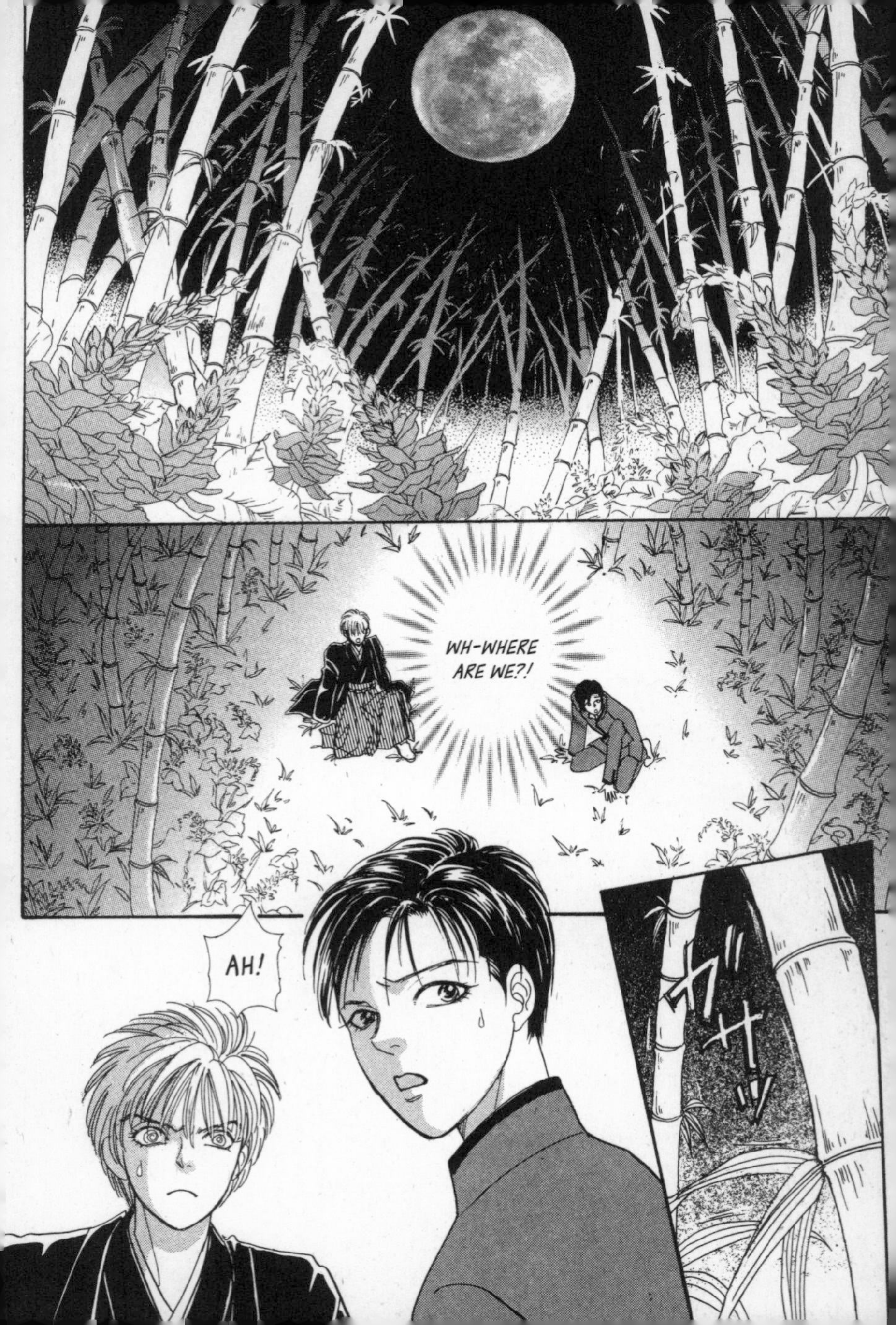
WH-WHERE ARE WE?!
AH!

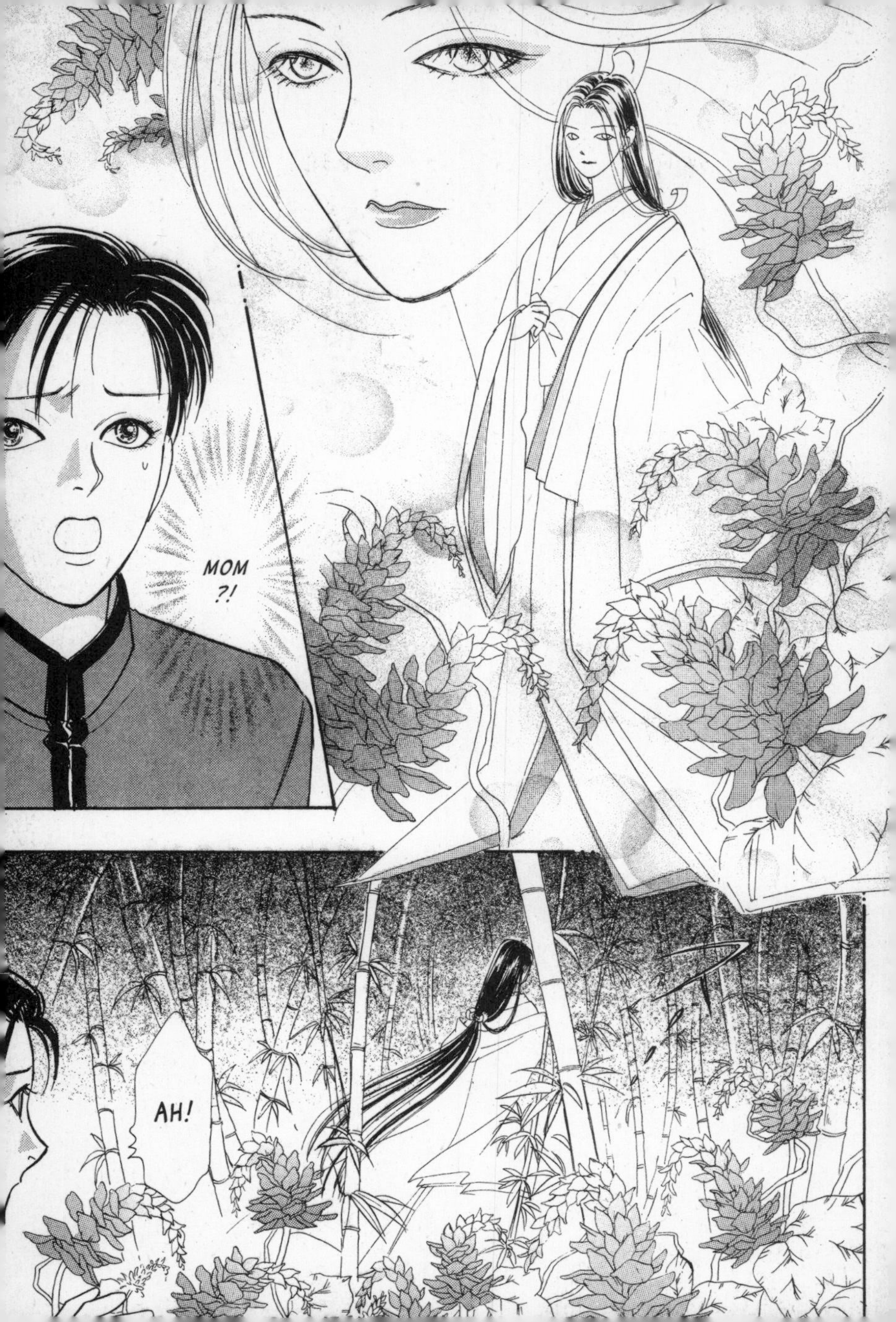
MOM ?!
AH!

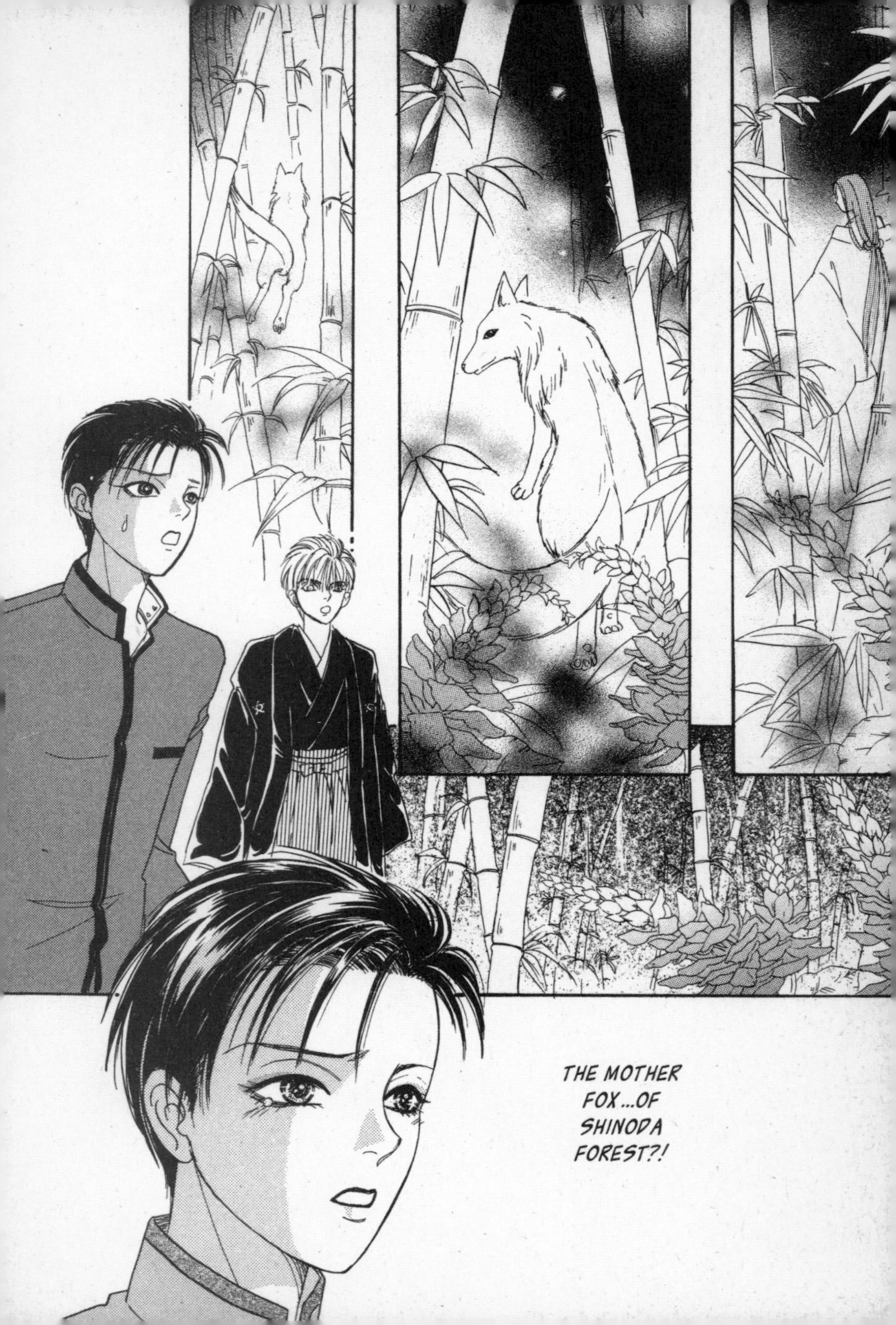
THE MOTHER FOX...OF SHINODA FOREST?!

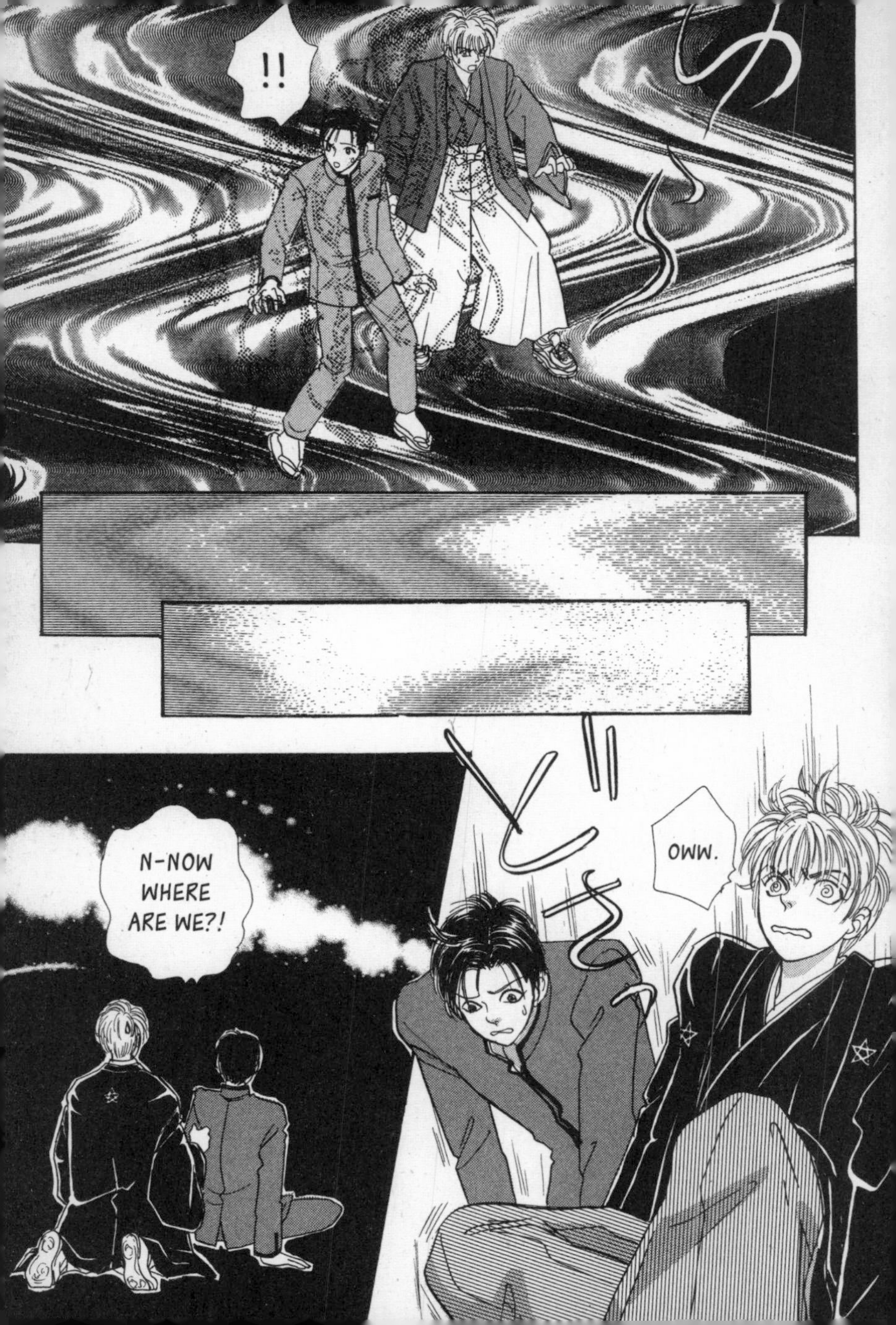
!!
OWW.
N-NOW WHERE ARE WE?!

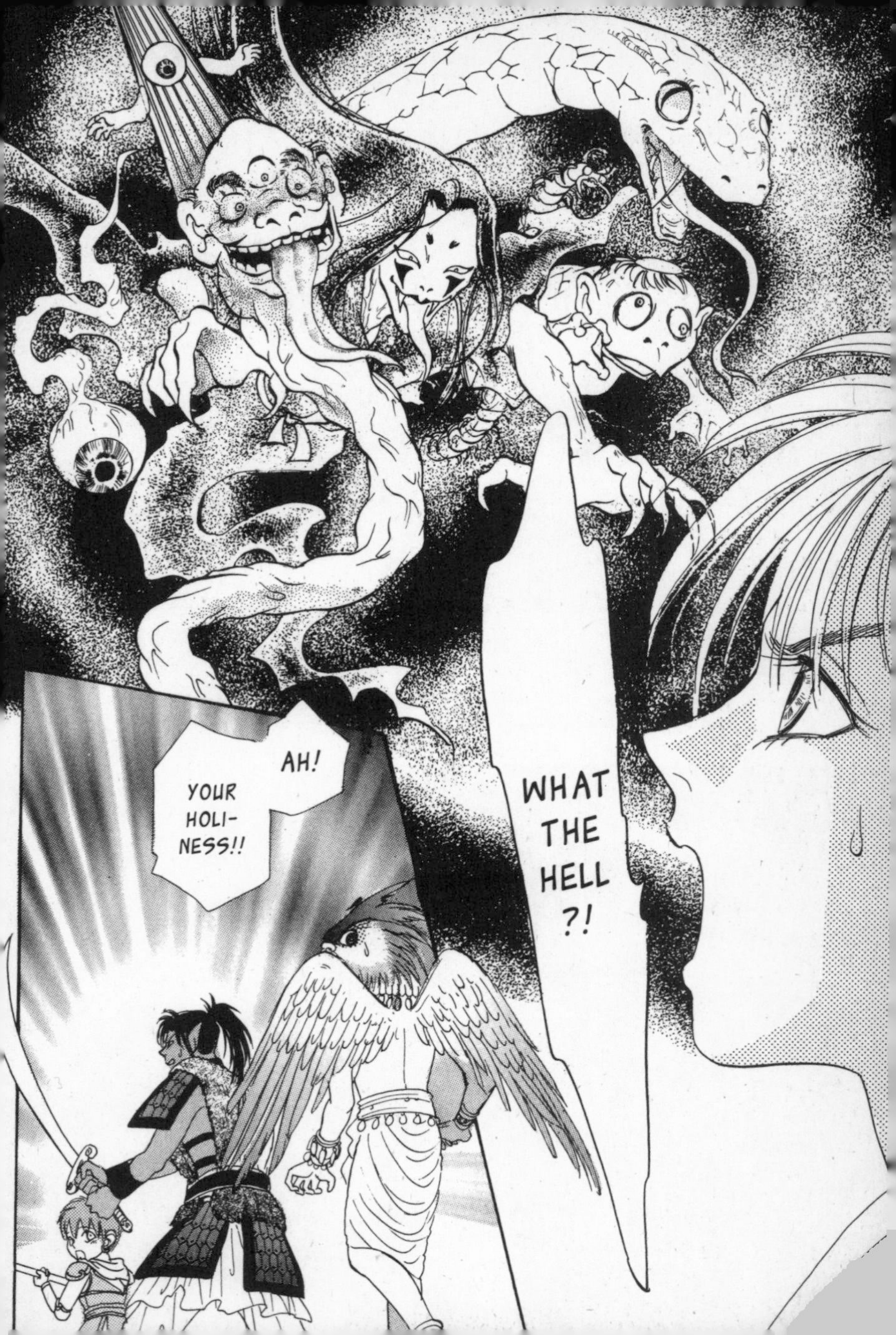
WHAT THE HELL ?!
AH! YOUR HOLI-NESS!!

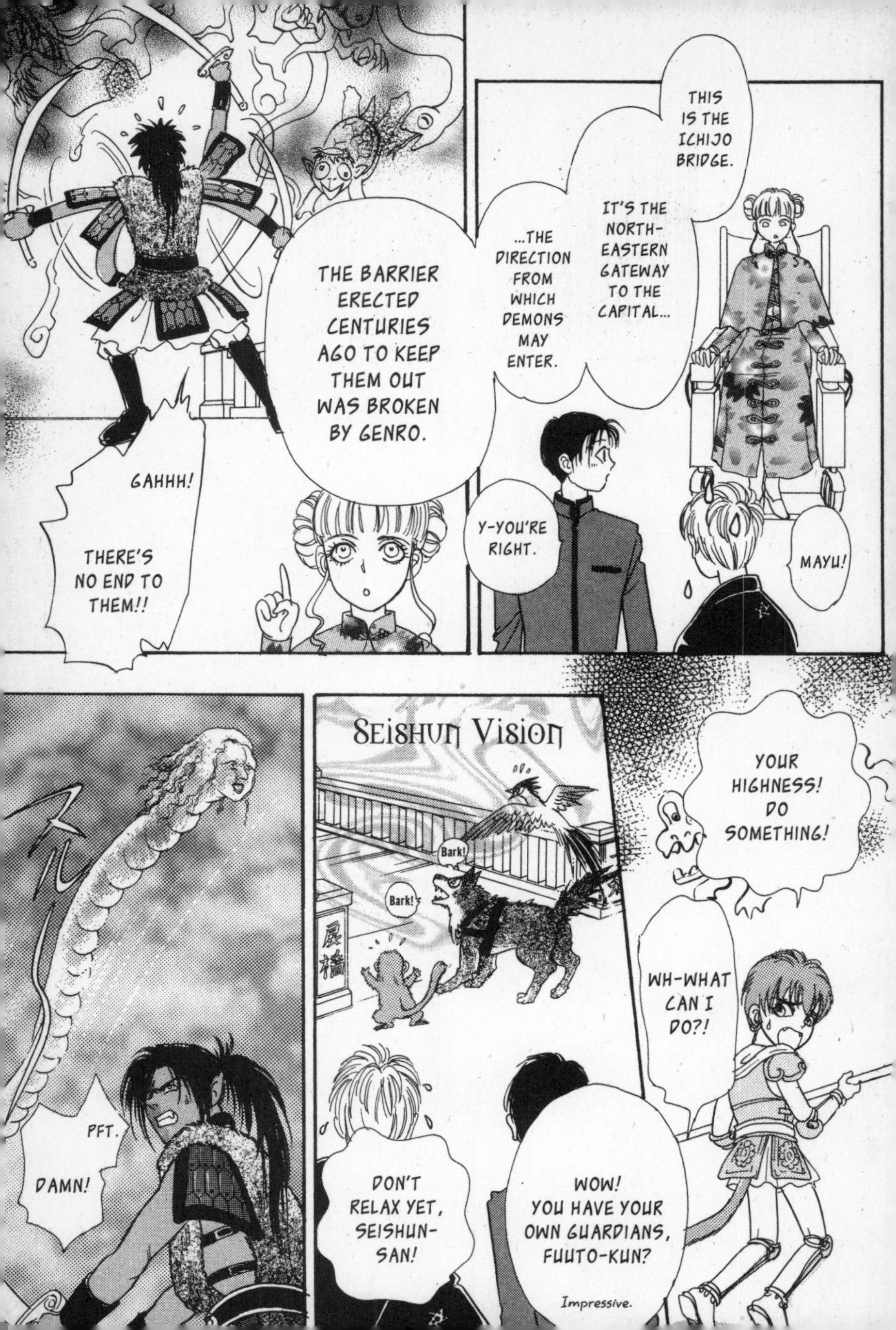
THIS IS THE ICHIJO BRIDGE.
IT'S THE NORTH-EASTERN GATEWAY TO THE CAPITAL...
...THE DIRECTION FROM WHICH DEMONS MAY ENTER.
MAYU!
Y-YOU'RE RIGHT.
THE BARRIER ERECTED CENTURIES AGO TO KEEP THEM OUT WAS BROKEN BY GENRO.
GAHHH!
THERE'S NO END TO THEM!!
YOUR HIGHNESS! DO SOMETHING!
WH-WHAT CAN I DO?!
Seishun Vision
Bark!
Bark!
WOW! YOU HAVE YOUR OWN GUARDIANS, FUUTO-KUN?
Impressive.
DON'T RELAX YET, SEISHUN-SAN!
PFT.
DAMN!

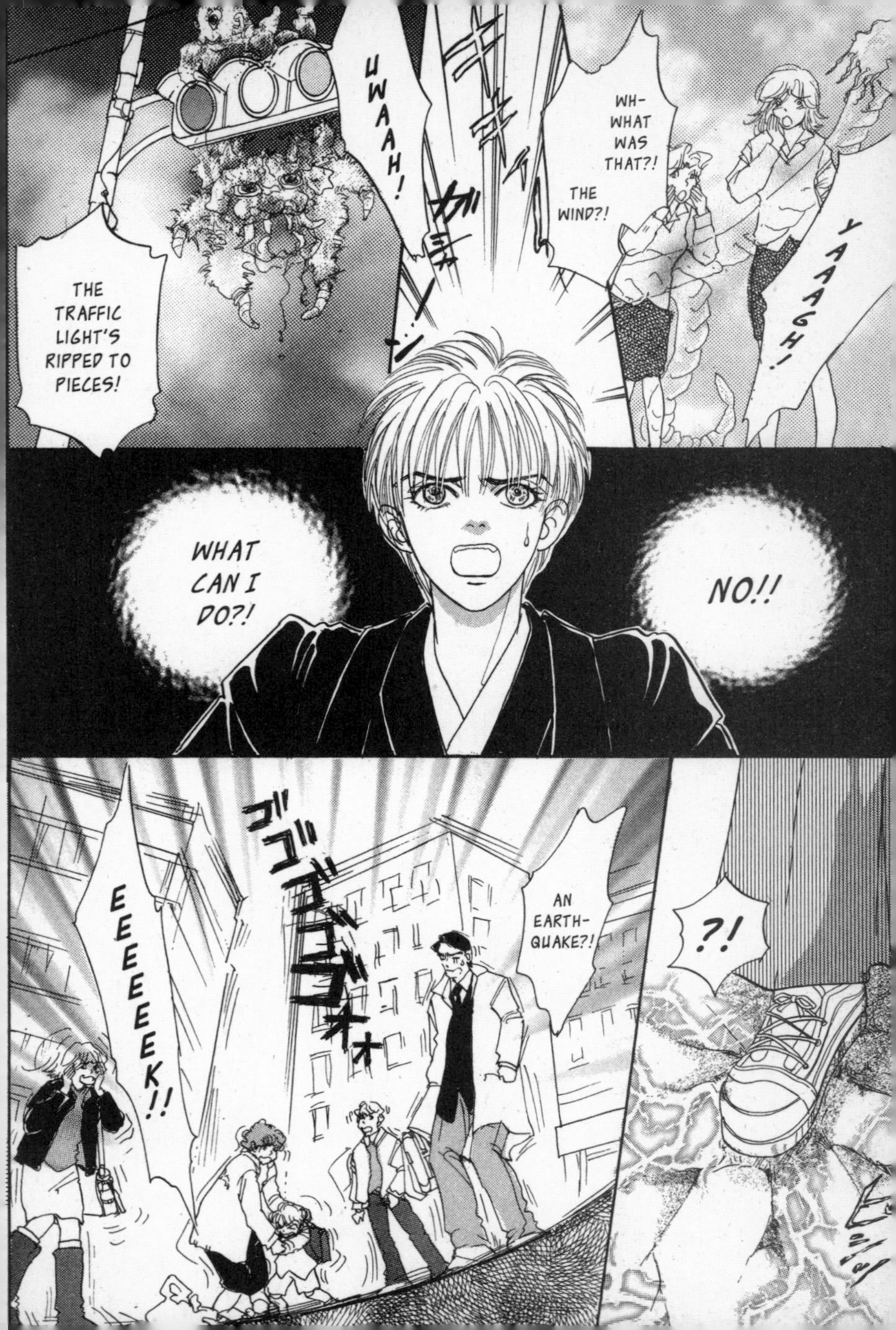
WH-WHAT WAS THAT?!
THE WIND?!
YAAAAGH!
UWAAAH!
THE TRAFFIC LIGHT'S RIPPED TO PIECES!
NO!!
WHAT CAN I DO?!
?!
AN EARTH-QUAKE?!
EEEEEEEK!!

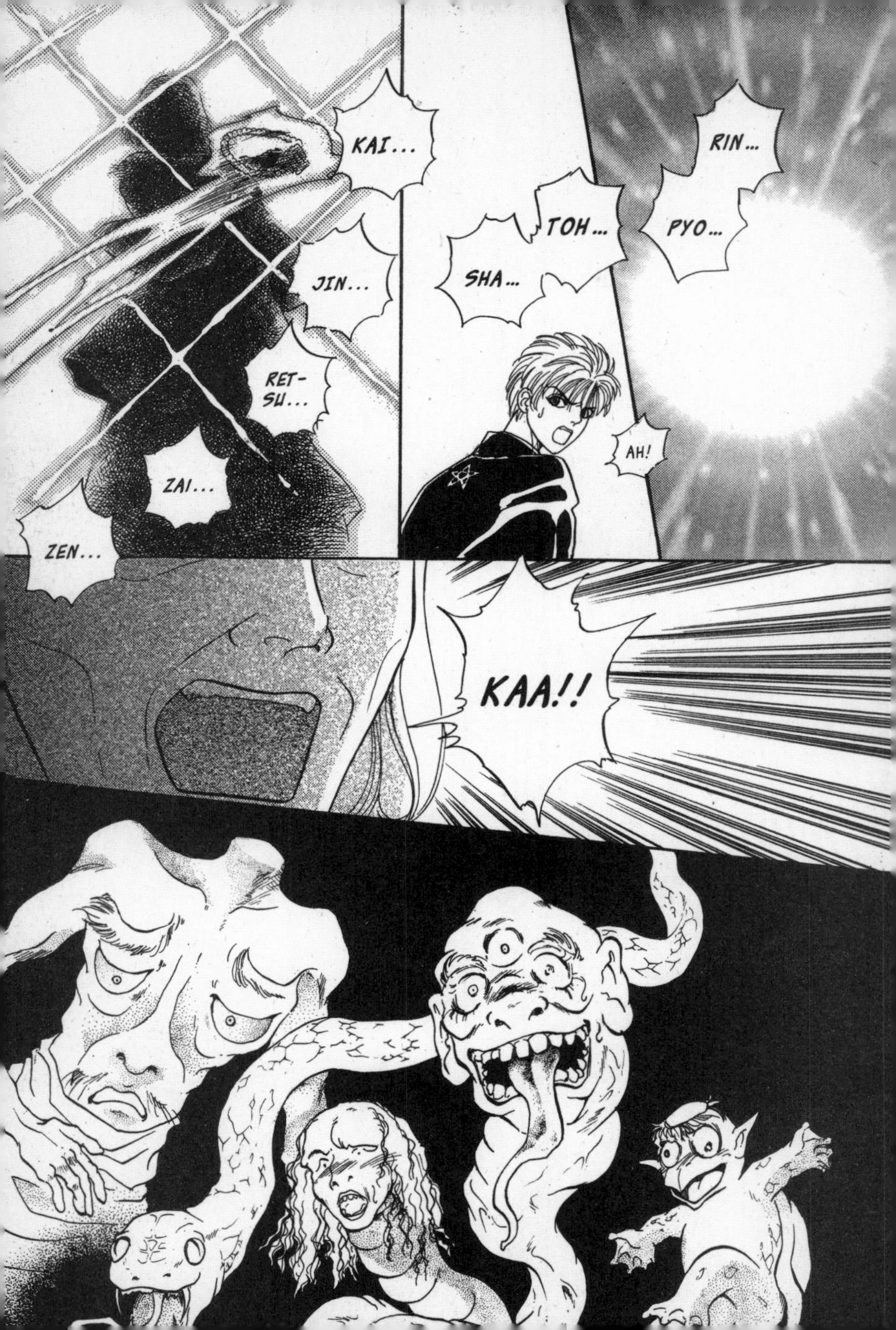
RIN...
PYO...
TOH...
SHA...
AH!
KAI...
JIN...
RET-SU...
ZAI...
ZEN...
KAA!!

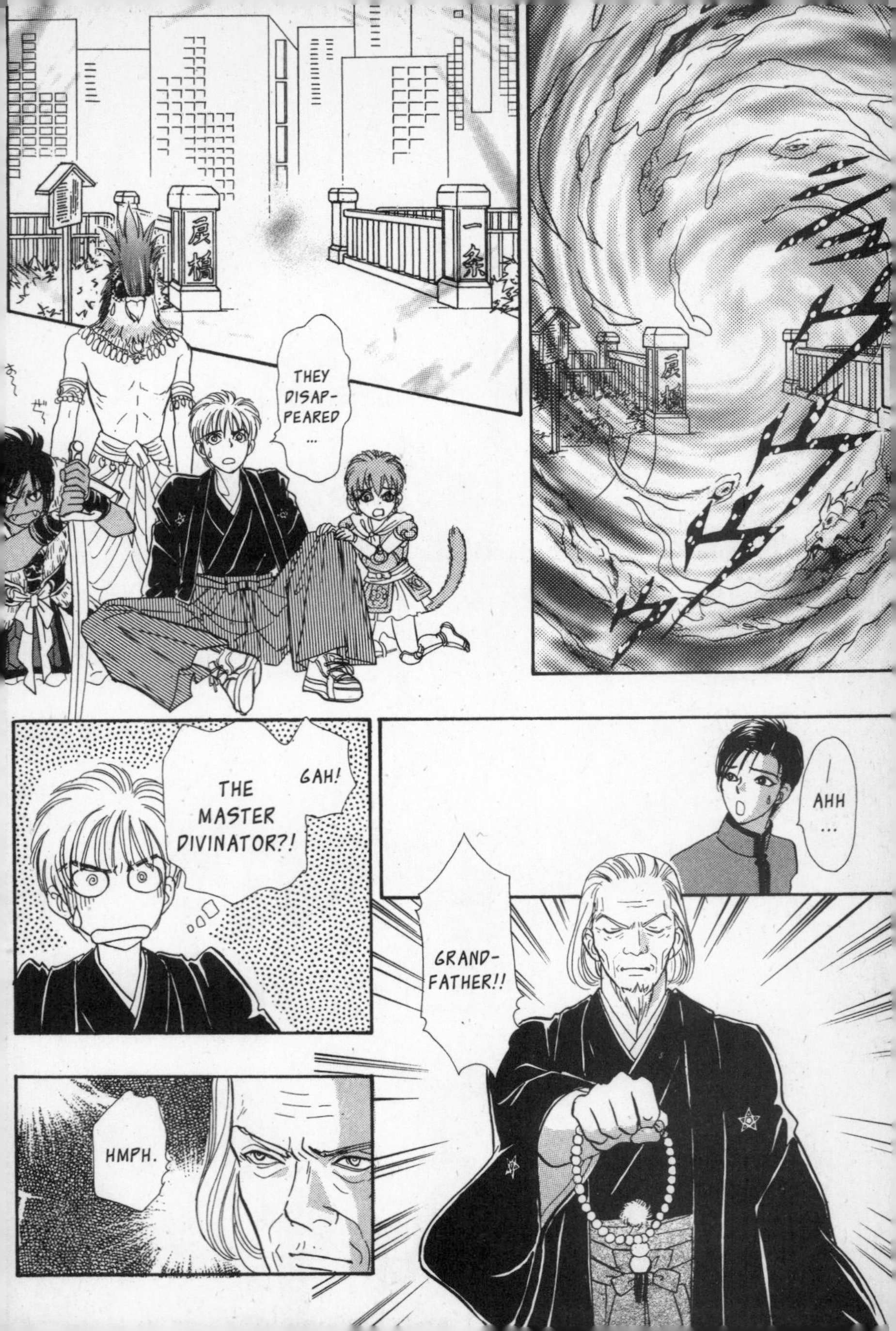
一条
戻橋
THEY DISAPPEARED...
AHH...
GRANDFATHER!!
GAH! THE MASTER DIVINATOR?!
HMPH.

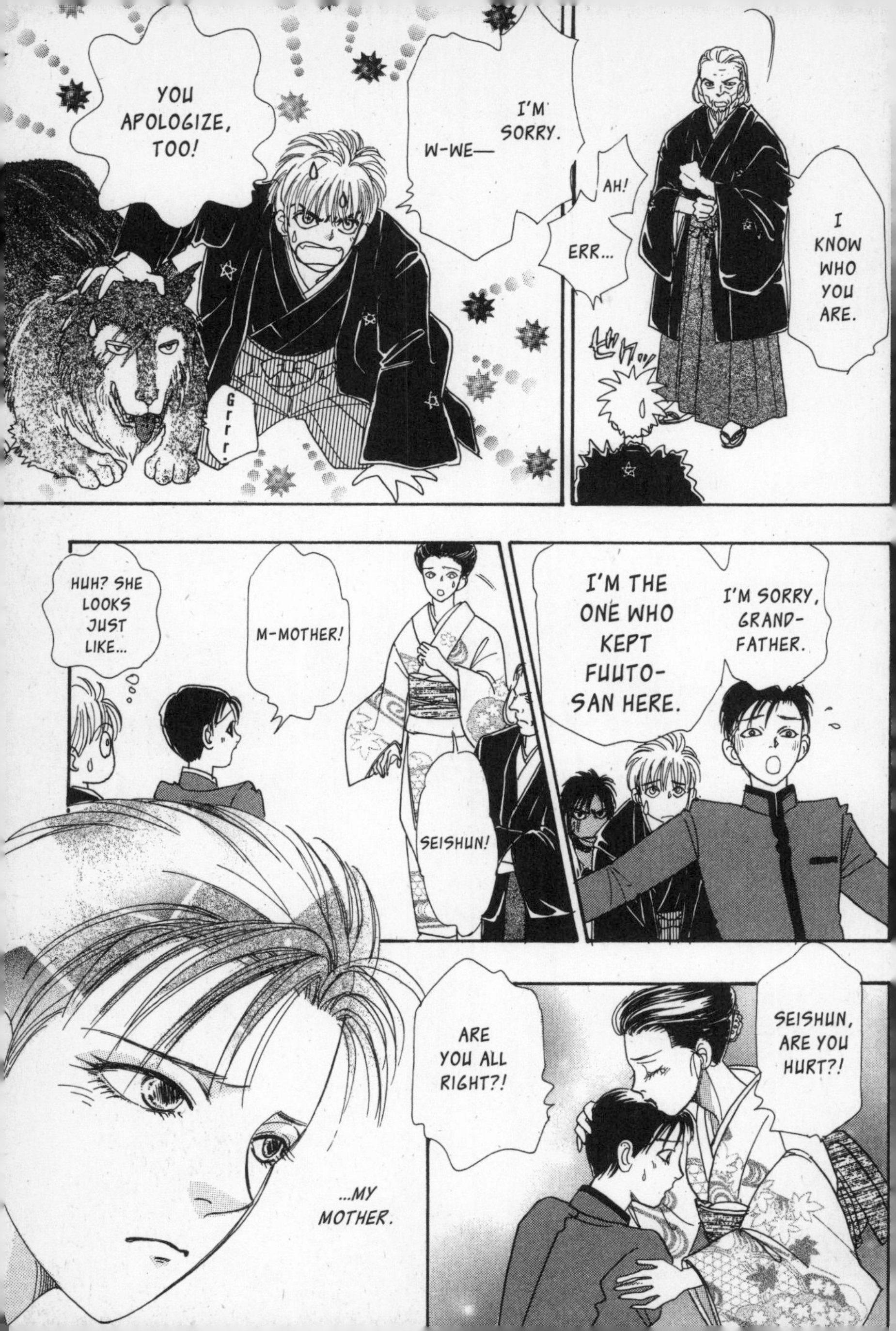
I KNOW WHO YOU ARE.
AH!
ERR...
W-WE— I'M SORRY.
YOU APOLOGIZE, TOO!
Grrr.
I'M SORRY, GRAND-FATHER.
I'M THE ONE WHO KEPT FUUTO-SAN HERE.
M-MOTHER!
HUH? SHE LOOKS JUST LIKE...
SEISHUN!
SEISHUN, ARE YOU HURT?!
ARE YOU ALL RIGHT?!
...MY MOTHER.

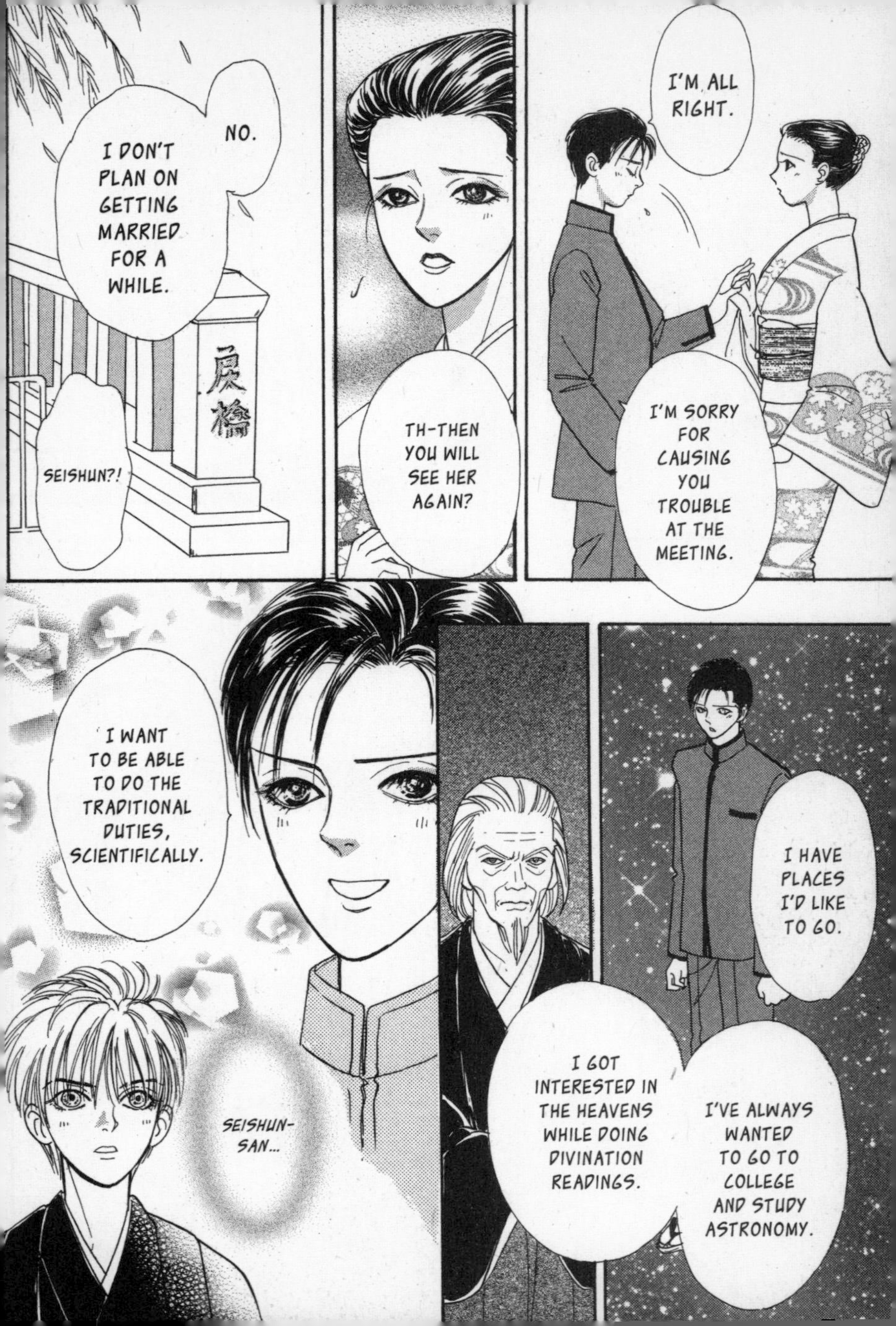
I'M ALL RIGHT.
I'M SORRY FOR CAUSING YOU TROUBLE AT THE MEETING.
TH-THEN YOU WILL SEE HER AGAIN?
NO.
I DON'T PLAN ON GETTING MARRIED FOR A WHILE.
戻橋
SEISHUN?!
I HAVE PLACES I'D LIKE TO GO.
I'VE ALWAYS WANTED TO GO TO COLLEGE AND STUDY ASTRONOMY.
I GOT INTERESTED IN THE HEAVENS WHILE DOING DIVINATION READINGS.
I WANT TO BE ABLE TO DO THE TRADITIONAL DUTIES, SCIENTIFICALLY.
SEISHUN-SAN...

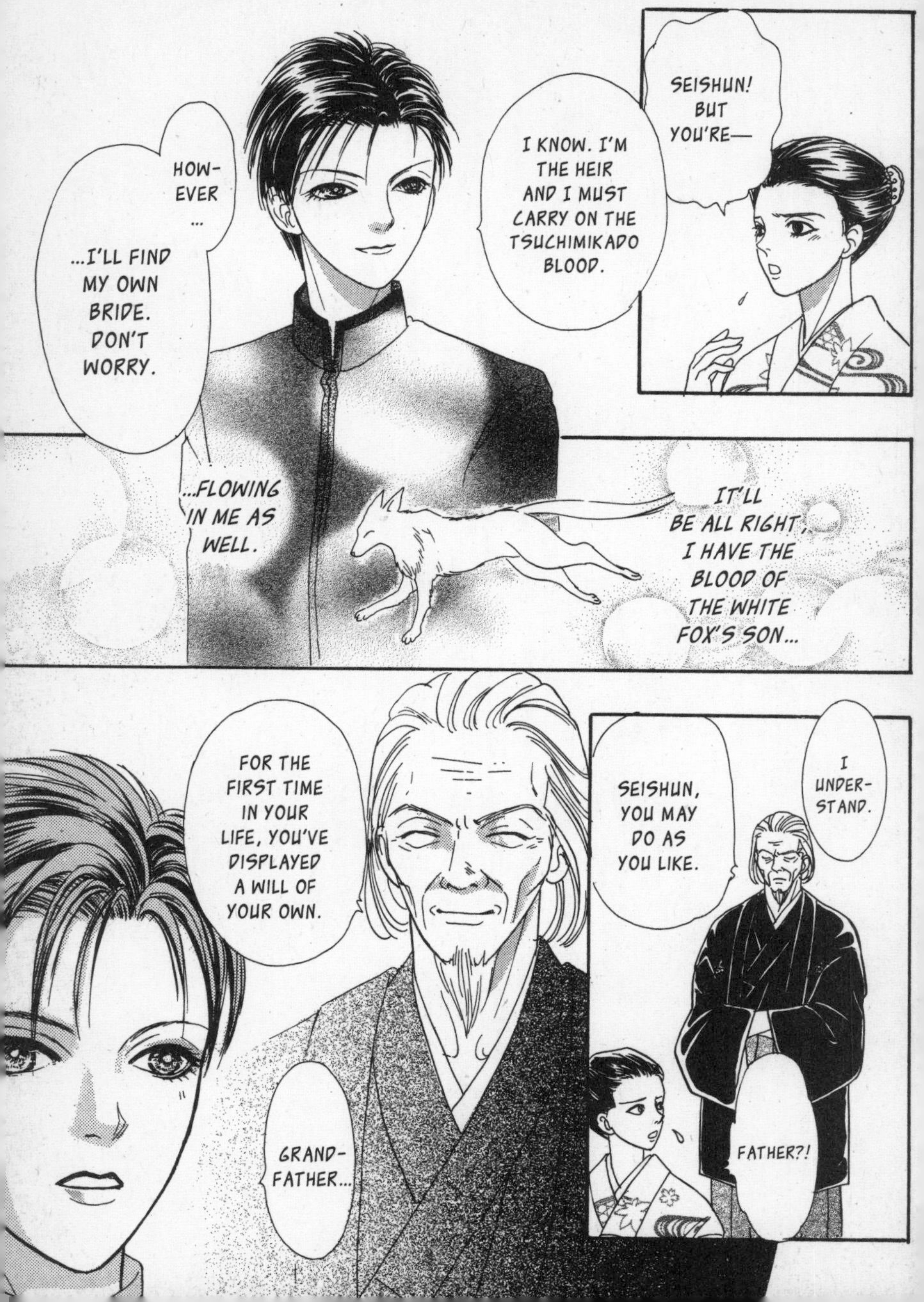
SEISHUN! BUT YOU'RE—
I KNOW. I'M THE HEIR AND I MUST CARRY ON THE TSUCHIMIKADO BLOOD.
HOW-EVER ...
...I'LL FIND MY OWN BRIDE. DON'T WORRY.
IT'LL BE ALL RIGHT, I HAVE THE BLOOD OF THE WHITE FOX'S SON...
...FLOWING IN ME AS WELL.
I UNDER-STAND.
SEISHUN, YOU MAY DO AS YOU LIKE.
FATHER?!
FOR THE FIRST TIME IN YOUR LIFE, YOU'VE DISPLAYED A WILL OF YOUR OWN.
GRAND-FATHER...

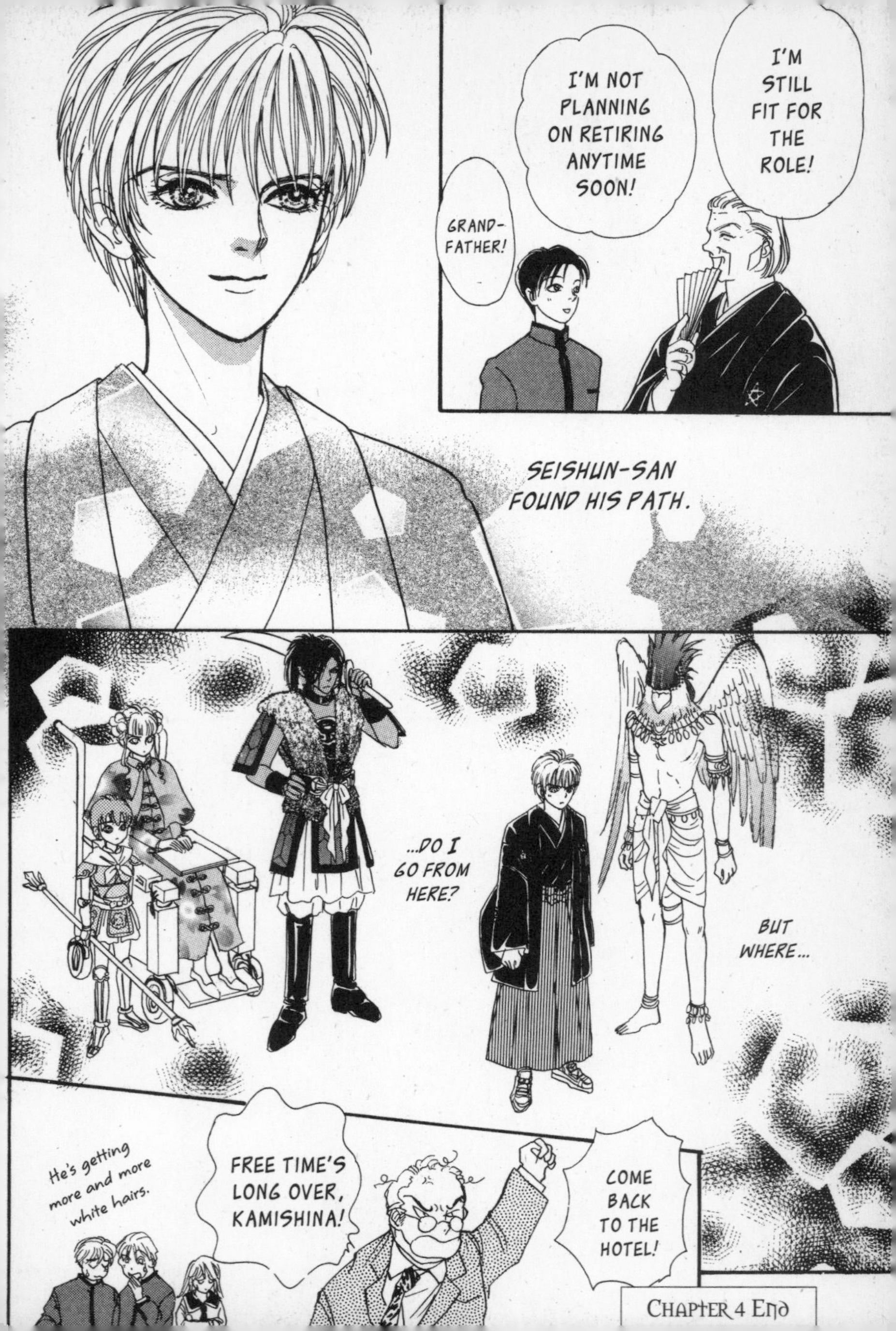
I'M STILL FIT FOR THE ROLE!
I'M NOT PLANNING ON RETIRING ANYTIME SOON!
GRAND-FATHER!
SEISHUN-SAN FOUND HIS PATH.
BUT WHERE...
...DO I GO FROM HERE?
COME BACK TO THE HOTEL!
FREE TIME'S LONG OVER, KAMISHINA!
He's getting more and more white hairs.
Chapter 4 End

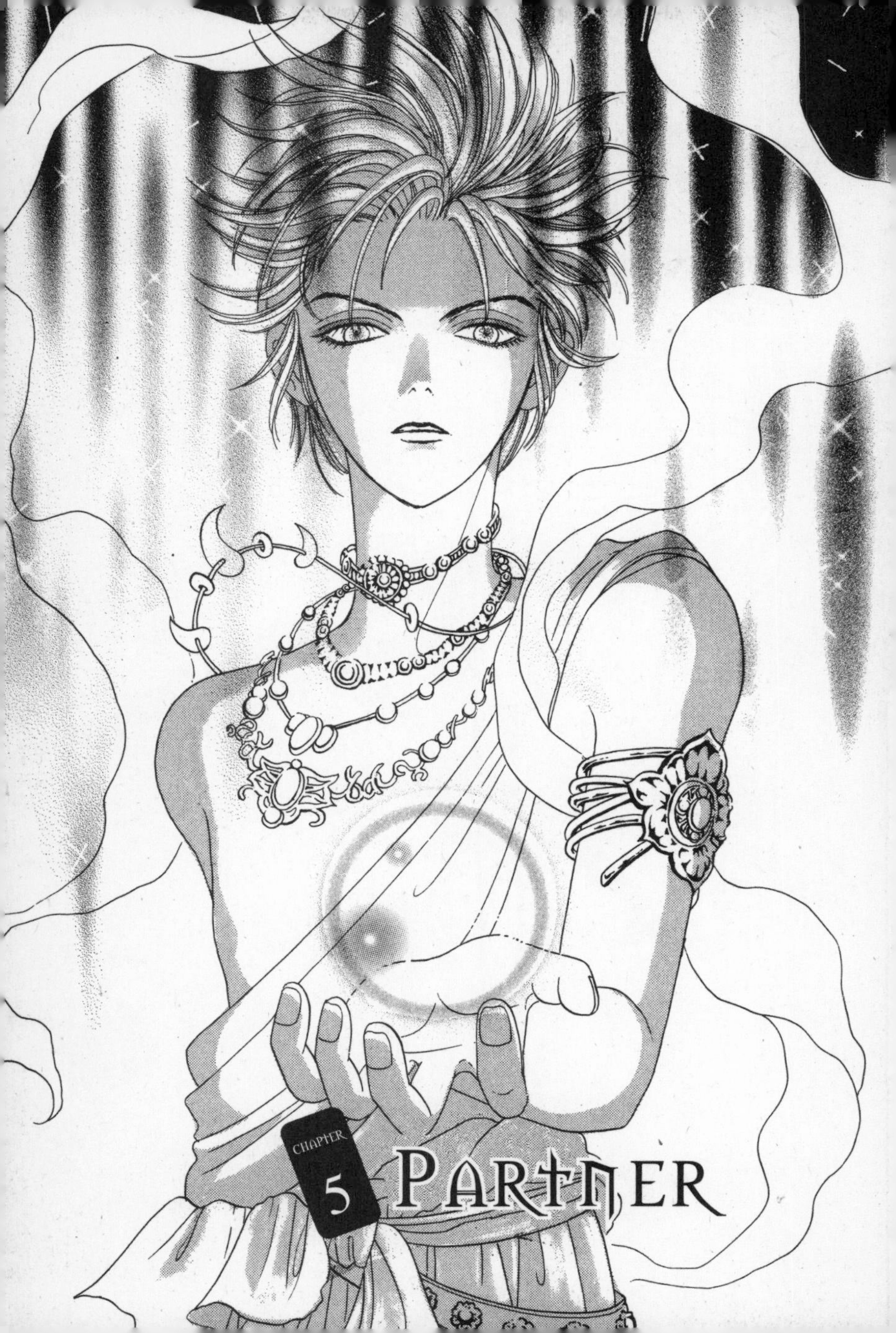
CHAPTER
5
PARTNER

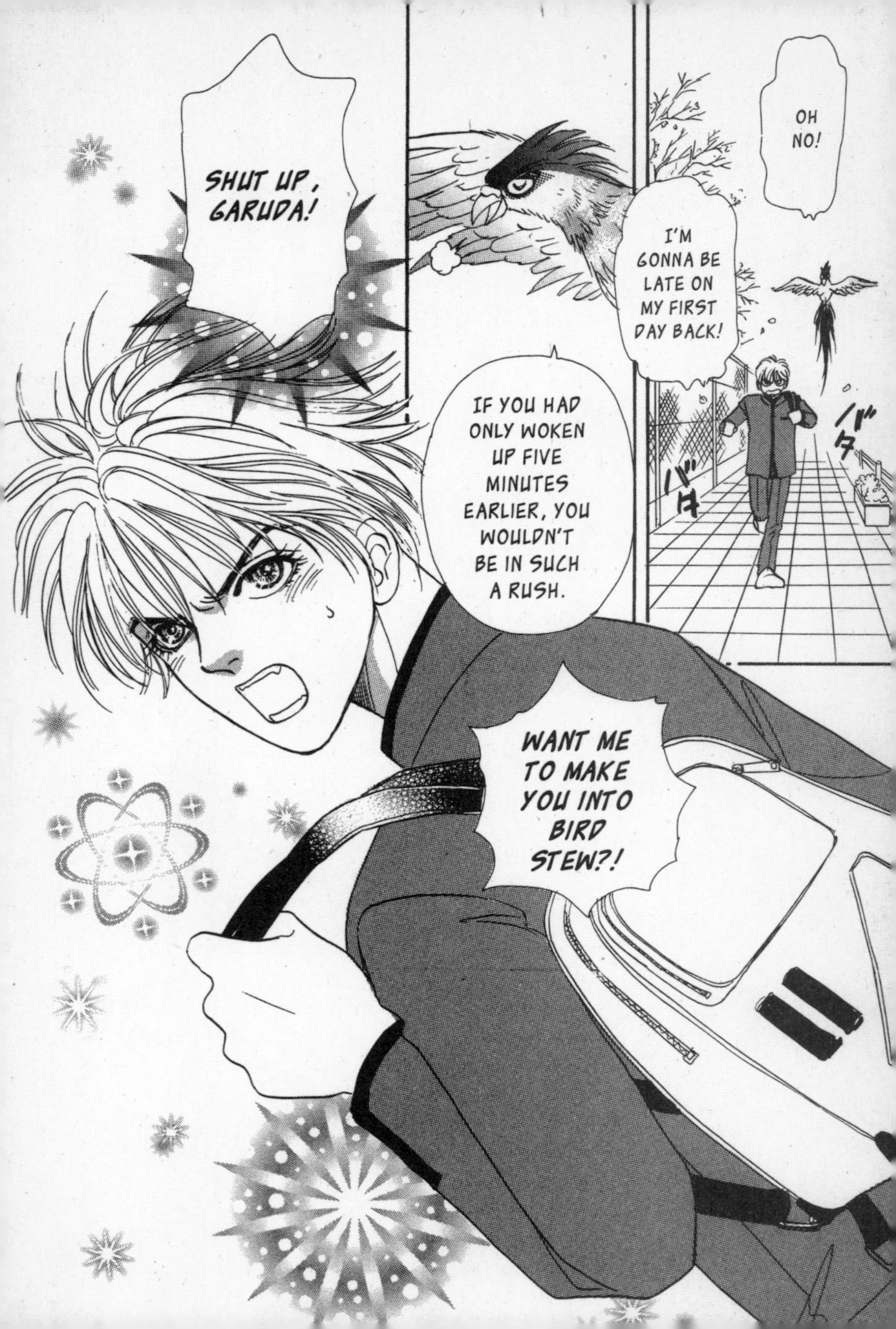
OH NO!
I'M GONNA BE LATE ON MY FIRST DAY BACK!
バタ
バタ
IF YOU HAD ONLY WOKEN UP FIVE MINUTES EARLIER, YOU WOULDN'T BE IN SUCH A RUSH.
SHUT UP, GARUDA!
WANT ME TO MAKE YOU INTO BIRD STEW?!

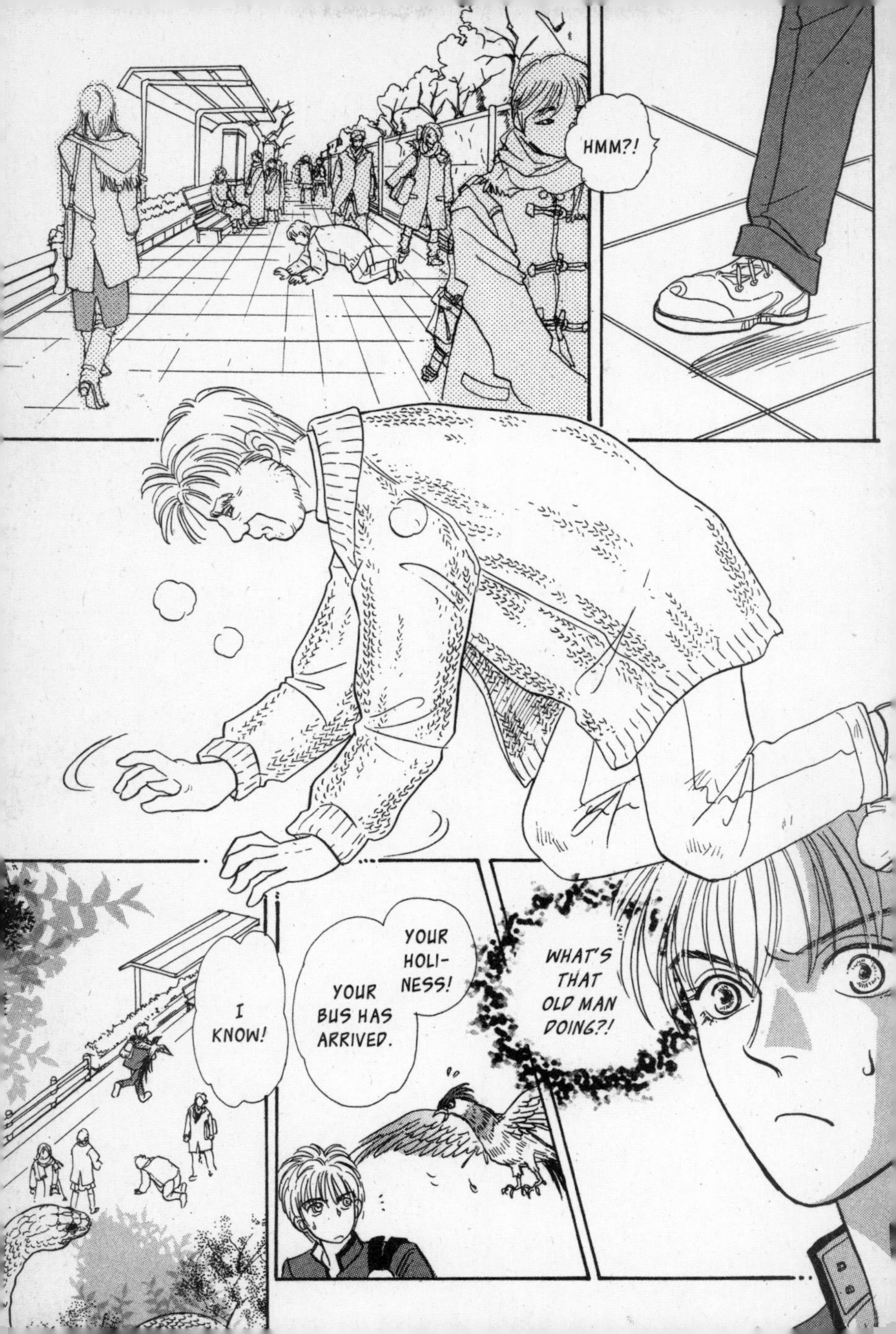
HMM?!
WHAT'S THAT OLD MAN DOING?!
YOUR HOLI-NESS!
YOUR BUS HAS ARRIVED.
I KNOW!

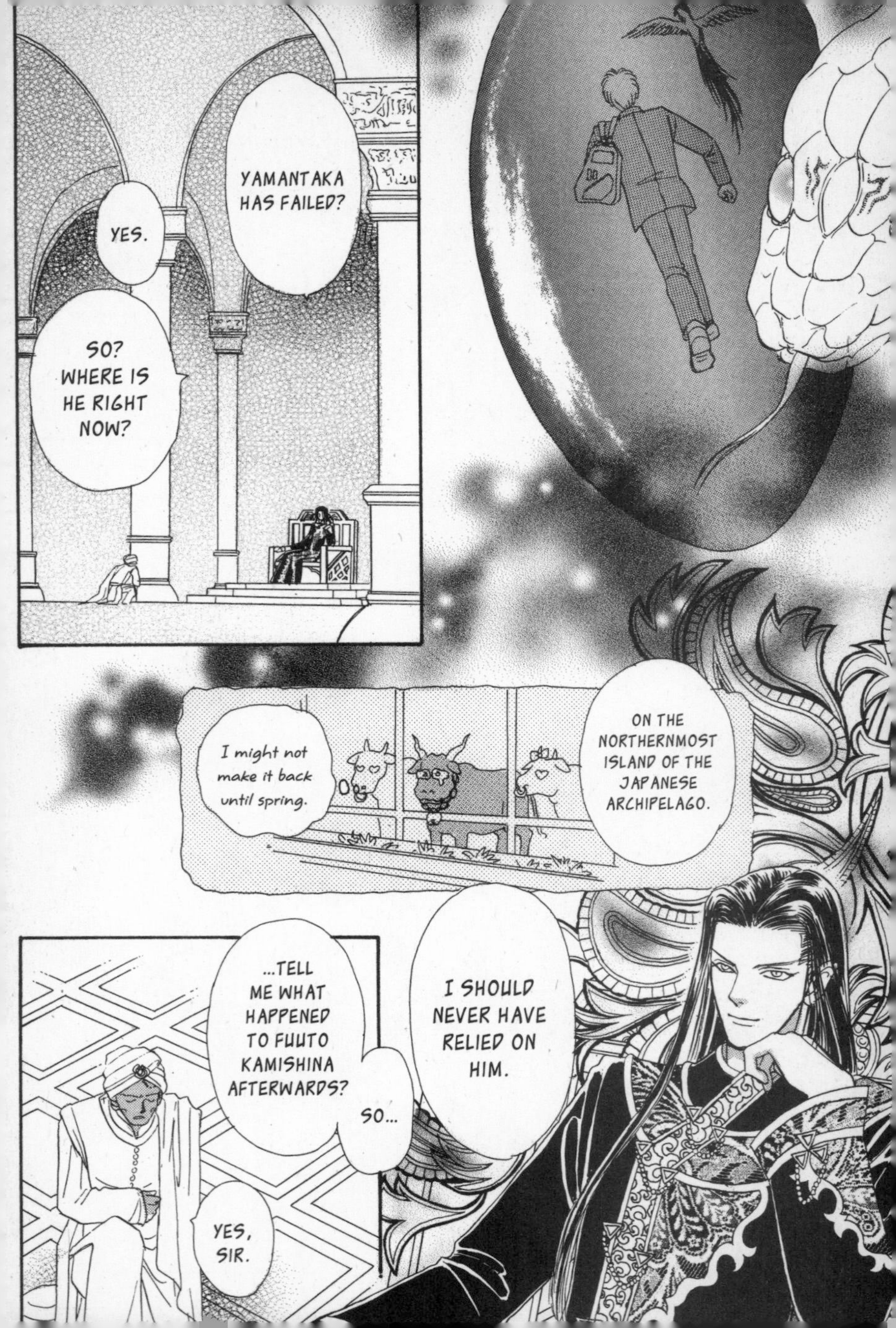
YAMANTAKA HAS FAILED?
YES.
SO? WHERE IS HE RIGHT NOW?
ON THE NORTHERNMOST ISLAND OF THE JAPANESE ARCHIPELAGO.
I might not make it back until spring.
I SHOULD NEVER HAVE RELIED ON HIM.
SO...
...TELL ME WHAT HAPPENED TO FUUTO KAMISHINA AFTERWARDS?
YES, SIR.

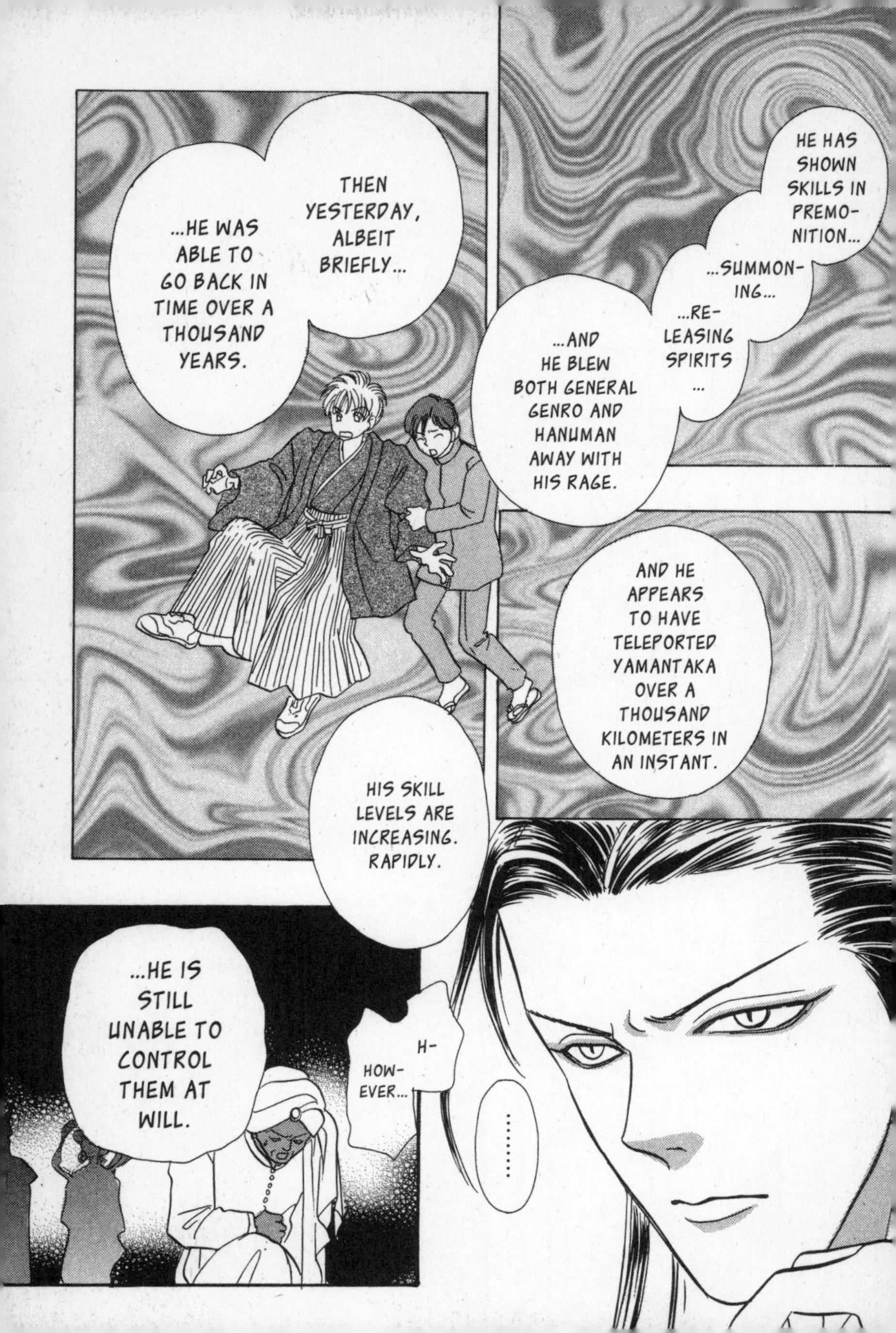
HE HAS SHOWN SKILLS IN PREMO-NITION...
...SUMMON-ING...
...RE-LEASING SPIRITS ...
...AND HE BLEW BOTH GENERAL GENRO AND HANUMAN AWAY WITH HIS RAGE.
AND HE APPEARS TO HAVE TELEPORTED YAMANTAKA OVER A THOUSAND KILOMETERS IN AN INSTANT.
THEN YESTERDAY, ALBEIT BRIEFLY...
...HE WAS ABLE TO GO BACK IN TIME OVER A THOUSAND YEARS.
HIS SKILL LEVELS ARE INCREASING. RAPIDLY.
......
H-HOW-EVER...
...HE IS STILL UNABLE TO CONTROL THEM AT WILL.

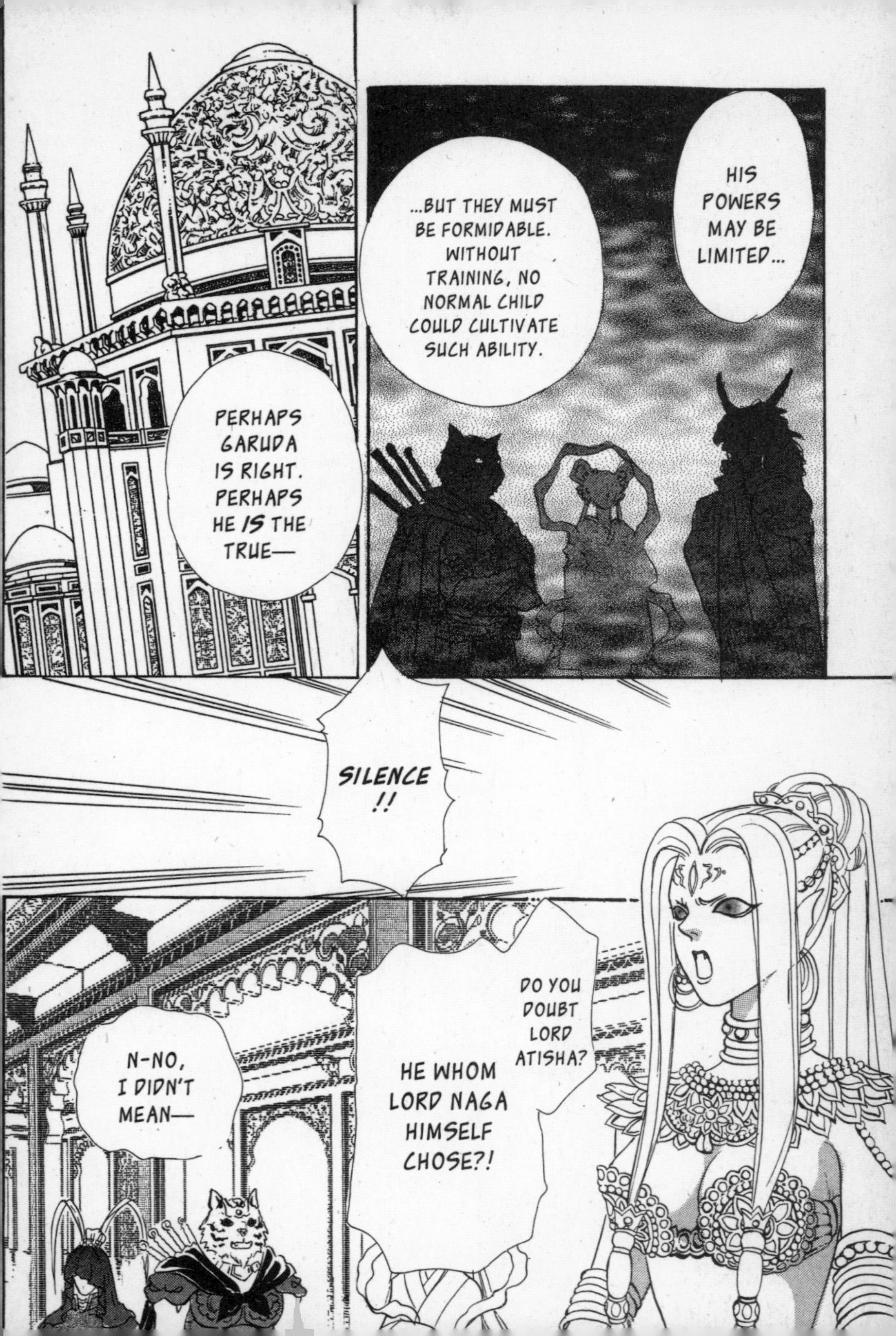
HIS POWERS MAY BE LIMITED...
...BUT THEY MUST BE FORMIDABLE. WITHOUT TRAINING, NO NORMAL CHILD COULD CULTIVATE SUCH ABILITY.
PERHAPS GARUDA IS RIGHT. PERHAPS HE *IS* THE TRUE—
SILENCE !!
DO YOU DOUBT LORD ATISHA?
HE WHOM LORD NAGA HIMSELF CHOSE?!
N-NO, I DIDN'T MEAN—

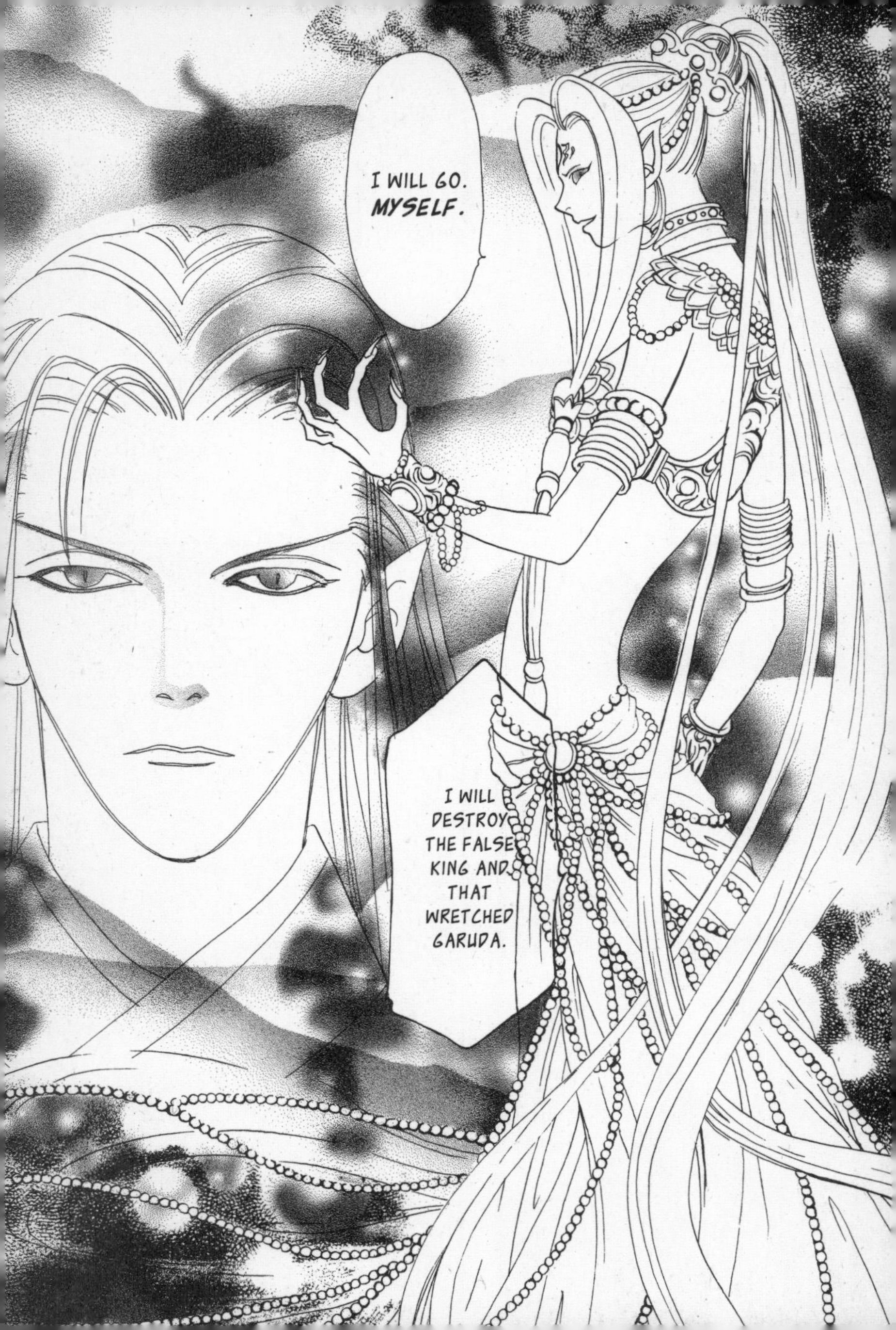
I WILL GO. MYSELF.
I WILL DESTROY THE FALSE KING AND THAT WRETCHED GARUDA.

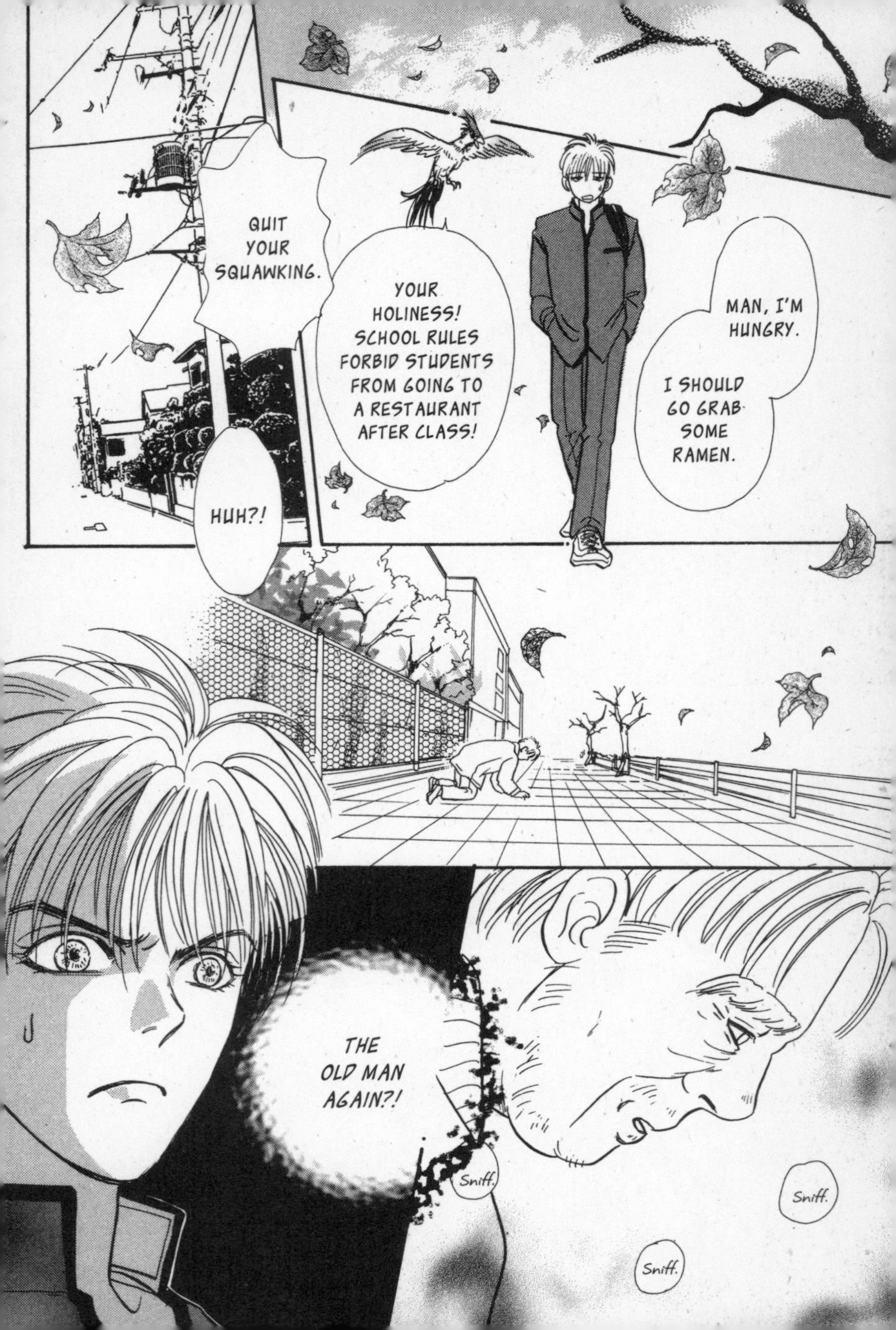
MAN, I'M HUNGRY.
I SHOULD GO GRAB SOME RAMEN.
YOUR HOLINESS! SCHOOL RULES FORBID STUDENTS FROM GOING TO A RESTAURANT AFTER CLASS!
QUIT YOUR SQUAWKING.
HUH?!
Sniff.
Sniff.
Sniff.
THE OLD MAN AGAIN?!

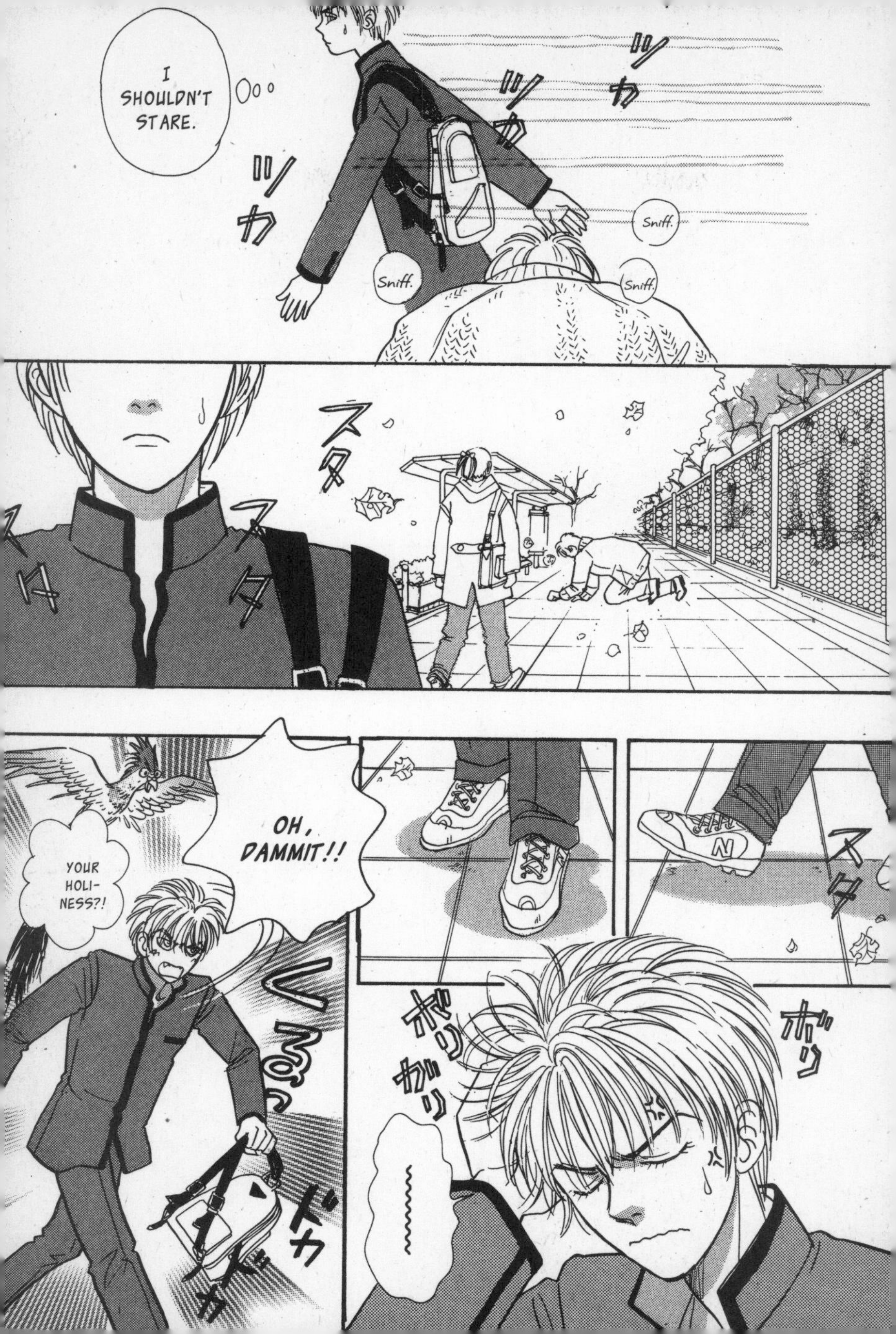
I SHOULDN'T STARE.
Sniff.
Sniff.
Sniff.
OH, DAMMIT!!
YOUR HOLI-NESS?!

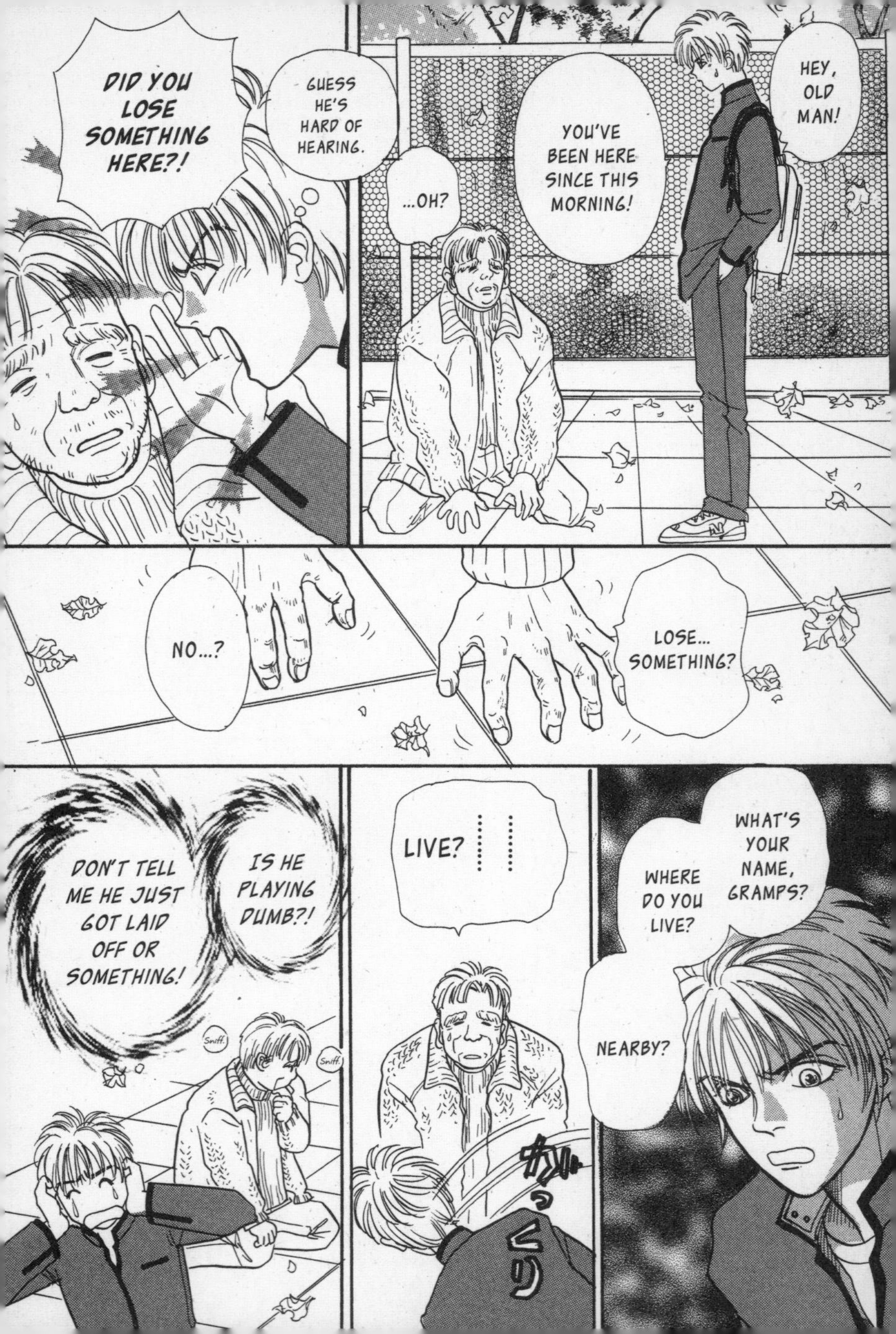
HEY, OLD MAN!
YOU'VE BEEN HERE SINCE THIS MORNING!
...OH?
GUESS HE'S HARD OF HEARING.
DID YOU LOSE SOMETHING HERE?!
LOSE... SOMETHING?
NO...?
WHAT'S YOUR NAME, GRAMPS?
WHERE DO YOU LIVE?
NEARBY?
LIVE? ......
IS HE PLAYING DUMB?!
DON'T TELL ME HE JUST GOT LAID OFF OR SOMETHING!
Sniff.
Sniff.

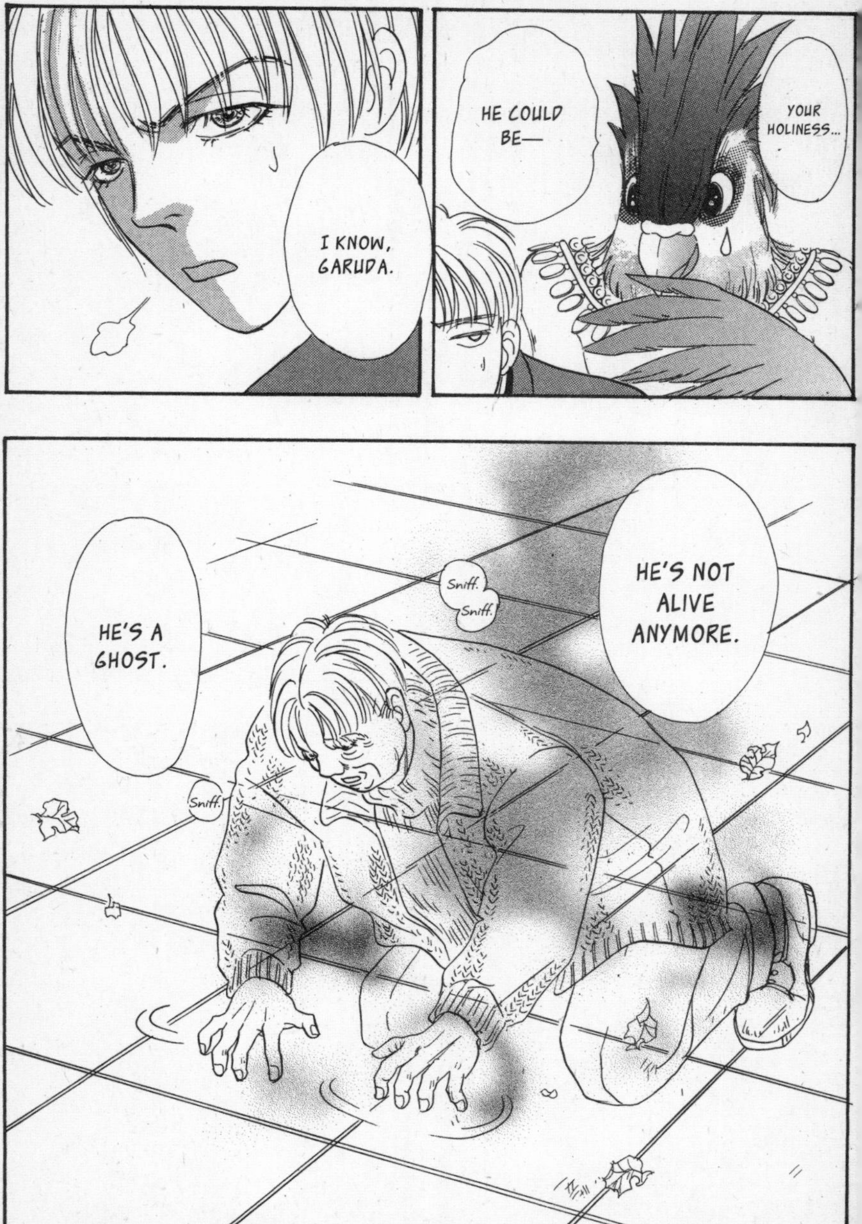
YOUR HOLINESS...
HE COULD BE—
I KNOW, GARUDA.
HE'S NOT ALIVE ANYMORE.
Sniff.
Sniff.
HE'S A GHOST.
Sniff.

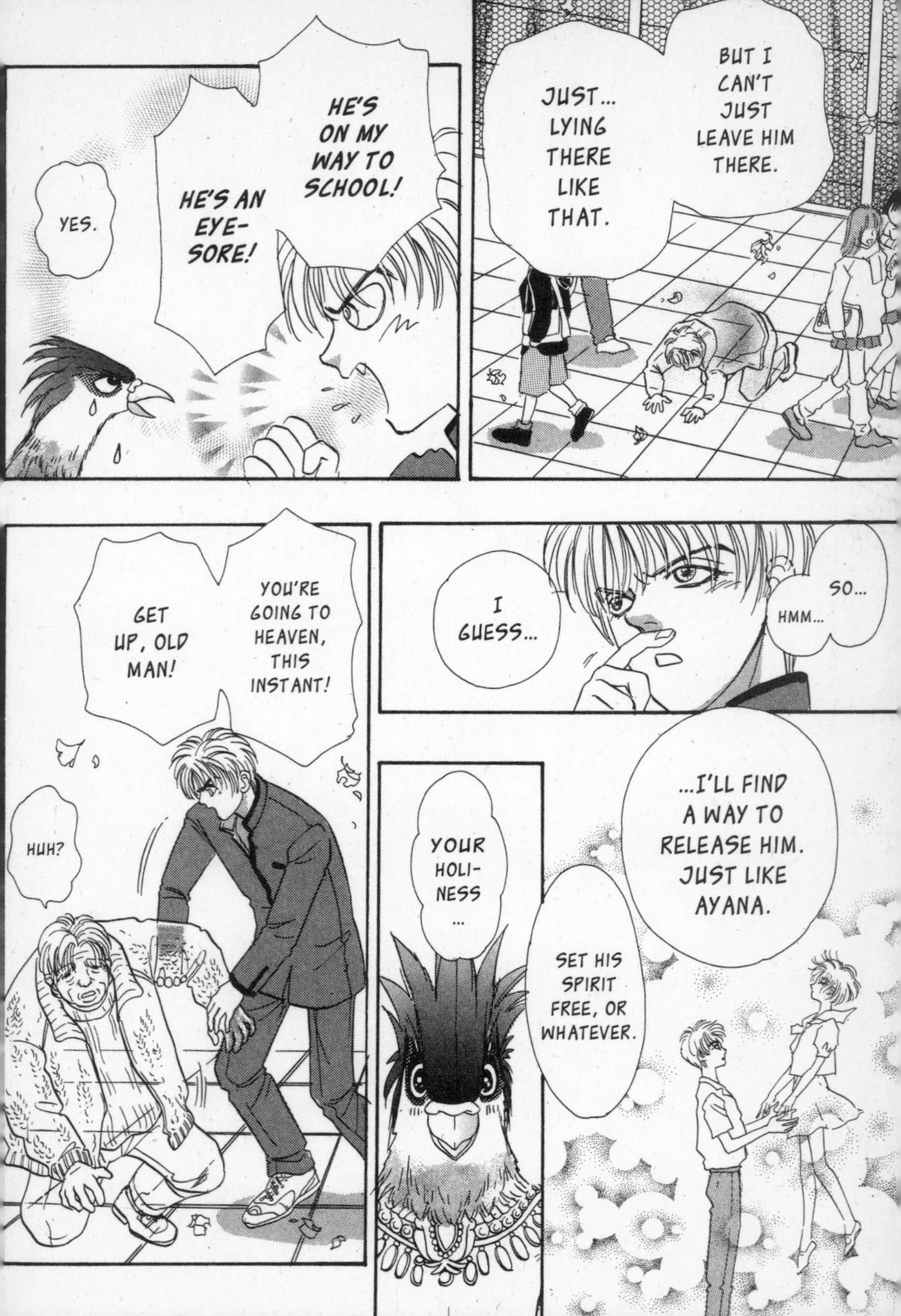
BUT I CAN'T JUST LEAVE HIM THERE.
JUST... LYING THERE LIKE THAT.
HE'S ON MY WAY TO SCHOOL!
HE'S AN EYE-SORE!
YES.
SO...
HMM...
I GUESS...
...I'LL FIND A WAY TO RELEASE HIM. JUST LIKE AYANA.
SET HIS SPIRIT FREE, OR WHATEVER.
YOUR HOLINESS...
YOU'RE GOING TO HEAVEN, THIS INSTANT!
GET UP, OLD MAN!
HUH?

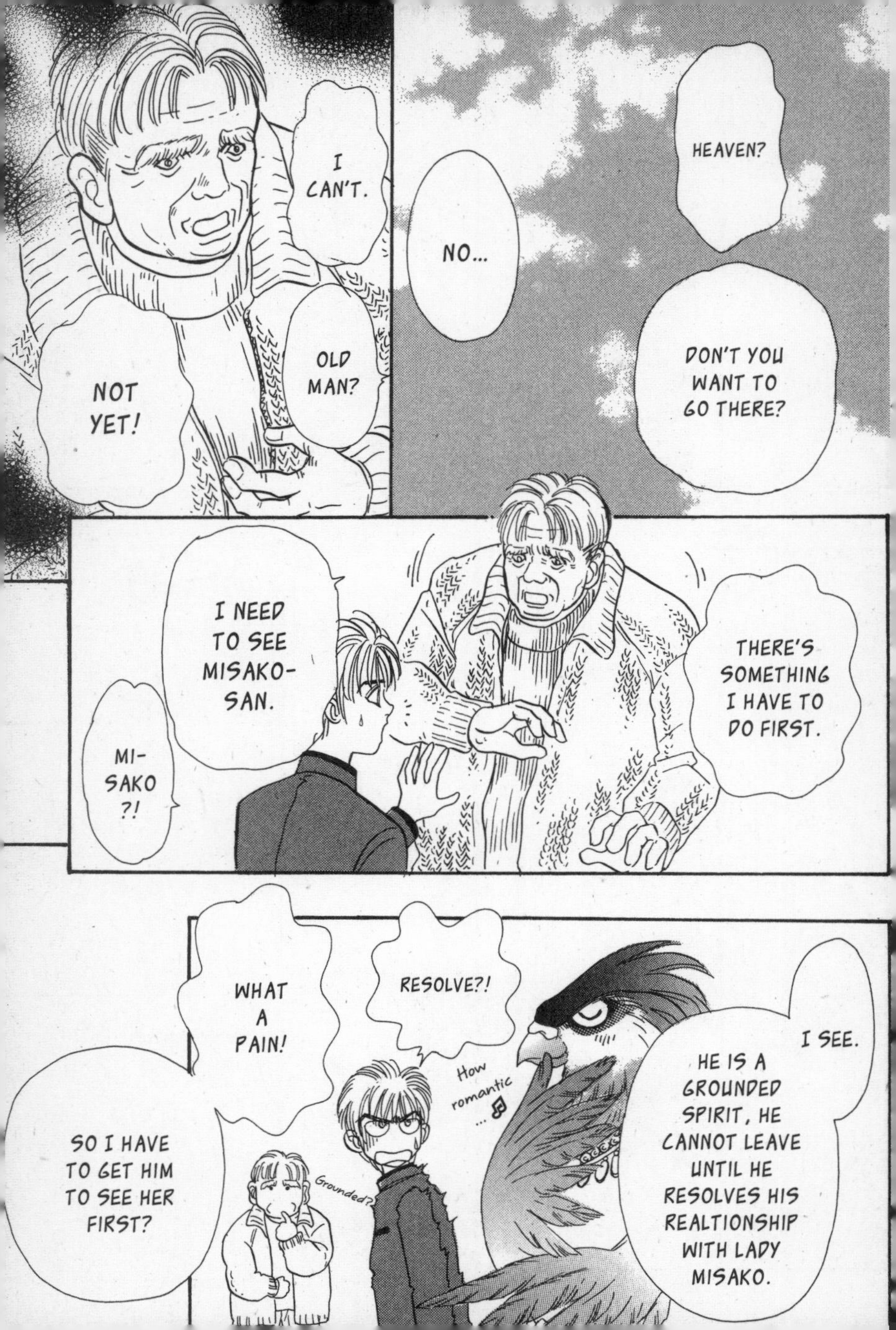
HEAVEN?
DON'T YOU WANT TO GO THERE?
NO...
I CAN'T.
OLD MAN?
NOT YET!
THERE'S SOMETHING I HAVE TO DO FIRST.
I NEED TO SEE MISAKO-SAN.
MI-SAKO?!
I SEE.
HE IS A GROUNDED SPIRIT, HE CANNOT LEAVE UNTIL HE RESOLVES HIS REALTIONSHIP WITH LADY MISAKO.
How romantic...
RESOLVE?!
Grounded?
WHAT A PAIN!
SO I HAVE TO GET HIM TO SEE HER FIRST?

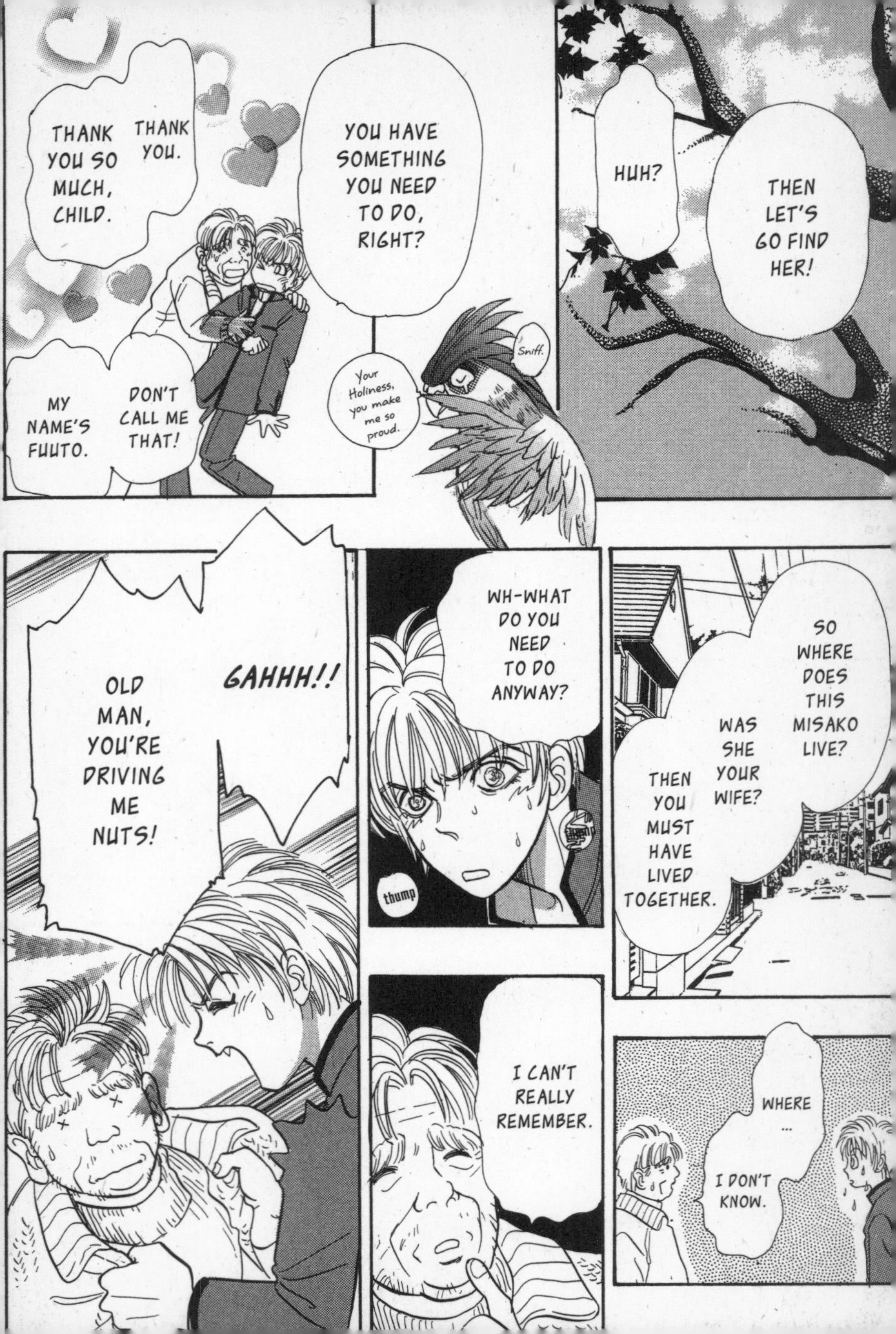
THEN LET'S GO FIND HER!
HUH?
YOU HAVE SOMETHING YOU NEED TO DO, RIGHT?
Sniff.
Your Holiness, you make me so proud.
THANK YOU.
THANK YOU SO MUCH, CHILD.
DON'T CALL ME THAT!
MY NAME'S FUUTO.
SO WHERE DOES THIS MISAKO LIVE?
WAS SHE YOUR WIFE?
THEN YOU MUST HAVE LIVED TOGETHER.
WHERE ...
I DON'T KNOW.
WH-WHAT DO YOU NEED TO DO ANYWAY?
thump
I CAN'T REALLY REMEMBER.
GAHHH!!
OLD MAN, YOU'RE DRIVING ME NUTS!

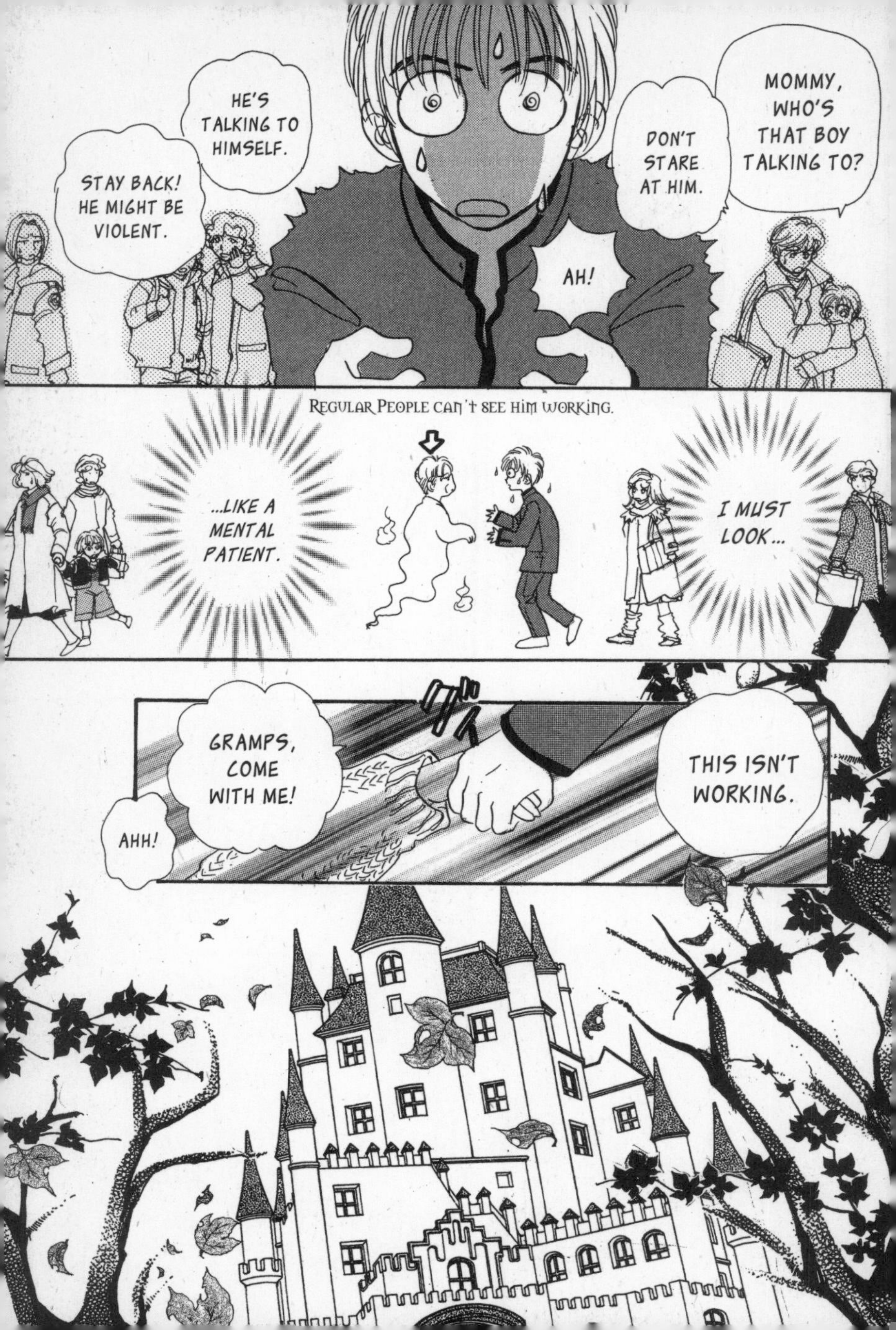
MOMMY, WHO'S THAT BOY TALKING TO?
DON'T STARE AT HIM.
HE'S TALKING TO HIMSELF.
STAY BACK! HE MIGHT BE VIOLENT.
AH!
REGULAR PEOPLE CAN'T SEE HIM WORKING.
I MUST LOOK...
...LIKE A MENTAL PATIENT.
THIS ISN'T WORKING.
GRAMPS, COME WITH ME!
AHH!

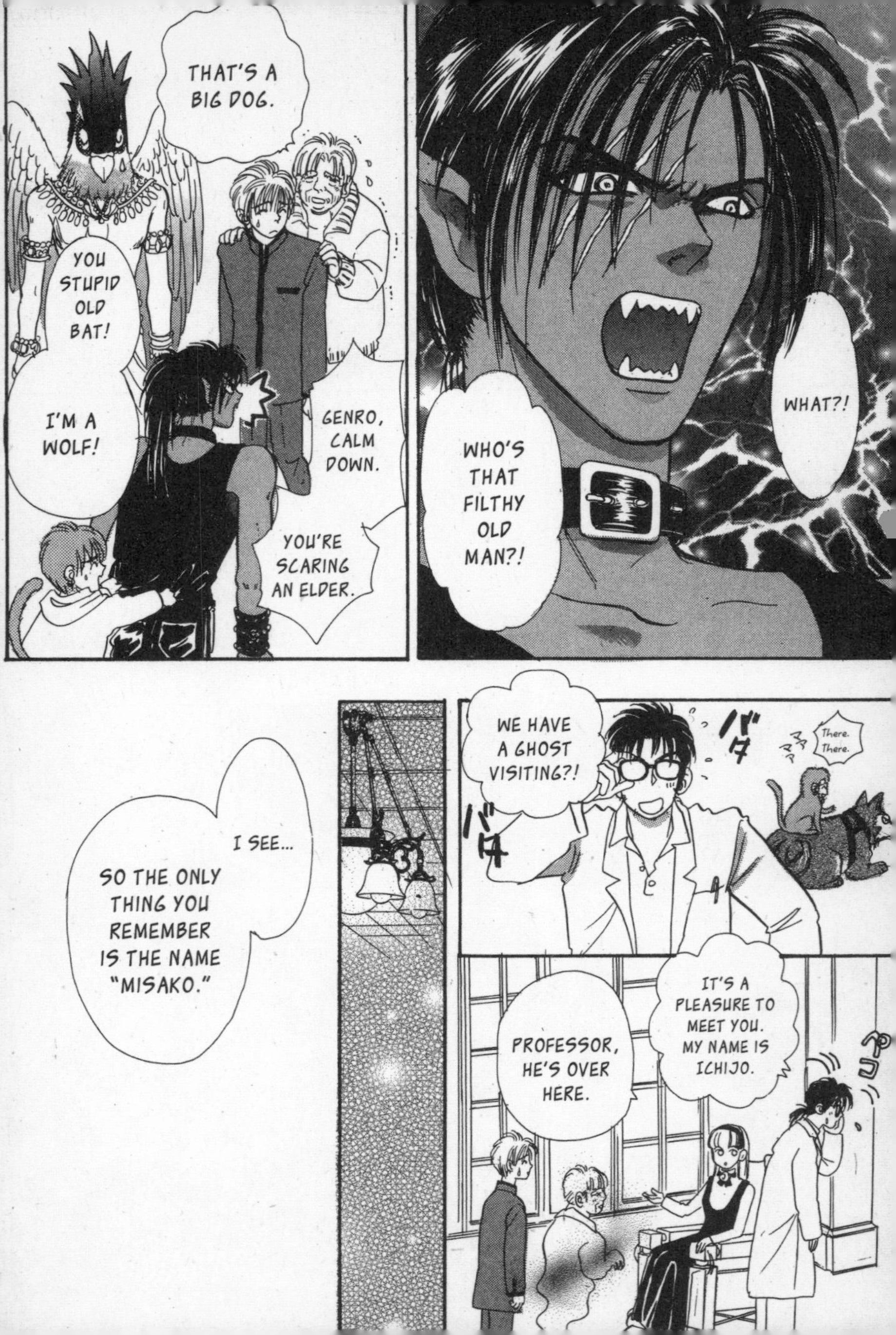
WHAT?!
WHO'S THAT FILTHY OLD MAN?!
THAT'S A BIG DOG.
YOU STUPID OLD BAT!
GENRO, CALM DOWN.
I'M A WOLF!
YOU'RE SCARING AN ELDER.
バタ
WE HAVE A GHOST VISITING?!
There. There.
バタ
ペコ
IT'S A PLEASURE TO MEET YOU. MY NAME IS ICHIJO.
PROFESSOR, HE'S OVER HERE.
I SEE...
SO THE ONLY THING YOU REMEMBER IS THE NAME "MISAKO."

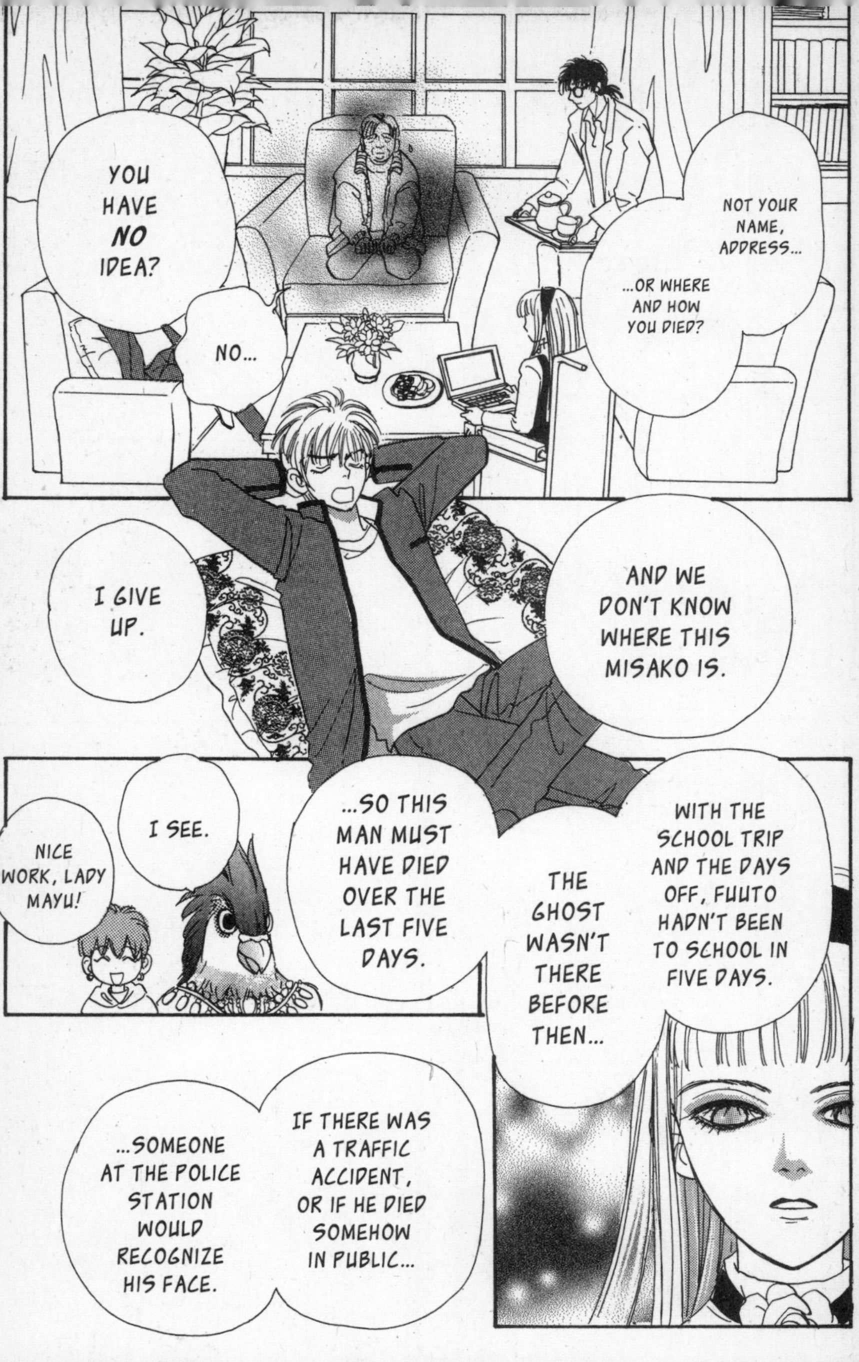
NOT YOUR NAME, ADDRESS... ...OR WHERE AND HOW YOU DIED?
YOU HAVE NO IDEA?
NO...
AND WE DON'T KNOW WHERE THIS MISAKO IS.
I GIVE UP.
WITH THE SCHOOL TRIP AND THE DAYS OFF, FUUTO HADN'T BEEN TO SCHOOL IN FIVE DAYS.
THE GHOST WASN'T THERE BEFORE THEN...
...SO THIS MAN MUST HAVE DIED OVER THE LAST FIVE DAYS.
I SEE.
NICE WORK, LADY MAYU!
IF THERE WAS A TRAFFIC ACCIDENT, OR IF HE DIED SOMEHOW IN PUBLIC...
...SOMEONE AT THE POLICE STATION WOULD RECOGNIZE HIS FACE.

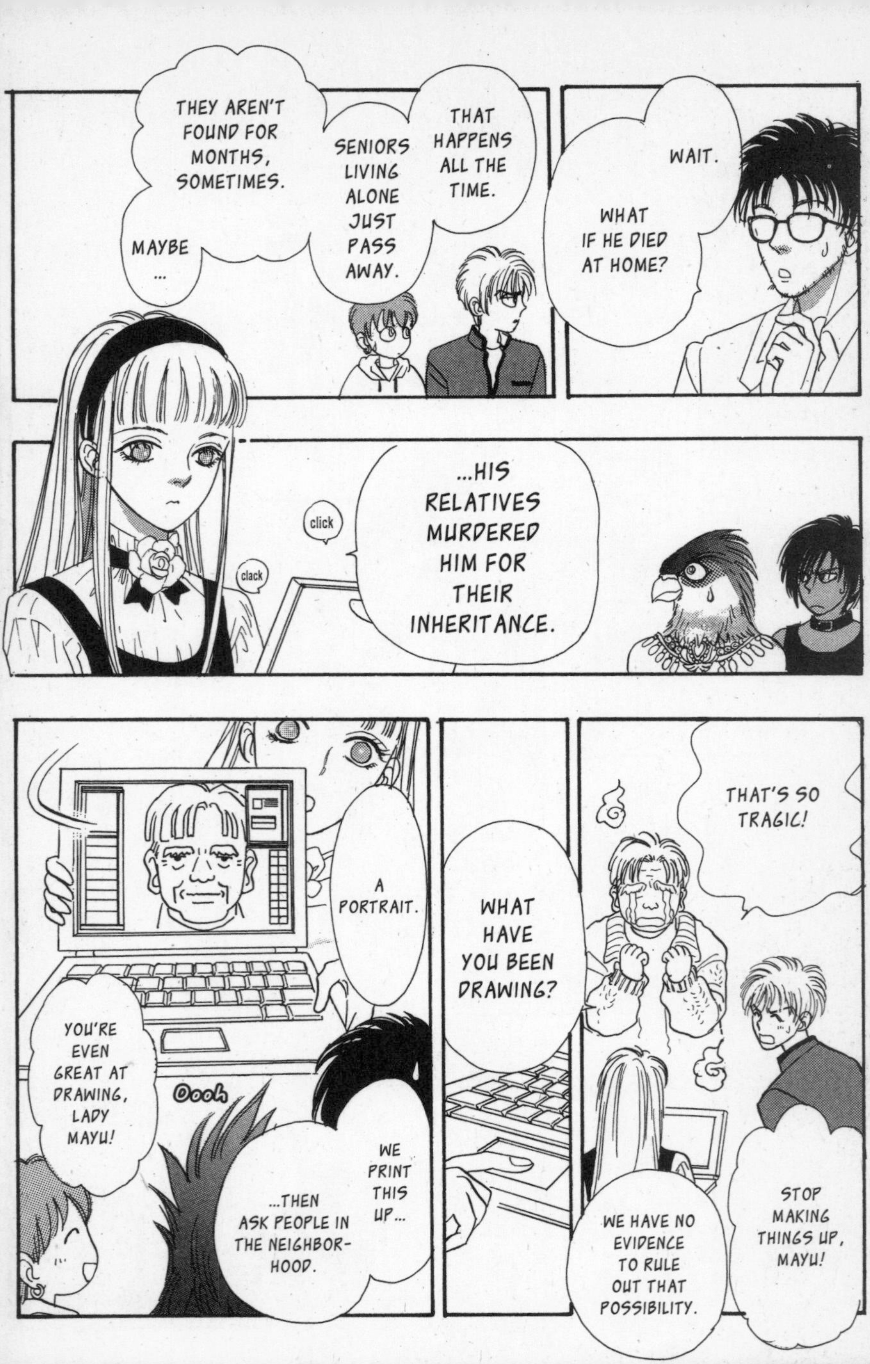
WAIT.
WHAT IF HE DIED AT HOME?
THAT HAPPENS ALL THE TIME.
SENIORS LIVING ALONE JUST PASS AWAY.
THEY AREN'T FOUND FOR MONTHS, SOMETIMES.
MAYBE ...
...HIS RELATIVES MURDERED HIM FOR THEIR INHERITANCE.
click
clack
THAT'S SO TRAGIC!
STOP MAKING THINGS UP, MAYU!
WE HAVE NO EVIDENCE TO RULE OUT THAT POSSIBILITY.
WHAT HAVE YOU BEEN DRAWING?
A PORTRAIT.
WE PRINT THIS UP...
...THEN ASK PEOPLE IN THE NEIGHBOR-HOOD.
YOU'RE EVEN GREAT AT DRAWING, LADY MAYU!
Oooh

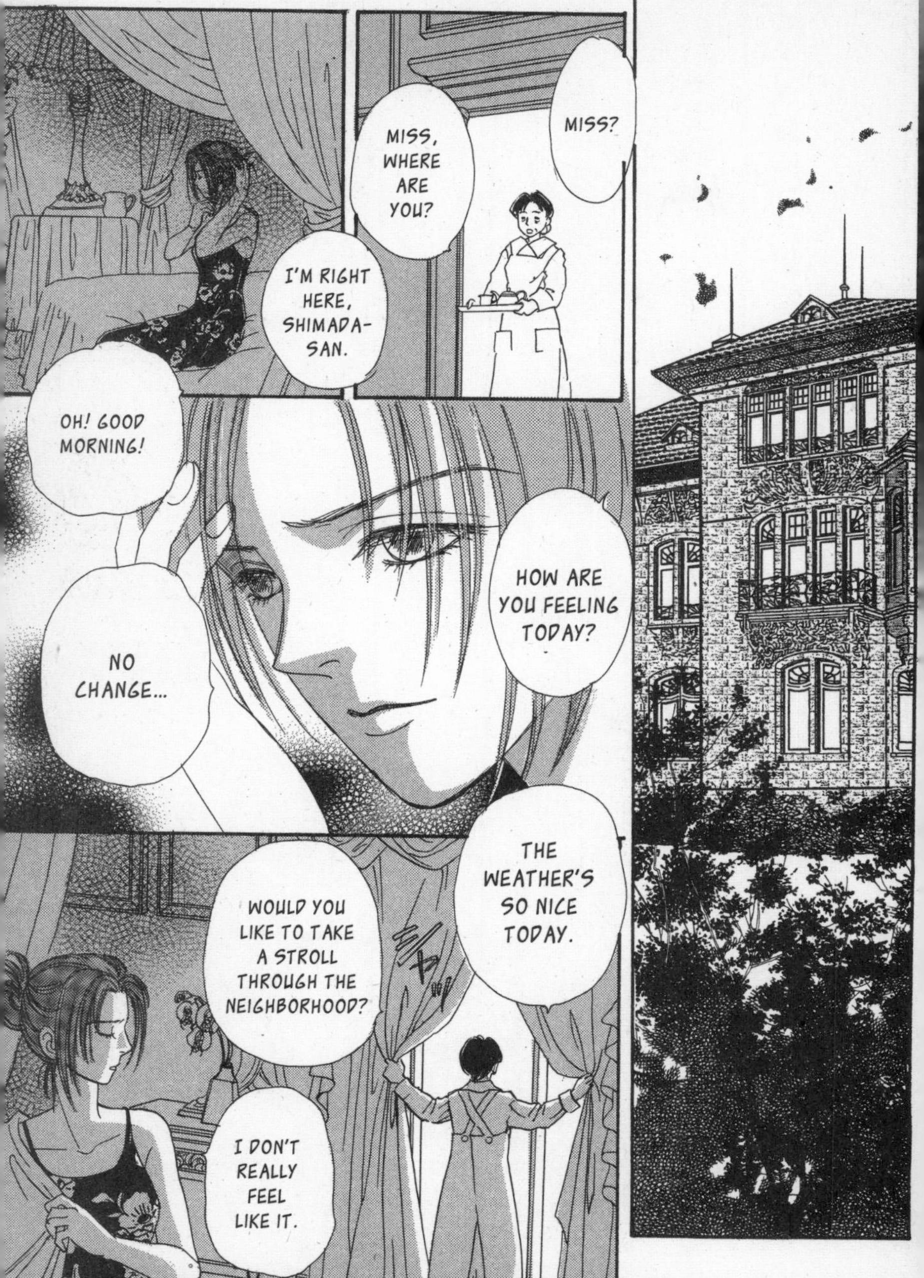
MISS?
MISS, WHERE ARE YOU?
I'M RIGHT HERE, SHIMADA-SAN.
OH! GOOD MORNING!
HOW ARE YOU FEELING TODAY?
NO CHANGE...
THE WEATHER'S SO NICE TODAY.
WOULD YOU LIKE TO TAKE A STROLL THROUGH THE NEIGHBORHOOD?
I DON'T REALLY FEEL LIKE IT.

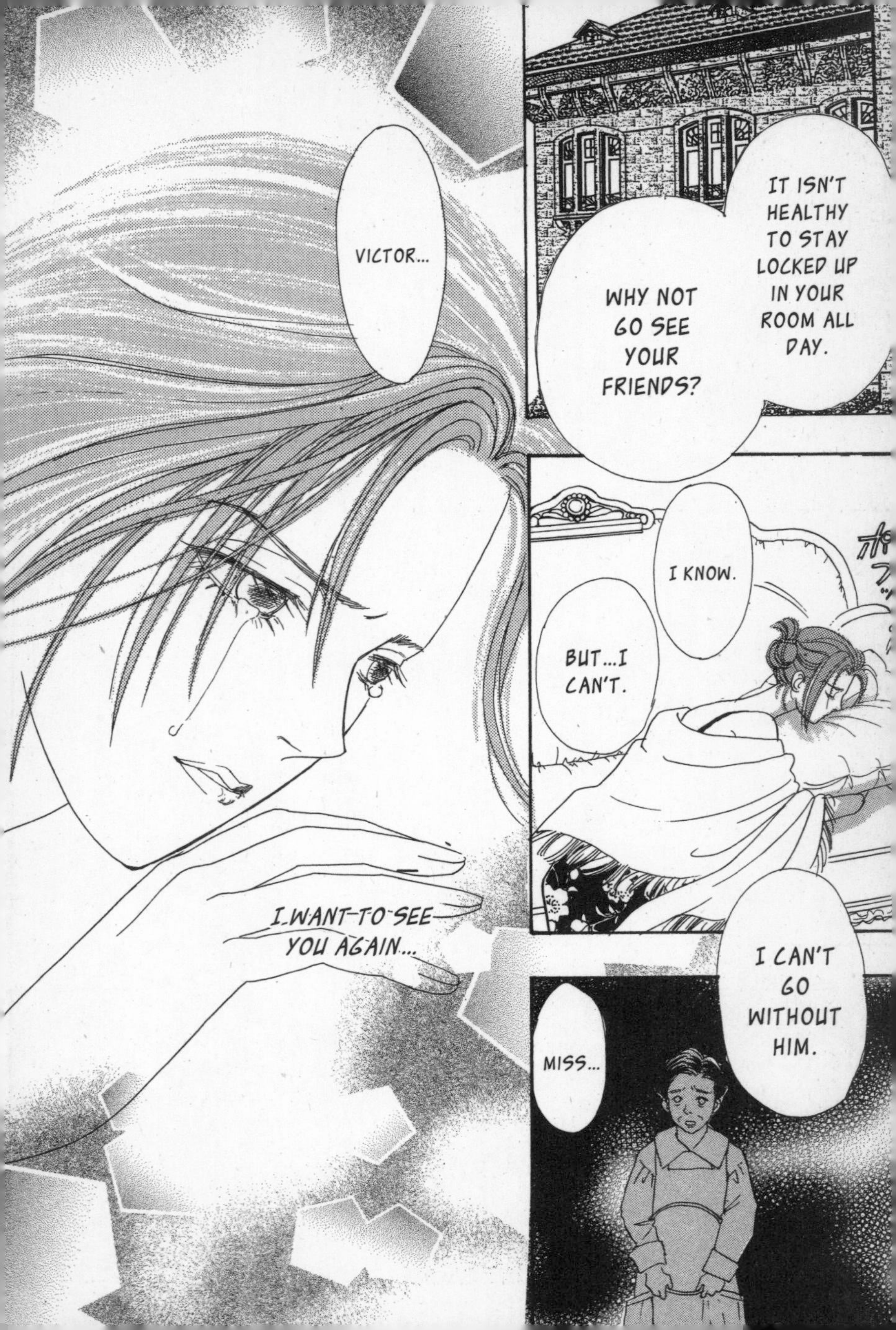

IT ISN'T HEALTHY TO STAY LOCKED UP IN YOUR ROOM ALL DAY.
WHY NOT GO SEE YOUR FRIENDS?
I KNOW.
BUT...I CAN'T.
I CAN'T GO WITHOUT HIM.
MISS...
VICTOR...
I WANT TO SEE YOU AGAIN...

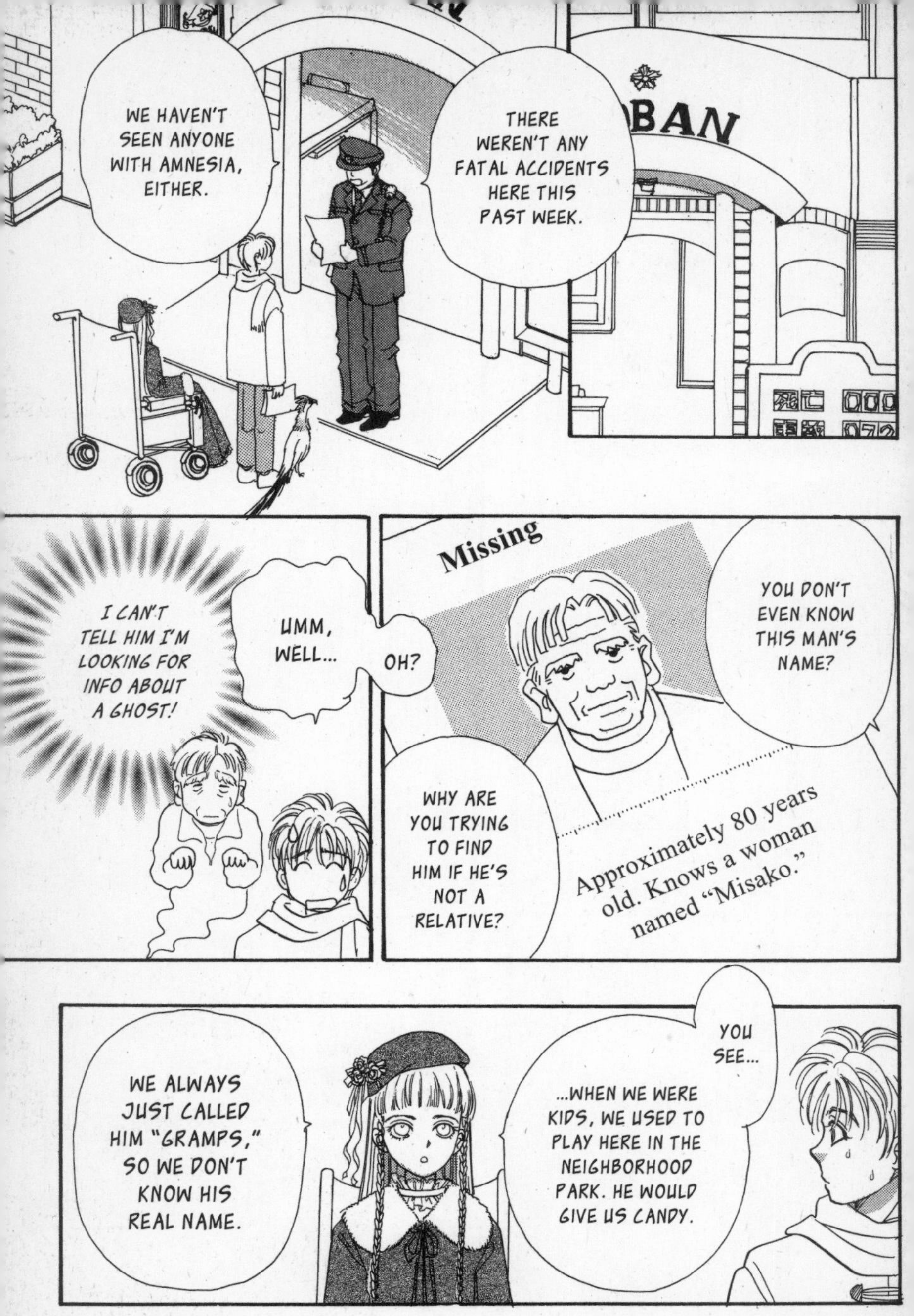
OBAN
THERE WEREN'T ANY FATAL ACCIDENTS HERE THIS PAST WEEK.
WE HAVEN'T SEEN ANYONE WITH AMNESIA, EITHER.
Missing
YOU DON'T EVEN KNOW THIS MAN'S NAME?
Approximately 80 years old. Knows a woman named “Misako.”
WHY ARE YOU TRYING TO FIND HIM IF HE'S NOT A RELATIVE?
OH?
UMM, WELL...
I CAN'T TELL HIM I'M LOOKING FOR INFO ABOUT A GHOST!
YOU SEE...
...WHEN WE WERE KIDS, WE USED TO PLAY HERE IN THE NEIGHBORHOOD PARK. HE WOULD GIVE US CANDY.
WE ALWAYS JUST CALLED HIM "GRAMPS," SO WE DON'T KNOW HIS REAL NAME.

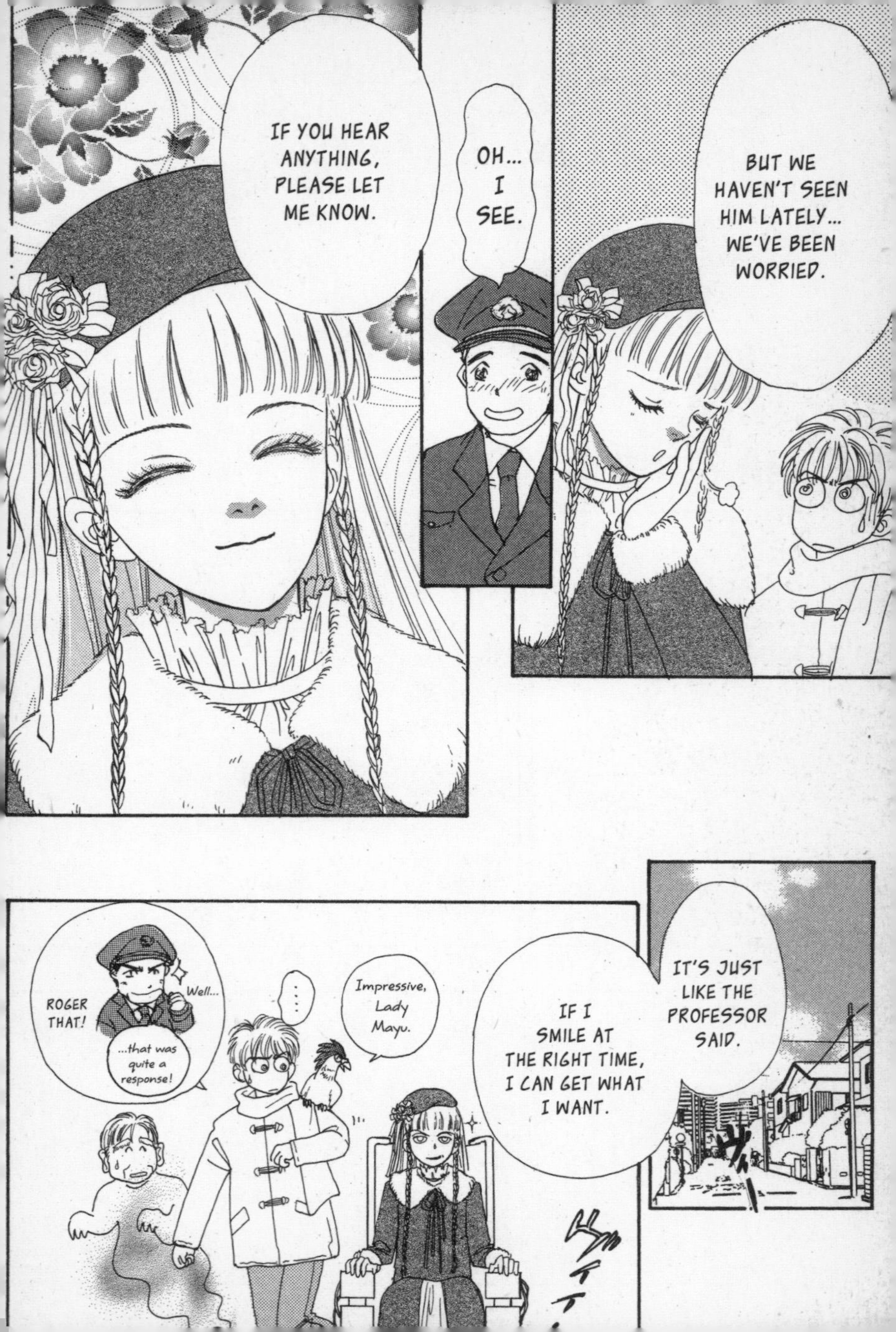
BUT WE HAVEN'T SEEN HIM LATELY... WE'VE BEEN WORRIED.
OH... I SEE.
IF YOU HEAR ANYTHING, PLEASE LET ME KNOW.
IT'S JUST LIKE THE PROFESSOR SAID.
IF I SMILE AT THE RIGHT TIME, I CAN GET WHAT I WANT.
Impressive, Lady Mayu.
....
ROGER THAT!
Well...
...that was quite a response!

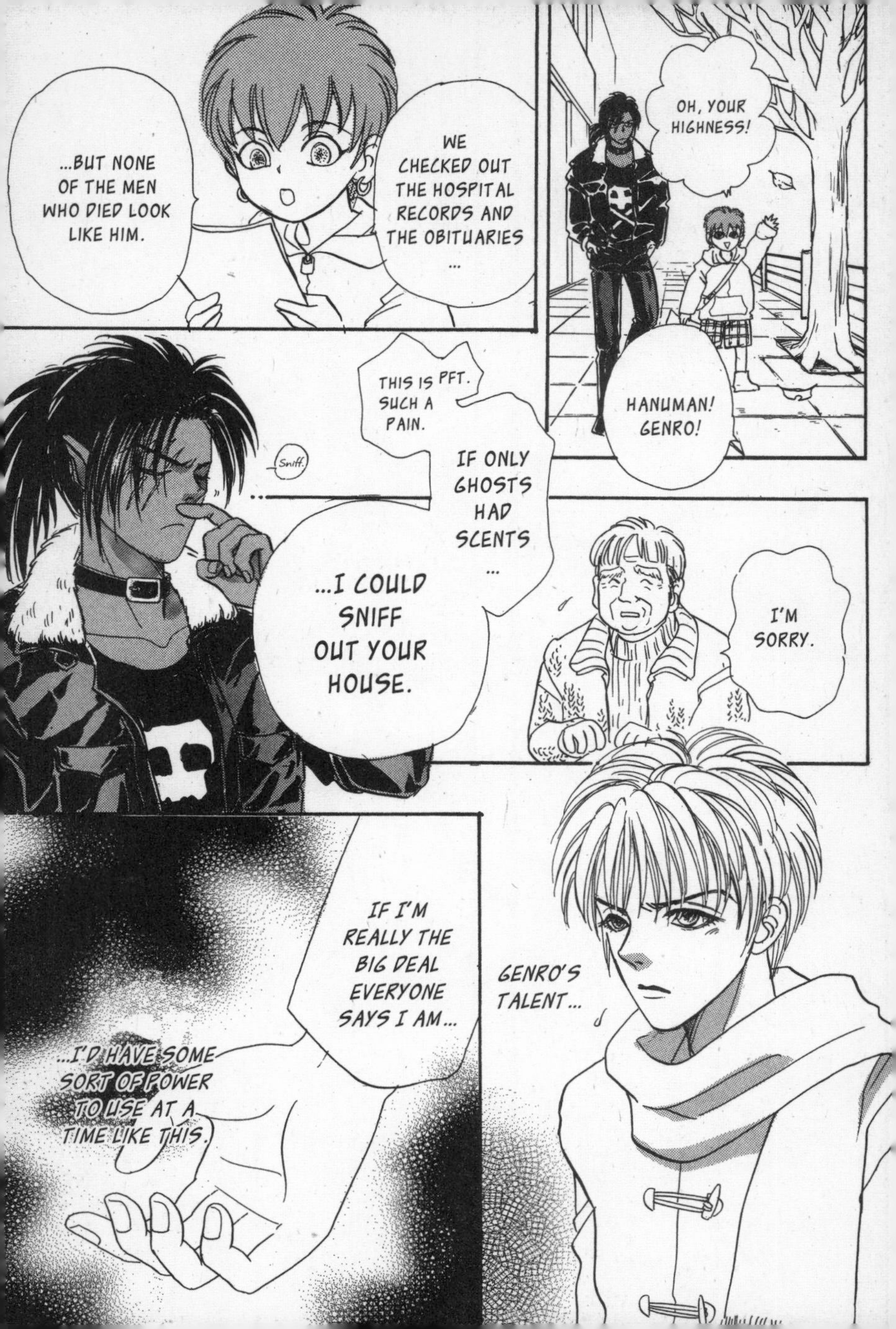
OH, YOUR HIGHNESS!
HANUMAN! GENRO!
WE CHECKED OUT THE HOSPITAL RECORDS AND THE OBITUARIES ...
...BUT NONE OF THE MEN WHO DIED LOOK LIKE HIM.
I'M SORRY.
THIS IS SUCH A PAIN.
PFT.
Sniff.
IF ONLY GHOSTS HAD SCENTS ...
...I COULD SNIFF OUT YOUR HOUSE.
GENRO'S TALENT...
IF I'M REALLY THE BIG DEAL EVERYONE SAYS I AM...
...I'D HAVE SOME SORT OF POWER TO USE AT A TIME LIKE THIS.

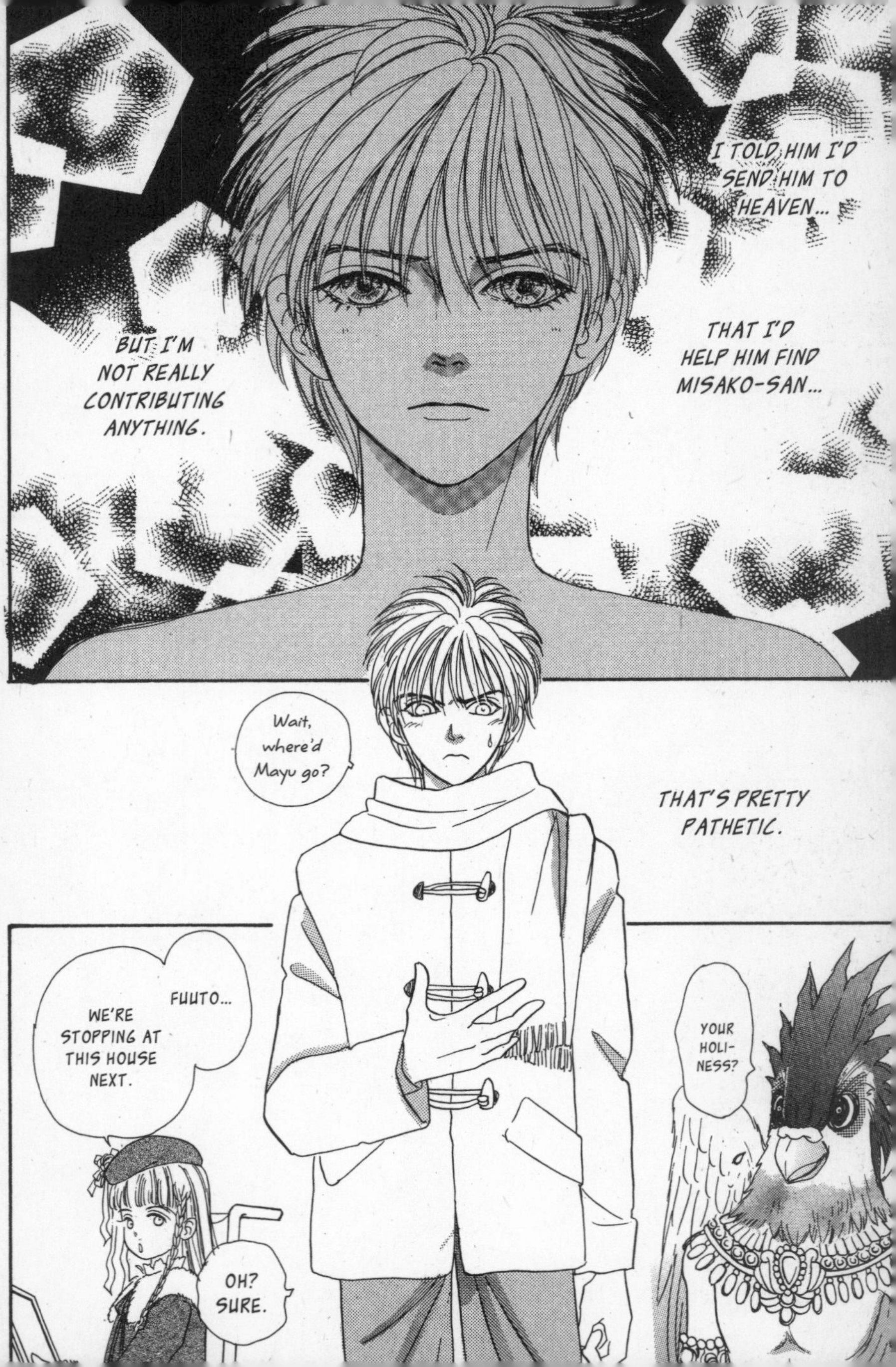
I TOLD HIM I'D SEND HIM TO HEAVEN...
THAT I'D HELP HIM FIND MISAKO-SAN...
BUT I'M NOT REALLY CONTRIBUTING ANYTHING.
THAT'S PRETTY PATHETIC.
Wait, where'd Mayu go?
YOUR HOLINESS?
FUUTO... WE'RE STOPPING AT THIS HOUSE NEXT.
OH? SURE.

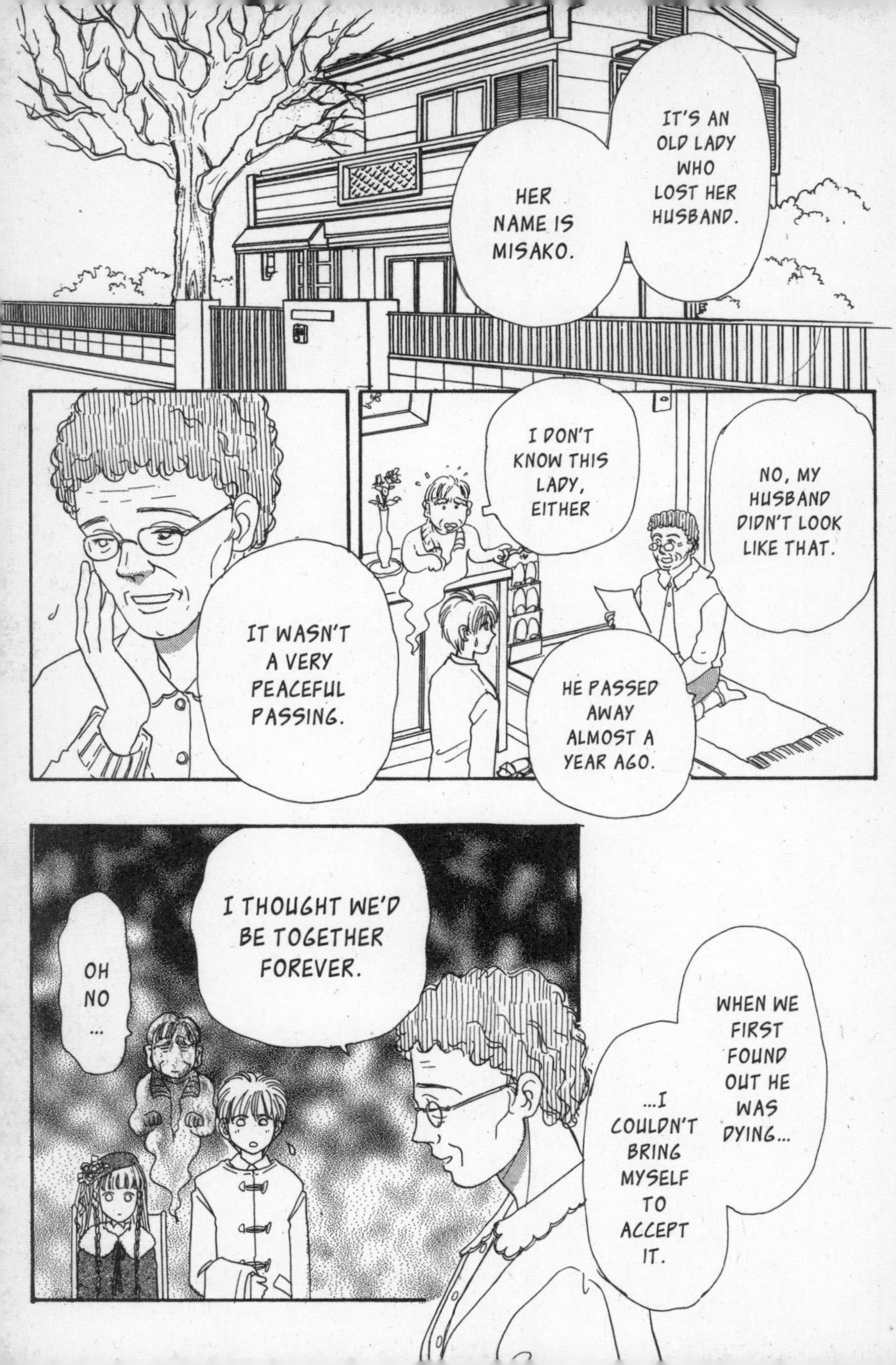
IT'S AN OLD LADY WHO LOST HER HUSBAND.
HER NAME IS MISAKO.
NO, MY HUSBAND DIDN'T LOOK LIKE THAT.
I DON'T KNOW THIS LADY, EITHER
HE PASSED AWAY ALMOST A YEAR AGO.
IT WASN'T A VERY PEACEFUL PASSING.
WHEN WE FIRST FOUND OUT HE WAS DYING...
...I COULDN'T BRING MYSELF TO ACCEPT IT.
I THOUGHT WE'D BE TOGETHER FOREVER.
OH NO ...

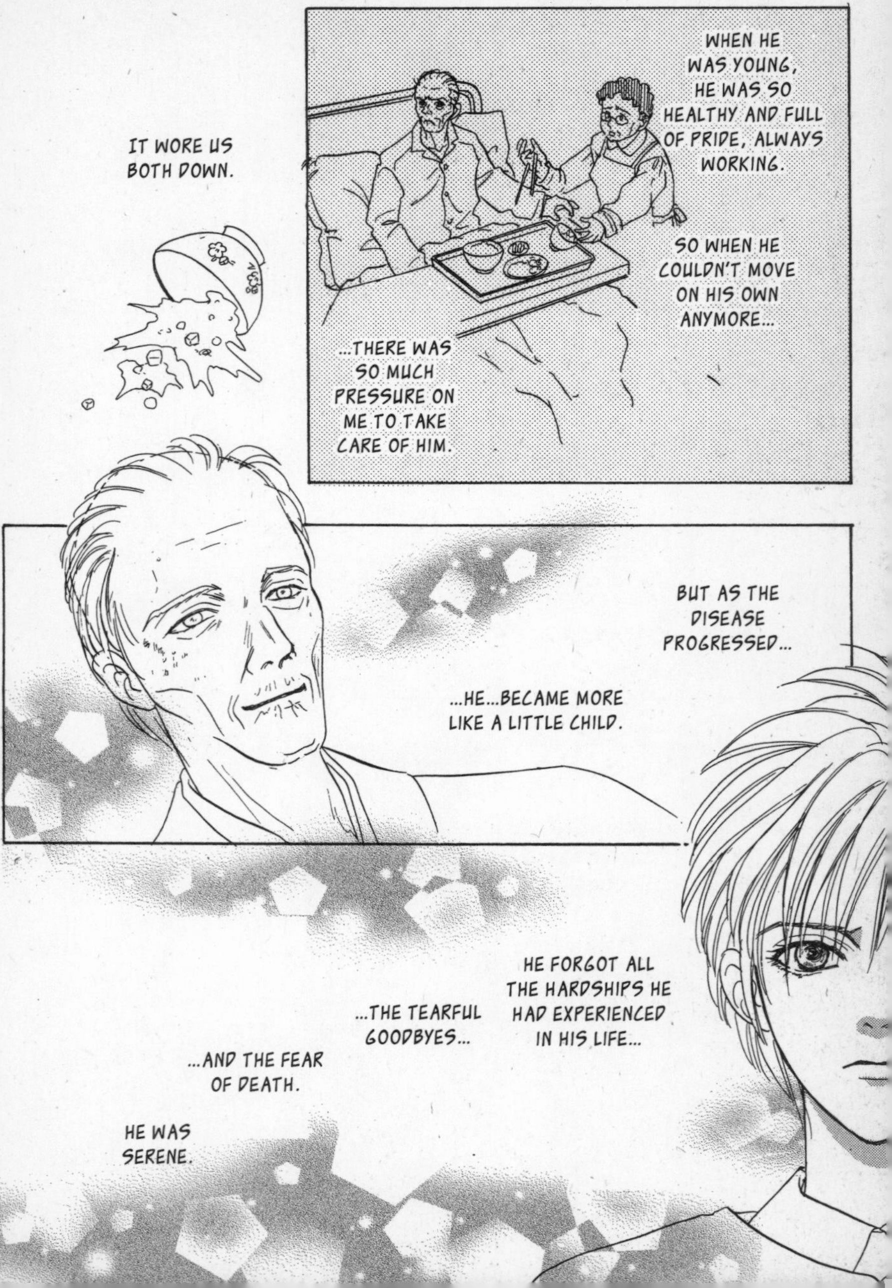
WHEN HE WAS YOUNG, HE WAS SO HEALTHY AND FULL OF PRIDE, ALWAYS WORKING.
SO WHEN HE COULDN'T MOVE ON HIS OWN ANYMORE...
...THERE WAS SO MUCH PRESSURE ON ME TO TAKE CARE OF HIM.
IT WORE US BOTH DOWN.
BUT AS THE DISEASE PROGRESSED...
...HE...BECAME MORE LIKE A LITTLE CHILD.
HE FORGOT ALL THE HARDSHIPS HE HAD EXPERIENCED IN HIS LIFE...
...THE TEARFUL GOODBYES...
...AND THE FEAR OF DEATH.
HE WAS SERENE.

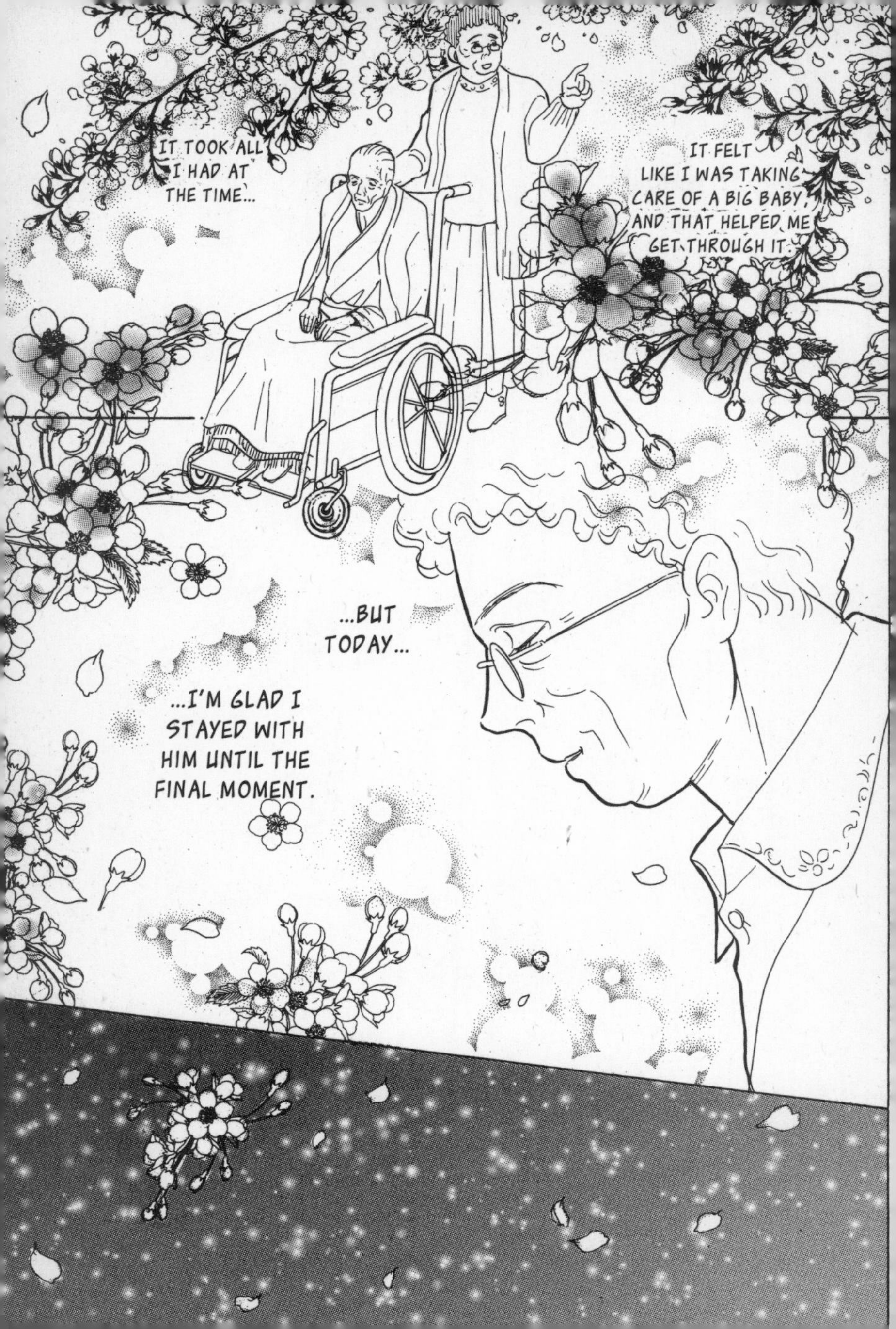
IT FELT LIKE I WAS TAKING CARE OF A BIG BABY, AND THAT HELPED ME GET THROUGH IT.
IT TOOK ALL I HAD AT THE TIME...
...BUT TODAY...
...I'M GLAD I STAYED WITH HIM UNTIL THE FINAL MOMENT.

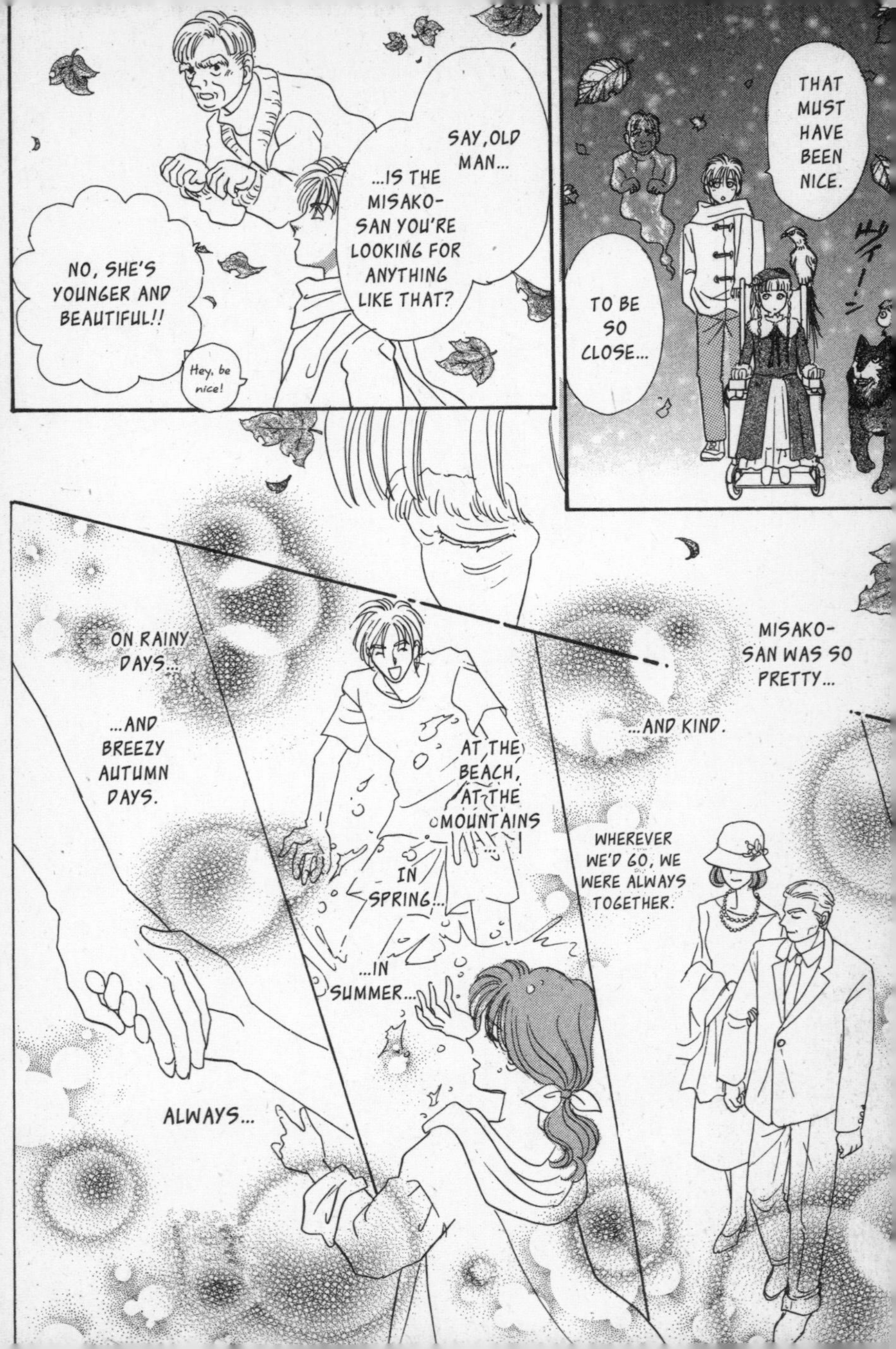
THAT MUST HAVE BEEN NICE.
TO BE SO CLOSE...
SAY, OLD MAN...
...IS THE MISAKO-SAN YOU'RE LOOKING FOR ANYTHING LIKE THAT?
NO, SHE'S YOUNGER AND BEAUTIFUL!!
Hey, be nice!
MISAKO-SAN WAS SO PRETTY...
...AND KIND.
WHEREVER WE'D GO, WE WERE ALWAYS TOGETHER.
AT THE BEACH, AT THE MOUNTAINS...
IN SPRING...
...IN SUMMER...
ON RAINY DAYS...
...AND BREEZY AUTUMN DAYS.
ALWAYS...

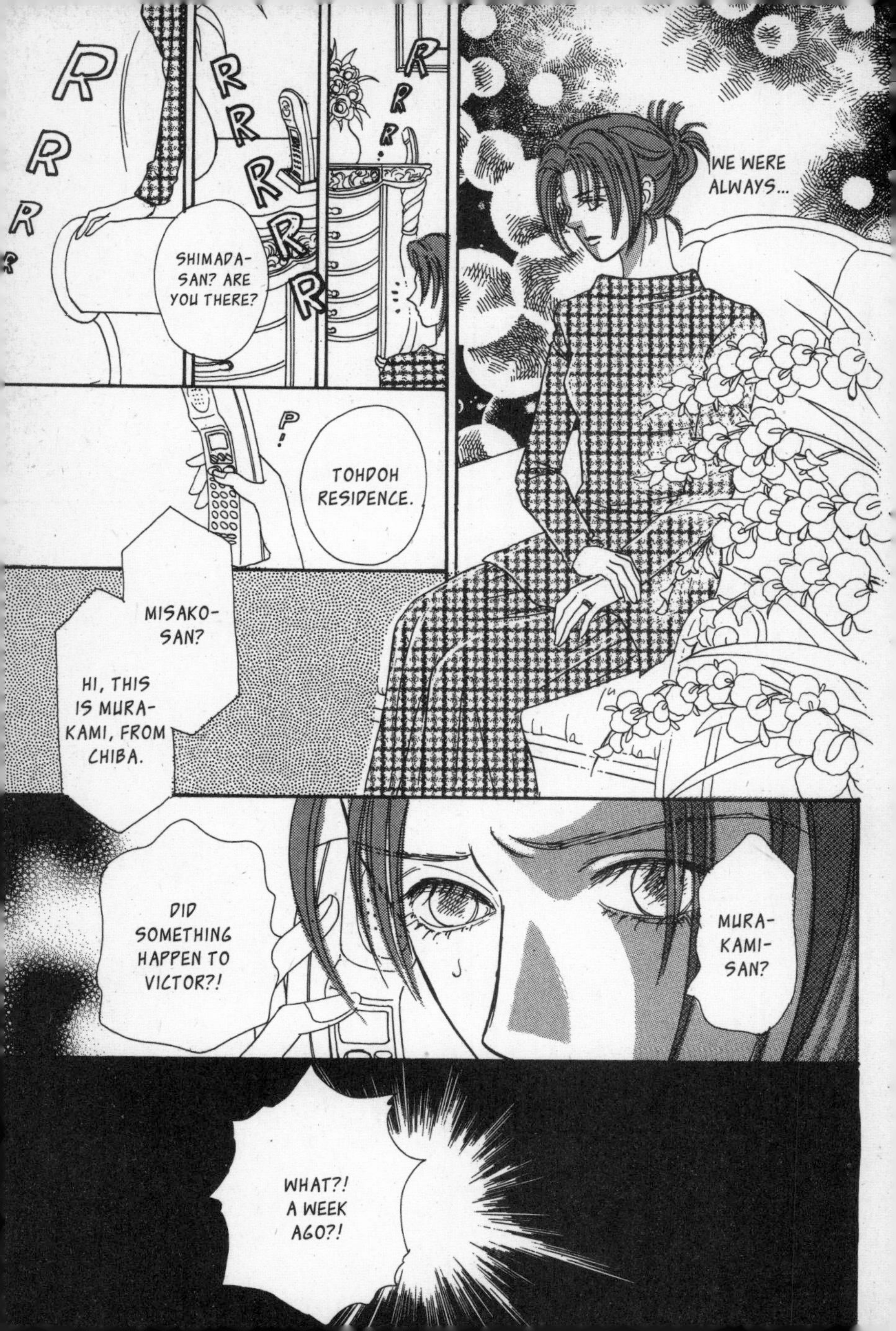

WE WERE ALWAYS...
R R R
RRRRR
R R R R
SHIMADA-SAN? ARE YOU THERE?
P!
TOHDOH RESIDENCE.
MISAKO-SAN?
HI, THIS IS MURA-KAMI, FROM CHIBA.
MURA-KAMI-SAN?
DID SOMETHING HAPPEN TO VICTOR?!
WHAT?! A WEEK AGO?!

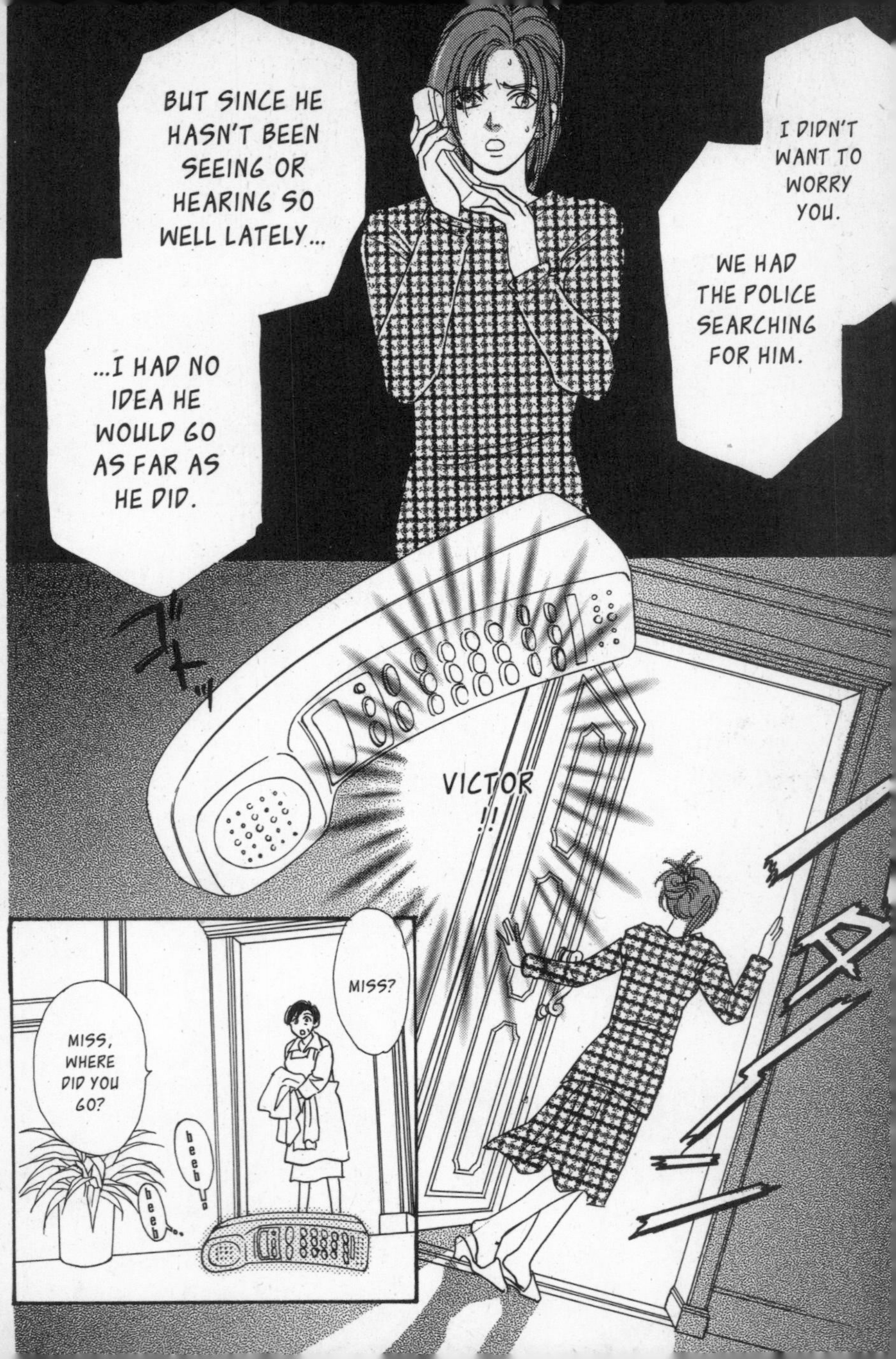

I DIDN'T WANT TO WORRY YOU.
WE HAD THE POLICE SEARCHING FOR HIM.
BUT SINCE HE HASN'T BEEN SEEING OR HEARING SO WELL LATELY...
...I HAD NO IDEA HE WOULD GO AS FAR AS HE DID.
ゴトッ
VICTOR !!
MISS?
MISS, WHERE DID YOU GO?
beeb
beeb

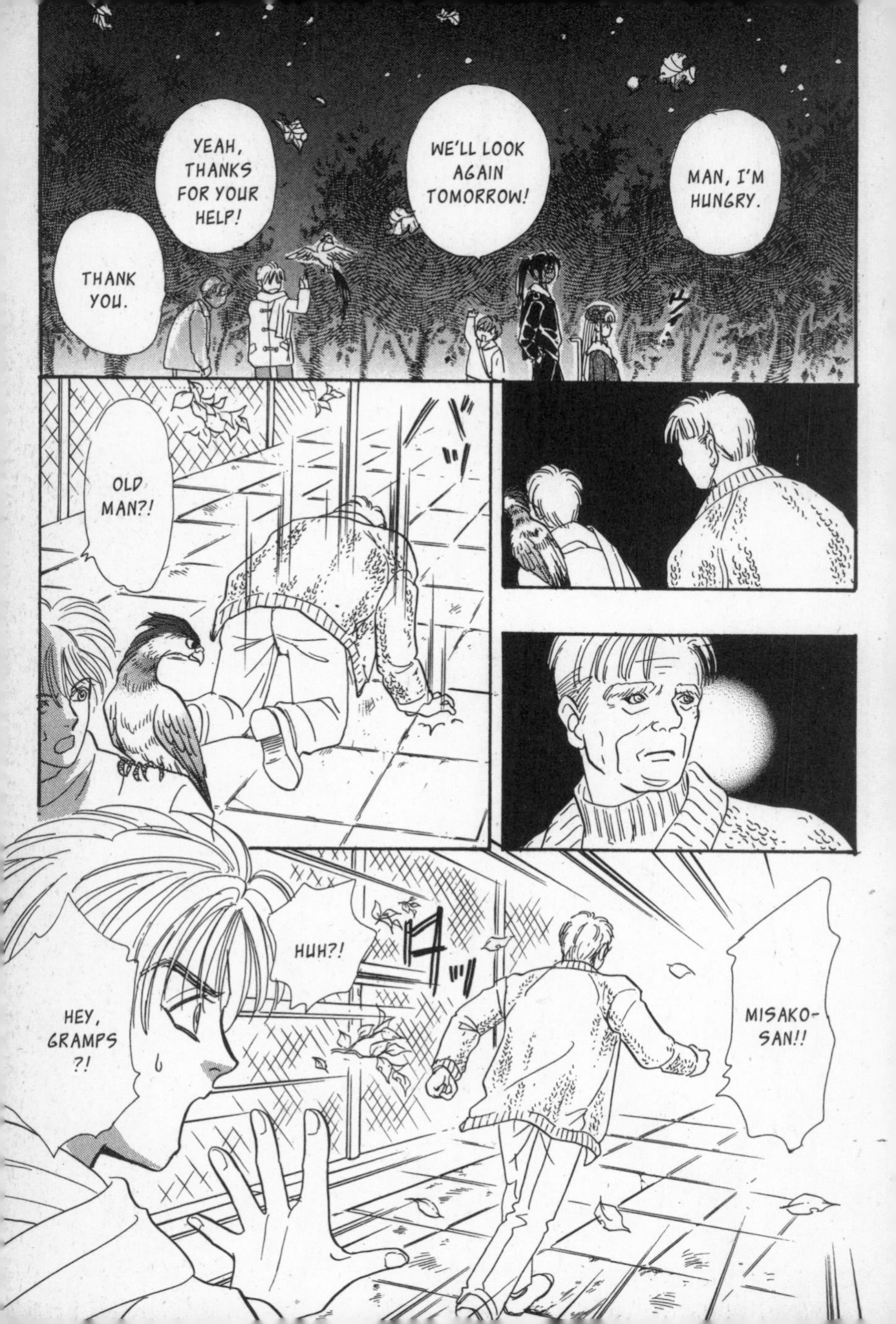
MAN, I'M HUNGRY.
WE'LL LOOK AGAIN TOMORROW!
YEAH, THANKS FOR YOUR HELP!
THANK YOU.
OLD MAN?!
MISAKO-SAN!!
HUH?!
HEY, GRAMPS ?!

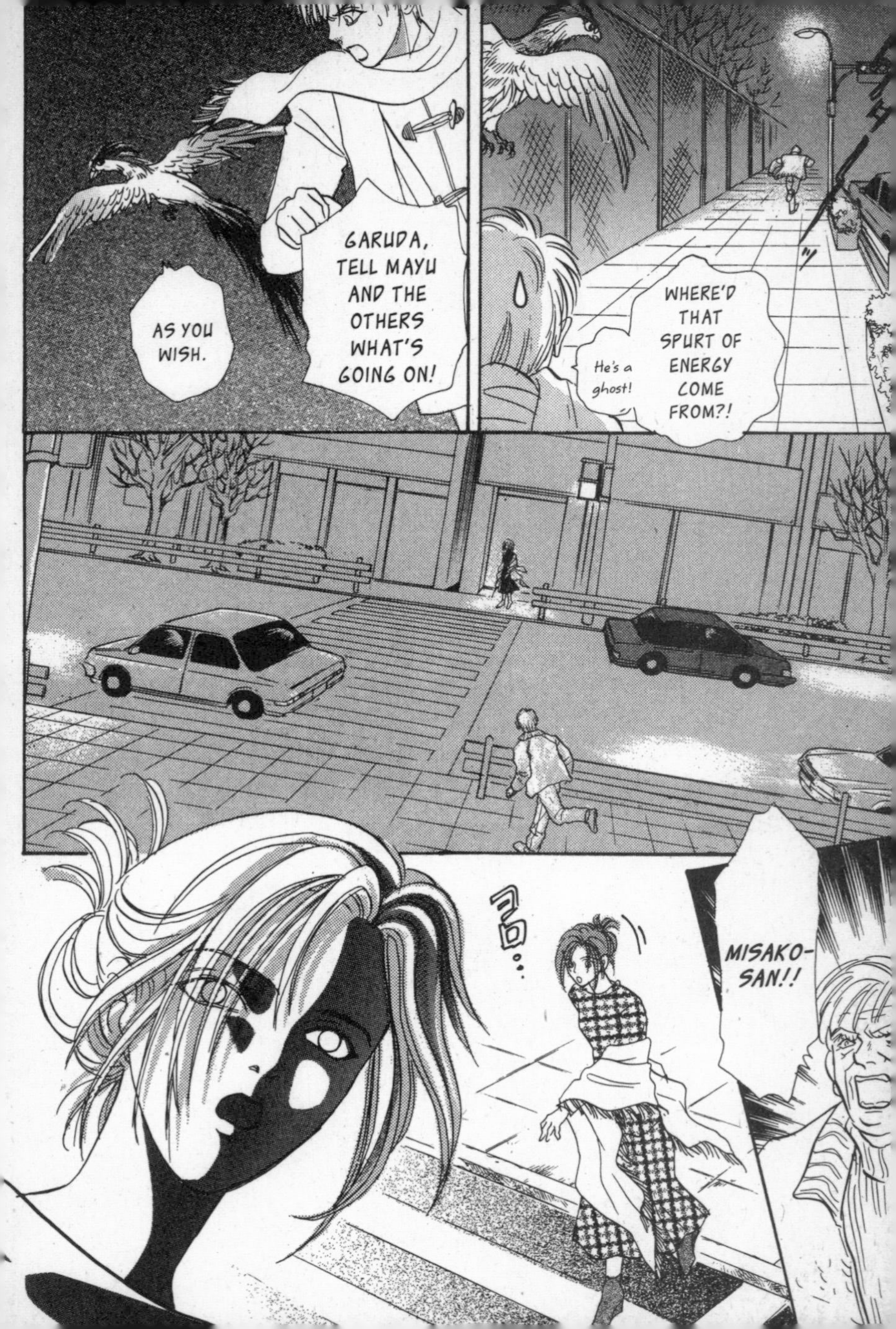
WHERE'D THAT SPURT OF ENERGY COME FROM?!
He's a ghost!
GARUDA, TELL MAYU AND THE OTHERS WHAT'S GOING ON!
AS YOU WISH.
MISAKO-SAN!!
ヨロ...

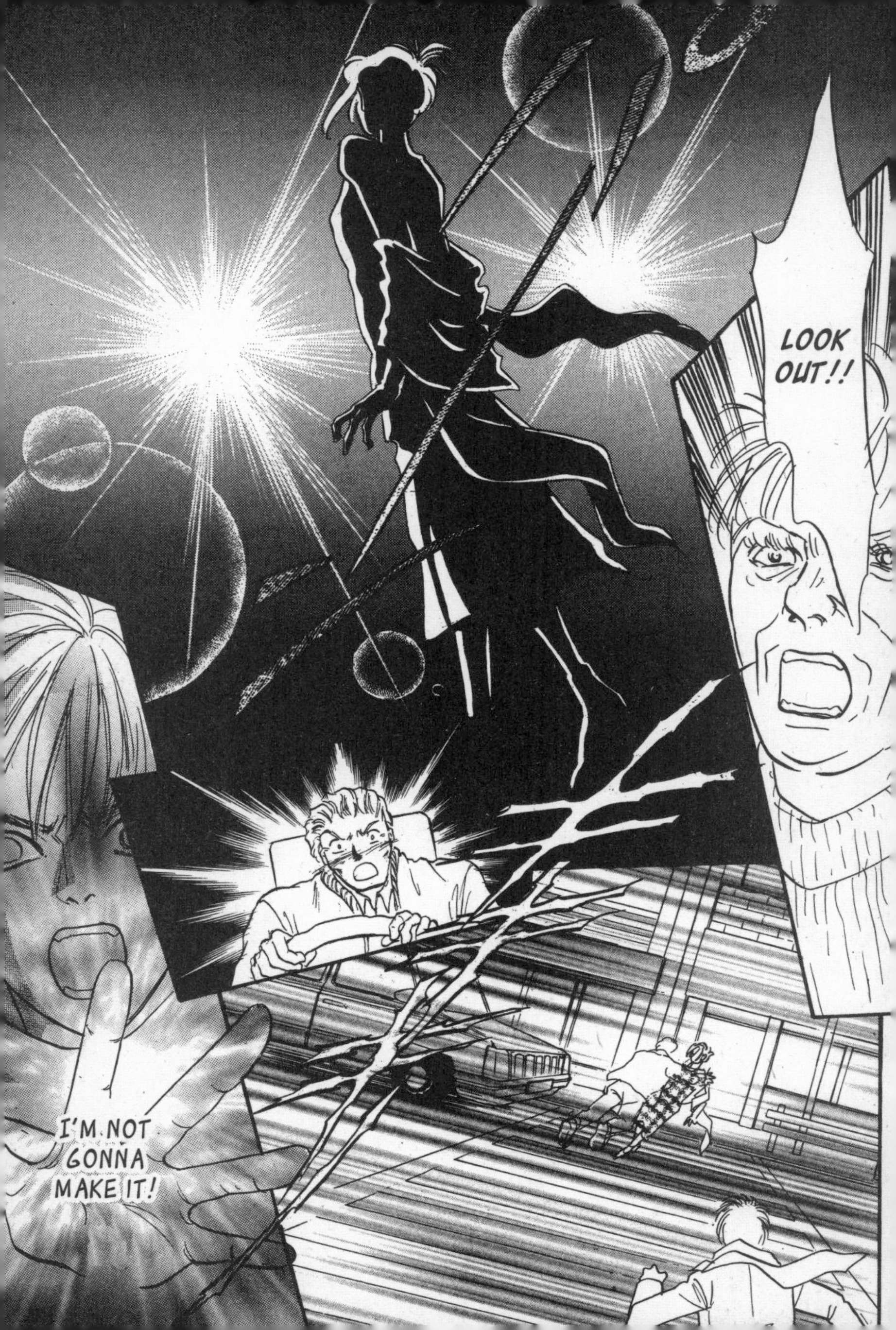
LOOK OUT!!
I'M NOT GONNA MAKE IT!

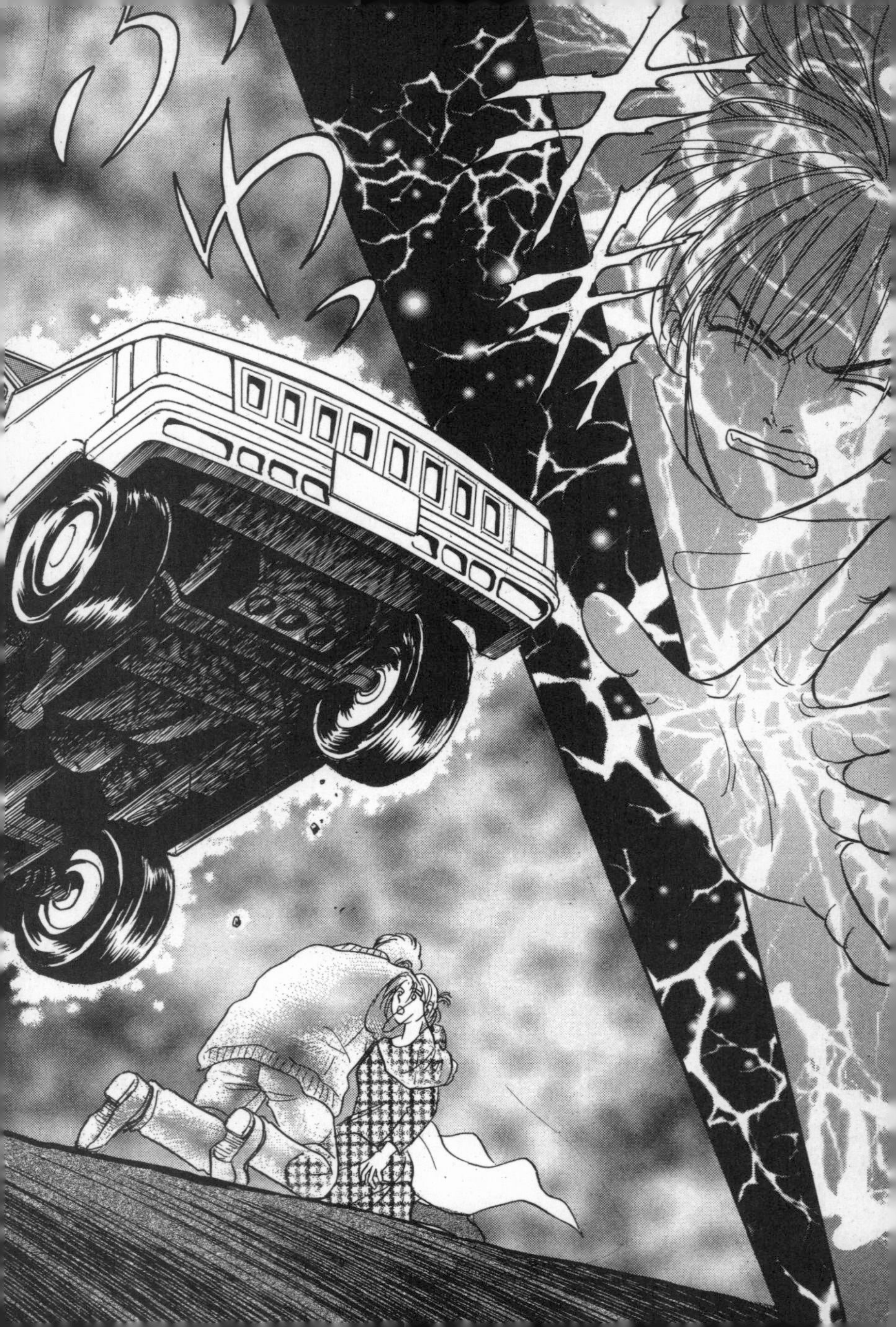
ゔわっ

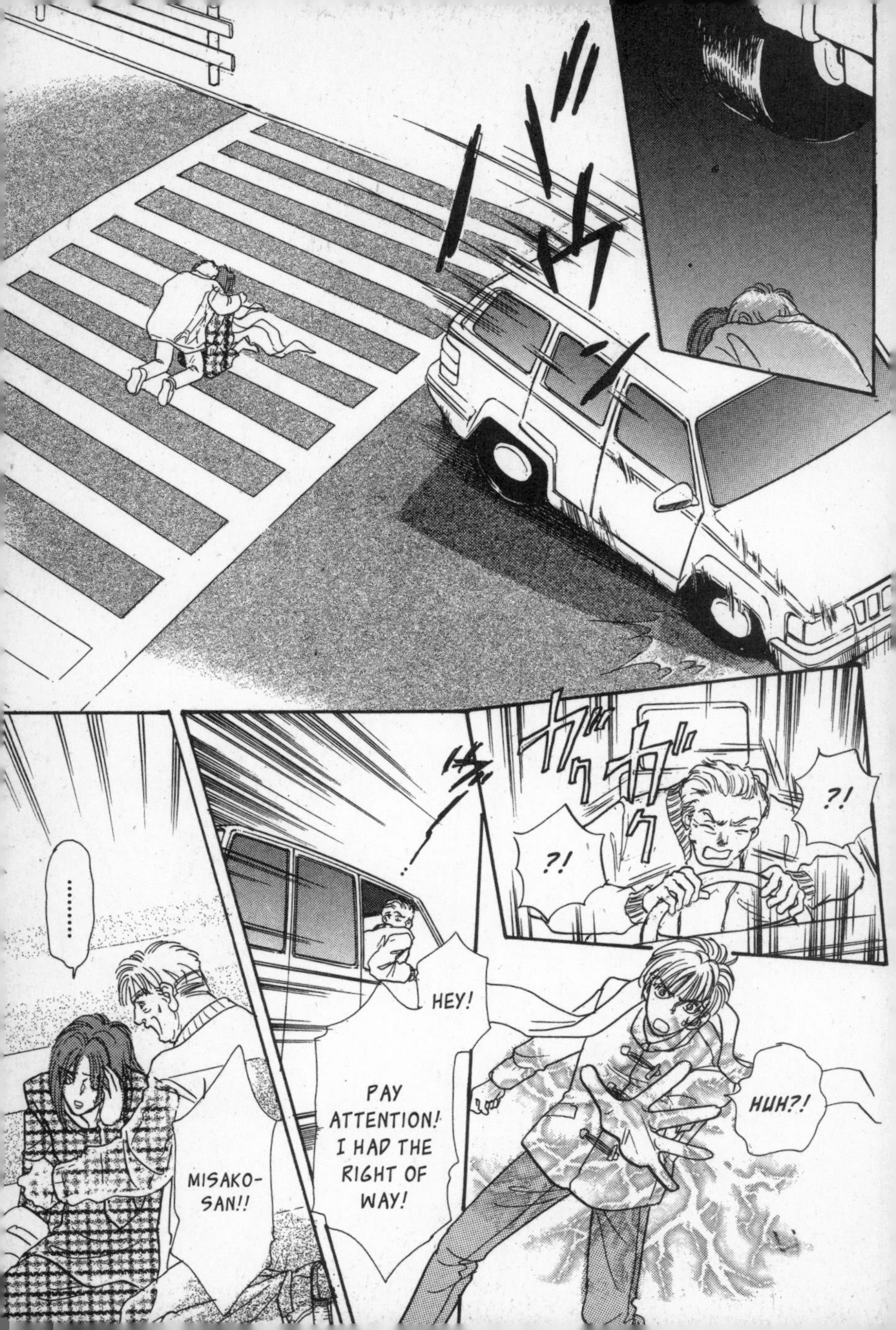
?!
?!
HUH?!
HEY!
PAY ATTENTION! I HAD THE RIGHT OF WAY!
......
MISAKO-SAN!!

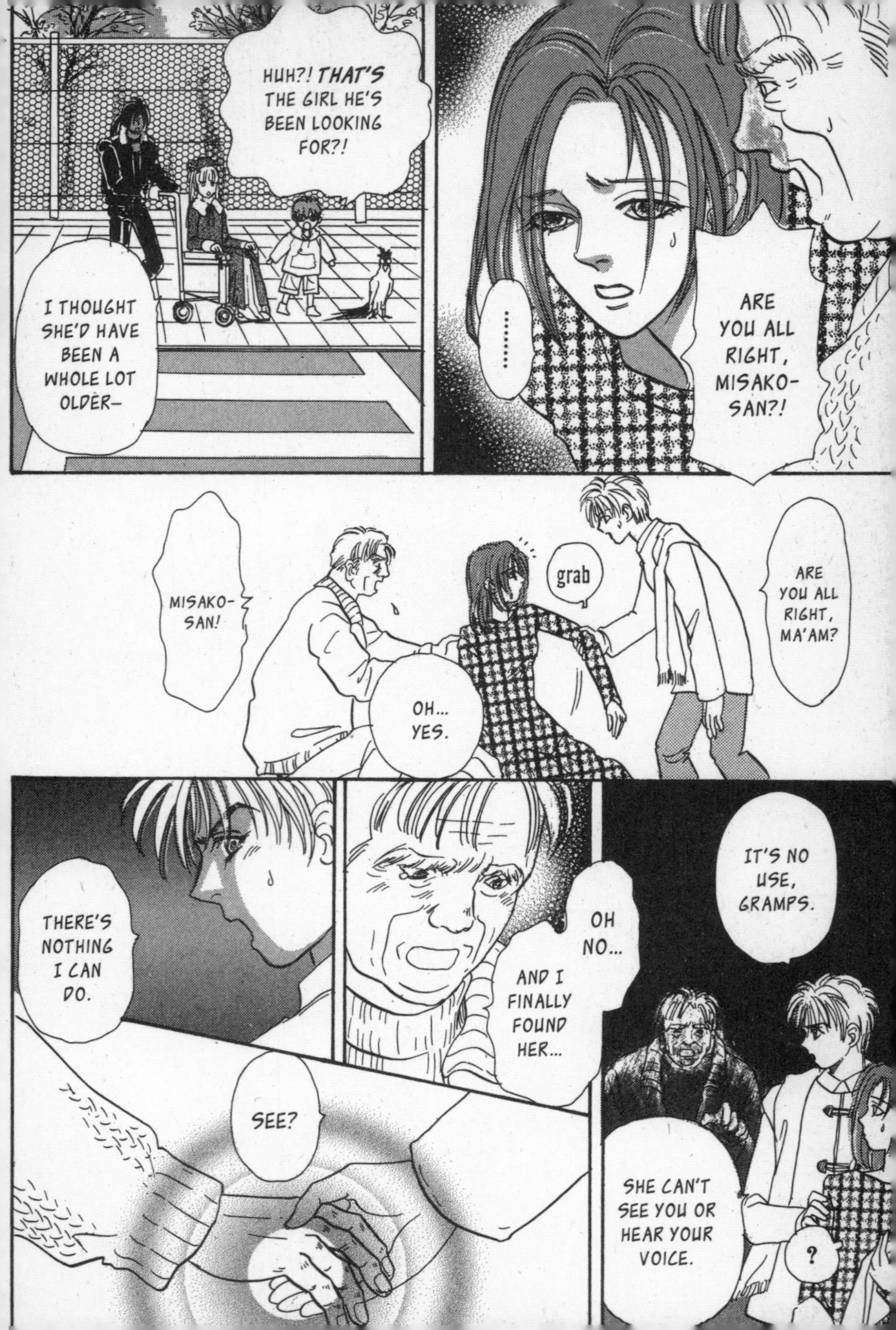
ARE YOU ALL RIGHT, MISAKO-SAN?!
……
HUH?! THAT'S THE GIRL HE'S BEEN LOOKING FOR?!
I THOUGHT SHE'D HAVE BEEN A WHOLE LOT OLDER—
ARE YOU ALL RIGHT, MA'AM?
grab
MISAKO-SAN!
OH... YES.
IT'S NO USE, GRAMPS.
SHE CAN'T SEE YOU OR HEAR YOUR VOICE.
?
OH NO...
AND I FINALLY FOUND HER...
THERE'S NOTHING I CAN DO.
SEE?

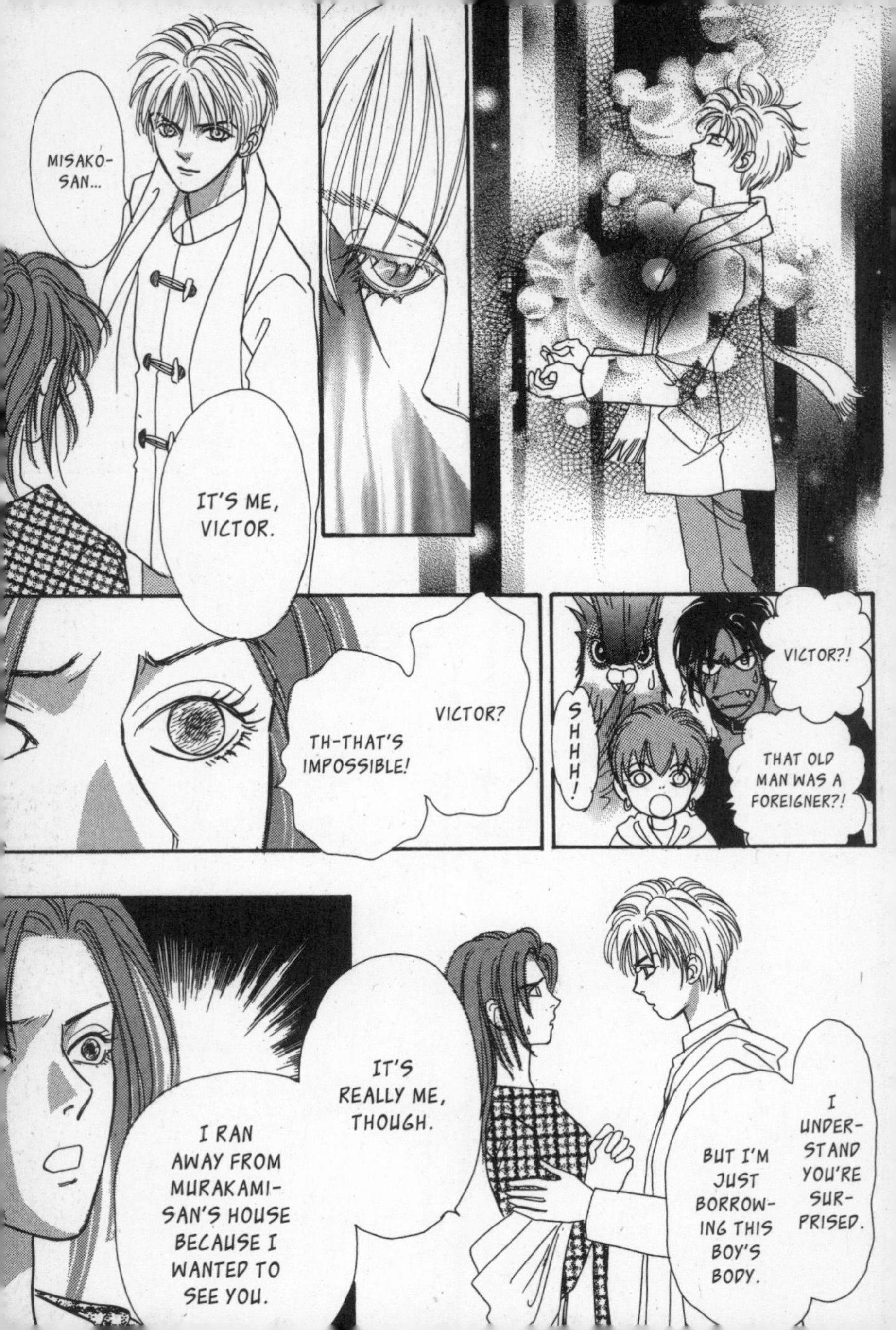
MISAKO-SAN...
IT'S ME, VICTOR.
VICTOR?!
THAT OLD MAN WAS A FOREIGNER?!
SHHH!
VICTOR?
TH-THAT'S IMPOSSIBLE!
I UNDERSTAND YOU'RE SURPRISED.
BUT I'M JUST BORROWING THIS BOY'S BODY.
IT'S REALLY ME, THOUGH.
I RAN AWAY FROM MURAKAMI-SAN'S HOUSE BECAUSE I WANTED TO SEE YOU.

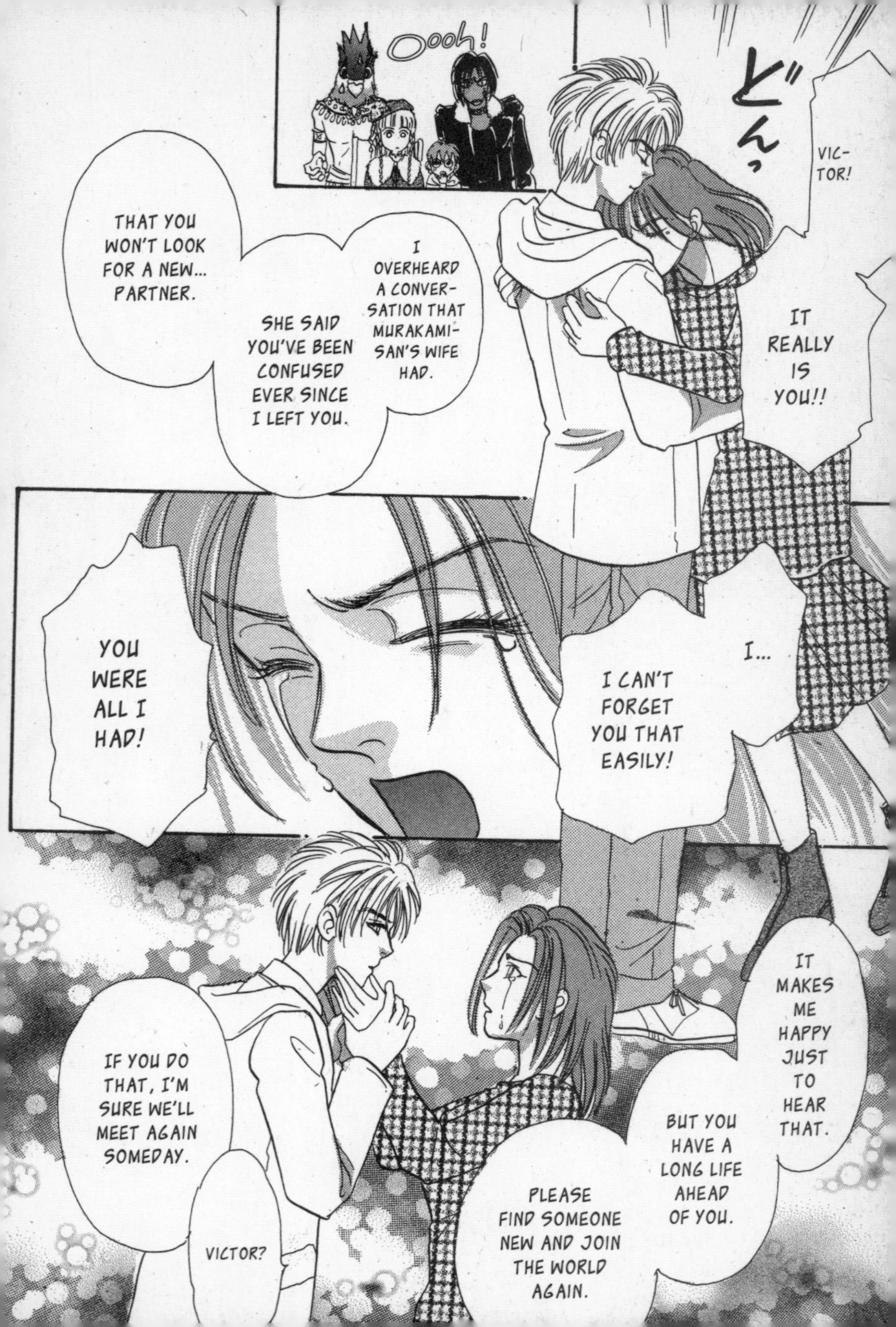
どん
VICTOR!
IT REALLY IS YOU!!
Oooh!
I OVERHEARD A CONVERSATION THAT MURAKAMI-SAN'S WIFE HAD.
SHE SAID YOU'VE BEEN CONFUSED EVER SINCE I LEFT YOU.
THAT YOU WON'T LOOK FOR A NEW... PARTNER.
I...
I CAN'T FORGET YOU THAT EASILY!
YOU WERE ALL I HAD!
IT MAKES ME HAPPY JUST TO HEAR THAT.
BUT YOU HAVE A LONG LIFE AHEAD OF YOU.
PLEASE FIND SOMEONE NEW AND JOIN THE WORLD AGAIN.
IF YOU DO THAT, I'M SURE WE'LL MEET AGAIN SOMEDAY.
VICTOR?

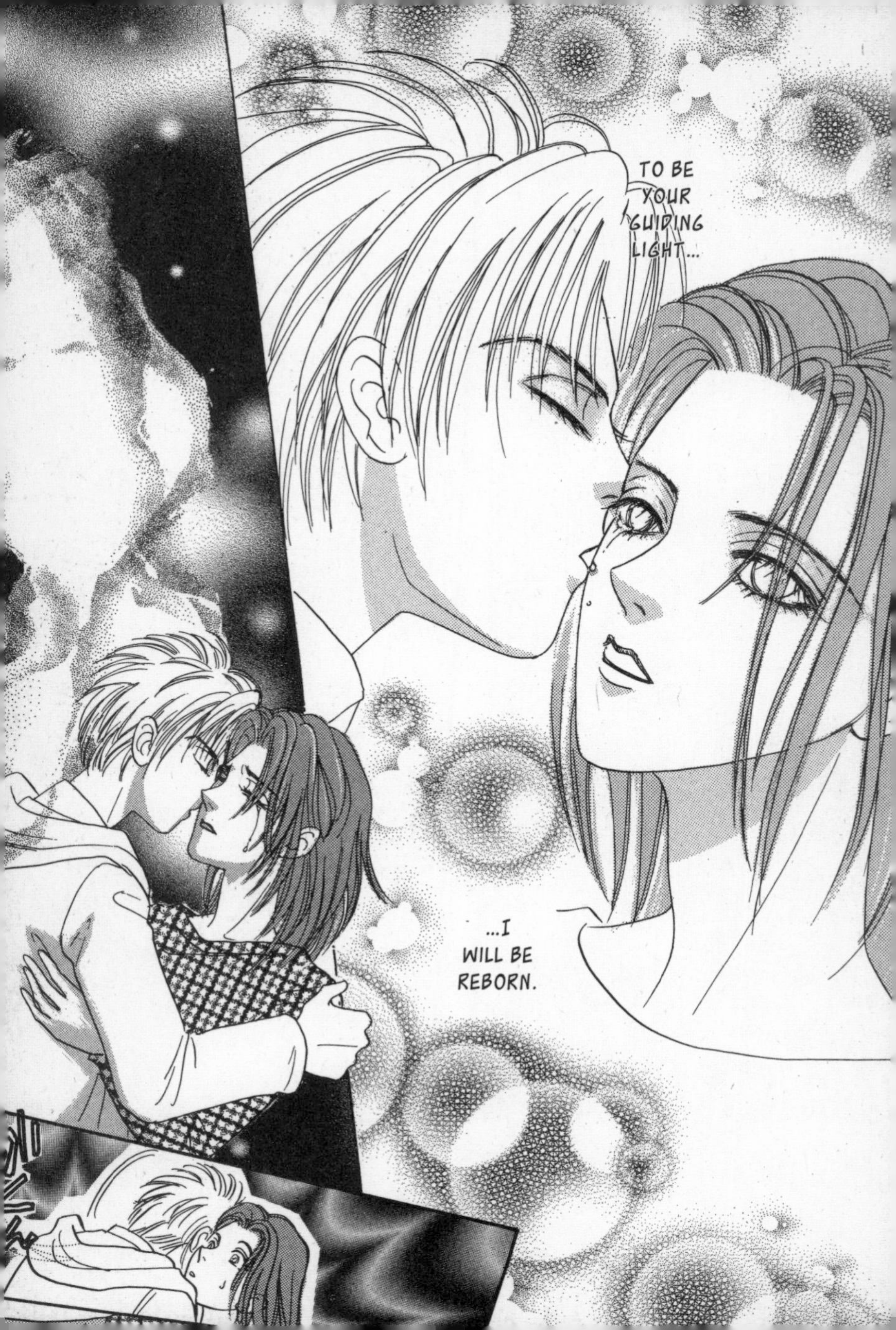
TO BE YOUR GUIDING LIGHT...
...I WILL BE REBORN.

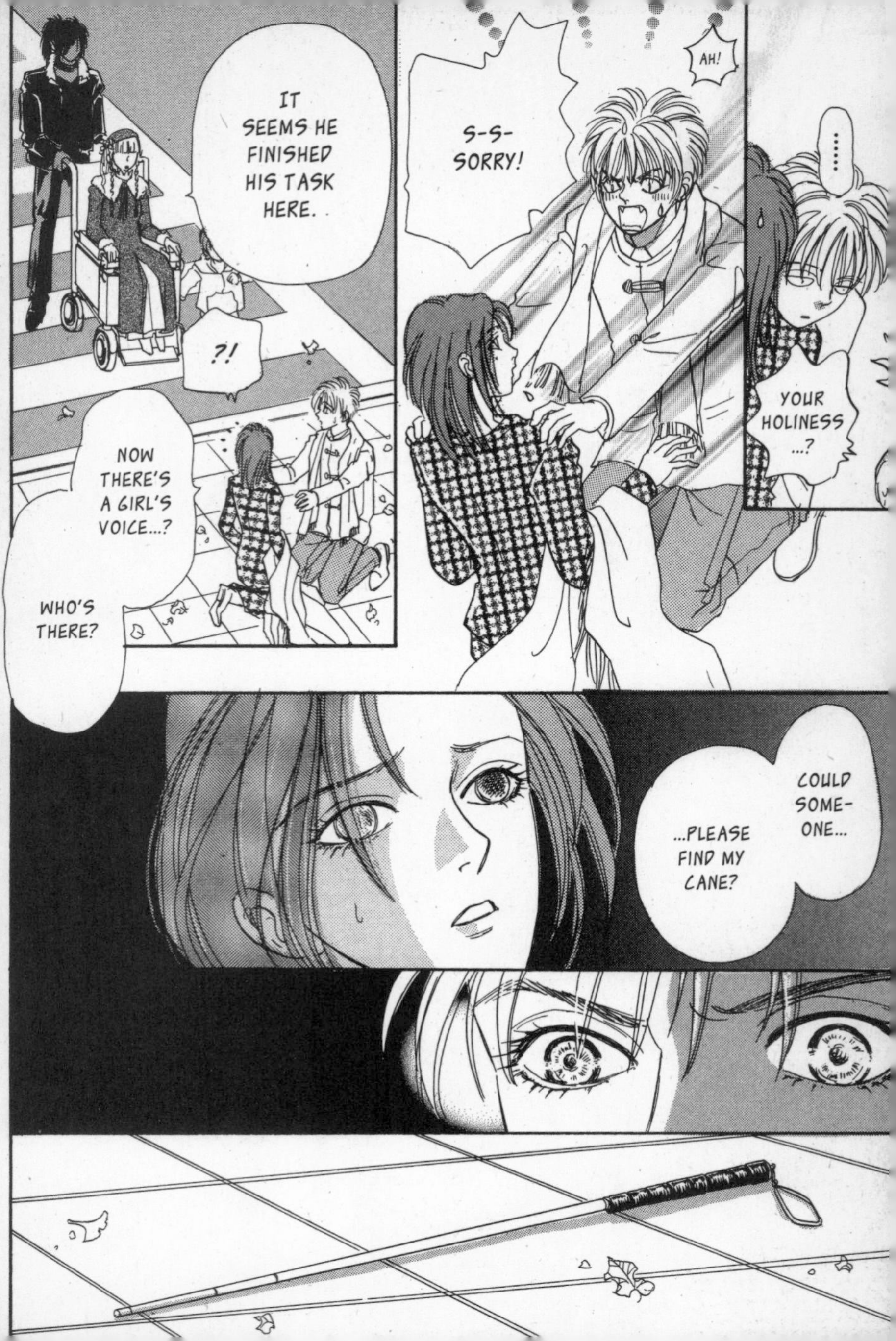
AH!
......
YOUR HOLINESS ...?
S-S-SORRY!
IT SEEMS HE FINISHED HIS TASK HERE.
?!
NOW THERE'S A GIRL'S VOICE...?
WHO'S THERE?
COULD SOME-ONE...
...PLEASE FIND MY CANE?

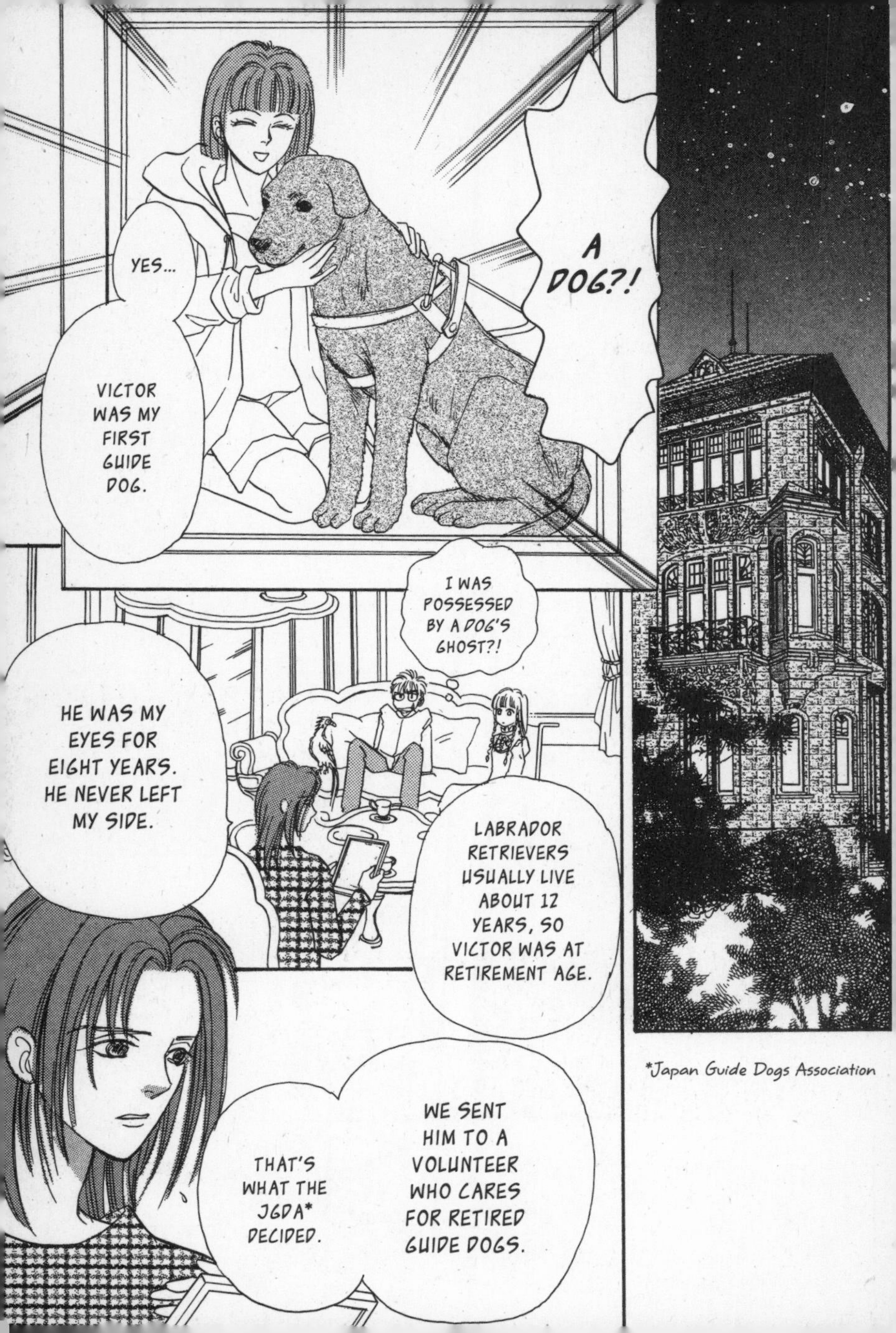
A DOG?!
YES...
VICTOR WAS MY FIRST GUIDE DOG.
I WAS POSSESSED BY A DOG'S GHOST?!
HE WAS MY EYES FOR EIGHT YEARS. HE NEVER LEFT MY SIDE.
LABRADOR RETRIEVERS USUALLY LIVE ABOUT 12 YEARS, SO VICTOR WAS AT RETIREMENT AGE.
WE SENT HIM TO A VOLUNTEER WHO CARES FOR RETIRED GUIDE DOGS.
THAT'S WHAT THE JGDA* DECIDED.

*Japan Guide Dogs Association

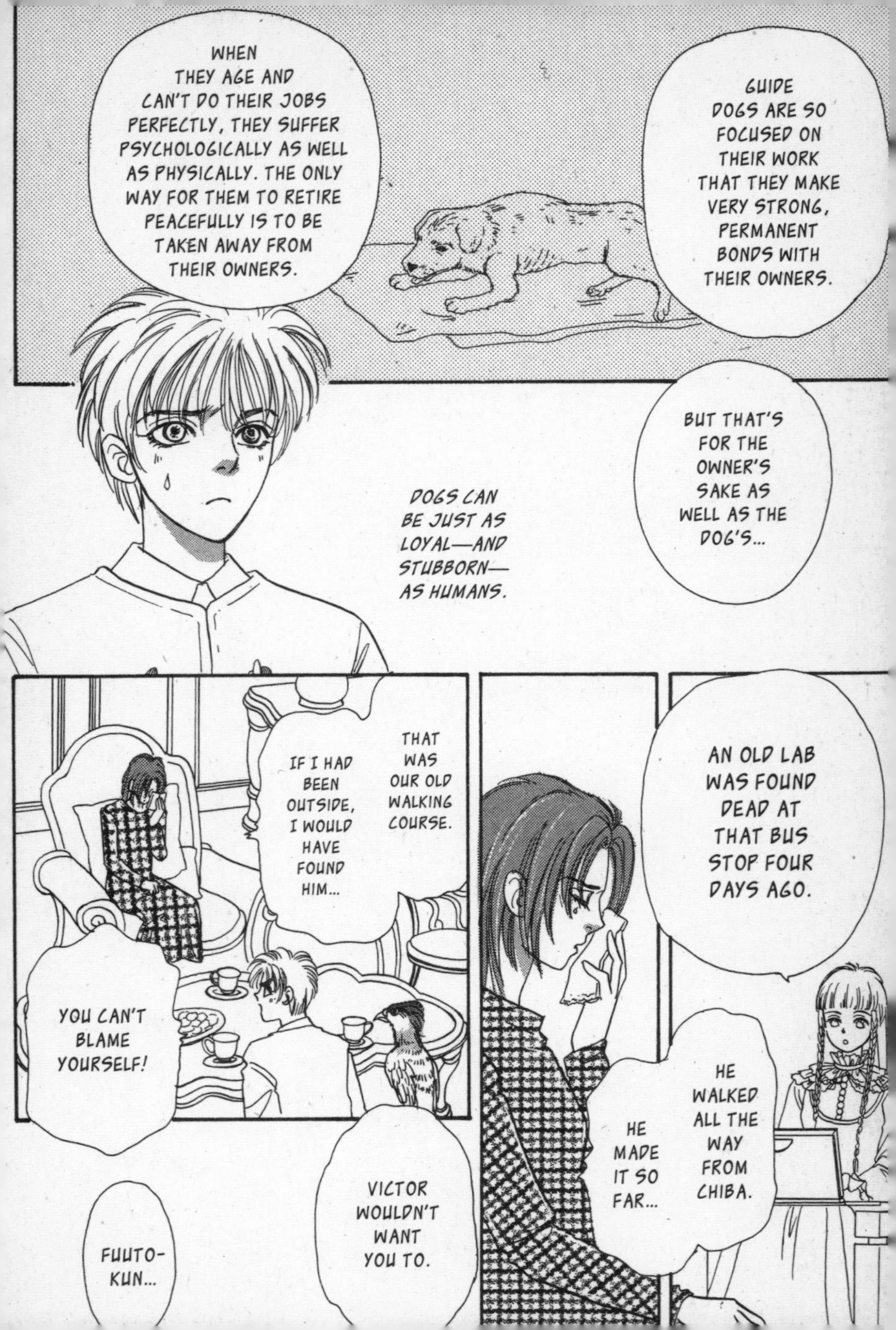
GUIDE DOGS ARE SO FOCUSED ON THEIR WORK THAT THEY MAKE VERY STRONG, PERMANENT BONDS WITH THEIR OWNERS.
WHEN THEY AGE AND CAN'T DO THEIR JOBS PERFECTLY, THEY SUFFER PSYCHOLOGICALLY AS WELL AS PHYSICALLY. THE ONLY WAY FOR THEM TO RETIRE PEACEFULLY IS TO BE TAKEN AWAY FROM THEIR OWNERS.
BUT THAT'S FOR THE OWNER'S SAKE AS WELL AS THE DOG'S...
DOGS CAN BE JUST AS LOYAL—AND STUBBORN—AS HUMANS.
AN OLD LAB WAS FOUND DEAD AT THAT BUS STOP FOUR DAYS AGO.
HE WALKED ALL THE WAY FROM CHIBA.
HE MADE IT SO FAR...
THAT WAS OUR OLD WALKING COURSE.
IF I HAD BEEN OUTSIDE, I WOULD HAVE FOUND HIM...
YOU CAN'T BLAME YOURSELF!
VICTOR WOULDN'T WANT YOU TO.
FUUTO-KUN...

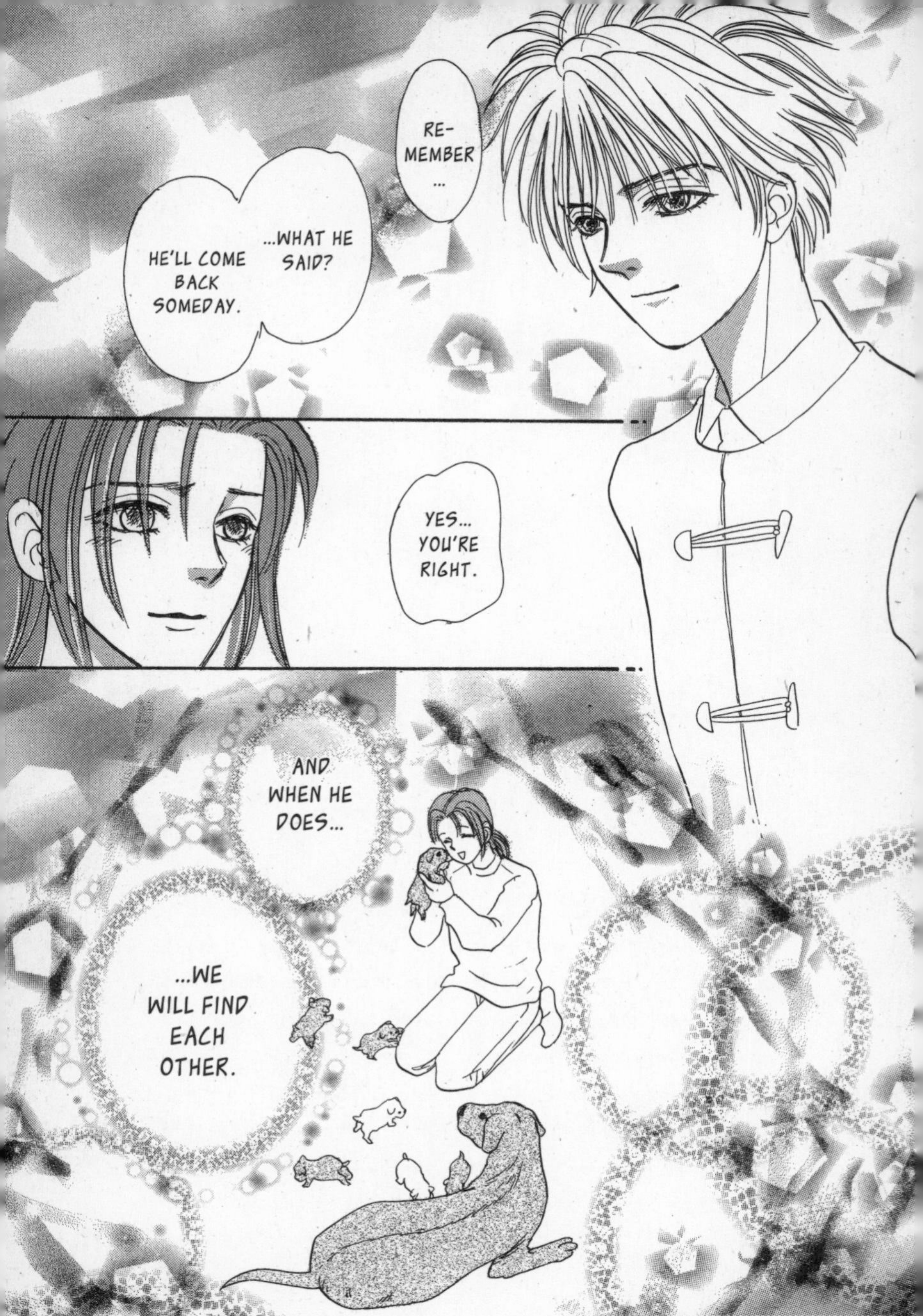
RE-MEMBER...
...WHAT HE SAID?
HE'LL COME BACK SOMEDAY.
YES... YOU'RE RIGHT.
AND WHEN HE DOES...
...WE WILL FIND EACH OTHER.

CHAPTER 5 END

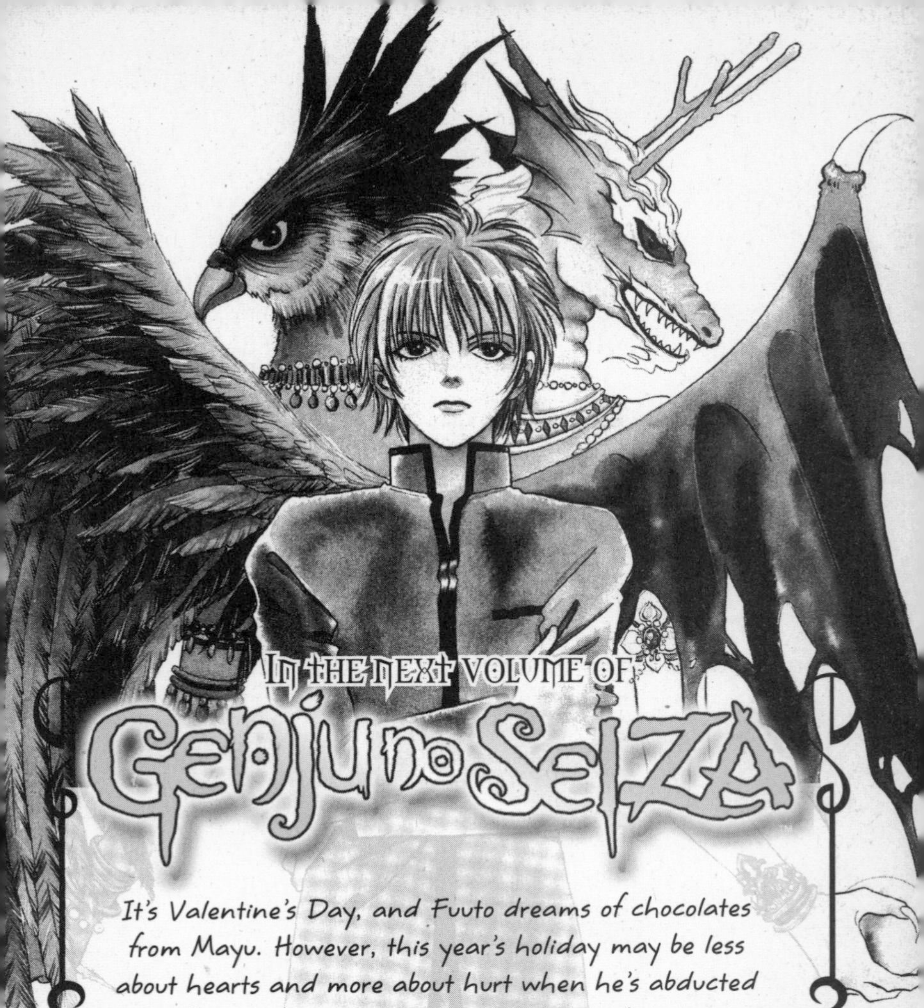

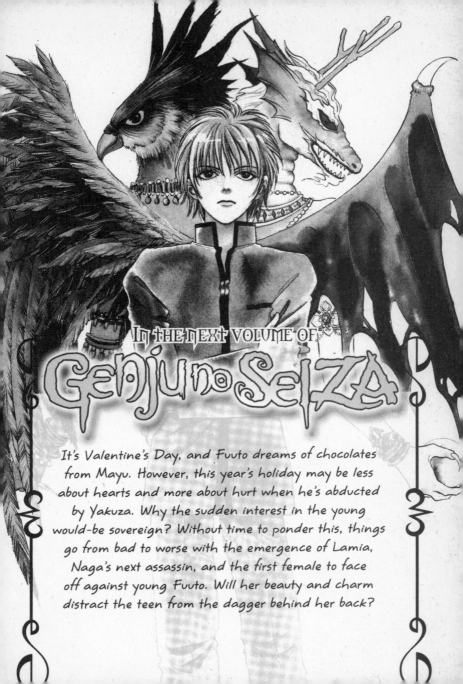

IN THE NEXT VOLUME OF

GENJU NO SEIZA

It's Valentine's Day, and Fuuto dreams of chocolates from Mayu. However, this year's holiday may be less about hearts and more about hurt when he's abducted by Yakuza. Why the sudden interest in the young would-be sovereign? Without time to ponder this, things go from bad to worse with the emergence of Lamia, Naga's next assassin, and the first female to face off against young Fuuto. Will her beauty and charm distract the teen from the dagger behind her back?

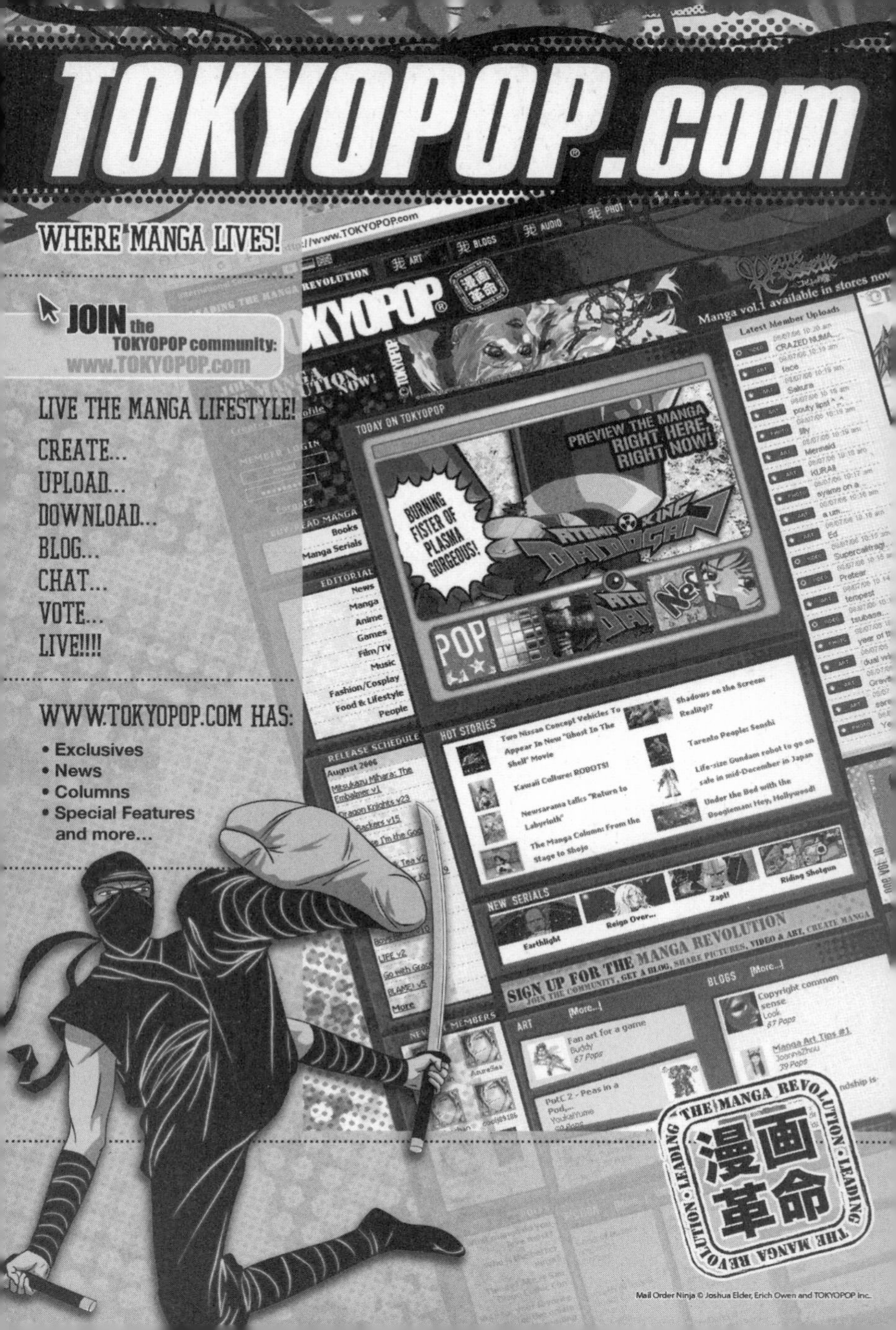

TOKYOPOP®.com
WHERE MANGA LIVES!
JOIN the TOKYOPOP community: www.TOKYOPOP.com
LIVE THE MANGA LIFESTYLE!
CREATE...
UPLOAD...
DOWNLOAD...
BLOG...
CHAT...
VOTE...
LIVE!!!!
WWW.TOKYOPOP.COM HAS:
• Exclusives
• News
• Columns
• Special Features and more...
PREVIEW THE MANGA RIGHT HERE. RIGHT NOW!
BURNING FISTER OF PLASMA GORGEOUS!
ATOMIC KING DAIDOGAN
TODAY ON TOKYOPOP
HOT STORIES
RELEASE SCHEDULE
NEW SERIALS
SIGN UP FOR THE MANGA REVOLUTION
THE MANGA REVOLUTION 漫画革命 LEADING THE MANGA REVOLUTION LEADING
Mail Order Ninja © Joshua Elder, Erich Owen and TOKYOPOP Inc.

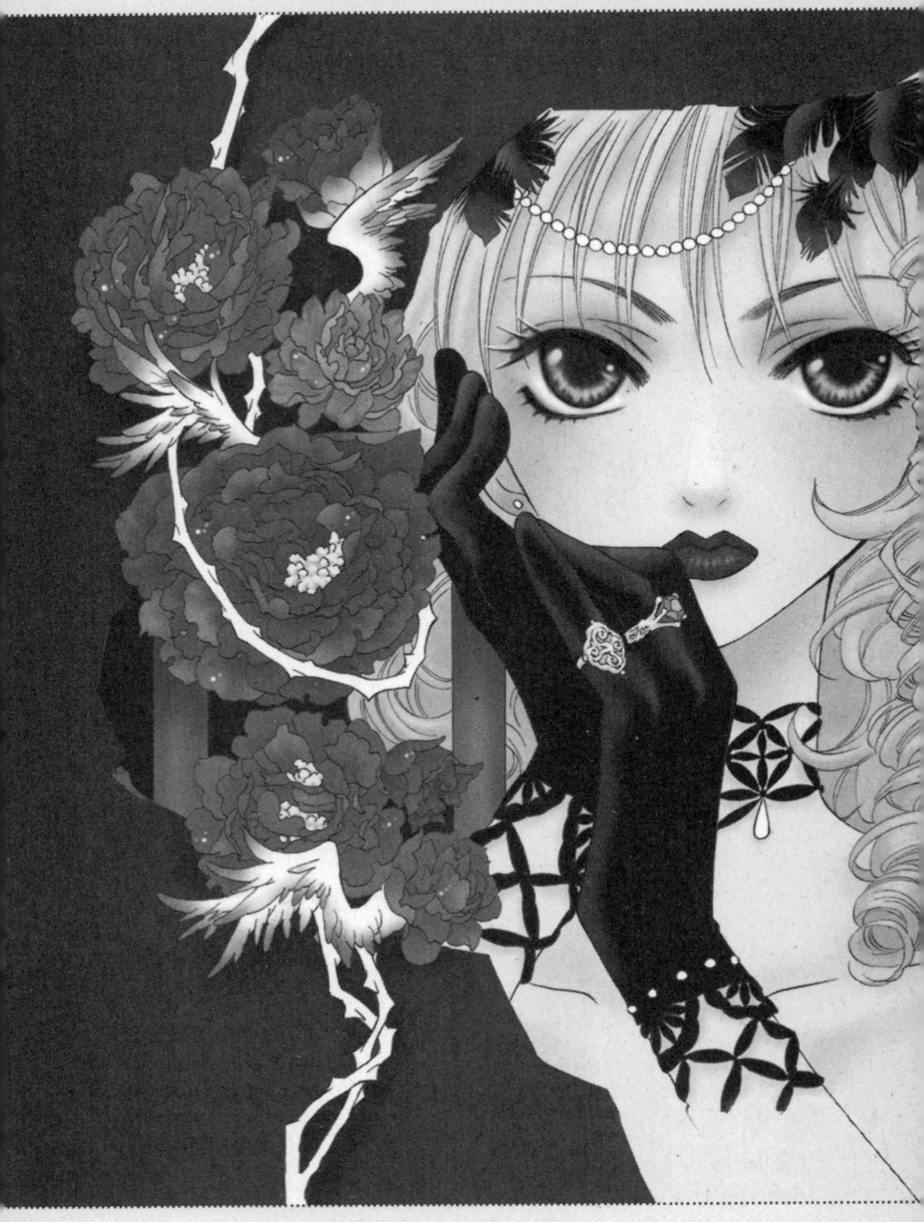

can BAD LUCK be A GOOD THING?

Shi-Hyun is a girl who has nothing but bad luck—at least that's what everyone believes. In some ways, Shi-Hyun herself believes this and tries to stay away from the people she loves the most. But when she transfers to a different high school, a fresh start brings unfamiliar characters—and new challenges—into her life.

good luck™

A romantic coming-of-age shojo!

© E-JIN KANG, DAIWON C.I. Inc.

STOP!

This is the back of the book.
You wouldn't want to spoil a great ending!

This book is printed "manga-style," in the authentic Japanese right-to-left format. Since none of the artwork has been flipped or altered, readers get to experience the story just as the creator intended. You've been asking for it, so TOKYOPOP® delivered: authentic, hot-off-the-press, and far more fun!

DIRECTIONS

If this is your first time reading manga-style, here's a quick guide to help you understand how it works.

It's easy... just start in the top right panel and follow the numbers. Have fun, and look for more 100% authentic manga from TOKYOPOP®!